INTERNATIONAL FASCISM

(

TITLES IN THE
ARNOLD READERS IN HISTORY SERIES

ALREADY PUBLISHED

THE ENGLISH CIVIL WAR
Edited by Richard Cust and Ann Hughes

THE FRENCH REVOLUTION IN SOCIAL AND
POLITICAL PERSPECTIVE
Edited by Peter Jones

GENDER AND HISTORY IN WESTERN EUROPE
Edited by Bob Shoemaker and Mary Vincent

THE IMPACT OF THE ENGLISH REFORMATION
1500–1640
Edited by Peter Marshall

THE ORIGINS OF THE SECOND WORLD WAR
Edited by Patrick Finney

THE TUDOR MONARCHY
Edited by John Guy

IN PREPARATION

BRITISH POLITICS AND SOCIETY 1906–1951
Edited by John Stevenson

WOMEN'S WORK: THE ENGLISH EXPERIENCE 1650–1914
Edited by Pamela Sharpe

INTERNATIONAL FASCISM

THEORIES, CAUSES AND THE NEW CONSENSUS

Edited by
ROGER GRIFFIN

Professor in the History of Ideas, Oxford Brookes University

A member of the Hodder Headline Group
LONDON • SYDNEY • AUCKLAND
Co-published in the United States of America
by Oxford University Press, Inc.

First published in Great Britain in 1998 by
Arnold, a member of the Hodder Headline Group
338 Euston Road, London NW1 3BH
http:\\www.arnoldpublishers.com

Co-published in the United States of America by
Oxford University Press, Inc.,
198 Madison Avenue, New York, NY 10016

British Library Cataloguing in Publication Data
A catalogue entry for this book is available from the British Library

Library of Congress Cataloging-in-Publication Data
A catalog entry for this book is available from the Library of Congress

ISBN 0 340 70614 7 (hb)
ISBN 0 340 70613 9 (pb)

Production Editor: James Rabson
Production Controller: Priya Gohil
Cover designer: Terry Griffiths

Typeset in 10/12pt Sabon by J&L Composition Ltd, Filey, North Yorkshire.
Printed and bound in Great Britain by J. W. Arrowsmith, Bristol

Contents

Preface   viii

Acknowledgements   xiii

Introduction   1

SECTION I THE LACK OF CONSENSUS IN FASCIST STUDIES

Presentation   22

1 Fascism
  Paul Wilkinson (1987)   27

2 Fascism
  Zeev Sternhell (1987)   30

3 Fascism
  Roger Griffin (1993)   35

SECTION II THE SEARCH FOR THE FASCIST MINIMUM

Presentation   42

The product of a crisis of capitalism

4 The terrorist dictatorship of finance capital
  Comintern (1933)   59

5 The counter-revolution of imperialist capitalism
  Leon Trotsky (1940)   67

6 A resurgence of Bonapartism
  Mihaly Vajda (1976)   75

7 An exceptional form of the capitalist state
  Nicos Poulantzas (1974)   86

The product of a crisis of modernization

8 Extremism of the centre
Seymour Martin Lipset (1960) 101

9 A metapolitical counter-revolution
Ernst Nolte (1965) 106

10 A revolt against modern civilization
Wolfgang Sauer (1967) 112

The emergence of a new consensus

11 A modernizing dictatorship
A. James Gregor (1974) 127

12 A politico-cultural revolution
George L. Mosse (1979) 137

13 A form of revolutionary ultra-nationalism
Stanley G. Payne (1996) 147

SECTION III CAUSAL FACTORS IN THE RISE OF FASCISM

Presentation 158

14 The crisis of *fin-de-siècle* thought
Zeev Sternhell (1976) 169

15 The crisis of democracy after the First World War
Juan Linz (1975) 175

16 The drive towards synthesis
Roger Eatwell (1992) 189

17 A sense-making crisis
Gerald M. Platt (1980) 204

18 The ecstasy of rebirth
Klaus Theweleit (1989) 216

19 A retrodictive theory of fascism
Stanley Payne (1996) 227

SECTION IV FASCIST THEORIES OF FASCISM

Presentation 238

20 The ideology of the twentieth century
Benito Mussolini (1932) 248

21 The third alternative
Claud Sutton (1937) 257

22 Between festival and revolution
   Marco Tarchi (1985)   264

23 Revolutionary charlatanism
   Bernadette Archer (1996)   275

SECTION V THE REBIRTH OF FASCISM?

Presentation   286

24 The revival of the fascist menace
   Chris Bambery (1992)   295

25 Fascism, neo-fascism, new radical right?
   Diethelm Prowe (1994)   305

   Afterword   325
   Index   327

Preface

Since fascist discourse abounds in extravagant metaphors, it might not be amiss to indulge in one now to evoke the consternation and bewilderment that fascism unleashed when it made its dramatic entry onto the stage of modern history. It was with the force of a violent shower of asteroids large and small that fascism[1] impacted on an inter-war Europe still quaking from the seismic aftershocks from the First World War and the Russian Revolution. The clouds of dust hurled into the atmosphere by the two largest meteorites, Fascism and Nazism, temporarily eclipsed the sun of liberal humanist understanding, though Marxists were quickly able to refocus their interpretive lens to dismiss it as yet another bombardment from the arch-enemy capitalism. Long after the Axis powers had been defeated, non-Marxist political scientists and historians struggled to devise new conceptual tools to make sense of what, for the liberal rationalist mind, was a totally unpredicted and shattering sequence of events. The span of a single generation had encompassed the establishment of authoritarian regimes in most European states, a total and genuinely global war, the Holocaust, the partition of Europe between the Empires of the Soviet Union and the 'Free World', and the outbreak of a Cold War which potentially signalled the self-destruction of humankind in a nuclear winter.

It took a long time for the dust to settle, and for most of the post-war period explanatory models of fascism bore the hallmarks either of extreme intellectual disorientation or crude reductionism. A situation prevailed which made any attempt to make a major contribution to fascist studies liable to be a thankless task. Even the most famous interpretive models, such as those of Nolte (Reading 9) or Sternhell (Reading 2), have hardly ever been applied by other scholars to empirical investigations of specific phenomena. Nor is this the result of lack of interest in resolving the problem. Indeed, with the possible exception of 'ideology', no other term in the political lexicon has spawned more rival definitions and causal theories or provoked more heated debate than 'fascism'. As a result every expert compiling a Reader on fascism can be expected to make a contrasting selection of 'key texts', and to be critical of the ones which would be chosen by a fellow specialist. Moreover, an anthology of primary sources relating to fascism is open to another charge, namely that reproducing lengthy excerpts of writings which epitomize the fascist mentality might indirectly bestow on it an unwarranted legitimacy by taking it seriously as a coherent 'world-view'. In other words, an exercise originally conceived as casting light on the internal logic and dynamics of fascism in the spirit of 'know thy enemy' might assume revisionist connotations: stressing its ideological cohesion could unwittingly rationalize and normalize it, diverting attention from the ruthlessly destructive results of bids to turn its utopia into reality.

However, at least an anthology of texts written by fascists themselves has the merit of allowing those who read them to confront directly the extremist ideas and radical values which inform a historical force that they are hopefully unlikely ever to encounter in the flesh, and so form their own judgement of the degree to which they provide a rationale for militant ultra-nationalism and organized hatred. By contrast, a secondary source Reader such as this offers none of the *frissons* that can be savoured when reading texts which have been written by the protagonists and victims of fascism themselves, and which not only cast a narrow beam of light on the murky concatenations of events with which they are associated, but evoke a link with human catastrophes and atrocities sometimes palpable in the words themselves. Instead, the linguistic register of academic analysis is generally the dry, theoretical one necessarily adopted by any intellectual bent on modelling and explaining events in rational terms, however steeped in irrationality and mythic forces they may be. (The use of an abstract, detached language to analyse phenomena associated with fanaticism and violence should not be seen as callousness, however, but rather as a means to counteract and exorcize the appalling threat which they have posed in the twentieth century to Enlightenment humanism and its legacy of tolerance and respect for human rights.)

There are, none the less, at least three good reasons for attempting to compile a secondary source Reader in fascism now, no matter how invidious and ultimately arbitrary the task of selecting 'key texts' is bound to be. For a start, while there are numerous surveys of fascist theories,[2] and several anthologies of such theories in German and Italian, no such source book has appeared in English to my knowledge.[3] Second, and more importantly, it is just possible that after seven decades in which the only island of agreement about the dynamics of fascism in an ocean of confusion, idiosyncrasy, and contradiction was to be found in Marxist territorial waters,[4] an archipelago of consensus may finally be surfacing among non-Marxists as well. In other words, a central thesis of this book is that, if not a sea-change, then a perceptible shift is taking place in the system of intellectual currents flowing within fascist studies. As recently as 1992 the authors of a historical dictionary of fascisms could assert without fear of contradiction that 'no universally accepted definition of the fascist phenomenon exists, no consensus, *no matter how slight,* as to its range, its ideological origins, or the modalities of action which characterize it'[5] I maintain that a slight but growing consensus does now exist on these issues, and in the Introduction (which is vital to an understanding of my selection of Readings) I attempt to clarify what constitutes it. The upshot is that a convergence of opinion or 'common sense' is beginning to develop among both theorists of generic fascism and specialists working on specific aspects of it, that it is to be treated on a par with other major political ideologies rather than as a special case defined primarily in terms of its negations, organizational forms, and style. In other words, like conservatism, anarchism, liberalism, or ecologism, fascism is definable as an ideology with a specific 'positive', utopian vision of the ideal state of society, a vision based on a matrix of core axioms about the contemporary world which can generate a number of distinctive forms determined by local circumstances. It is these axioms which condition fascism's various external characteristics, and which in particular account for its extreme hostility towards the values of liberal and socialist humanism, as well as towards various 'out groups' in society, which is manifested when attempts are made to realize the fascist utopia. Many representatives of an older generation of scholars will doubtless persist in seeing fascism as essentially nihilistic, barbaric, reactionary, anti-modern, lacking an ideology and purely action-oriented, or as basically (petty) bourgeois. Yet, there is at least some prospect that as a new generation of scholars leavens traditional fascist studies and demonstrates the empirical value of a recognition of these axioms when applied to specific aspects of fascism, the embryonic consensus about the heuristic value of this approach will grow ever stronger. It may even percolate eventually into what can sometimes be the most retrograde stronghold of outdated paradigms, history school text books and exam revision manuals written for sixth forms and high schools.

If this scenario is not an unconscious piece of wishful thinking on my part, then the appearance of this Reader is indeed timely. For the first time since fascism burst unannounced into contemporary history it is possible for the editor to choose texts not in a spirit of defiant individualism or apologetic relativism, but on the basis of an organizing principle which corresponds to the intuition of many non-Marxist scholars currently working in the field. As I explain in the Introduction, there is thus an overt sub-text to the anthology which follows, a 'thesis' about the nature of fascism which informs both the selection of Readings and their 'Presentations'. No Reader can claim to be value-free, and this one in particular is in a very real sense a work of both exegesis and propaganda. It presents but a small sample of writings culled from literally hundreds, if not thousands, of potentially relevant texts, but which I hope includes at least several which would be recognized by my colleagues in the field as being 'seminal' to, or at least representative of, the history of the debate about what constitutes fascism, even if there are many more whose absence they will doubtless regret and which they would certainly have substituted for some I have chosen. At the same time it is a selection oriented to trace the evolution of fascist studies towards the 'new consensus' (which I emphasize once again is as yet embryonic and one whose very existence some academics would dispute). Indeed, by making the emerging paradigm the organizing principle of a documentary Reader for undergraduate and postgraduate students, it deliberately sets out to widen and deepen that consensus.

The third reason for undertaking the task of assembling this Reader has been to produce not just an anthology of texts representative of fascist studies, but also a 'self-instruction manual' in them (a guide, that is, in how to understand a fascist movement, not how to join one!). The way it is structured should make it possible for a student embarking on fascist studies without previous experience of the subject first to grapple with the bewildering array of conflicting positions generated when the Babel effect still prevailed in fascist studies; then to sample some of the pioneer-ing works written when academics started to take fascism seriously as a field of enquiry, but still were deeply confused or ill-informed about its ideology and social base; then to see how a new consensus has started to form over the last few years and how empirical research into several causal aspects of fascism is corroborated by the general approach it suggests. Thus the anthology not only makes available some 'classic' texts in fascist studies which are often hard to track down outside the larger university libraries (e.g. the Comintern's or Mussolini's definition of fascism), and gives a flavour of the latest research on the topic, but also offers a sort of 'do-it-yourself course' in the subject for those who want to delve below the surface of the debate.

A final piece of advice to the user of this book. 'Grey, grey is all theory' exclaims Goethe in expressing Faust's longing for the understanding which comes from 'lived' experience. Unfortunately, generic fascism cannot be conceptualized, let alone comprehended, unless it is investigated with an appropriate theoretical apparatus. Nevertheless, students who use this book are urged to study as much as possible of the 'real' history of specific fascisms (i.e. examples of the ideology they produce and accounts of the actions and events they have given rise to). Only in this way can they see how useful those conceptual tools really are, and access the curious cognitive and emotional experience of at least partially understanding fascism from the inside, even if it remains anathema to everything they personally stand for.

If this Reader fulfils its objectives, those who have been able to retain something from working their way through most if not all of the volume (whether with guidance or alone) should reach a point where they are able to follow the general argument expounded in the demanding final article by Prowe, as well as recognizing some of his references to various positions and experts. Furthermore, they will be hopefully able to engage with his basic thesis in an informed and critical spirit, despite the authoritative tone with which it is written. Even more importantly they will understand why such a gulf divides it from the preceding piece on how to fight the 'Nazi menace' written by a Marxist activist. In short, they will have gained a clearer idea not only of what fascism is, but of their own response to it. And they should be able to do so not just intellectually, but, which is considerably more important, as enlightened citizens of society and morally aware human beings.

Notes

1 As is now standard practice, lower case 'fascism' designates international, 'generic' fascism, as opposed to upper case 'Fascism', which refers exclusively to Mussolini's movement and regime.
2 In English the principal surveys are A.J. Gregor, *Interpretations of Fascism*, (Cambridge, Mass., General Learning Press, 1974); Renzo de Felice, *Interpretations of Fascism*, (Morristown, NJ, Harvard University Press, 1977); B. Hagtvet and R. Kühnl, 'Contemporary approaches to fascism: a survey of paradigms', in S. U. Larsen, B. Hagtvet, J. P. Myklebust (eds), *Who Were the Fascists* (Oslo, Universitetsforlaget, 1980); and Stanley Payne, *A History of Fascism, 1914–1945* (London, UCL Press, 1996), Part II.
3 For a list of the anthologies of theoretical positions published in Italy and Germany: see S. Payne, *A History of Fascism, 1914–1945* (London, UCL Press, 1996), footnote to page 442. Section IV of Roger Griffin, *Fascism* (Oxford, Oxford University Press, 1995) also contains some 25 brief samples of different theoretical responses to fascism since 1922.
4 Even in the Marxist camp a wide range of nuanced positions have been evolved, despite a basic consensus on the fact that fascism is the offspring of capitalism. See especially D. Beetham, *Marxists in Face of Fascism* (Manchester, Manchester University Press, 1983).
5 P. Milza and S. Bernstein, *Dictionaire historique des Pascisme's et du nazisme* (Brussels, Editions Complete, 1992), p. 7 (my emphasis).

Acknowledgements

Several drafts of the proposed structure and contents of this book were tried out on experts in the field of fascist studies, whose reports to the editor naturally remain anonymous. The final scheme, for which I must take full responsibility, has been considerably influenced by their reactions, which ranged from unbounded enthusiasm to scathing disdain, and I offer them my thanks. If the resulting Reader helps those uninitiated into the debate over fascism without offending the intelligence of the initiated, then I must thank Christopher Wheeler of Arnold Publishers. It was he who overcame my initial reluctance to undertake yet another anthology of texts relating to fascism so soon after the publication of my primary source Reader *Fascism* by Oxford University Press in 1995.

Over the years in which I have been refining and applying the new model of fascism which I first expounded in *The Nature of Fascism* in 1991, a number of scholars have shown me an intellectual (and sometimes personal) generosity beyond the norm which prevails in academia, and hence contributed in an indirect and yet vital way to sustaining my zeal for this field of studies (even if some of them harbour reservations about the value, or even the sound, of the concept 'palingenetic ultra-nationalism'!). I would like to take the opportunity to acknowledge here their support and friendship: in broadly chronological order they are Tudor Jones, Robert Murray, Detlef Mühlberger, Peter Pulzer, Martin Conway, Tom Buchanan, Ian Kershaw, Richard Thurlow, Martin Blinkhorn, Mario Sznajder, António Costa Pinto, George Mosse, Zeev Sternhell, Emilio Gentile, Berndt Hagtvet, Mike Cronin, David Baker and Andreas Umland. David Baker, Roger Eatwell and Stanley Payne not only belong to this list, but provided valuable feedback at the manuscript stage. I also want to thank Colin Cook for acting as guinea pig for the final draft of the book, Antonella Bestaggini for tracking down copright holders and proof-reading the final text, as well as cohorts of students who down the years have attended the course on generic fascism which enabled me to try out theories and documentary material relating to fascism. The support of the School of Humanities at Oxford Brookes University has also been invaluable, while the encouragement of Peter, Gillian, and Paul deserves special mention. The person who sustains my enthusiasm for work and life more than anyone remains, of course, Mariella.

The editor and the publisher would like to thank the following for permission to use copyright material in this volume:

Blackwell Publishers for Paul Wilkinson, 'Fascism', from V. Bogdanor (ed.), *Blackwell Encyclopedia of Political Institutions* (Oxford, 1987), pp. 226–8; Blackwell Publishers for Zeev Sternhell, 'Fascism', from D. Miller (ed.), *Blackwell Encyclopedia of Political Thought* (Oxford, 1991), pp. 148–50; Blackwell Publishers for Roger Griffin, 'Fascism', from W. Outhwaite and T. Bottomore (eds), *Blackwell Dictionary of Social Thought* (Oxford, 1993), pp. 223–4; The Royal Institute of International Affairs for Extracts from the Theses of the Thirteenth ECCI Plenum on Fascism, the War Danger, and the Tasks of Communist Parties, from J. Degras (ed.), *The Communist International, 1919–1943*, vol. III, 1929–1943, published by Oxford University Press for the Royal Institute of International Affairs (London, 1965), pp. 296–303; Pathfinder Press for Leon Trotsky, 'Bonapartism, Fascism, and War', from *The Struggle against Fascism in Germany* (New York, 1971), pp. 445–52, copyright 1971 by Pathfinder Press, reprinted by permission; Verso and Editions La Découverte for Nicos Poulantzas, *Fascism and Dictatorship: The Third International and the Problem of the Exceptional State* (London, 1974), pp. 312–19, 331–5 © Editions La Découverte; Seymour M. Lipset for ' "Fascism" – Left, Right, and Center', from *Political Man* (Baltimore, Johns Hopkins University Press, 1981), pp. 131–7; The Orion Publishing Group Ltd and Piper Verlag, Munich for Ernst Nolte, *Three Faces of Fascism* (London, Weidenfeld & Nicolson, 1965), pp. 429–30, 433–4, 450–4; The American Historical Association for Wolfgang Sauer, 'National Socialism: Totalitarianism or Fascism?', *The American Historical Review*, vol. 73, no. 2 (Dec. 1967), pp. 408–11, 412–24; Johns Hopkins University Press for A. James Gregor, 'Fascism and Modernization: Some Addenda', *World Politics*, 26 (1976), pp. 370–9, 383–4, copyright The Johns Hopkins University Press; Sage Publications Ltd for G. L. Mosse, 'Towards a General Theory of Fascism', from G. L. Mosse (ed.), *International Fascism: New Thoughts and New Approaches* (New York, Howard Fertig, 1979), pp. 1–6, 15–17, 25–7, 36–41; The University of Wisconsin Press and Taylor & Francis Group for Stanley G. Payne, *A History of Fascism, 1914–45* (Wisconsin, University of Wisconsin Press, 1996 (London, UCL Press, 1996)), pp. 6–14, 487–95; Scolar Press for Zeev Sternhell, 'Fascist Ideology', in Walter Laqueur (ed.), *Fascism: A Reader's Guide* (Harmondsworth, 1979; first published by Wildwood House Ltd., 1976), pp. 332–8; Professors Fred J. Greenstein and Nelson W. Polsby for Juan Linz, 'Totalitarian and

Authoritarian Regimes', in F. J. Greenstein and N. W. Polsby (eds), *Political Science*, vol. 3, Macropolitical Theory, (Mass., Addison-Wesley Longman, 1975), pp. 313–321; Sage Publications Ltd for Roger Eatwell, 'Towards a New Model of Generic Fascism', *Journal of Theoretical Politics*, vol. 4, 1992, pp. 174–85, 189–90; The Lexington Press for Gerald M. Platt, 'Thoughts on a Theory of Collective Action: Language, Affect, and Ideology in Revolution', in M. Albin (ed.), *New Directions in Psychohistory* (Mass., Lexington Books, 1980), pp. 78–88, 92–4, copyright 1980 Jossey-Bass Inc. Publishers, first published by Lexington Books, all rights reserved; University of Minnesota Press and Blackwell Publishers for K. Theweleit, *Male Fantasies* (Minneapolis, University of Minnesota Press, 1989: 2 Vols) (Cambridge, Polity Press, 1989: 2 Vols) Vol. 2, pp. 227–43; Marco Tarchi for 'Between festival and revolution' from *Diorama letterario*, no. 31, May–June 1985, p. 29–34; the English Nationalist Movement (Head Office: BM Box LCRN, London WC1N 3XX) for Bernadette Archer, 'Were 'Fascisms' Outside Germany and Italy Anything More than Imitators?', *The Crusader*, no. 6, 1996, pp. 20–3; Bookmarks Publications and Chris Bambery for 'Killing the Nazi Menace: How to Stop the Fascists', (a Socialist Workers Party pamphlet, London, February, 1992), pp. 7–14, 35–41; Cambridge University Press and Diethelm Prowe for D. Prowe, '"Classic" Fascism and the New Radical Right in Western Europe: Comparisons and Contrasts', *Contemporary European History*, vol. 3, no. 3, (Nov. 1994), pp. 289–96, 303–13.

Every effort has been made to obtain permission to reproduce copyright material. If any proper acknowledgement has not been made, copyright holders are invited to contact the publishers.

Introduction

'It is to be expected that this century may be that of authority, a century of the "Right", a Fascist century.'[1] So wrote Mussolini in his famous 1932 Encyclopedia definition of Fascism, suggesting that by then he had convinced himself, at least at some level of his complex personality, that the new type of state he was creating in Italy was a role model for other modern nations whose liberal political and economic institutions had been plunged into crisis by the Great Depression. Nor was there any shortage of admirers of Fascism at home and abroad prepared to devote their energy to turning international fascism, or what the regime itself called 'Universal Fascism', into a reality, notably the Englishman J. S. Barnes.[2] Indeed, as early as 1928, five years after The March on Rome and only three years after the Fascist dictatorship had been inaugurated, the International Centre of Fascist Studies had been set up in Switzerland, and over the next few years Italy produced a steady flow of books, periodicals, and conferences campaigning for the birth of a fascist[3] Europe, or even the fascistization of the entire West.

The climax of fascist internationalism was the congress held in Montreux by CAUR (Action Committees for the Universality of Rome) in December 1934, which attracted delegates from the ultra-right movements or circles of thirteen countries. However, the congress was conspicuously boycotted by Europe's new fascist regime, the Third Reich,[4] and the bid to arrive at a coherent strategy for collaborative action floundered on the problem of agreeing a shared set of doctrinal principles. The congress's failure highlights the paradox that this book is seeking to illuminate. Clearly the participants who gathered on the shores of Lake Geneva believed there was a common denominator between their political ideals and the ones pursued by Fascism in Italy, yet precisely what constituted this was far from self-evident. After all, the Fascist new order in Italy was not the attempted realization of an ideological blueprint in the way that the French Revolution invoked liberal and Enlightenment principles or Soviet Russia claimed to be implementing Marxism–Leninism. As a result, when the role which biological racism or anti-Semitism should play in the concept of the nation proved highly contentious at Montreux, no canonic texts could be cited to resolve the dispute. Other issues, such as the relationship of a fascist state to the Christian Church, the importance of 'socializing' capitalism for the sake of the national community, the commitment to corporatism, or the need for territorial expansion and hence war, were potentially equally divisive. There was also the stubborn fact that coordinating an International made up of movements all committed to their own self-assertive form of hyper-nationalism was always going to be problematic to say the least.

As far as Italy was concerned, Mussolini cut the Gordian knot of what precisely constituted 'international fascism' with the sword, or rather with the invasion of Ethiopia followed by ever closer alignment with Hitler. By the time the Spanish Civil War broke out a 'Universal Fascism' centred on Rome had become a dead letter[5], though the military support which Mussolini and Hitler gave Franco on the erroneous assumption that he would actively collaborate with them after victory points to the persistence of a more pragmatic and cynical type of fascist internationalism. In reality the *Führer*'s own imperial ambitions precluded anything but a grim travesty of the harmonious ecumenicalism of equals aspired to by Universal Fascists, even if Third Reich diplomacy and propaganda often paid lip service to a Germano-centric version of it in order to encourage collaboration by the more virulently ultra-right, anti-communist, and sometimes fascist, constituencies of the countries they so brutally integrated into their 'New European Order'.

The post-war era has seen a marked trend towards trans-national linkages between fascist groups and the trickle of pan-European initiatives has swelled into a major current of neo-fascism,[6] but post-war fascists have been no more successful than their inter-war predecessors at reaching a consensus about what precisely their myriad different groupings have in common.[7] As a result, the task of identifying the 'fascist minimum' has mainly fallen to opponents of the extreme right, whether the ideologues of rival political movements, or academics working in the human sciences. Once conceived as a strictly academic issue, however, the terminology changes. Rather than refer to 'international fascism', the convention is to talk of 'generic fascism', because the central theoretical problem is to establish the definitional characteristics of the *genus* fascism, of which each variety is a different manifestation. Moreover, in contrast to intellectuals or political activists, 'liberal' academics are not primarily motivated to embark on their quest for the fascist minimum with an ideological axe to grind, or with the thirst for the type of knowledge which will allow them to orient themselves on their enemy's terrain, and spot the weak points in his defences. Instead, they are intent on inferring 'disinterestedly' from the empirical data associated with the history of different 'putative' fascisms (i.e. phenomena generally thought to be fascist) the key elements or patterns that distinguish them from other, apparently similar, but in reality distinct, phenomena. Only then can 'fascism' be used as a discrete category of political thought which makes it possible to supply answers to such questions as: What is the relationship of fascism to totalitarianism or ultra-right conservatism? Were Nazism or Peronism fascist movements? Were Franco or Salazar fascist leaders? Was Vichy a fascist regime? Are Le Pen's Front National, Fini's Alleanza Nazionale, or Zhirinovsky's Liberal Democratic Party of Russia fascist, whatever their spokesmen say to the contrary? Is fascism rising or falling, spreading or shrinking in the contemporary world? If fascism has changed since 1945, what are the essential traits which allow it still to be recognized?

Such questions cannot be answered without an explicit or implicit definition of fascism based on something more articulate and empirically testable than a gut-feeling, for while most people believe instinctively that they know what facism is, once verbalized their intuitions generally give rise to a wide range of nebulous and conflicting characterizations. Nor should it be assumed that these questions are purely theoretical. Once journalists or politicians start asking what threat fascism poses to democracy, or what the USA, the European Union, or the new Russia can do to inhibit its spread, then some measure of agreement over the nature of the beast becomes a prerequisite for evaluating the overall situation and formulating policies to tackle it. In an ideal world they would be able to turn to academics for clear guidance.[8] The trouble is that for the last seven decades the more academics who have trained their mind on the study of fascism, the more explanatory models have proliferated, and the more confusion has been generated over the most appropriate approach to adopt.

It should be stressed that for one intellectual and academic tradition at least the fascist riddle has never existed. It would have required a major overhaul of the Marxist scheme of history to admit that revolutionary socialism had a brand new arch-enemy to contend with other than capitalism, especially one which shared with it an essentially anti-bourgeois, revolutionary dynamic. It was much more tempting to accommodate Mussolini's Fascism within communist theology by treating it as a reactionary movement born directly of the crisis of capitalism and charged with the mission to postpone at all costs the imminent victory of the proletariat. Since capitalism itself was an international force, Marxists had few problems recognizing in fascism a potentially global threat liable to materialize whenever the ramparts of bourgeois liberalism seemed about to be breached by the 'people'. Thus, as early as 1921, two years before Hitler's abortive putsch in Munich, the Italian Marxist Antonio Gramsci was already convinced that 'on an international scale' fascism was 'the attempt to resolve the problems of production and exchange with machine guns and pistol-shots', its troops being provided by 'the petty and middle bourgeoisie'.[9] Thus a tradition was soon established which attributed to fascism a particular class base of support (sections of the bourgeoisie), a particular ideology (a form of aggressive, pseudo- or counter-revolutionary nationalism), and particular natural enemies (the working classes, socialists). When Hitler became increasingly prominent in the politics of Weimar Germany, a country whose stability had been seriously threatened by Bolshevik revolutionaries in 1919 and which still boasted the most powerful trade union movement in the world, Marxists were quick to classify the NSDAP as 'German fascism': after all it was demonstrably even more ruthless than Italian Fascism in its drive to wipe out international socialism and destroy the power of the workers as a discrete social class. With a minimum of theoretical agonizing or in-fighting Marxists have gone on to categorize under the same heading all the more virulently anti-communist paramilitary movements and authoritarian regimes which have sprung up in Europe, Latin America, Asia, and Southern Africa in the course of the twentieth century.

As is to be expected from such a broad ideological church, there are nevertheless significant variants of the Marxist analysis of fascism. An important difference separates the 'vulgar' Marxists, who see fascism as directly spawned by capitalism and identical with its interests, from their 'sophisticated' comrades who concede to fascism an autonomous (even revolutionary!) dynamic, but see it being hijacked and exploited by 'agents' of capitalism for their own ends. Furthermore, the prime agents who manipulate fascism in this way can be variously seen as 'the petty bour-geoisie', 'the bourgeoisie', 'finance capital'(see Reading 4), 'big business', 'the industrial classes', 'imperialism' (see Reading 5), or 'state monopoly capitalism' (see Reading 7). (By the late 1950s such was the prevalence of Marxist assumptions about the essentially bourgeois nature of fascist support that even non-Marxists sometimes based their theory of fascism on it, despite the poor empirical evidence to corroborate it, notably Seymour Lipset: see Reading 8). Another permutation of Marxist inter-pretation focuses instead on the parallels between Mussolini's seizure of power in 1922 and that of Louis-Napoleon in 1852: in both cases a crisis in the capitalist state was resolved by the installation of a dictatorship which operated in populist and nationalist key largely independently of the domination of any one class, even if bourgeois economic interests were clearly safeguarded at the expense of proletarian ones. Hence fascism becomes a twentieth-century form of 'Bonapartism' (see Reading 6).

The hallmark of all Marxist approaches is the axiomatic assumption that fascism is primarily to be understood in relation to the crisis of the capitalist state, and as long as Marxism survives as an active ideological force, Marxist interpretations of fascism will continue to be produced (see Reading 24). They are destined to go on appearing long after the last communist state, whether through dramatic collapse or stealthy transfor-mation, has been inextricably woven into the world-wide web of global capitalism. Even to the non-believer ('bourgeois intellectual') there can be something reassuring about a Marxist interpretation of fascism. Its assumptions involve such plausible causal factors as the vulnerability of elites to socio-economic and political crises, and their readiness to resort to authoritarianism and military violence to ward off any challenge from below. More particularly, it offers a compelling narrative about how the forces of reaction with a vested interest in the perpetuation of the capitalist system responded to the prospect that revolutionary socialism might take advantage of the chaos following the First World War to liberate the world's dispossessed from their enforced hardship, humiliation, and alienation.

Marxist studies are perhaps at their most penetrating when they demonstrate empirically how any apparent victory of what they categorize as fascism can only be won at the cost of systematically deceiving the popular masses about the true nature of its rule and of carrying out atrocities against its chosen victims. The Marxist conviction that all capitalist ideology is an elaborate mystification of the real forces governing society has proved an excellent starting-point to exposing the yawning gap between fascist rhetoric and reality, the monumental façade and the squalid edifice which lies behind it. However much fascism claims to be a revolutionary solution to the class divisions in society, or presents all material and spiritual privations as 'sacrifices' necessary for the nation's higher destiny to be fulfilled, in practice a fascist regime pursues policies leading to persecutions and wars which vastly intensify the degree of misery and dehumanization which liberal capitalism has already inflicted 'systemically' on the masses under parliamentary democracy. The other important feature of Marxist dissections of fascism is that they are never intended to be purely theoretical. Their subtext is that, since even the most humanistic liberals who see through the fascist conjuring trick are prevented by their blindness to the true nature of capitalism and by their instinctive fear of collectivism from taking a united stand against fascism, it falls to the activists of the revolutionary left to maintain a relentless struggle against fascism, whatever ploys it adopts. The purpose of fascist studies is thus never confined purely to the academic and educational: they are to provide the theory and knowledge which inform the praxis of resistance.[10]

Epic accounts of fascism as the incarnation of the enemy which bars the way to the next stage of progress are not confined to Marxists. Christian intellectuals such as Jacques Maritain, idealizing philosophers such as Benedetto Croce, and moralizing historians such as Friedrich Meinecke have offered equally dramatic analyses centring on the struggle between evil and good, between the forces of nihilism and humanism, between barbarism and civilization, between pathology and sanity.[11] Few such stirring tales have been offered by professionals of the 'liberal' camp, however. Before the 1950s there was considerable bewilderment about the dynamics of fascism amongst those academics with no clearer idea of what the direction of history should be other than that there should be a general expansion in freedom, rights, prosperity, technology, and parliamentary systems. Moreover, the unprecedented scale of calculated destruction and inhumanity associated with the Third Reich probably created a psychological block even to recognizing the possibility that anything as positive as utopian idealism or as rational as an ideology could lie behind them. As a result, they tended to concentrate on the pathologies of the individual paths towards modern nationhood which had allowed extreme forms of nationalism to conquer power in Italy, Germany, and elsewhere.[12] The closest equivalent which liberal historians and political scientists have offered to the Manichaean vision of dark forces bent on snuffing out the light for ever, has been to define fascism primarily in terms of what it is against. Thus fascism is 'anti-liberal', 'anti-positivist', 'anti-socialist', 'anti-conservative', 'anti-materialist'. Alternatively, it is the negation of modernity, of progress, of reason, of the Enlightenment, of humanism, of civilization itself. Given the pervasive belief during the Cold War that history was a life or death struggle between the 'Free World' and state tyranny, it is not surprising that many found it convenient to treat fascism as essentially a form of totalitarianism, with little in its social dynamics or state system which merited further probing beyond the mechanisms of oppression.[13] As for fascist ideology, it was commonplace for it to be described as a hotch potch, or even treated as non-existent.

The breakthrough in treating fascism as a generic concept outside the Marxist camp is generally attributed to someone who also treated it primarily in negative key. In 1963 the German scholar Ernst Nolte offered a definition in terms of 'anti-Marxism' and resistance to 'transcendence', the human impulse to reach out to 'the universal' rather than retrench into the particular and familiar. What distinguished Nolte's study from those of so many of his precursors is that to arrive at this apparently negative conclusion he carried out a detailed investigation of the history of three samples of putative fascism. Not only did the scholarly intensity and originality of his analysis vindicate the importance of taking the generic phenomenon seriously, but the scrupulous attention he paid to their individual doctrines implicitly demonstrated the need to give due attention to fascism's ideological contents and their roots in intellectual history. Furthermore, he treated generic fascism as a highly prolific force in inter-war Europe to the point of being able to speak of the period as 'the fascist era'. Finally, his argument that fascist practice embodied the attempt to destroy Marxism through 'a radically opposed yet related ideology' implied that fascism had by opposing communism absorbed through osmosis some of its revolutionary thrust. What emerged was a 'metapolitical' drive to transcend the present crisis-torn state of society which had somehow become involuted, so that it turned in on the nation rather than work outwards towards 'the universal' (see Reading 9). Even if Nolte's own 'fascist minimum' (a phrase he seems to have pioneered) was couched in such abstruse language that it failed to gain currency, he had legitimated the social scientist's search for a more precise and user-friendly one.

A year before Nolte's theory started attracting (respectful but mostly critical) attention in its English translation (*Three Faces of Fascism*, 1965), a slim and highly readable volume had been published by the American academic Eugen Weber which may well have had an even greater practical impact on fascist studies. *Varieties of Fascism* (1964), while not providing a concise definition of the key concept, nevertheless offered a discursive account of its salient traits, establishing its credentials as an 'opportunistic activism inspired by dissatisfaction with the existing order, but unwilling or unable to proclaim a precise doctrine of its own'.[14] In fleshing out the ideological dimension of this activism he highlighted its anti-liberalism, its exaltation of violence, its celebration of a 'collectivistic nationalism' or the idea of the national community, its tendency to fuse ideas taken from both the left and right in a nationalistic form of socialism, and the key role played in its revolutionary ethos by a mixture of utopia and myth, used here in the sense given them by the French thinker Georges Sorel. Fascism thus combined a brand of utopianism, or 'the imaginative construction of a possible future' with strong mythic elements 'whose very unreality makes it possible to keep up a violent, intransigent, doctrinaire position'.[15] He went on to distinguish the pragmatically activist 'Fascist' variant of fascism from the 'theoretically motivated' 'National Socialist' one, a distinction which chimes in with Nolte's stress on the way Nazism implemented a preconceived doctrine, while Fascism elaborated one only after the event. Weber illustrated the value of his approach by citing brief samples from the writings of ideologues of Fascism, Nazism, the Hungarian Arrow Cross, the Romanian Iron Guard, the British Union of Fascists, the Spanish Falange, Belgian Rexism, and the French Faisceau and Rassemblement National Populaire.

Between them Nolte and Weber made a convincing case for approaching fascism as an ideologically driven, or at least myth-driven, movement of essentially revolutionary (and hence anti-conservative) nationalism with a number of variants in inter-war Europe, only two of which actually formed regimes, namely the highly contrasting Fascism and Nazism. The next few years saw a spate of publications from scholars all over the non-Marxist world whose investigations of international fascism were broadly congruent with this cluster of premises, even if few acknowledged any conscious debt to either Nolte or Weber.[16] Indeed, it is tempting to infer that, like so many ideas which become fashionable, their currency shows they were 'in the air' rather than due to the impact of a particular thinker. One of the most influential collections of essays by scholars from all over the world who were now taking fascism seriously as a generic political force was *Fascism: A Reader's Guide*, edited by Walter Laqueur and published in 1976. The book broke new ground by including a sustained analysis of putative fascist phenomena outside Europe, namely in Latin America, and, thanks to the tacit acceptance of fascism's nature as a revolutionary and populist form of anti-communist nationalism, the author, Alistair Hennessy, was able to distinguish between fascism proper and both the military dictatorship of Vargas in Brazil and the populist authoritarianism of

Perón in Argentina without fear of stirring up excessive controversy.[17] What was still conspicuous by its absence from this landmark in fascist studies – apart from any reference to how fascism had evolved in the post-war era – was a succinct, or at least precise, definition which could be widely adopted as the basis of a working consensus for work on particular fascisms. Instead, individual contributors applied their own implicit definition.

There is one exception. Juan Linz's brilliant chapter on the comparative study of fascism offers a lengthy 'multi-dimensional typological definition' of fascism which stresses as core components hypernationalism, anti-parliamentarism, anti-liberalism, anti-communism, populist anti-proletarianism, partial anti-capitalism and anti-clericalism.[18] It is a sign of how far fascist studies had advanced since the immediate post-war years, however, that, while conceding fascism is 'an anti-movement', Linz argues that 'this antithesis in the minds of the ideologists should lead to a new synthesis integrating elements from the political creeds they so violently attack'.[19] He identifies the aim of fascism as that of bringing about 'national social integration through a single party' using an ideology and rhetoric which 'appeals for the incorporation of a national cultural tradition selectively in the new synthesis in response to new social classes, new social and economic problems, and with new organizational conceptions of mobilization and participation,' all of which 'differentiate them from conservative parties.'[20]

Yet the lack of consensus which still prevailed in the mid-1970s is underlined by Zeev Sternhell's equally ground-breaking chapter on fascist ideology,[21] a topic which, as he points out, was practically unthinkable two decades earlier.[22] His article contains the type of observation which has become almost *de rigueur* in contributions to the fascist debate for non-Marxists since 1945 when they start out on their contribution to the debate. He states that few concepts in political terminology are so 'notoriously blurred and imprecise in outline' as fascism, and that 'there still exists no definition of fascism acceptable to all, or recognized as universally valid'.[23] As for the definition which he (implicitly) applies in his own contribution, it conflicts with Linz's article, with the chapters by Hans Mommsen and Karl Bracher on National Socialism, and with Alan Milward's discussion of 'fascism and the economy' by excluding Nazism from consideration altogether. The rationale which Sternhell provides for this omission is clearly stated, if somewhat laconic: 'Nazism cannot, as I see it, be treated as a mere variant of fascism: its emphasis on biological determinism rules out all efforts to deal with it as such.'[24] In a similar vein Francis Carsten concludes his extensive survey of 'interpretations of fascism' with the verdict that 'there is no generally accepted theory of fascism which could apply to the many countries in which fascist movements developed in the 1920s and 1930s', and that 'the present trend among the historians is towards more detailed studies of single fascist parties and movements, and away from any generalization'.[25] It was a situation which caused some scholars at the time, notably G. Allardyce,[26] to go into print suggesting that the quest for a definition of generic fascism was futile.

However, the ghost of generic fascism could not be laid so easily. Not only was it firmly established in common parlance even if only as a synonym for repressive authoritarianism or a term of abuse, but Marxist scholars were keeping it very much alive as a category of chauvinistic capitalism applicable, for example, to apartheid in South Africa or to Latin American dictatorships. There was also the awkward fact that some ultra-right movements of the inter-war period deliberately appropriated the term, notably Georges Valois' Le Faisceau and Mosley's British Union of Fascists, not to mention such advocates of Universal Fascism as J. S. Barnes whom we encountered earlier. Moreover, by the end of the 1970s the comparative fascist studies industry had built up such a global momentum of productivity that it was not to be closed down by a few dissenting voices. In any case, scholars seemed able to make headway in their research without a clearly formulated consensus or working definition of fascism, in the same way that the British parliamentary system seems to function adequately without a written constitution.

It is thus not surprising if the same year in which Allardyce attempted to take the wind out of the sails of generic fascist studies also saw the launch of a new volume of collected essays called *International Fascism: New Thoughts and New Approaches* (1979), shortly followed by the monumental *Who Were the Fascists* (1980), which brought together over 50 essays on the dynamics of fascism, both generic and in individual countries, from a truly international team of scholars. At about this time specialists in individual fascisms were trying their hand at cracking the definitional conundrum. In 1977 the biographer of Mussolini, Renzo de Felice, had published *Interpretations of Fascism*, which offered an elaborate check-list of basic features, a popular approach to this day.[27] G. L. Mosse too, the world's foremost expert on the cultural and ideological dynamics of Nazism, wrote a wide-ranging and incisive essay on the topic as his introduction to *International Fascism*, emphasizing how, in pursuing an activist mode of national mystique, fascism sought a 'third way' between Marxism and capitalism which would produce a 'new man' (see Reading 12). In his major new work on French fascisms, *Ni droite, ni gauche* (1983), Sternhell too proposed a definition, again of the discursive variety. It started by declaring the essence of fascism to be 'a synthesis of organic nationalism with anti-Marxist socialism, a revolutionary ideology' which 'aimed at bringing about a total spiritual revolution'. This involved 'a simultaneous rejection of liberalism, Marxism, and democracy', all three of which were 'regarded as merely the three faces of one and the same materialist evil'. Not only was this synthetic definition an advance on the cumbersome check-list type, it also summarized the thrust of his earlier essay on fascist ideology by stressing the centrality of the bid to bring about the renewal of the national community:

> fascism [. . .] sought to lay the foundation of a new civilization, a communal, anti-individualist civilization that alone would be capable of perpetuating the existence of a human collectivity in which all layers and classes of society are perfectly integrated. The natural framework of such a harmonious, organic collectivity was the nation.[28]

Sternhell's definition is refreshingly concise.[29] He also showed unusual methodological sophistication in the introduction to his book by recognizing that, at bottom, a fascist state and a fascist party are, in Weberian terms, 'ideal types' which no actual historical phenomenon will match entirely. He pointed out too that, 'compared to communism or socialism', the problem of arriving at an ideal type of fascism is compounded by 'the lack of a single source comparable to Marxism'. As a result,

> the historian has to try to discern the common denominator of 'fascist minimum' shared not only by the various political movements and ideologies that claimed to be fascist but also by those that disclaimed the title but nevertheless belonged to the family.[30]

Seen from this point of view, Nolte's emphasis on 'anti-Marxism' and 'the resistance to transcendence', Mosse's stress on the quest for the 'Third Way' and the cult of the 'new man', or Sternhell's emphasis on the 'fusion of organic nationalism with anti-Marxist socialism' are all products of a process of 'idealizing abstraction'. In each case this process, so indispensable to the social sciences, has singled out perceived attributes of generic fascism from the welter of traits which can be associated with it empirically, and welded them into an artificially tidy conceptual model, much as a colour-coded and stylized underground or subway map simplifies the topographical messiness of the actual routes so that passengers can find their way around them. In this perspective there are no 'true' and 'false' definitions of fascism, only ones of more or less heuristic value, i.e. more or less useful for investigating the topic and making sense of evidence. The proliferation of rival theories about its nature results naturally from the fact that different minds will identify different patterns in the data relating to different putative fascisms on the basis of different (often subliminal) assumptions, and hence will create different ideal types.

A scholar who made a methodological breakthrough of parallel importance contemporaneously with Sternhell was Stanley Payne, who earned his academic spurs as a historian of inter-war Spain. His essay on 'The Concept of Fascism' for *Who Were the Fascists* (1980) presents fascism as a subspecies of 'the broader genus of modern revolutionary mass movements'.[31]

This is characterized in what he terms a 'typological description', which he stresses 'does not by any means exhaust the inventory of major character- istics or goals of individual movements', or that they will necessarily exhibit *all* the qualities the typology specifies to count as fascist. In other words, what Payne offers is also an ideal type, a deliberately schematized and simplified model which identifies what fascisms have in common rather than highlighting their undeniable complexity and uniqueness. Following up a suggestion by Juan Linz, he groups these qualities under three headings: Fascist Negations, Ideology and Goals, and Style and Organization. This schematization allows him cumulatively to build up an identikit picture of fascism as a revolutionary form of trans-class nationalism which, though prepared to ally itself with authoritarian conservatism, was ultimately hostile to it.[32]

Of all the ideal types of fascism produced outside the Marxist camp, Payne's was for many years the one which corresponded most closely to the tacit assumptions made by most historians when working on inter-war fascism. Sometimes academics specifically acknowledged their debt to it,[33] but even these occasionally implied that they used Payne's model only because there was nothing more suitable available.[34] Thus it was that in 1985 Ian Kershaw, a major expert on Nazism, was still stressing the 'need for a generic ideal-type concept of fascism'.[35] Not that there had been a shortage of tenders to supply one. A. J. Gregor, for example, turned two major assumptions about Fascism on their head: he portrayed Mussolini's movement, not as an ideological rag-bag or vacuum, but as the relatively coherent synthesis of theories about the nature of 'man' and society which had emerged at the turn of the century; not as anti-modern, but as the product of the tensions engendered in a traditional society by the forces of modernization which could not be resolved by liberal democracy. Indeed, he presented Fascism as the prototype of a 'mass-mobilizing, development- al dictatorship' which he saw cropping up in so many areas of the developing world since 1900 that, on condition that his definition is accepted, Mussolini's vision of a 'century of Fascism' suddenly might seem to be vindicated after all, and even applies to Marxist–Leninist Russia to a remarkable degree.[36]

Yet the impact of Gregor's approach was the same as that of Nolte's and Sternhell's: it became famous within the debate as yet another original and highly sophisticated contribution, but was not applied as a conceptual tool or heuristic device by scholars working at the coal-face of research into the fascist phenomenon. If Nolte's was too abstruse, Sternhell's stress on the left-wing origins of fascism and exclusion of Nazism was too idiosyn- cratic, while Gregor's, apart from giving Fascist ideology an intellectual coherence and gravity which flew in the face of the acute pluralism and frequent vagueness which demonstrably characterized it, inflated the gen- eric phenomenon to a point where it became so universal that crucial distinctions between movements and regimes seemed to be erased. The same fate befell other attempts to resolve the debate. Whether fascism was treated as a utopian form of anti-modernism,[37] or as the latest product of the age of activistic, violence-oriented, and theatrical politics inaugurated by the French Revolution,[38] academics politely noted the book's publication and carried on regardless.

A symptom of the prevailing confusion was the British intellectual Roger Scruton's definition of fascism in his *Dictionary of Political Thought* which appeared in 1982. We are assured that 'From the intellectual point of view fascism remains an amalgam of disparate conceptions, often ill-understood [one is prompted to ask 'by whom?], often bizarre', and that it has 'the form of an ideology but without specific content (other than can be provided by admiration towards the leader)'.[39] In case the reader thinks that the problem only prevailed in the English-speaking world, it must be pointed out that the fascist debate has been dominated by Anglophone theorists, with the notable exception of Zeev Sternhell, and that dismay at its inconclusiveness of the issue thus percolated into the commentaries of academics all over the non-Marxist world. Typical is the observation of the German academic W. Wippermann in the essay 'What is fascism? On the history and problematic of a concept' which forms the introduction to his book on European fascism published in 1983:

> The search for a global theory of fascism which it is possible to use as a master-key to explain the form and function of the different manifestations of fascism and fascisms has to this day led to no satisfactory and generally accepted result.[40]

Reflecting the mood of resignation which reigned at the time, Wippermann concludes by alluding to the now famous verdict of the Italian historian Angelo Tasca that 'to define fascism is above all to write its history', and that a comparative method is necessary 'to indicate a certain number of common characteristics susceptible of being incorporated into a general definition of fascism'.[41] While this might seem at first sight a pragmatic solution to the problem, on closer inspection the statement has a Kafkaesque quality, because without a working definition it is impossible to identify the fascisms to research in order to extract the empirical data on which to base a definition.

The 1980s thus presented the paradoxical situation of a mushrooming academic interest in comparative fascism which only tended to intensify the 'Babel effect' surrounding the central concept. The more scholars worked on it, the more the lack of consensus intensified. The result was that in Italy and Germany the bulk of historians remained highly suspicious of the value of the whole concept of generic fascism in researching the history of Fascism and Nazism, which were accordingly treated as products of the unique histories of each country. The possibility that they can profitably be treated *both* as unique *and* simultaneously as manifestations of a generic force with supra-national dynamics tended to be actively rejected or simply ignored. Nevertheless some prominent academics voiced their unease at the state of affairs. One of them, the prominent historian of Nazism, Tim Mason, swam against the current in an article entitled 'Whatever happened to fascism?' (1991). In what was to be one of his last essays, he bemoaned the loss of a comparative dimension in Nazi studies and associated it with the fall from grace of the generic concept of fascism. In the conclusion he exhorted his colleagues to realize that 'if we can do without much of the original contents of the concept of fascism, we cannot do without comparison', and reasserted a fundamental conviction which had informed his life's work on the Third Reich, namely that 'fascism was a continental phenomenon and that Nazism was part of something much larger'.[42]

In what was surely an example of coincidence rather than synchronicity, the very same year that Mason's essay was published, my own attempt at offering a heuristically useful ideal type of fascism saw the light of day. With hindsight, the theory it expounded seems to have signalled something of a breakthrough in fascist studies, at least in the sense of articulating and crystallizing some premises about fascism which were increasingly 'in the air'. A dictionary definition which derives from my theory is included in this selection,[43] so that there is no need for a lengthy exposition of it here. It is perhaps appropriate, though, to point out its idiosyncratic features: (a) it specifically recognizes that every definition of fascism is an 'ideal type'; (b) it defines fascism exclusively in terms of its mobilizing 'mythic core' which has been abstracted from primary source evidence relating to the ideology of Italian Fascism and other putative fascisms; (c) this core myth is treated as the matrix of each individual fascism's 'surface' ideology, programme, policies, organizational and institutional structures, and style, all of which are assumed to vary considerably from movement to movement because of the unique contemporary situation and historical conditions in which they arise; (d) it presents the mythic core as a fusion of ultra-nationalism with the longing for renewal and rebirth (palingenesis). Since the national renewal is to be brought about as far as possible in a spirit of populist 'people power', my definition of fascism can be formulated in three words: 'palingenetic populist ultra-nationalism' (or 'palingenetic ultra-nationalism' for short).

On the basis of this approach, fascism emerges as an ideology with: (a) its own revolutionary and modernizing agenda which sets it apart from authoritarian forms of both conservatism and capitalism, and also conditions what fascism is against (the fascist 'anti-' dimension) which thus becomes the target of its destructiveness and oppression; (b) a drive towards mobilizing the energies of all those considered part of the national community, something which distinguishes it from right-wing military regimes which are content to impose the 'new order' from above without a genuine social revolution, whatever pseudo-populist façade they erect to legitimize themselves; (c) an organic concept of the nation which, certainly in the inter-war period, rejected dynastic tradition and liberal rationalism in favour of the charismatic energies seen in the leader cult and the pervasive use of theatrical and ritual elements in politics.[44]

Without any formal association between them, several academics concerned with the theory of generic fascism[45] have published analyses over the last few years which are broadly congruent with my approach.[46] Taken as a loosely constituted 'school of thought', we seem to converge on the following axiomatic assumptions: *fascism is a genus of modern, revolutionary, 'mass' politics which, while extremely heterogeneous in its social support and in the specific ideology promoted by its many permutations, draws its internal cohesion and driving force from a core myth that a period of perceived national decline and decadence is giving way to one of rebirth and renewal in a post-liberal new order.* An interesting symptom of how these assumptions are now being unwittingly absorbed even by scholars who still consciously reject them is an article by Robert Paxton, an outstanding expert on the Vichy regime. Having rather pointedly given the definitions offered by Stanley Payne, Roger Eatwell, and myself the cold shoulder, he suggests instead that fascism is to be regarded as 'a political practice intended by its leaders to serve quite specific functions: to unite, purify, and energize nations or ethnic groups that have been put under strain by internal divisions, by the fear of decadence, or by tumultuous social changes.'[47] But both these policies and their implied rationale correspond precisely to an ideology aspiring towards 'renewal in a post-liberal new order' after 'a perceived period of national decline and decadence,' and hence Paxton's own approach is entirely compatible with the definitions proposed by all three of us.[48]

All the components of the paradigm[49] of fascism implied by the new consensus would have been highly contentious until the mid-1970s. Within the next few years they had come to be recognized by the major fascist scholars (Weber, Sternhell, Linz, Payne, Gregor, Mosse), but had been expressed as parts of lengthy check-lists or discursive definitions where they rubbed shoulders with several peripheral elements (such as the 'anti-' aspects or style), so that their heuristic value as definitional features had been diluted or neutralized. Moreover, both Sternhell and Gregor had introduced idiosyncrasies which made their theories as unusable as Nolte's for the practical purposes of research. The consensus view throughout the 1980s was still that expressed by Richard Robinson at the beginning of the decade: 'Although enormous amounts of research time and mental energy have been put into the study of it [. . .] fascism has stubbornly remained the great conundrum for students of the twentieth century.'[50] By the mid-1990s, however, the situation had been transformed. Stanley Payne[51] and

Roger Eatwell[52] even took it upon themselves to deliver single-sentence definitions of generic fascism (both broadly consistent with my own), something which until recently would have been thought foolhardy, heretical, or downright impossible. Yet it underlines just how embryonic the new consensus is that both Payne and Eatwell have shown more zeal in emphasizing the differences between the scholars who represent it than what unites them. Roger Eatwell has written a review article criticizing shortcomings in the definitions offered by Sternhell, Payne and myself,[53] while Payne, though he cities my work approvingly, also finds fault with the single-sentence version of my ideal type,[54] despite the palpable affinity between our approaches. Notwithstanding some genuine differences, I believe that time will show that in the context of the debate over fascism as a whole, what our ideal types have in common is more significant than what separates them. A promising sign of this is that some specialists are demonstrating how the new paradigm can be applied to studying particular fascist phenomena with encouraging empirical results.[55]

The principle of selection and organization underlying this book should now have become apparent. It is the conviction that contributors to fascist studies are finally in a position to treat fascism like any other political ideology rather than as a 'special case' in which its negations or the apparatus and style of exercising power when it is implemented become paramount. In short they need no longer indulge in ritual lamentations over its lack of a consensus, or at least working, definition. The anthology illustrates the deep divisions and confusion which reigned about the term fascism till recently (Section I); the long struggle by academics from various disciplines, Marxist and non-Marxist, to evolve a coherent conceptual model with which to investigate it, and the embryonic consensus about (or emerging paradigm of) its definition which is now discernible (Section II); and how that consensus correlates to positions adopted on particular causal issues raised by fascism, such as the relationship between fascism and modernity or the psychology of fascism (Section III). For good measure, I have also included three texts by fascists themselves which underline the close correspondence between their own understanding of fascism and that implied by the 'new consensus' (Section IV). The fourth text in that section demonstrates that not all the groups which the new paradigm would classify as fascist would accept the label. The book ends with two pieces on contemporary fascism whose approaches, though at loggerheads, should be intelligible in the light of the rest of the book, even though they too contradict the definition we have proposed (Section V). I should point out that in most cases I have not used the original titles of the pieces selected. Instead I have used phrases which indicate the central point of the extract, and should help the reader become aware of how each text fits into the thematic structure of the anthology as a whole.

There are various strategies which can be adopted to make the best use of this Reader. Some lecturers already conversant with the subject may use it simply to have available a few key texts which they can use in any sequence to throw light on the particular aspect of fascist studies they want to present. Students at undergraduate and postgraduate level may find it useful to have some sustained samples of different approaches from which to quote in the context of an essay or dissertation on a particular issue. Yet it should also be possible for someone with a grounding in modern political history or the social sciences but only a minimal familiarity with fascist studies to use this book as a self-instruction manual or work-book which leads into the core of the continuing controversy over fascism's nature and dynamics. By reading the texts in sequence the labyrinthine intricacies of the debate soon reveal themselves. Yet hopefully the sense of progression towards what I have identified as the 'new consensus' offers a thread of Ariadne to help the more tenacious students not only to find their way around the labyrinth, but to exit gulping in the fresh air of what has become *their* own approach.

In other words, by the time readers reach the last two highly contrasting pieces (the last one also highly demanding) on neo-fascism, they should be in a position to sense where their authors are 'coming from', and have some idea where they themselves are going in their own explorations of the subject. However they make use of the anthology, I wish them an enlightening journey. I hope too that, despite the academic register which necessarily prevails throughout, they will find that the texts cumulatively deepen rather than exhaust their fascination with fascism, a phenomenon which combines a shattering potential for destructiveness with causal dynamics of extraordinary complexity.

Notes

1 See Reading 20.
2 J. S. Barnes, *The Universal Aspects of Fascism* (London, Williams and Northgate, 1928). The preface was by Benito Mussolini, showing that he toyed with the vision of Fascism's 'universality' several years before commiting himself to it in the Encyclopedia definition of fascism with which this introduction opened.
3 As indicated in the Preface, the lower case will be used throughout this book to distinguish 'international' or 'generic' fascism, a label which can be applied to movements in many countries, irrespective of what they call themselves, from Mussolini's Fascism, which was a particular political movement and regime referred to as such by its members and opponents. In other words Fascism was a 'historical singularity' while 'fascism' is a 'genus' of phenomena that can assume various forms. Thus Fascism could be described as the Italian variant of fascism.
4 There is, of course, considerable controversy about whether Nazism is a form of fascism or not. The reasons why it is treated as fascist here will hopefully become clearer when the operational definition which informs the organization

of the present text becomes familiar in the course of using the Reader. See Ian Kershaw, *The Nazi Dictatorship* (3rd edition, London, Edward Arnold, 1993), Chapter 2; Roger Griffin, 'Was Nazism Fascist?', *Modern Historical Review*, 5: 1, (September 1983), pp. 15–17.

5 For an account of Universal Fascism see M. Ledeen, *Universal Fascism* (New York, Howard Fertig, 1972).

6 The post-war period has seen a number of (equally ineffectual) internationalist fascist initiatives: see R. D. Griffin, *Europe for the Europeans: Fascist Myths of the New European Order, 1922–92*, Humanities Research Centre Occasional Papers, No. 1 (Oxford, Oxford Brookes University, 1993). Available on request from R. D. Griffin, School of Humanities, Oxford Brookes University, Oxford, OX3 0BP.

7 It is significant in this respect that in June 1985 the most ideologically sophisticated periodical of the Italian radical right, *Diorama letterario* (no. 83), dedicated an entire issue to the topic 'Fascism: a general theory' which presented the problems which the concept poses very much in terms all too familiar from the debate within liberal academia. For example, the editorial stresses that 'an empirical general theory of fascism which makes it intelligible and identifiable without involving any value judgement needs the convergence of several approaches', and identifies four areas to be considered: structures (or institutions), political space, ideology, and sociology. The experts cited by the various contributors are nearly all 'liberal', or certainly non-fascist, academics. The contribution of the editor, Marco Tarchi, who by this time had himself moved away from neo-fascism, forms Reading 22 of this collection.

8 For a practical example of cooperation between academics and politicians in the attempt to understand and counteract international fascism (and the problems of arriving at a consensus on the nature of fascism), see the 'Evrigenis report' produced for the European Parliament: D. Evrigenis (ed.), *Report Drawn Up on Behalf of the Committee of Inquiry into the Rise of Fascism and Racism*, Report no. 2–160/85 (PE 97.547), 2 vols, (Strasbourg, European Parliament, 1986).

9 Cited in D. Beetham, *Marxists in Face of Fascism* (Manchester University Press, Manchester, 1983), p. 82.

10 Reading 24 provides a good example of the Marxist (in this case Trotskyite) nexus between theoretical analysis and practice.

11 See S. Payne, *A History of Fascism, 1914–1945* (London, UCL Press, 1996), pp. 451–4.

12 See ibid., p. 455.

13 See ibid., pp. 447–9.

14 E. Weber, *Varieties of Fascism* (New York, Van Nostrand, 1964), p. 28.

15 Ibid., p. 17.

16 For an excellent account of the stage the debate about fascism had reached by the mid–1970s, see Zeev Sternhell, 'Fascist Ideology', in W. Laqueur (ed.), *Fascism: A Reader's Guide* (Harmondsworth, Penguin, 1979; 1st edition 1976), p. 385–99.

17 Alistair Hennesy, 'Fascism and Populism in Latin America', ibid., pp. 248–99.

18 Juan Linz, 'Some Notes towards a Comparative Study of Fascism in Sociological Historical Perspective', ibid., pp. 13–78.

19 Ibid., p. 29.

20 Ibid., pp. 23–4. See Reading 15 for another sample of Linz's sophisticated analysis of fascism.

21 An extract from this chapter forms Reading 14.

22 Sternhell, 'Fascist Ideology', op. cit., p. 326: 'For many years it was common form to see fascism either as completely wanting in concepts or as having gotten itself up for the sake of the cause in a few rags of doctrine, which therefore need not be taken seriously, nor allowed even the minimal importance that is attached as a rule to the ideas professed by a political movement.'

23 Ibid., p. 326.

24 Ibid., p. 328.

25 Francis Carsten, 'Interpretations of Fascism', in W. Laqueur (ed.), *Fascism: A Reader's Guide*, op. cit., p. 428.

26 G. Allardyce, 'What Fascism is Not: Thoughts on the Deflation of a Concept', *The American History Review*, 84(2) (1979).

27 A highly sophisticated 10-point check-list definition was offered by the outstanding scholar of Fascism, Emilio Gentile, in the latest edition of *Enciclopedia Italiana* in 1992, sixty years after his namesake Giovanni Gentile had written the first part of the definition of Fascism for the first edition of the encyclopedia, a major product of Fascist culture. See S. Payne, *A History of Fascism*, op. cit., pp. 5–6 for the full definition.

28 Zeev Sternhell, *Neither Right nor Left*, paperback of English edition, (Princeton, Princeton University Press, 1996; hardback edition, 1986; original French edition, 1983), p. 27.

29 It formed the basis of the expanded version which appears as the encyclopedia definition reproduced in Reading 2.

30 For a brief account of Max Weber's theory of ideal types see R. Griffin, *The Nature of Fascism* (London, Pinter, 1991), pp. 8–12.

31 S. U. Larsen, B. Hagtvet, J. P. Myklebust (eds), *Who Were the Fascists* (Oslo, Universitetsforlaget, 1980), p. 20. Payne made the same definition the basis of his monograph *Fascism: Comparison and Definition* (Madison, University of Wisconsin Press, 1980), the prototype of *A History of Fascism, 1914–1945*, op. cit.

32 The slightly modified version of Payne's typology, which has now been supplemented by a single sentence definition, is provided in Reading 13.

33 For example, G. J. Kasza, 'Fascism from Below? A Comparative Perspective on the Japanese Right 1931–1936', *Journal of Contemporary History*, 19(4) (1984); G. Botz, 'Austria', in D. Mühlberger (ed.), *The Social Basis of European Fascist Movements* (London, Croom Helm, 1987).

34 For example, in 'Leaders and Martyrs: Codreanu, Mosley, and José Antonio', *History*, 71 (1986), S. M. Cullen uses Payne's definition with the qualification that 'the academic search for some workable definition of fascism that embraces the various manifestations of the phenomenon will be a long one'.

35 Ian Kershaw, *The Nazi Dictatorship* (London, Edward Arnold, 1985), p. 150.

36 See especially A. J. Gregor, *The Fascist Persuasion in Radical Politics* (Princeton, Princeton University Press, 1974). See also Reading 11.

37 H. A. Turner, 'Fascism and Modernization', in H. A. Turner (ed.), *Reappraisals of Fascism* (New York, Franklin Watt, 1975).

38 Neil O'Sullivan, *Fascism* (London, J.M. Dent & Sons, 1983). O'Sullivan supplements this approach with another check-list of definitional features drawn from Fascism and Nazism, something resorted to also a decade earlier by Paul Hayes, *Fascism* (London, George Allen & Unwin, 1973).

39 Roger Scruton, *Dictionary of Political Thought* (London, The Macmillan Press, 1982), p. 169.

40 W. Wippermann, *Europäischer Faschismus im Vergleich, 1922–1982* (Frankfurt am Main, Suhrkampf, 1983), pp. 19–20.

41 A. Tasca, *Nascita e avvento del fascismo* (Bari, Laterza, 1965), vol. 2, pp. 553–4.
42 Jane Caplan (ed.), *Nazism, Fascism and the Working Class: Essays by Tim Mason* (Cambridge, Cambridge University Press, 1995), p. 331.
43 Reading 3.
44 The post-war period has seen some forms of ideological fascism which apparently reject a charismatic style of politics, though it is difficult to see how the vision of the new society would be enacted through a 'rational' parliamentary system. See R. Griffin, *Fascism* (Oxford, Oxford University Press), pp. 5–6.
45 For example, P. Ignazi, *L'Estrema destra in Europa* (Bologna, Il Mulino, 1994); R. Eatwell, *Fascism: A History* (London, Chatto & Windus, 1995); S. G. Payne, *A History of Fascism, 1914–45*, op. cit. In his *Fascism, Past, Present, Future* (New York, Oxford University Press, 1996), Walter Laqueur, despite his scepticism concerning definitions of generic fascism, grudgingly accepts that one based on rebirth ultra-nationalism is difficult to improve on (p. 9). To take another example, the approach of M. Neocleous, though its main focus is to locate fascism within the nexus of modernity and capitalism, is broadly consistent with what we are calling here 'the new paradigm', and he is happy to adopt the term 'palingenetic'. See his *Fascism* (Buckingham, Oxford University Press, 1997), especially pp. 72–3.
46 It is perhaps worth adding that the representative of one ultra-right organization which I would classify as fascist, the English Nationalist Movement (see Reading 23), was sufficiently impressed by my *Fascism*, op. cit. to praise my theory for the understanding it implied for the dynamics of fascism, even though he recognized that I was hostile to fascism (and naturally repudiated any suggestion that his movement was to be included in that category in the first place). Such a reaction is important, since it has been one of the anomalies of academic definitions of fascism that they were all too often couched in terms which were alien or incomprehensible to fascists themselves, whereas every other political ideology is defined in terms which reflect the world-view of its protagonists, no matter how much it clashes with the values of the author responsible for devising the definition. One of my aims in developing my theory was precisely to generate a definition of fascism from the writings of fascists themselves, which they could recognize as valid, without any implication that I was sympathizing with the object of my study. The ENM's reaction also emphasizes that a number of ideologues whom my ideal type classifies as fascist still vehemently repudiate such a suggestion, an understandable reaction given the term's overwhelmingly negative connotations for the vast majority.
47 Robert O. Paxton, 'The Uses of fascism', *New York Review of Books*, 43(19), 28 November (1996), p. 48. Another interesting example of the unwitting absorption of the new paradigm is provided by Alexander De Grand. In his *Fascist Italy and Nazi Germany. The 'Fascist' Style of Rule* (Routledge, London, 1995) he states that much ink has also been spilled in the search for some 'generic fascism' but that 'it seems no consensus will ever be reached' (p. 2). Yet he later recognizes that the common denominator to Fascism and Nazism was that both offered a 'quasi-religious alternative to Marxism' central to which was 'the idea of a national rebirth in a new social and political system' which 'sought to shape a new type of humanity' (pp. 77–8).
48 See Readings 3, 13, and Roger Eatwell, *Fascism: A History* (London, Chatto & Windus, 1995), p. 11.
49 'Paradigm' can be used in two related ways: (a) it refers to the 'classic' example of a phenomenon which holds the key for the understanding of all

other versions of it: hence Nazism can be treated as the 'paradigm' of generic fascism; (b) it also can mean the conceptual framework and value system used (often unconsciously) to understand aspects of the world and investigate them: hence each phase of fascist studies can be seen to have been dominated by a particular 'paradigm' which determined how it was approached.

50 R. A. H. Robinson, *Fascism in Europe* (London, The Historical Association, 1981), p. 1.
51 S. G. Payne, *A History of Fascism, 1914–45*, op. cit. See Reading 13.
52 R. Eatwell, *Fascism: A History,* op. cit., p. 11: here he defines fascism as 'a form of thought which preaches the need for social rebirth in order to forge a *holistic-national radical Third Way*'.
53 Roger Eatwell, 'On Defining the "Fascist Minimum"': The Centrality of Ideology', *Journal of Political Ideologies*, 1(3) (1996), pp. 303–19.
54 Payne, *A History of Fascism, 1914–45*, op. cit., p. 5.
55 Notably N. Copsey, 'Fascism: the Ideology of the British National Party', *Politics*, 14(3) (1995); Mike Cronin, *The Blueshirts and Irish Politics* (Cork, Cork University Press, 1997); D. Baker, *Ideology of Obsession: A. K. Chesterton and British Fascism* (London, Tauris, 1996); A. Costa Pinto, *Salazar's Dictatorship and European Fascism* (New York, Columbia University Press, 1995); Thomas P. Linehan, *East London for Mosley: The British Union of Fascists, 1933–40* (Portland, Oregon, Frank Cass, 1996); M. Affron and M. Antliff (eds), *Fascist Visions: Art and Ideology in France and Italy* (Princeton, New Jersey, Princeton University Press, 1997).

THE LACK OF CONSENSUS IN FASCIST STUDIES

Presentation

The three Readings in this section are intended to initiate the reader into the debate over generic fascism at the point where many conscientious undergraduates first encounter it, namely by consulting general reference works in the social sciences. If not forearmed or forewarned by lectures which have prepared the ground in advance, this can be a confusing and chastening experience. The editors of such reference works generally (though not always!) bring in academics with some record of publishing specialist studies in the area, who therefore write in an authoritative style and make a number of valid points. However, when the subject is as unwieldy and contentious as fascism, the result for the 'consumer' is predictable. The first encyclopedia consulted will give a fairly clear line on what the term means and suggest several books for further study. The second will contradict it in some important respects, and suggest a conflicting approach backed up by a different bibliography. Any illusion that matters resolve themselves once a third expert definition is consulted is then quickly dispelled when the new approach turns out to be strikingly different again.

It is important to reflect for a moment on why this is so, because even some postgraduates cling to the touching assumption that experts are somehow right, or that the fact that their essay is published as an article in a reference work, often with their name reduced to cryptic initials, confers on their analysis the quality of objective authority. In reality, each essay is exactly that: an attempt to take stock of the meaning of a term by someone familiar with the major schools of scholarly thought concerning its use within the discipline. There is nothing definitive or sculpted in stone about the verdict thus produced, even if convention dictates that the reader is not bombarded with the intricacies of the controversy surrounding a particular term in a dictionary article, so that each one tends to convey an artificially definite, coherent sense of its meaning and usage. In reality, as explained in the Introduction, every definition of a generic term in the social sciences is at bottom an ideal type, and even when there is a broad consensus within the discipline about what the most heuristically useful ideal type is, it only points to a high degree of interpersonal subjectivity (i.e. conventional agreement) about how the word is to be used, rather than to the existence of an impersonal truth about it.

Generic 'fascism' is similar to words such as 'ideology', 'culture', 'race', 'class', 'history', and 'progress', in that a bewilderingly wide range of ideal types of their essential definitional traits has accumulated over time, and there is no objective way of resolving the differences between them. This dilemma is a major handicap to researching fascism at any level of naïvety or expertise until the dynamics of the controversy have been understood. To illustrate it I have chosen three discursive definitions of fascism taken from three companion volumes in the series of reference works published by the Oxford-based academic publishers, Blackwells.

Paul Wilkinson is best known for his pioneering research on terrorism, though in 1981 he published *The New Fascists*, a survey of extreme right-wing activity in Europe without pretensions to furthering the debate over what exactly constituted fascism. His definition in the *Blackwell Encyclopedia of Political Institutions* (1987) thus reflects some of the preconceptions commonly held by academics at the time. It starts with a brief account of Italian fascism (i.e. Fascism), which incidentally contains two factual errors: 'fascist' did not derive from the *fasces*, but from the term *fascio* or league chosen by Mussolini to describe his cellular movement of war-veterans and ultra-nationalist revolutionaries, the *Fasci di combattimento*, which were founded in March 1919, not 1921. He goes on to attribute Fascism's success less to its 'nebulous ideology' than to its ritualistic, militaristic style of politics, and rightly points out the tensions at the heart of the Fascist movement and its dependency for success on the collusion of Italy's powerful conservative forces.

Turning to the thorny issue of generic fascism (not that he hints that it is thorny), Wilkinson produces a check-list of basic ideological tenets which implies it is best seen as a totalitarian form of ultra-nationalism largely modelled on Nazism (note the reference to 'Führer'). As for its manifestations, there is a cryptic reference to the notion that Mussolini's black-shirted paramilitaries had imitators 'throughout Europe and Latin America', a highly debatable assertion, since the main wave of European fascism arguably came in the wake of the success of Hitler's NSDAP, while most experts agree that in Latin America right-wing militarism and conservatism effectively reduced the political space for fascism to a minimum.[1] The specific examples he gives of generic fascism are the Spanish Falange (though not Franco's regime), Nazism, as well as unnamed mass movements in Rumania and Hungary (presumably the Iron Guard and Arrow Cross respectively). He stresses the uniqueness of Nazism's virulent racism (though the Iron Guard was also fanatically anti-Semitic), and the extraordinary degree of success it had in implementing its policies. Wilkinson then expresses surprise at the survival of small pockets of neo-fascism since 1945, attributing this to the perverse 'religious-cult' aspect of fascism which breeds a fanaticism nourished by its very alienation from democratic norms. As for electoral fascism, he cites the German NDP, Italian MSI, and French FN as examples of contemporary political parties which have perpetuated the neo-fascist success in capitalizing on the structural problems of modern democracy. Wilkinson's article has the advantage of at least being accessible to most readers. After all, its judgement that fascism is to be treated as a violent and oppressive form of nationalist regime devoid of ideological depth corresponded to the prevailing common sense view within and outside academia in the 1980s.

Zeev Sternhell's approach to fascism has already been discussed at some length in the Introduction. In contrast to Wilkinson his definition for *The Blackwell Encyclopedia of Political Thought* (1987) presents it, not as 'nebulous', but as a relatively coherent ideological synthesis of 'organic nationalism and anti-Marxist socialism' with no reference to its ritual, militaristic style of politics. He also stresses the revolutionary thrust towards a 'new civilization' rooted in the values first expounded by the intellectuals who broke radically with Enlightenment values in what he terms the 'revolt against positivism',[2] highlighting the celebration of the power of myth in the Sorelian sense already identified by Eugen Weber.[3] He goes on to stress how the transformation of both nationalism and socialism at the turn of the century in the spirit of overtly irrational myth laid the foundation of fascism, which he sees as being first converted into political reality in Italy. Italian fascism (Fascism) is thus treated as the first manifestation of a generic, 'pan-European' ideological force (fascism) prefigured in France, and then espoused by other militants in inter-war France, Spain, Belgium, Romania, and Britain. If it is noticeable that France, Belgium, and Britain are not mentioned by Wilkinson, it is much more telling that Germany is conspicuous by its absence from Sternhell's essay. Rather than explain why Nazism is not to be treated as a member of fascism's extended family, Sternhell chooses to dwell on the structural conditions which, though they did not produce fascism as such, did cause it to crystallize as the major new political ideology of the inter-war period: the rise of the masses as agents of socio-political change, the Great Depression, but above all the First World War. Typical of Sternhell's insistence on the importance of the history of ideas in the understanding of fascism is the way he then concentrates on the 'political philosophy of fascism' (which many scholars refuse to take seriously), rather than consider non-European fascism or post-war fascism. This excursus leads to the important conclusion that fascist totalitarianism was consistent with its conception of the state rather than a perversion of it, as in the case of Stalinism. Despite the aberrant judgement on Nazism's fascist credentials and a one-sided preoccupation with the contribution to fascism of the revolutionary left, Sternhell's article reveals his basic approach to be a major forerunner of the 'new consensus' on generic fascism, in stark contrast to Wilkinson's.[4]

Another variant of this consensus is embodied in my own definition for *The Blackwell Dictionary of Social Thought* (1993), though in the context of Section I the contrasts are more significant than the parallels. I too present fascism as a synthesis of ultra-nationalism with another component, though where Sternhell identifies this as 'anti-Marxist socialism', I see it as the myth of rebirth or 'palingenesis'. By my reckoning this has formed the basis of movements in at least ten European and two non-European countries, and has survived into the post-war era as a shadow of its former self. My article specifically cites National Socialism as a form of fascism, and as the only movement other than Fascism to seize power, though it stresses that even in Italy and Germany it retained power only in extensive collusion with conservative forces. It also stresses the distinction between fascist and pseudo-fascist, essentially conservative ('para-fascist'), regimes, and points out that the natural constituency for fascism is always a minority, so that the attempt to impose its values through social engineering inevitably leads to totalitarianism. At this point the contentious nature of my definition is pointed out as an inevitable consequence of its ideal-typical character,[5] and the reader is invited to compare it to conflicting definitions offered in companion works of reference. Attention then turns to various ways in which the core myth of national decadence and rebirth can be rationalized in accordance with the peculiar conditions prevailing in the national culture where it arises, stressing its tendency to exploit mythic notions of past glories to mobilize national energies in the present. This section concludes by pointing out that contemporary fascisms continue to evolve ideologically, giving the example of how some have appropriated ecologism and New Age culture (I would now also refer to the extensive neo-fascist use of the Internet, and cannot understand why at the time I omitted to refer to the important role played by Holocaust denial and revisionism in post-war fascist discourse).

My analysis then turns to the way the sociological complexity of fascism reflects its extreme ideological heterogeneity, and how neo-fascism has disguised itself with the trappings of democratic party politics. I draw particular attention to the influence of the French New Right (Nouvellé Droite) and pan-Europeanism on the more sophisticated variants of neo-fascism, and the way fascism is bound to continue as an ingredient of modern politics, especially in countries undergoing structural crises, such as immediate post-Wall Germany and the new Russia (the flare-up of neo-Nazi activity in reunified Germany probably deserved more comment). Since the article was written for a volume on social thought, the final paragraph is devoted to some observations on the success of fascism, especially in its two regime forms, in producing academic rationales for its essentially mythic, anti-rational world-views. I conclude with the suggestion that certain intellectual traditions within the liberal social sciences provide important tools with which to study fascism as a myth-driven (but not millenarian and hence genuinely religious) revolutionary phenomenon.

Left to their own devices, uninitiated readers in search of a clear, definitive idea of what constitutes fascism would be liable to emerge from a close study of these three articles disillusioned, bewildered, and frustrated. Why is there no reference to Britain in the first, or Nazism in the second? Why is Latin America referred to in the first but only Brazil in the third (though I should in fact have alluded to Chilean fascism as well)? Why do the second and third spend so long on the ideological complexity of fascism when the first dismisses the subject out of hand? Why is post-war fascism given short shrift in the first, ignored entirely in the second, and then dwelt on in the third? Why is the revolutionary thrust of fascism left out of account in the first, focused on in the second as the fruit of a distinctive intellectual current, and then portrayed in the third as a force that can concoct its rationale from a vast range of cultural traditions. Given the fact that all three of us suggest our own books for further reading, it would be forgivable to see them as exercises in self-advertising written in an arrogant, even obfuscating register. Sociologists might be dismayed at the scant attention given to the social base of fascism, and historians at the weight given to ideological rather than strictly institutional, political, and economic considerations, or the impact of national histories and outstanding personalities. Feminists might well point out that there are no female sources cited, and no reference to the fascist denigration of women, or to *machismo* as a vital ingredient of the fascist mindset. Marxists would be equally scathing: where is there a single reference to the centrality to fascism of capitalism and the bourgeoisie, or to the economic dimension of the causes of fascism and the policies pursued by fascist regimes?

The reason for the diversity of the approaches has been covered in the Introduction: the three passages are expressions of conflicting ideal types of fascism generated at a time (late 1980s–early 1990s) when outside the Marxist camp few ingredients of consensus could be found and the Babel effect of ever intensifying scholarly preoccupation with fascism was at its height. Having deliberately muddied the waters, the opening Readings of Section II will fill in one of the significant gaps left by these three articles by focusing on persuasive, if arguably misleading, Marxist approaches. The gender dimension will only be encountered specifically much later (in a text on the psycho-dynamics of fascism). For the moment it is important for readers to familiarize themselves with the analyses offered here, which sow a number of seeds which will hopefully germinate in the course of Sections II and III. These three definitions should thus read quite differently by the time they have worked their way through to the end of Section V.

Notes

1 For example, Alistair Hennessy, 'Fascism and Populism in Latin America', in W. Laqueur, *Fascism: A Reader's Guide* (Harmondsworth, Penguin, 1979), pp. 248–99.
2 A term pioneered by H. S. Hughes in his *Consciousness and Society,* (London, McGibbon and Kee, 1958).
3 See Introduction p. 7.
4 On the 'new consensus' see Introduction, pp. 13–15.
5 See Introduction, p. 10.

1

*Fascism**

PAUL WILKINSON

fascism A term designating a wide variety of violently nationalistic and authoritarian movements that reached the peak of their strength between 1930 and 1945. The term fascist derives from the *fasces* which were bundles of elm or birch rods bound with red cord and carried by the lictors in ancient Rome in attendance upon magistrates: the rods symbolized unity and authority.

The original fascist movement was that of Mussolini in Italy, organized in March 1921, although its origins lie in the First World War and, more deeply, in the intellectual reaction against liberalism which began in the latter half of the nineteenth century. The movement acquired various ideas and slogans which were to have a popular appeal among those hit by post-war disillusion and depression, and somewhat resentful of Italy's second-class status as a European power. It was ultra-patriotic, ultra-nationalist and pro-militarist in policy and style. Italian fascism was to some extent revolutionary: for example in its desire to shake off the constraints of bourgeois liberal democratic values and practices, in its dedication to modernization and industrial growth, in its exaltation of the role of youth. In other respects it was counter-revolutionary and reactionary: for example Mussolini offered the capitalists and the church a bulwark against Bolshevism, the style and practice of fascism favoured the continuance of the privileges and status of the Italian monarchy and aristocracy, the structure of fascist rule was rigidly elitist; Mussolini followed a colonialist policy traditionally associated with the Right.

Mussolini's Black Shirts had many imitators throughout Europe and Latin America – indeed nearly every European country had a fascist party in the 1930s – though there were enormous variations in ideology and programme. It was not so much the rather nebulous ideology of Italian fascism that proved so appealing (though certainly ultra-nationalism and anti-Bolshevism became identifying characteristics of all fascisms), but rather its mass revolutionist techniques. Drawing on his experience as a socialist party organizer and propagandist, Mussolini proved able to use the techniques of the mass movement with enormous *élan* and propaganda

* Reprinted in full from V. Bogdanor (ed.), *The Blackwell Encyclopedia of Political Institutions* (Oxford, Basil Blackwell, 1987), pp. 226–8.

success. He learnt to use the symbolism and ritual of para-military organizations, uniforms, mass parades, demonstrations and the whole para-
phernalia of youth movement and media manipulation, to consolidate his
personal charisma and political power as dictator. In the long process of
this consolidation, between 1921 and 1928, the inherent ambiguities and
internal contradictions of fascism became apparent.

There was a running conflict over political aims and methods between
the fascist movement's grass-roots militants and members of Mussolini's
para-military militia, and the more conservative traditionalist forces in
Italy which Mussolini was not powerful enough to destroy or control and
upon whose tacit support the Mussolini regime depended for its survival.
These were the army, the church, the monarchy, large landowners and
major capitalist interests. There was, furthermore, an internal conflict
within the fascist movement between the impetuous revolutionary zeal
of the mass movement and the needs of the movement-regime to establish
a stable, disciplined and centrally controlled party bureaucracy. There is
evidence that not only the fascist movement organizers, but also Mussolini
himself, became confused, baffled and vacillating, in the search for a fascist
political strategy in the mid-1920s, on the eve of the 'second wave' of
fascist illegality and intimidation.

The other European fascisms did not necessarily follow the Italian
historical pattern. This does not, however, mean that we should abandon
the term fascism. All these movements combined, to some degree, mass
revolutionist strategies with reactionary ideologies compounded of virulent ultra-nationalism, exaltation of irrationality, illegality, violence and
fanatical anti-communism. In Spain, the Falange only became temporarily
dominant in the right wing coalition of the 'national movement' between
1936 and 1941–42. During this period, its ideological militancy and sympathy with its brother movements, Nazism and Italian fascism, were of
indispensable value in acquiring the resources for Franco's Civil War
victory. But the 1950s the ideological fanaticism of the Falange was an
embarrassment to the Spanish regime.

Spanish and Italian fascisms also lacked the *völkisch* racialist and anti-
Semitic ideology of Hitler's Nazism. (Italian fascism was not explicitly
anti-Semitic until 1938, and did not engage in anti-Semitic persecution on
a major scale until the SS itself directly intervened under the German
occupation.) Furthermore, Hitler was vastly more successful both in his
use of mass revolutionist strategies, mass propaganda and party organization, and the control of mass communications media, nationalist symbolism and slogans. He appealed to German youth, to the German
propensities for authoritative dictatorial government and military glory,
and to the German desire for revenge against the humiliations imposed by
the Versailles powers. Hitler used the full repertoire of mass revolutionism
both to further his racialist aims of pathological anti-Semitism and to

bolster his own charisma and power as leader of the new 'revolution'. Through the agency of the Nazi para-military terror organizations, the SA, the SS and later the Gestapo, the Hitler regime was able to indulge in violent and sadistic mass terrorism, mass liquidation, racial persecution and racial extermination, secure in the knowledge that all popular bases for organized mass political opposition had been eliminated within the first twelve months of the Nazi revolution in 1933. Despite the considerable evidence that Hitler continued to meet stiff resistance to his will among individual members of the top military and state bureaucracy, the overwhelming actual and potential power over German society which fell to the Nazi party passed the threshold of totalitarianism appallingly rapidly after 1933. In Spain, Italy, Rumania and Hungary, fascist movements, despite their considerable influence as mass movements, did not achieve the scale of the Nazi hegemony.

It is not difficult to summarize the crude tenets of fascist ideology: the belief in the supremacy of the chosen national group over all other races and minorities; the total subordination of the individual to an absolute state under an absolute leader or Führer figure; the suppression of all autonomous secondary institutions; the rejection of the values and institutions of parliamentary democracy and their replacement by fascist dictatorships; total opposition to peaceful internationalism; a foreign policy of expansionism and conquest as the natural 'destiny' of the nation. As George Orwell observed in *The Road to Wigan Pier*: 'It is usual to speak of the fascist objective as the "beehive state", which does a grave injustice to bees. A world of rabbits ruled by stoats would be nearer the mark.'

Historians and social scientists have been baffled by the stubborn survival of small pockets of fascist belief and activity over forty years after the defeat of Hitler. The phenomenon of small neo-fascist movements, scattered not only in western Europe and North America but as far away as Australia and South Africa, defies all the established theories of political participation and rational political choice elaborated by political scientists. We perhaps come closer to explaining their continued existence if we view tham as ideological–religious cult movements, sustained by a crude set of irrational dogmas, and paradoxically strenghthened in their fanaticism by their total alienation from the norms and values of democratic societies. Wilkinson (1983) surveys the growth of tiny groups of this type and the problems they can create in liberal democratic societies.

But it would be dangerous to assume that neo-fascism will inevitably be confined to the role of tiny conspiratorial groups. There have been a number of remarkably effective attempts in western Europe since 1945 to develop neo-fascist parties with mass support, under a veneer of respectability. These include the National Democratic Party (NPD) in West Germany, the Italian Social Movement (MSI) in Italy (which managed to get fifty-six Deputies elected to the Chamber of Deputies in the 1972 elections), the National Front (NF) in Britain and the *Front National* in France. These movements have not succeeded in capturing power but they have shown their capacity to exploit certain populist fears and prejudices such as hostility to immigrants, racial prejudice, fear of large communist movements (in Italy and France), and general frustration with economic conditions in a period of recession.

References

Felice, R. de 1977: *Interpretations of fascism*. Cambridge, MA: Harvard University Press.

Gentile, G. 1973: The origins and doctrine of fascism. In Lyttleton, A. (ed.), *Italian Fascisms*. London: Cape.

Gregor, A. J. 1976: *The ideology of fascism: the rationale of totalitarianism*. New York: Free Press.

Hagtvet, B., Larsen, S. U. and Myklebust, J. P. 1980: *Who were the Fascists: Social Roots of European Fascism*. Oslo: Universitetsforlaget.

Laqueur, W. (ed.), 1976: *Fascism: a reader's guide*. London: Wildwood.

Lyttleton, A. (ed.), 1973: *Italian Fascisms from Pareto to Gentile*. London: Cape.

Mussolini, B. 1935: *The political and social doctrines of fascism*. London: Hogarth.

Nolte, E. 1965: *Three faces of fascism*. London: Weidenfeld & Nicolson.

Payne, S. G. 1980: *Fascism: comparison and definition*. Madison: University of Wisconsin Press.

Weber, E. 1964: *Varieties of fascism*. New York: Van Nostrand.

Wilkinson, P. 1983: *The new fascists*, rev. edn. London: Pan Books.

Woolf, S. (ed.), 1981: *Fascism in Europe*. London: Methuen.

2

*Fascism**

ZEEV STERNHELL

fascism Of all the major ideologies of the twentieth century, fascism was the only one to come into being together with the century itself. It was a synthesis of organic nationalism and anti-Marxist socialism, a revolution-

* Reprinted in full from D. Miller (ed.), *The Blackwell Encyclopedia of Political Thought* (Oxford, Basil Blackwell, 1987), pp. 148–50.

ary movement based on a rejection of liberalism, democracy and Marxism. In its essential character, fascist ideology was a rejection of materialism—liberalism, democracy and Marxism being regarded simply as different aspects of the same materialist evil. It was this revolt against materialism which, from the beginning of the century, allowed a convergence of anti-liberal and anti-bourgeois nationalism and a variety of socialism which, while rejecting Marxism, remained revolutionary. This form of socialism was also, by definition, anti-liberal and anti-bourgeois, and its opposition to historical materialism made it the natural ally of radical nationalism. The fascists synthesis symbolized the rejection of a political culture inherited from the eighteenth century and the French Revolution, and it aimed at laying the foundations of a new civilization. Only a new communal and anti-individualistic civilization was deemed capable of assuring the permanence of a human collectivity in which all strata and all classes of society would be perfectly integrated, and the natural framework for such a harmonious, organic collectivity was held to be the nation – a nation enjoying a moral unity which liberalism and Marxism, both agents of warfare and disunity, could never provide.

An organic, tribal, exclusive nationalism based on biological determinism was a translation into political terms of the intellectual revolution of the turn of the century. With Barrès, Maurras and Corradini (who created the idea of the 'proletarian nation'), nationalism became a coherent political theory. It converged quite naturally with the second element in the fascist equation: the revision of Marxism undertaken at the beginning of the century by Georges Sorel and the theoreticians of Italian revolutionary syndicalism. If one fails to take into account this initially socialistic revolt against materialism, fascist ideology can hardly be understood. Intellectually, it was greatly influenced by social Darwinism, by the anti-Cartesian and anti-Kantian philosophy of Bergson and Nietzsche, by the psychology of Le Bon and the sociology of Pareto. Its immediate context was the enormous changes which were taking place in the capitalist economy, in bourgeois society and in the life of the working class – changes which ran quite contrary to Marxist expectations.

Sorel replaced the rationalistic, Hegelian foundations of Marxism with anti-materialist, voluntarist, vitalist elements. This form of socialism was a philosophy of action based on intuition, and the cult of energy and *élan*, activism and heroism. To activate the masses, thought Sorel, one did not require reasoning but myths, systems of images which strike the imagination. When it became obvious that the myth of the general strike and proletarian violence was ineffective because the proletariat was incapable of fulfilling its role as a revolutionary factor, the Sorelians had no option but to abandon Marxism and to replace the proletariat with the great rising force: the nation as a whole. One arrived in this way at a socialism for all, embodying a new idea of revolution – a national, moral and psychological revolution, the only kind of revolution which does not bear the characteristics of class struggle. This was the real contribution of Sorel and the revolutionary syndicalists and non-conformists of France and Italy to Fascism.

Among these were the theoreticians of revolutionary syndicalism such as Arturo Labriola, Robert Michels, Sergio Panunzio and Paolo Orano, and their fellow-traveller Benito Mussolini. The connection between Mussolini and the revolutionary syndicalists was already very strong in 1902 and, throughout the period prior to the First World War, Mussolini's development took place under their shadow. In 1914, Mussolini and the revolutionary syndicalists together with Corradini's nationalists constituted the spearhead of the interventionist movement: the synthesis of a radial nationalism and a new type of socialism thus became a political reality. During the war, revolutionary syndicalism turned into national syndicalism and then into fascism.

In the sphere of political theory, this synthesis was already clearly expressed around the years 1910–12 in such publications as *Les Cahiers du Cercle Proudhon* in France, and above all *La Lupa* in Italy. The nationalists and revolutionary syndicalists wished to replace the mercantile civilization of their day with a civilization of monks and warriors, a warlike, virile and heroic civilization in which a sense of sacrifice would replace bourgeois hedonism and egoism. This new world would be created by an elite conscious of its duties which alone would be capable of leading the masses, who in turn were only a herd, to battle.

These constitutive elements of the fascist ideology, elaborated previous to August 1914, reappeared in an almost identical form in the 1920s and 1930s both in Italy and elsewhere: among the French fascists who had come from the right such as Georges Valois, Robert Brasillach and Pierre Drieu La Rochelle, and former French socialists and communists such as Marcel Deat or Jacques Doriot. Other examples were José Antonio Primo de Rivera in Spain, Léon Degrelle in Belgium and Corneliu Zelia Codreanu in Rumania.

From this perspective, it is clear that fascism was a pan-European phenomenon, and it existed on three levels – as an ideology, as a political movement, and as a form of government. From the point of view of the history of ideas, the First World War was not the watershed it appears to have been in so many other areas. Fascism did not belong only to the inter-war era but to that whole period of history which began with the modernization of the European continent at the end of the nineteenth century. The intellectual revolution of the turn of the century, the entry of the masses into politics, produced fascism as a system of thought, as a sensibility, as an attitude to the essential problems of civilization. The First World War and the economic crisis of the 1930s produced the sociological and psychological conditions necessary to the construction of the fascist movement, but they did not produce fascist ideology.

The war did, however, contribute to the final crystallization of fascist ideology, not only because it provided a proof of the capacity of nationalism to mobilize the masses, but because it displayed the tremendous power of the modern state. It revealed quite new possibilities of economic planning, and of mobilizing the national economy as well as private property in the service of the state. The state was regarded as the expression of national unity and its might depended on the spiritual unanimity of the masses, but at the same time the state was the guardian of this unity which it fostered with every means possible. The war revealed how great the capacity of the individual for sacrifice could be, how superficial was the idea of internationalism, and how easily all strata of society could be mobilized in the service of the state. It demonstrated the importance of unity of command, of authority, of leadership, of moral mobilization, of the education of the masses, and of propaganda as an instrument of power. Above all, it had shown how easily democratic liberties can be suspended and a quasi-dictatorship gain acceptance.

The fascists felt that in many respects the war had proved the validity of the ideas expressed by Sorel, Michels, Pareto and Le Bon, namely, that the masses need a myth, they only want to obey, and democracy is merely a smokescreen. The First World War, the first total war in history, was a laboratory in which the ideas they put forward throughout the first decade of the century proved themselves in practice. Thus the fascism of the 1930s, as found in the writings of Gentile and Mussolini, José Antonio and Oswald Mosley, Léon Degrelle and Drieu La Rochelle, was made up both of the theoretical contribution of the pre-war nationalists and syndicalists, and of the experience of the war.

Basic to the political philosophy of fascism was a conception of the individual as a social animal. For Gentile the human individual is not an atom; in every respect man is a political animal. In so far as man is outside the organization of society with its system of reciprocal rules and obligations, he has no significant freedom. Ultimately, for Gentile and Mussolini, man has existence only in so far as he is sustained and determined by the community.

Fascist thought did not stop there, however, but went on to develop a conception of liberty that in Mussolini's terminology was 'the liberty of the state and of the individual within the state'. This is the reason why, according to Alfredo Rocco, Mussolini's minister of justice, individual rights were only recognized in so far as they were implied in the rights of the state. It was by way of such arguments that fascism arrived at the concepts of the new man and the new society so admirably characterized by the French fascist Marcel Déat: 'the total man in the total society, with no clashes, no prostration, no anarchy'. Fascism was a vision of a coherent and reunited people, and it was for this reason that it placed such emphasis on march-pasts, parades and uniforms, on a whole communal liturgy where deliberation and discussion were supplanted by songs and torches, by the cult of physical strength, violence and brutality. This unity found its most perfect expression in the quasi-sacred figure of the leader. The cult of a leader who embodied the spirit, will, and virtues of the people, and who was identifed with the nation, was the keystone of the fascist liturgy. Gentile was quite correct when he defined fascism as a revolt against positivism.

Preserving the integrity of the nation and solving the social question means destroying the dictatorship of money. Wild capitalism must be replaced by the classic tools of national solidarity: a controlled economy and corporate organization topped by a strong state, a decision-making apparatus that represents the victory of politics over economics. The fascist state, creator of all political and social life and of all spiritual values, would of course be the undisputed master of the economy and of social relations.

The reform of the relations of power was the cornerstone of the fascist revolution. The most striking aspect of that moral and political revolution was totalitarianism. 'Ours will be a totalitarian state in the service of the fatherland's integrity,' said José Antonio. Innumerable passages in an identical vein are to be found throughout fascist literature. Totalitarianism is the very essence of fascism, and fascism is without question the purest example of a totalitarian ideology. Setting out as it did to create a new civilization, a new type of human being and a totally new way of life, fascism could not conceive of any sphere of human activity remaining immune from intervention by the state. 'We are, in other words, a state which controls all forces acting in nature. We control political forces, we control moral forces, we control economic forces . . .,' Mussolini wrote, and, 'everything in the state, nothing against the state, nothing outside the state' (p. 40). For Mussolini and Gentile the fascist state is a conscious entity and has a will of its own – for this reason, it can be described as 'ethical'. Not only does the existence of the state imply the subordination of the individual's rights, but the state asserts the right to be 'a state which necessarily transforms the people even in their physical aspects' (p. 39). Outside the state, 'no human or spiritual values can exist, much less have value'; 'no individuals or groups (political parties, cultural associations, economic unions, social classes) outside the state' (p. 11).

The concrete consequences of such a conception of political power and the physical and moral repression it would engender are not hard to imagine. Here we see how communist and fascist totalitarianisms differ: whereas the Stalinist dictatorship could never be described as an application of the Marxist theory of the state, fascist terror was doctrine put into practice in the most methodical way. Fascism constitutes one of the best examples of the unity of thought and action.

References

Gentile, G. n.d.: The philosophic basis of fascism. In *Readings on Fascism and National Socialism*. Denver, Col.: Swallow.

Gregor, A. J. 1979: *Young Mussolini and the intellectual origins of Fascism*. Berkeley and Los Angeles: University of California Press.

Hamilton, A. 1971: *The appeal of fascism: a study of intellectuals and fascism 1919–1945*. New York: Macmillan.

Laqueur, W. (ed.), 1979: *Facism: a reader's guide: analyses, interpretations, bibliography*. Harmondsworth: Penguin.

Lyttelton, A. (ed.), 1973: *Italian Fascisms from Pareto to Gentile*. London: Cape.

Mosse, G. L. 1980: *Masses and man*. New York: Howard Fertig.

Mussolini, B. 1968: *Fascism: doctrine and institutions*. New York: Howard Fertig.

Nolte, E. 1969: *Three faces of fascism: Action française, Italian Fascism, National Socialism*. New York: New American Library.

Payne, S. G. 1980: *Fascism: comparison and definition*. Madison: University of Wisconsin Press.

Primo de Rivera, J. A. 1972: *Selected writings*, ed. and intro. H. Thomas. London: Cape.

Rocco, A. 1925: *La dottrina politica del fascismo*. Rome: Aurora.

Sternhell, Z. 1986: *Neither right nor left: Fascist ideology in France*. Berkeley and Los Angeles: University of California Press.

Turner, H. A. Jr (ed.), 1975: *Reappraisals of fascism*. New York: New Viewpoints.

Weber, E. 1966: *Varieties of fascism*. New York: Van Nostrand.

3

*Fascism**

ROGER GRIFFIN

fascism Used generically, fascism is a term for a singularly protean genus of modern politics inspired by the conviction that a process of national rebirth (palingenesis) has become essential to bring to an end a protracted period of social and cultural decadence, and expressing itself ideologically

---

* Reprinted in full from W. Outhwaite and T. Bottomore (eds), *The Blackwell Dictionary of Social Thought* (Oxford, Basil Blackwell, 1993), pp. 223–4.

in a revolutionary form of integral nationalism (ultra-nationalism). Confined to publicistic writings and groups of activists on the margins of political life prior to the outbreak of World War I and since the end of World War II, fascism provided the rationale for the formations and political parties of the ultra-right which surfaced to combat liberalism, socialism and conservatism in practically every European country between 1918 and 1945. Notable fascist movements appeared in Austria, Belgium, Britain, Finland, France, Germany, Hungary, Italy, Romania and Spain, as well as further afield in South Africa and Brazil. Though some of these temporarily broke through to become the nucleus of popular movements, or to play a part in collaborationist regimes under National Socialism, only in Italy and Germany did particular conjunctures of events enable fascism to seize power autonomously through a combination of legality with violence, giving rise to Mussolini's Fascist State (1925–43) and Hitler's Third Reich (1933–45).

These two regimes exhibited the marked contrasts both in surface ideology and in potential for ruthless brutality in the pursuit of domestic and foreign policy which distinguish different permutations of fascism. However, their drive to regenerate the whole nation through a popular reawakening set both apart generically from the many contemporary authoritarian states of the ultra-right which, though adopting many of the trappings of fascist Italy and Germany, were essentially opposed to the social revolution envisaged by fascism and hence are best seen as 'fascistized' or 'para-fascist' regimes (for example, Dolfuss's Christian Social Austria or Salazar's *Estado Novo* in Portugal). The anti-conservative dimension of fascism is partly obscured by the extensive collusion with traditional power elites (such as the army, the church, industry) which both Fascism (best spelt with a capital to distinguish it from generic fascism) and Nazism were forced to make on pragmatic grounds (see Blinkhorn, 1990). Similarly, the genuine populism intrinsic to their ideology is easily lost from view because of the extensive social engineering (involving intensive propaganda and state terror) necessitated in practice by the bid to turn the utopia of a homogeneous and revitalized national community into a reality. Any fascist revolution is doomed to fail since it is the outstanding example of a palingenetic or regenerationist modern political movement with a small natural constituency seeking to operate as the exclusive truth system for the whole of a pluralistic society. When such an ideology becomes the basis of a regime it leads inevitably to systematic inhumanity and totalitarianism.

This definition of fascism is inevitably contentious since it is an ideal type, and as yet no consensus has emerged among academics about which of the many rival ideal types of the phenomenon is the most useful (compare the definitions in the companion volumes to this one: Sternhell, 1987; Wilkinson, 1987). What distinguishes the present approach is that it locates the 'fascist minimum' in a core myth of the reborn nation which can express itself in a wide range of rationalizations and permutations. Historically there has been a high level of agreement among different fascists on which forces threaten the health of the nation, namely Marxism–Leninism, materialism, internationalism, liberalism, individualism, but considerable variation in what forces are advocated as their remedy and the degree of imperialist and racist violence envisaged in order to impose it. Being ultra-nationalist in inspiration, each fascism will inevitably draw on the history and culture of the country in which it arises so as to legitimize its assault on the status quo, as exemplified in the Nazi vision of Germany as an Aryanized Third Reich or the Fascist claim that Italy was renewing its Roman heritage. In the past fascisms have incorporated elements of militarism, technocracy, ruralism, imperialism, neoclassicism, avant-garde art, syndicalism, national socialism, neo-romanticism, politicized Christianity, paganism, occultism, biological racism, anti-Semitism, voluntarism, social Darwinism, or more recently elements of 'alternative culture' (for instance of 'New Ageism' and the green movement). In the 1980s a convention of Italian neo-fascists was held at Camp Hobbit, and a British neo-fascist stood as a 'green-wave' candidate.

Though the rampant eclecticism of fascism makes generalizations about its specific ideological contents hazardous, the general tenor of all its permutations places it in the tradition of the late nineteenth-century revolt against liberalism and positivism which impart to it a strong emphasis on the primacy of vitalism and action over intellect and theory. Consistent with the ideological complexity of fascism, the social basis of individual movements is highly heterogeneous, and by no means restricted to the lower middle or capitalist classes (see Mühlberger, 1987), despite a persistent assumption to the contrary. Fascism also draws on the tradition of elite theory, though the self-appointed activist and paramilitary vanguards of its interwar variants were convinced of their mission to revolutionize society not just 'from above', but from below through a mass movement capable of transforming the alleged chaos and degeneracy of modern society into a coordinated and healthy national community.

Since the war nearly every Westernized country has seen the appearance of small and often ephemeral groups modelling themselves on Nazism or Fascism to agitate for crude versions of racism and chauvinism in what might be called 'mimetic' fascism. More significantly, perhaps, a number of parties have arisen which, even when officially dissociated from inter-war fascism, campaign for a palingenetic version of ultra-nationalism adapted to post-war conditions, as for example Italy's MSI (Movimento Sociale Italiano) and the German Republicans. In France Le Pen's spectacularly successful Front National has some fascist followers, but its official platform is a racist perversion of conservative liberalism rather than a revolutionary creed. In terms of its direct impact on mainstream politics, perhaps the most significant fascist formation in the early 1990s was the Afrikaner Weerstandsbeweging in South Africa.

The post-war period has also seen the emergence of new rationalizations of palingenetic ultra-nationalism. The most influential of these are the post-Nietzschean vision of a 'conservative revolution' preached by De Benoist on behalf of the French 'New Right' (to be distinguished from Anglo-American neoliberalism) and Julius Evola's 'Traditionalist' fusion of Hindu and occultist pseudo-science adopted by many currents of the Italian 'Radical Right' (see Sheehan, 1981), both of which have influenced contemporary neo-fascism in Britain (see for example the periodical *Scorpion*). Characteristic of much European neo-fascism is the theme of a new Europe made up of a league of regenerated nations acting as a bastion against the twin decadent powers, America and (till 1990) Russia, a theme already explored by some elements of inter-war fascism. The tenaciousness of illiberal nationalism even in the most stable liberal democracies (see Ó Maoláin, 1987, and current issues of *Searchlight*) makes it likely that fascism and neo-fascism will be a perennial ingredient of modern politics, and it was to be expected that after the autumn of 1989 minute neo-Nazi and neo-fascist movements surfaced in several of the 'new democracies' (for example, Pamyat in Russia). However, the conjuncture of structural forces that allowed Fascism and Nazism to conquer state power no longer obtain, and it is condemned to lead a highly marginalized existence for the foreseeable future (see Cheles *et al.*, 1991).

In terms of fascism's contribution to social thought, some of its theorists, notably in Germany, Italy and France, produced relatively elaborate theories on such themes as the organic concept of the state, the leader principle, economics, corporatism, aesthetics, law, education, technology, race, history, morality and the role of the church. Though they all neglect fundamental liberal (and Marxist) methodological principles, they offer important case studies in the application of nationalist and irrationalist myth to academic discourses as a contribution to the legitimation and normalization of revolutionary politics. As for the light thrown on fascism by orthodox social thought, the Durkheimian concept of anomie, the Weberian concept of charismatic politics and leadership, research in sociology, social anthropology and social psychology on the complex dynamics of revolutions, personal dictatorships, youth movements and authoritarianism, all have a bearing on fascism. So do studies which investigate the mythic dimension of nationalism and the utopian component in all revolutionary ideologies without confusing them with religious millenarianism.

References

Blinkhorn, M. (ed.) 1981: *Fascists and conservatives*. London: Unwin Hyman.

Cheles, L., Ferguson, R. and Vaughan, M. (eds) 1991: *Neo-fascism in Europe*. London: Longman.

Griffin, R. D. 1991: *The nature of fascism.* London: Pinter.

Laqueur, W. (ed.) 1979: *Fascism: a reader's guide*. Harmondsworth: Penguin. 1st edn 1976.

Mosse, G. L. (ed.) 1979: *International fascism: new thoughts and approaches*. New York: Howard Fertig.

Mühlberger, D. (ed.) 1987: *The social basis of European fascism*. London: Croom Helm.

Ó Maoláin, C. 1987: *The radical right: a world directory.* London: Longman.

Payne, S. G. 1980: *Fascism: comparison and definition*. Madison: University of Wisconsin Press.

Sheehan, T. 1981: Myth and violence: the fascism of Julius Evola and Alain de Benoist, *Social Research* 48 (1).

Sternhell, Z. 1987: Fascism. In D. Miller (ed.), *The Blackwell encyclopedia of political thought*. Oxford: Basil Blackwell.

Wilkinson, P. 1987: Fascism. In V. Bogdanor (ed.), *The Blackwell encyclopedia of political institutions*. Oxford: Basil Blackwell.

SECTION

II

THE SEARCH FOR THE
FASCIST MINIMUM

Presentation

Section II falls into three subsections. The first samples variations on the Marxist approach to fascism. The second gives examples of liberal academics attempting to explain fascism as a by-product of modernization. The third traces the gradual development of what has come to be a new consensus about the nature of fascism outside the Marxist camp.

The product of a crisis of capitalism

The next four Readings are a minute sample of the extensive writings by Marxists on fascism.[1] The first contains the nub of the Comintern definition of 1933 which was to be canonic within the Soviet Empire till it collapsed in the late 1980s, and is followed by an article by the arch-critic of Stalinism, Leon Trotsky, who was assassinated in Mexico (presumably by Stalinist agents) in the year he wrote it. The third was published in the 1970s by the Hungarian writer, Mihaly Vajda, while the fourth is by Nicos Poulantzas, a Western Marxist. The common denominators between them, typical of Marxist analyses in general, are that: (a) fascism is the product of a crisis of capitalism and as such it has no genuinely revolutionary dynamic, but merely a counter-revolutionary one; (b) it is to be treated essentially as a form of reactionary (totalitarian) state power, rather than as a movement; (c) as the tool of repressive capitalist interests it does not have an ideology worth investigating in any depth; and (d) Nazism is to be understood as the most radical and successful historical manifestation of fascism: indeed, it forms the paradigmatic[2] fascist regime on which all analyses are based.[3]

However, significant differences emerge even in these four accounts over whether fascism (a) is identifiable with a particular class (the bourgeoisie), or rather with a state operating with a degree of autonomy from any social grouping; (b) is unique with respect to nineteenth-century history, or actually represents a modern(-ized) form of Bonapartism;[4] (c) has been realized in a regime form only in Italy and Germany, or elsewhere in Europe/the rest of the world; (d) possessed any sort of genuine ideology.

For the Comintern (Reading 4), meeting in December 1933, only months after Hitler's take-over of power in Germany, fascism is the result of a systemic crisis of capitalism which has led the bourgeoisie in individual nations, threatened by the internal collapse of their system and the external threat posed by international communism, to resort to ruthless dictatorship and imperialism. It is portrayed as already established in Italy, Germany, Japan and 'a number of other capitalist countries' (possibly an allusion to other authoritarian regimes in Europe such as those in Poland, Hungary, and Yugoslavia) with the goal of crushing the proletariat and preserving the forces of finance capital. Typical of the Comintern stance on fascism is the way the declaration (a) presents fascism as bringing, not a new order to the workers as it claims, but economic and political slavery at the hands of the established ruling elites; (b) portrays social democracy (i.e. reformist Marxism) as an enemy on a par with fascism, since by splitting the proletariat between revolutionaries and reformists they are playing into the hands of fascism to the point of meriting the title 'social fascists' (the allusion to the 'Second and Amsterdam Internationals' refers to international socialist organizations set up before Marxism–Leninism existed). Note that, reversing its earlier position which rejected collaboration with reformist socialism out of hand, the Comintern now recognizes for pragmatic reasons that its main task is to create a 'popular front' between all leftists dedicated to the defeat of fascism. The passage also expresses overwhelming confidence in the imminent overthrow of capitalism by the international proletariat under the leadership of Soviet Russia, not just in Europe, but in China too.

Writing in exile a year into the Second World War, Trotsky (Reading 5) rejects the allegation that he sees fascism as a form of Bonapartism, citing Giolitti's domination of liberal Italy and Hindenburg's presidency in Germany as evidence that Bonapartism *precedes* fascism (Pétain, the head of the Vichy regime in France is also seen as a Bonapartist). Instead he presents fascism as the product of the same capitalist imperialism which led to the First World War, arguing that when the proletariat fails to seize power, this force will immediately organize its energies in an openly dictatorial way, thus giving rise to the fascist state. He associates the ascendancy of fascist imperialism with a cycle in which the bourgeoisie initially encourages reformist socialism, but once hit by economic and political crisis sets out to crush the very proletarian revolution which it has originally helped set in train. Typical of the fierce infighting which had broken out within the ranks of international socialism by the 1930s (and which had such tragic consequences for the Republican cause in the Spanish Civil War) is the rancour Trotsky reserves for fellow Marxists who criticize his analysis of fascism. In his conclusion he attacks the Comintern and Social Democrats for having made Hitler's seizure of power possible by disrupting the proletarian revolution – previously he has made a tantalizing allusion to the prospect of a socialist breakthrough in the USA with the right (i.e. Trotskyite) leadership.

By the time Mihaly Vajda made his contribution to the debate (Reading 6), the Comintern position had become orthodoxy throughout the Eastern bloc. It is perhaps a symptom of Hungary's relative independence from Russian dogma that he presents another contrasting picture, taking issue with both the Comintern and Trotskyite definitions. While the crisis of capitalism cannot be left out of any analysis of fascism, he states, unusually for a Marxist, that it established a regime only in Italy and Germany, and was not the dictatorship *of* the bourgeoisie. Rather, it was created when the bourgeoisie handed over power to the state which served its interests, their renunciation of direct political power being the price they willingly paid in order to retain their socio-economic power. This interpretation builds on the pre-war theories of a number of Marxists, notably the Austrian August Thalheimer, who stressed the relative autonomy of the fascist state from any one class (the only example initially was in Italy). The 'Austro-Marxists' in turn were inspired to adopt this approach by Marx's seminal analysis of the nexus of political, economic and social conditions which first brought Louis-Napoleon to power, and hence see fascism as a form of Bonapartism. An important consequence of this analysis is first that Vajda is able to recognize that the fascist elite was drawn from all classes (even if he clings to the fallacious assumption that the mass base of Nazism was middle class), and second, that the Fascist and Nazi regimes, far from being mere puppets of the middle classes, actually annihilated their traditional parties. This leads Vajda to the curious paradox that fascism ended up serving the interests of the 'leading bourgeois circles even against the bourgeoisie itself'!

The French theorist Nicos Poulantzas demonstrates just how sophisticated an analysis of fascism can be based on Marxist premises. His dissection of fascism (Reading 7) is elaborated in a lengthy monograph which has had to undergo draconian editing to produce the extract printed here. Again, fascism is assumed to be a form of repressive regime produced by specific political crisis and class relations, but it has a complex make-up. According to Poulantzas' analysis the reality of fascist politics cannot be reduced to the dictatorship of monopoly capitalism, imperialism, or the petty bourgeoisie, while its 'relative autonomy' from a particular class base has been misunderstood by upholders of the Bonapartist school of thought, because the conditions of class equilibrium which were the premise to the rule of Napoleon III did not prevail in inter-war Europe. Instead, the fascist regime should be seen as combining elements of a capitalist state, an exceptional state, and an imperialist state. As an exceptional state attempting to manage a deep crisis in capitalism, the fascist regime intervenes heavily in the economy. Furthermore, since the economic crisis in turn causes an ideological crisis (in liberalism), it also develops a specific set of values imposed by an ideological and repressive (terror) apparatus which subordinates the various institutional ideologues which coexist in times of 'normal capitalism' to that of the now hegemonic (dominant) fascist elite.

Other important features of fascism singled out by Poulantzas are: (a) it is characterized in power by a mass party which forms part of the ideological State apparatus and which aims to ensure the permanent mobilization of the masses; (b) it invades the existing (liberal) state from without; (c) the party and state never fuse: instead, in a first stage the party achieves domination over part of the state, leading on to a second stage in which one branch of the state, now transformed from within, dominates both the party and ideology, using a political police as one instrument with which to do so; (d) propaganda becomes a central feature of the ideological state apparatus, a concomitant of which is the weakening of the role played by educational and religious apparatuses; (e) the progressive transformation of the liberal state by fascism means that it was endowed with in-built mechanisms of stability, and thus it was not destined to rapid disintegration as might have been expected had it been only an emergency state. This resilience confounded the predictions and tactics of the Comintern analysts of the 1930s.

Poulanztas's analysis is certainly an advance on the simplistic, reductionist theories put forward by most Marxists grappling with the dilemma of fitting fascism into their scheme of history. However, he too operates with an axiomatic assumption that fascism is to be seen as a counter-revolutionary and oppressive *regime*, rather than an extra-systemic *movement* which only in the most unusual circumstances can ever mount an effective assault on state power: in fact to be the basis of a regime at all is fascism's 'exceptional state'. This assumption has two important consequences. First, it leads to a typically Marxist neglect of the actual contents of fascist ideology, even though in principle Poulantzas' theory accords it a greater role in shaping the regime than in Comintern, Trotskyite, or Bonapartist interpretations. Second, his analysis of the fascist state 'as a form of exceptional regime' creates the strong suspicion that he has created his generic model by generalizing from one historical, 'singularity', namely the Third Reich, with the occasional glance at Mussolini's Fascist Italy where it strengthens his argument (though not where it weakens it). We never learn what other regimes, let alone movements, the model applies to, and end up with little more than an abstract, 'X-ray' picture of the Nazi state with all the surface texture of historical reality removed. To non-Marxists it is tempting to see the aridly conceptualized tone of the analysis as symptomatic of the general Marxist refusal or inability to come to terms with the concrete phenomenon of fascism in its own terms as something distinct from capitalism, rather than treat it on a par with liberalism as another of its disguises. But if Marxists have been hard put to accommodate fascism within their philosophy of history, liberals have, until comparatively recently at least, been experiencing equally stubborn problems of their own. Again what hampered progress for so long was simplistic assumptions about fascism's social and ideological dynamics.

The product of a crisis of modernization

The perception of fascism as an essentially middle-class, reactionary phenomenon has not been confined to the Marxist theorists. Some liberals and socialists were emphazising the central role played by middle-class interests in the support and ideology of Fascism even before it established itself as a regime in 1925, and the assumption that this held true underlay most non-Marxist analyses till comparatively recently. It is only in the last decade that irrefutable empirical evidence has been accumulated to destroy the 'middle-class thesis', at least to the satisfaction of academics, though the myth will doubtless be perpetuated in text books for years to come.[5]

Reasons for the persistence of this myth can only be speculated about. One may be the fact that the Marxist theory of fascism as being essentially bourgeois rang true, given fascism's retention of private property (capitalism), its destruction of working-class organizations, its virulent hostility to communism, and the cult of the family as the mainstay of the national community. Another is the marked tendency of many scholars theorizing about generic fascism until the 1960s to avoid grappling with empirical data relating to the membership, policies, or ideology of a specific movement, and to work with a composite image of the phenomenon based on the Fascist and Nazis regimes, in whose social base the middle classes were indeed over-represented, though never to the exclusion of other classes. Pictures of Mussolini as prime minister in a top-hat and tails, the embourgeoisement of many among the Nazi elite, and the kitsch versions of classical art sponsored by the Third Reich only served to reinforce this image. The middle-class thesis also harmonized well with the image of fascism as basically reactionary, nostalgic for the stability of the past, and hence 'anti-modern'.

Once academics conceived fascism in this way, it was a small step to seeing as the key to its dynamics a dysfunction in the process which by the late 1950s had become such a fashionable topic in Western social sciences: modernization. If the middle classes were the mainstay of fascism, then fascism could be neatly explained by seeing them as a social group which in some countries had lost out as a result of the ascendancy of industry and big business, and felt threatened by the rise of socialism and mass democracy. The resentment and disorientation which resulted could all too easily express themselves in commitment to an ideology which identified a range of scapegoats as the true reason for their failure, and which furthermore announced an ultra-nationalist vision which promised to restore their sense of power and worth. Thus 'a crisis in the process of modernization' acquired for many non-Marxists the same sort of overarching explanatory power which the 'crisis of capitalism' had for Marxists.

A classic statement of assumptions prevalent by the early 1960s is Seymour Lipset's 'Fascism, Left, Right and Centre' (Reading 8). The preamble which precedes the extract printed here suggests yet another factor in the appeal of the middle-class thesis: the aesthetic one of symmetry.

> The extremist movements of the left, right, and centre (Communism and Peronism, traditional authoritarianism, and fascism) are based primarily on the working, upper, and middle classes, respectively. The term 'fascism' has been applied at one time or another to all of these varieties of extremism,[6] but an analytical examination of the social base and ideology of each reveals their different characters.[7]

The ensuing analysis is curious in several respects. First, the examples of fascism discussed are Nazism, the *Großdeutsche Volkspartei* in Austria (but not the far more extreme *Heimwehren*, the Austrian Nazis, or even the *Vaterlandsfront*, the single party of the Dolfuss regime), and Poujadisme in France (but not Doriot's *Parti Populaire Français* or Déat's *Rassemblement National Populaire* which are generally acknowledged as fascist). Second, since Lipset was writing at a time when little serious empirical research had been done into the sociology of the Nazi voter and member, he is forced to infer the middle-class composition of NSDAP support from the collapse of the traditional 'middle-class parties' of the centre and the defection of their electoral support to the Nazis between 1928 and 1933, something which, as I have pointed out, later scholarship has revealed to be a highly suspect methodology.

In the subsequent analysis the success of Nazism is attributed to its appeal to reactionary 'small businessmen' who are liable to express *en masse* a radical disaffection with parliamentary democracy in times of acute political and economic crisis, such as the one which hit the Weimar Republic in the Depression years. Such crises are specifically associated with the destabilizing consequences of industrialization and modernization. In the light of the new consensus two fallacies are detectable in this passage: fascism is once more identified essentially with Nazism, and it is denied any revolutionary dynamic. Moreover, the psychological dynamics of paradigmatic fascism are explained in remarkably simplistic terms: the Third Reich's bid to create a racial state at the cost of millions of lives is accounted for in terms of lower middle-class fear of economic rationalization. Apart from the extraordinary (and disturbing) model of human psychology this explanation implies, it also suggests that angst-ridden small businessmen were sufficiently numerous in inter-war Germany to enable Hitler's party to gain 37.3 per cent of the poll (over eleven million votes) in the elections of July 1932. In short, the very success achieved by Lipset's article (frequently cited and reprinted in 1981) points to the considerable disarray among non-Marxist political scientists in the early 1960s about the nature of fascism, which, since Lipset nowhere defines it explicitly, apparently refers to any political manifestation of illiberal, anti-communist nationalism with conspicuous lower middle-class support.

Middle-class support for fascism is also one of the premises assumed by Ernst Nolte in *Three Faces of Fascism*, first published in English in 1965 and in German two years earlier (Reading 9). However, whereas Lipset's analysis has the hallmark of an Anglo-Saxon political sociologist at work, Nolte's has that of a German intellectual steeped in a native tradition of 'the philosophy of history'[8] for whom political events naturally tend to be endowed with a 'metapolitical' dimension – a dimension which transcends the strictly political sphere. The upholders of this tradition (which is deeply bound up with the peculiar genius of the German language for spawning abstract concepts resonant with meanings which largely evaporate in translation) operate on the premise that such a dimension, too subtle to be discerned by the conventional empirical historian, can best be explored by those trained in the 'phenomenological' method of identifying the role which key ideas play in the unfolding of events. These are not just any ideas, such as the ones which operate as causal factors in history on a par with economic, social, and political ones. They are ideas which operate as spiritual forces informing the deep structure or matrix of surface phenomena. Thus Nolte defines fascism on three planes of reality: first, the political one where its basic constituent is a virulent anti-Marxism which has appropriated something of its arch-enemy – by implication a crusade against the status quo and a readiness to resort to violence to overthrow it; second, the social or sociological one where it expresses the struggle of the 'sovereign, martial, inwardly antagonistic group': this seems to be a cryptic reference to the most backward-looking, reactionary elements in established (i.e. bourgeois?) society, elements prepared to resort to violence in defence of their interests, namely the army and military caste; third, the metapolitical one of 'resistance to transcendence'.

Using a fair amount of guess-work, Nolte's exposition of this concept, which to a non-Hegelian Anglo-Saxon mind is extremely arcane, might be paraphrased as follows: the basic driving force behind fascism is the impulse to seal off society from the impact of liberalism and communism, which in conflicting ways are based on a thrust towards 'transcendence'. In other words, liberalism and communism, both in theory and in practice, pursue the ultimate goal of liberating human society from the material, political, and cultural constraints of traditional ('primitive', religious, closed) societies by forging links between all human beings within a global technology, a global economy, a global political system, and a global human-istic culture. He alludes to the Russians' success in putting the first man (Yuri Gagarin) into space in 1961 as emblematic of the 'transcendent' thrust of (Soviet) communism. Fascism radically denies this transcendence, both theoretically (by asserting the primacy of the national community or race over 'humanity', and the state's right and need to exercise as total a monopoly as possible over ideology and culture), and practically (by creating a society hermetically closed off from others through a radically authoritarian economic, political, and cultural regime). Yet paradoxically, since fascism resists transcendence from within that transcend-ence (i.e. is part and parcel of the modern world), it ends up (in its Nazi form, at least) pursuing its own perverse version of transcendence by attempting to achieve world domination (hegemony) for itself.

Thus translated into the, admittedly far more banal, but hopefully more trans-parent, discourse of 'non-phenomenological' social science, Nolte's theory has remarkable parallels to Lipset's. In the 'era of fascism' (inter-war Europe), both seem to be saying, segments of the middle classes in some countries felt acutely threatened materially and psychologically by the major economic, political, and social upheavals being generated by modernization[9] whether in their liberal–capitalist or socialist–communist manifestations. They reacted by retrenching into an ideology of radical nationalism which effectively denied full humanity to other nationalities or ethnic groups, and formed the basis of a fortress-like, and sometimes tank-like, state geared to enforcing conformity on the civilian popula-tion at home, and to subjugating (and in the Nazi case enslaving or exterminating) enemies abroad. Fascism is thus an essentially negative phenomenon: anti-liberal, anti-Marxist, anti-modern, anti-global, anti-humanist, anti-transcendent. What these two very different theorists also have in common is that neither supply a serviceable definition of fascism. Both discursively evoke its dynamics in terms so general (Lipset) or abstruse (Nolte) that no academic could use their descriptions, 'operationally', to distinguish between a fascist and non-fascist movement or regime, and no academic ever has. However, the very fame (notoriety?) of Nolte's book encouraged other academics to take generic fascism seriously as a subject worth investigating. The challenge was to refine a conceptual framework which would identify the 'fascist minimum' (Nolte's phrase) and allow its complex dynamics to become more apparent.

The parameters of the challenge were delineated clearly by Wolfgang Sauer, whose article (Reading 10) captures well the state of ferment that fascist studies were in by the mid-1960s. His stated purpose in writing is to help develop a more appropriate conceptual framework for the study of Nazism than 'totalitarianism', which despite its many shortcomings had gained considerable currency within non-Marxist research into the Third Reich after 1945.[10] It was a concept particularly in vogue as long as the Cold War mentality encouraged the regimes of Stalin and Hitler to be treated as twin monoliths of repression and inhumanity when contrasted with those of the 'Free World'. This article explores the possibility that the concept 'fascism' might provide the answer, even if Marxist theories of it had proved wanting – hence the reference to the critique of them put forward by Iring Fetscher. Sauer points to publications by Seymour Lipset, Eugen Weber, Arthur Schweitzer, and Ernst Nolte as the 'first serious attempt to develop a workable, non-Marxist definition of fascism', and proceeds to outline several criteria which a successful definition would embrace: it would (a) allow for the fact that its basic dynamics are not restricted to manipulation by monopoly capitalism; (b) recognize that the social support of fascism is not exclusively middle class; (c) distinguish between fascism as a movement and as a regime; (d) acknowledge the revolutionary, and not just counter-revolutionary, thrust of fascism in principle, however meagre its results in practice. Implicit in these axioms is a fundamental shift in the perception of fascism, an early glimpse of 'the new consensus' identified in the Introduction. Fascism is finally being approached as an ideologically driven, and socially heterogeneous, political movement which, like all true revolutionary forces, aims at the creation of a new order, not just the restoration of an old one.

What Sauer does not attempt to do is identify the content of the revolutionary vision, though his sustained critique of Nolte goes some way towards at least clarifying the type of revolution he thinks it was not. He summarizes Nolte's basic thesis as the claim that fascism was 'a revolt against secularization, democratization, and international integration in the modern era' (i.e. modernization), and expresses a number of misgivings about the cogency of his overall approach. These centre on the 'phenomenological method', the concept 'resistance to transcendence', the alleged 'anti-modernism' this implies, and the neglect of a concrete socio-economic analysis of fascist support. Sauer argues that Nolte's detailed examination of the 'first face of fascism', the *Action Française*[11] serves only to set up the argument that fascism is to be located within a counter-revolutionary tradition. This, Sauer claims, distorts the analysis by disguising the fact that fascism was 'a revolution from below' (i.e. a genuinely populist movement geared to renewal rather than restoration). He then goes on to explore the possibility that a sophisticated theory of modernization, and in particular, industrialization, may hold the key. In the course of his reflections he declares fascism to be the 'revolt of the *déclassés*', i.e. anti-urban peasants and 'middle-class losers'. In terms of sophistication, this seems something of a retrograde step, since the article has earlier stated that these groups were no more than 'one of the major social components of fascist movements', and accepted that workers, big business, aristocrats and top bureaucrats were also involved.

The discussion is further complicated by Sauer's attempt to draft his own model of fascism based on modernization theory,[12] thus following in the steps of Nolte and Lipset, whose attempts to define fascism also turn out to be little more than causal explanations. In this case its appearance is explained as stemming from the conjuncture of two basic factors: the pervasive militarization of society in the wake of the First World War, and the economic, social, and psychological disruption caused by industrialization when it impacted on societies where pre-industrial traditions were still strong. It is at this point that it finally becomes clear that Sauer sees fascist regimes as having established themselves not just in Italy and Germany, but in 'the regions of Central, Eastern, and Southeastern Europe' (presumably an allusion to the authoritarian regimes in Hungary, Romania, Yugoslavia, and Greece?). The article thus exhibits a struggle to break free from the gravitational pull exerted by the interpretation of fascism as a middle-class movement of radicalized anti-capitalism and anti-modernism, but curiously ends up doing little more than restate this position – the insight expressed early on that fascism contained a genuine revolutionary dimension seems to have got lost along the way. Yet whatever criticisms Sauer's article might prompt now, what still makes it impressive three decades on is the academic seriousness with which he takes the concept of generic fascism, and how zealously he applies himself to elaborating an empirically cogent, non-Marxist, and non-reductionist explanatory framework for its investigation.

The emergence of the new consensus

A. J. Gregor moves the debate on in an important respect. His 1974 article (Reading 11) is conceived as the rebuttal to the theory of fascism put forward in a widely read article by fellow American academic, Henry A. Turner. In it Turner had rehearsed and radicalized the Lipset/Nolte/Sauer line of argument that fascism was born of an animus against modernization, defining it as a form of 'utopian antimodernism', though one which in the very pursuit of anti-modern ends paradoxically introduced its own form of modernization. Gregor sets about systematically refuting this position in respect of Fascism, citing some of the abundant evidence for its deliberately modernizing ideals, policies, and practices. He argues that even the cults of *Romanità* and of rural life which were conspicuous features of Mussolini's Italy cannot be taken at face value: in fact ancient glories and past values were appealed to so as to mobilize popular energies for modernization.[13] Gregor goes further by proposing that fascism be seen as one example of the many mass-mobilizing and modernizing dictatorships which have been set up in societies caught up in the throes of rapid transition from traditional to industrialized society ('developmental dictatorships'). Seen though this lens Mussolini's Italy suddenly appears to have had more in common with Stalin's Russia, Mao's China, or Castro's Cuba than with conservative authoritarian regimes such as Franco's Spain or Pétain's Vichy France.

Gregor had recently published *The Fascist Persuasion in Radical Politics*[14], a book which elaborated the thesis advanced in the article and used the term 'fascist' to cover 'the entire class of mass-mobilizing developmental dictatorships under single-party auspices'. In his last note to the essay (no. 41 on p. 137) he now claims he was quite aware that such a usage would cause outrage among colleagues whose common sense dictated that Marxism and fascism are mutually exclusive. How far he presented this thesis as a deliberate act of provocation he does not tell us. Certainly Gregor's reworking of the term means it could apply to many Third World and Latin American dictatorships whether of the left and right, thus rivalling Marxist definitions of fascism in the sheer number of regimes which it potentially covers – though it is noteworthy that he too makes no attempt to offer a concise definition of fascism which might establish precise criteria to govern its usage.[15] Needless to say, such an idiosyncratic and counter-intuitive deployment of the term has meant that Gregor has been a lone, if highly audible, voice in the fascist debate, though no more so than Sternhell, Turner, or Nolte. What remains of abiding importance, however, is that fascism was treated in Gregor's article as a 'generic term' (note his use of this phrase in the concluding paragraph of his essay) to refer to a historical force which, far from being based on a pathological horror of modernity, actively pursued its own path of modernization, one based on a clear ideological commitment to an alternative future to the one offered by liberalism.

It was with two essays on generic fascism published within a year of each other that fascist studies arguably came of age, the first in 1979 by George Mosse, an eminent historian of Nazism, the second in 1980 by Stanley Payne, a historian of inter-war Spain. George Mosse wrote his (Reading 12), as the editor of a collection of articles on a variety of inter-war fascisms. Given the essay's seminal importance in the history of the debate over fascism, it is perhaps appropriate that the book's title – *International Fascism: New Thoughts and Approaches* – anticipated the one chosen for the present volume, and unfortunate that considerations of space have caused it to be drastically cut.[16] It opens with the stark declaration, practically unthinkable a decade earlier, that fascism is to be seen on a par with Marxism as a revolutionary movement. In expanding on this assertion Mosse alludes to the prevalent suspicion among academics of general theories of fascism, and, like Sauer before him, draws attention to shortcomings in the term 'totalitarianism' as a key concept in fascist studies, stressing the way it not only conceals important differences between fascism and bolshevism, but obscures the way fascism evolved over time. In particular, by placing undue emphasis on the oppressive state system created by fascism in a couple of instances, rather than on the dynamics of the many fascist movements which have attempted to seize power (but generally failed to do so), the 'totalitarianism' paradigm[17] encourages scholars to neglect fascism's internal logic as a comprehensive value system and world-view. Hence the almost exclusive concentration in fascist studies on the external manifestations of fascist power, such as the leader cult, propaganda, militarism, terror, and the forces of (counter-revolutionary) conservatism. Instead, Mosse extrapolates his conceptual framework for investigating fascism precisely from a study of the goals, world-view, and direct manifestations of fascist movements, which he takes at face value, rather than interpret them in the light of extraneous concepts such as 'capitalism', 'transcendence', or 'modernization'. He is not the first to proceed in this way: Sternhell's extended essay on fascist ideology[18] had been published several years earlier and anticipates much of Mosse's argument. In stark contrast to Sternhell, however, Mosse has no reservations in treating Nazism as a major example of the genus of politics he is trying to define.

Consistent with his stress on fascism's revolutionary dynamics, Mosse accepts at face value fascism's claim to represent a Third Way between capitalism and communism. It is a trail blazed by a new constituency or Third Force in European politics, the generation for whom the World War had revealed a new kind of solidarity forged by the shared experience of heroism and activism in the cause of the nation. In the cultic, mythic mindset typical of this self-appointed elite, fascism was an attempt to perpetuate in peace time the spirit of the trenches so as to revitalize the life of the nation. Rejecting parliamentary processes, its power to transform the old order had to be channelled not through a party but through a movement led by a charismatic leader, and whose dynamism was regularly recharged in the liturgies of mass meetings where irrational forces of the choral and the symbolic took over from individualism and rationality.

Mosse came to fascist studies as the author of several major works of scholarship exploring the Nazi bid to replace liberalism by an entirely new type of civic religion in which politics, myth, and culture fused. He was thus predisposed to see generic fascism essentially as a movement whose primary goal was to generate an ecstatic sense of national community and mystique, not as part of a 'repressive ideological state apparatus', or of a bid to hold back the tide of modernization, but as an end in itself. The ultimate fascist utopia was not just a new order, but the birth of a 'new man' who experienced a heightened sense of meaning and intensity by living for and through the nation. This utopia embraced a cult of the male principle, of youth, of the national community, of the Third Way, clothing itself as it did so in an ideology synthesized, or rather loosely assembled, from various elements scavenged from nineteenth-century European culture and science. Crucial to an understanding of fascism, therefore, are less its individual doctrines and policies than a particular type of mentality, one not confined to any particular social group or class, for which the dream of national revolution was irresistible. The Nazi nightmare was the direct consequence of attempting to turn that dream into reality.

Though Mosse claimed, modestly enough, only to have offered 'a general framework for a discussion of fascism', his analysis is truly ground-breaking, establishing several points which herald a new phase in fascist studies. First, though Nazism is to be conceived as unquestionably a manifestation of generic fascism, it is no longer to be seen as paradigmatic of it or its quintessential manifestation.

Second, at bottom fascism is neither a regime, nor a movement, but first and foremost an ideology, a critique of the present state of society and a vision of what is to replace it. Third, when this vision is dissected it reveals fascism to be a revolutionary form of nationalism, one which first emerged in inter-war Europe with the aim of creating a new type of modern society and a new type of human being. Fourth, its ideology expresses itself primarily not through theory and doctrines, but through a bizarre synthesis of ideas whose precise content will vary significantly from nation to nation but whose appeal will always be essentially mythic rather than rational. Equally importantly, it is an ideology which expresses itself through a liturgical, ritualized form of mass political spectacle. Taken together, the characteristics which Mosse identifies set fascism apart both from communist regimes, and from all right-wing dictatorships which are essentially conservative or militaristic in nature.

Mosse's essay, while pivotal for the emergence of the new consensus, stops short of providing a synthetic definition of fascism. It was Mosse's colleague at the University of Wisconsin, Stanley Payne who moved a step nearer to doing so by providing a highly condensed and schematic 'typological description'. This tidied up version of the check-list approach and the explanatory chapter which accompanied it were published in 1980 both in his highly influential book *Fascism: Comparison and Definition* and in *Who Were the Fascists*, a collection of essays on the sociology of international fascism whose very size and comprehensiveness are an indicator of the way fascist studies had become a thriving international enterprise by the late 1970s. In 1996 Payne updated his earlier book with *A History of Fascism, 1914–1945*, the most comprehensive and thoughtful work on generic fascism yet to see the light of day. In the introductory chapters which establish a working definition of his subject, he presents the contents of the three sections which make up his 'typological description' unchanged, but they are accompanied by a new explanatory chapter extensively modified in the light of contributions from scholars to the subject over the last fifteen years. It also delivers for the first time a single sentence definition of fascism. All in all Payne's new chapter, an extract from which concludes this section (Reading 13), is the most concise and authoritative expression of the 'new' paradigm to date.

Payne now refers to his tripartite typology of fascism specifically as an ideal type, something only implicit in the 1980 version,[19] grouping what he sees as the salient traits of generic fascism under three headings: *ideology and goals*, i.e. what were to fascists themselves the positive ideals they pursued? *negations*, i.e. the values and ideologies they rejected or combated in the pursuit of those ideals; and *style and organization*. But if the contents of the three sections have not changed, their order has. Consistent with the recognition of the primacy of the positive over the negative in the 'new paradigm', the ideology is now placed first, the negations coming second as their logical corollary. Payne stresses that fascist ideology is essentially eclectic, irrational, utopian, and varies significantly from country to country, but that these traits do not disqualify it from being taken seriously as the key to understanding the nature of fascism. As for the defining features of the ideology, the text stresses the creation of a 'new man' (highlighted by Mosse and myself), and the aim of overcoming decadence (highlighted by Sternhell[20] and myself[21]), through the creation of a civic religion (an aspect explored brilliantly both by Mosse in the case of Nazism[22] and Emilio Gentile in the case of Fascism[23]). But because Payne has chosen to leave his 1980 typology unaltered except for the sequence of subsections, these crucial elements are not included in it.

The rest of Payne's chapter is taken up with a new text elucidating the individual components alluded to schematically in the typology, which ends in contrast to all the other contributions to the debate except for the one provided by Comintern (Reading 4) with a single-sentence definition. Leaving aside the awkwardness of the phrase 'a form of revolutionary ultra-nationalism for national rebirth', the signifi-cance of this definition is that fascism is characterized (a) as a revolutionary ideology which is (b) bent on bringing about the rebirth of the nation in an anti- and post-liberal spirit of 'ultra-nationalism'. The other features specified (vitalism, elitism, mass mobilization, leader principle,[24] the cult of violence and war) can all be seen as fleshing out the contents of the ultra-nationalism and the organizational style which fascism adopted in the aftermath of the First World War (though there have been considerable modifications in its ideology, style and organization since 1945). Indeed, the colouring Payne has given his core definition of 'rebirth ultra-nationalism' may well reflect the fact that his expertise as an empiricist is in the history of inter-war Spain. Whatever the contingent aspects of the definition, it epitomizes how far fascist studies have come since Mussolini first seized power in October 1922. Though some might quibble at some of Payne's assertions or point to omissions, for example the need to build a more extensive socio-economic dimension into any causal account of fascism, most scholars now active in the field of comparative fascist studies would agree with the broad lines of his argument.

A new generation of academics has grown up into the post-war era free of the blind spot which prevented most of their predecessors from recognizing that it was fascism's inherent utopianism, not its nihilism, which bore such poisonous fruits. For this generation Payne's chapter sets up a superbly positioned and equipped base camp from which to carry out gruelling scholarly expeditions, whether to scale the forbidding rock-faces of particular fascist events or to explore hidden caverns of their inner socio-psychological dynamics. His typological description, though perhaps in need of minor updating to bring it in line with developments in his own thinking, is made fully intelligible by a discursive commentary on fascism informed by the latest research, and has now been supplemented by a synthetic definition which sums it up in a single phrase. Payne's chapter provides the conceptual framework to a intellectually cohesive and meticulously researched synoptic history of individual fascist movements and regimes which subsumes the major contributions to individual topics made by scholars the world over right up to the mid-1990s. A following section then provides a critical account of the evolution of the debate which has grown up about the precise nature of generic fascism, while yet another traces the broad outlines of how fascism has evolved since the Second World War.

Payne's *A History of Fascism, 1914–1945* thus provides triumphant vindication of the premise, heretical till recently, that fascism is to be treated on a par with any other modern ideology (socialism, anarchism, etc.): it is no 'special case' which needs to be handled differently from all other political movements because its alleged lack of a genuine ideological core turns it into the historical equivalent of a voracious black hole. Moreover, Payne's model, and hence the 'new consensus' of which it is the most comprehensive and sophisticated expression, are entirely compatible with existing research into the various factors which together constitute the causes of fascism, as Section III will show.

Notes

1 For a comprehensive anthology of Marxist writings on fascism see David Beetham, *Marxists in Face of Fascism* (Manchester, Manchester University Press, 1983).
2 See above Introduction note 49.
3 This is particularly apparent in Poulantzas's characterization of the 'fascist state' in Reading 7, which at bottom turns some salient features of the Third Reich into a generic type of state system.
4 That is, a dictatorship with the same dynamics as the authoritarian Second Empire in France created by Louis-Napoleon Bonaparte after a military coup in 1851.
5 Over the last 15 years a number of scholars have collaborated in the systematic demolition of the 'middle-class thesis' based on thorough empirical research. See, for example, Detlef Mühlberger's *Hitler's Followers* (London, Routledge, 1991), which establishes conclusively that the NSDAP was a genuine transclass *Volkspartei* before 1933 (after which statistics are meaningless for gauging true support).
6 This is a somewhat cryptic observation. To my knowledge the only serious academic who has suggested that Communism is, if not identical to, at least closely related to fascism, is A. J. Gregor, and then (a) in a deliberately provocative spirit; (b) some 14 years after Lipset's essay was published. See Reading 11.
7 M. S. Lipset, ' "Fascism" – Left, Right, and Centre', *Political Man* (expanded edition, Baltimore, Johns Hopkins University Press, 1981), p. 131.
8 There is evidence in Nolte's book for the influence of Kant, Hegel, and Heidegger.
9 Modernization embraces such processes as secularization, rationalization, democratization, globalization, massification or the 'levelling' down of society to create mass conformity.
10 For a critical history of the concept 'totalitarianism', see Simon Tormey, *Making Sense of Tyranny* (Manchester, Manchester University Press, 1995).
11 An arch-conservative, royalist, and elitist political movement which emerged in France in the 1890s under the leadership of Charles Maurras.
12 Modernization theory enjoyed considerable vogue in the social sciences in the 1960s and 1970s.

13 See Roger Eatwell, *Fascism: A History* (London, Chatto & Windus, 1995), pp. 4–5.

14 Princeton, Princeton University Press, 1974.

15 Some anti-Stalinist Marxists might not balk at the idea that Stalinism represented a form of fascism!

16 Note that the last line is taken from the otherwise identical version of the text when it was reproduced in his collection of essays *Masses and Man* (New York, Howard Fertig, 1980).

17 Here used in the second sense outlined in note 1 of the Introduction.

18 'Fascist Ideology', in W. Laqueur (ed.), *Fascism: A Reader's Guide* (Harmondsworth, Penguin, 1979), pp. 325–406. See also Reading 14 and Introduction, p. 8.

19 See Introduction, pp. 10–11.

20 See Reading 14.

21 See Reading 3, and the General Introduction to Roger Griffin, *Fascism*, (Oxford, Oxford University Press, 1995).

22 Especially in his *The Nationalization of the Masses* (New York, Howard Fertig, 1975).

23 Especially in his *The Sacralization of Politics in Fascist Italy* (Cambridge, MA., Harvard University Press, 1996).

24 Note that Payne refers to the leader principle as the *Führerprinzip*, suggesting that Nazism is still playing the paradigmatic role in defining this aspect of fascism it had for Wilkinson in Reading 1.

THE PRODUCT OF A CRISIS
OF CAPITALISM

4

*The terrorist dictatorship of finance capital**

COMINTERN

I. Fascism and the maturing of the revolutionary crisis

1. Fascism is the open, terrorist dictatorship of the most reactionary, most chauvinist and most imperialist elements of finance capital. Fascism tries to secure a mass basis for monopolist capital among the petty bourgeoisie, appealing to the peasantry, artisans, office employees and civil servants who have been thrown out of their normal course of life, and particularly to the declassed elements in the big cities, also trying to penetrate into the working class.

The growth of fascism and its coming into power in Germany and in a number of other capitalist countries means:

(a) that the revolutionary crisis and the indignation of the broad masses against the rule of capital are growing;

(b) that the capitalists are no longer able to maintain their dictatorship by the old methods of parliamentarism and of bourgeois democracy in general;

(c) that, moreover, the methods of parliamentarism and bourgeois democracy in general are becoming a hindrance to the capitalists both in their internal politics (the struggle against the proletariat) and in their foreign politics (war for the imperialist redistribution of the world);

(d) that in view of this, capital is compelled to pass to open terrorist dictatorship within the country and to unrestrained chauvinism in foreign politics, which represents direct preparation for imperialist wars.

Born in the womb of bourgeois democracy, fascism in the eyes of the capitalists is a means of saving capitalism from collapse. It is only for the purpose of deceiving and disarming the workers that social-democracy denies the fascization of bourgeois democracy and draws a contrast in

* Extract from 13th Enlarged Executive of the Communist International (ECCI) Plenum (held in December 1933) on 'Fascism, the War Danger, and the Tasks of Communist Parties', in J. Degras (ed.), *The Communist International 1919–1943* (Oxford, Oxford University Press, 1965), Vol. 3, pp. 296–303.

principle between the democratic countries and the countries of the fascist dictatorship. On the other hand, the fascist dictatorship is not an inevitable stage of the dictatorship of the bourgeoisie in all countries. The possibility of averting it depends upon the forces of the fighting proletariat, which are paralysed by the corrupting [disintegrating] influence of social-democracy more than by anthing else.

2. While the general line of all bourgeois parties, including social-democracy, is towards the fascization of the dictatorship of the bourgeoisie, the realization of this line inevitably gives rise to disagreements among them as to forms and methods of fascization. Certain bourgeois groups, particularly [including] the social-fascists, who in practice stick at nothing in their acts of police violence against the proletariat, urge the maintenance of parliamentary forms when carrying through the fascization of the bourgeois dictatorship. The fascists, however, insist on the full or partial abolition of these old, shaken forms of bourgeois democracy, on carrying through fascization by means of the establishment of an open fascist dictatorship and by a wide application of both police violence and the terrorism of fascist gangs. Having come to power, fascism pushes aside, splits and disintegrates the other bourgeois parties (for instance, Poland) or dissolves them (Germany and Italy). This striving of fascism for political monopoly intensifies the discord and conflicts in the ranks of the ruling classes which follow from the internal contradictions in the position of the bourgeoisie who are becoming fascized.

3. The establishment of the fascist dictatorship in Germany has unmasked German social-democracy before the whole world. From the bloody crushing of the proletarian revolution in 1918, through an uninterrupted chain of treachery and strike-breaking, through all the coalition governments, the savage police massacres of revolutionary workers, voting for Hindenburg as the 'lesser evil', to servile endeavours to co-operate openly with the fascist gangs – such is the record of German social-democracy, the leading party in the Second International. [. . .]

Social-democracy continues to play the role of the main social prop of the bourgeoisie also in the countries of open fascist dictatorship. In fighting against the revolutionary unity of the proletariat and against the USSR, it helps the bourgeoisie to prolong the existence of capitalism by splitting the working class. In the majority of countries, however, it is already in the process of disintegration. The radicalization of the social-democratic workers intensifies the squabbles among the leading circle of the social-fascists. Avowed neo-fascist groups are arising; 'left' fragments break away and try to patch together a new Two-and-a-half International. Trotsky, the lackey of the counter-revolutionary bourgeoisie, is unsuccessfully trying to prevent the soical-democratic workers from coming over to the side of communism by his despicable attempts to form a Fourth International and by spreading anti-Soviet slanders. On the basis of the sharp antagonisms between the imperialist countries, the international organization of social-democracy is disintegrating. The crisis of the Second International is a fact.

4. The economic policy of the financial oligarchy for overcoming the crisis (the robbery of the workers and peasants, subsidies to the capitalists and landlords) is unable to restore the stabilization of capitalism; on the contrary, it is helping still further to disintegrate the mechanism of capitalist economy (disorganization of the money system, of the budget, state bankruptcies, a further deepening of the agrarian crisis), and to sharply intensify the fundamental contradictions of capitalism.

In this situation, all the capitalist countries are developing their war industries to unprecedented dimensions, and are adapting all the principal branches of industry, as well as agriculture, to the needs of war. The 'demand' thus created for means of extermination and destruction, combined with open inflation (USA, Great Britain and Japan), super-dumping (Japan), and hidden inflation (Germany), has in the past year caused an increase in output in some branches of industry in a number of countries (particularly iron, steel, non-ferrous metals, the chemical and textile industries). But this whipping up of production for non-productive purposes, or the speculative leaps in production on the basis of inflation, is accompanied by stagnation or a fall in production in a number of other branches (machine construction, building, the production of articles of [mass] consumption), and in the near future cannot but lead to the still greater disturbance of state finances and to a still further intensification of the general crisis of capitalism.

The furious struggle for foreign and colonial markets has already assumed the form of an actual international economic war.

5. Therefore the social-democratic estimation of the present world situation as one in which capitalism has succeeded in consolidating its position, in which it is already on the path towards overcoming its general crisis, is completely wrong. As distinguished from the first wave of the fascization of capitalist states which took place at the time of the transition from a revolutionary crisis to partial stabilization, the capitalist world is now passing from the end of capitalist stabilization to a revolutionary crisis, which determines other perspectives of development of fascism and the world revolutionary movement of the toilers.

Even the most savage terror, which the bourgeoisie employs in order to suppress the revolutionary movement cannot, in the conditions when capitalism is shaken, for long frighten the advanced strata of the toilers and restrain it from taking action; the indignation which this terror has roused even among the majority of the workers who followed the social-democrats, makes them more susceptible to communist agitation and propaganda. When the bourgeoisie reorganizes its tottering dictatorship on a fascist basis in order to create a firm, solid government, this, in the present conditions, leads to the strengthening, not only of its class terror-ism, but also of the elements which disrupt its power, to the destruction of the authority of bourgeois law [legality] in the eyes of the broad masses, to the growth of internal friction among the bourgeoisie and to the accelera-tion of the collapse of its main social support – social-democracy. Finally, when the bourgeoisie tries, by an aggressive war policy, to strengthen its foreign position, it extremely intensifies international antagonisms and the danger for capitalism which arises from them.

6. It would, therefore, be a right opportunist error to fail to see, now, the objective tendencies of the accelerated maturing of a revolutionary crisis in the capitalist world. But the presence and operation of these tendencies, both economic and political, do not imply that revolutionary development is proceeding upwards by itself, or unhindered, without resistance from counteracting forces. Revolutionary development is simul-taneously hindered and accelerated by the fascist fury of the bourgeoisie. The question of how soon the rule of bankrupt capitalism will be over-thrown by the proletariat will be determined by the fighting preparedness of the majority of the working class, by the successful work of the com-munist parties in undermining the mass influence of social-democracy. [. . .]

The mainstays of capitalism are already being destroyed by virtue of its profound, insoluble contradictions. The world economic crisis is most closely interwoven with the general crisis of capitalism, and sharpens all the cardinal contradictions of the capitalist world to such an extent that a turn may take place at any moment, a turn which will signify the trans-formation of the economic crisis into a revolutionary crisis. The great task of the international proletariat is to turn this crisis of the capitalist world into the victory of the proletarian revolution.

II. The imperialist preparations for a new world war

The growing uncertainty of the bourgeoisie as to the possibility of finding a way out of the crisis only by the intensified exploitation of the toilers of their own countries has led the imperialists to put their main stake on war. The international situation bears all the features of the eve of a new world war.

1. The flames of a new world war are flaring up in the Pacific. The Japanese militarists, spurred on by the profound internal crisis which the bourgeois-landlord monarchy is undergoing, are continuing the predatory war against China and, with the aid of the Kuomintang, are subjugating Northern China and are preparing a blow against the Mongolian People's Republic. British imperialism is stretching out its hand to the Southeastern

provinces of China, Tibet, Szechwan, while French imperialism is stretching out its hand towards Yunnan. The fascist military clique of Japan is acting as the battering ram against the anti-imperialist and agrarian revolution in China. The American, Japanese and British imperialism[s] are behind the Kuomintang in its sixth campaign against the only people's government in China, against the Chinese Soviets. The victories of the Soviet revolution in China, the partisan war in Manchuria, the growth of the revolutionary forces in Japan and of the liberation movement of the colonial peoples, create a new front in the rear of the imperialists. The Soviet revolution in China has become a big factor in the world revolution.

2. The Japanese militarists are calling to the German fascists and the British imperialists to unleash a counter-revolutionary war against the USSR from the East and from the West. [. . .]At the same time, German fascism is inviting the international bourgeoisie to purchase its national-socialist mercenaries to fight against the USSR, intriguing with British, Italian and Polish imperialism (the German–Polish negotiations). The British imperialists at the present time have taken the place of the French as the chief organizers of an anti-Soviet war.

The Soviet Union has achieved considerable successes in the unswerving and firm policy of peace it has pursued in the interests of all the toilers (a number of pacts of non-aggression, a number of new recognitions, the definition of the aggressor, the forced raising of the embargo by Great Britain). The land of the Soviets is the only bulwark of peace and of the independence of the weak states against the attacks of the predatory imperialists. [. . .]

3. The fascist government of Germany, which is the chief instigator of war in Europe, is provoking trouble in Danzig, in Austria, in the Saar, in the Baltic countries and in Scandinavia and, on the pretext of fighting against Versailles, is trying to form a *bloc* for the purpose of bringing about a new bloody carving up of Europe for the benefit of German imperialism. Imperialist *blocs*, headed either by France or Italy or by Great Britain which intrigues behind their backs, are being feverishly reorganized around the key-points of imperialist contradictions. Europe has become a powder-magazine which may explode at any moment. [. . .]

4. In this situation social-democracy sticks at nothing in the support of the imperialist interests of its own bourgeoisie and combines this support with service to international capital against the USSR. [. . .]

At the same time, the Second and Amsterdam Internationals are adapting their policy to the situation of the eve of war, trying to safeguard the interests of their own bourgeoisie and to ensure that the main blow will be directed at the USSR; they hypocritically mask this by expressing readiness to reply to war by a general strike and a boycott, but they declare in advance that they will do so only against the government that will be declared the aggressor by the League of Nations. They pretend to be leading a boycott against goods from fascist Germany, but they persecute the workers who really carry out this boycott. Under the slogans of pacifism and of a fight against war and fascism, they act as pioneers in working up public opinion in the capitalist countries in favour of a counter-revolutionary war against the USSR.

The bourgeoisie want to postpone the doom of capitalism by a criminal imperialist war and a counter-revolutionary campaign against the land of victorious socialism. The great historical task of international communism is to *mobilize the broad masses against war even before war has begun, and thereby hasten the doom of capitalism.* Only a Bolshevik struggle before the outbreak of war for the triumph of revolution can assure the victory of a revolution that breaks out in connection with war.

III. The tasks of the communist parties

In the conditions of the maturing of the world revolutionary crisis, when the bourgeoisie is trying to divert the ferment, the discontent and the indignation of the masses into the channel of fascization and war in order to strengthen its dictatorship, the main task of the communists is to direct this mass movement towards the fight for the overthrow of the dictatorship of the exploiting classes.

A. *The fight against fascist ideology*

The communist must:

(a) daily and concretely expose chauvinism to the masses in every country and oppose it by proletarian internationalism;

(b) in the imperialist countries, come out determinedly for the independence of the colonies, for the liberation of the dependent nations from all national oppression; in the keypoints of national antagonisms communists must struggle against imperialist occupation and violence, for the right of self-determination (Upper Silesia, the Saar, Northern Bohemia, etc.), coming out in all these regions, and also in Austria and Danzig, against the chauvinism of their national bourgeoisie and against incorporation in the hangmen's 'third empire' of German fascism;

(c) widely popularize the solution of the national question in the USSR and the tremendous economic social and cultural successes achieved by the peoples which were liberated by the October Revolution.

B. *The fight against the fascization of the bourgeois governments and against war*

In the fight against the fascization of the so-called 'democratic' countries, the communist parties must first of all brush aside [repudiate] the fatalist, defeatist line of the inevitability of a fascist dictatorship and imperialist war and also the opportunist underestimation of the tempo of fascization and the threat of imperialist wars, which condemn the communist parties to passivity.

In carefully explaining the economic and political slavery which the fascist dictatorship is bringing to the toilers, in showing the masses that the fascists are not socialists and are not bringing in a new [social] order, but are lackeys, lickspittles of capital, the communists must: rouse the masses in time for the defence of the trade unions, of the labour press, of the workers' clubs, of freedom to strike and of workers' meetings, organizing protests, demonstrations, strikes and setting up fighting self-defence detachments to resist the terrorist gangs.

In the fight against the fascist dictatorship, the communists must:

(a) taking as the starting point the defence of the everyday economic and political interests of the toilers, rouse the masses against the fascist dictatorship which deceived the workers, the peasants and the urban toilers; expose the demagogy and all provocations of fascism (the burning of the Reichstag, the faking of the Reichstag elections, etc.), stirring up strikes and leading the proletariat up to mass political strikes;

(b) penetrate all the *fascist mass organizations* and also carry on revolutionary work in the forced labour camps; while fighting against the revolutionary workers leaving the fascist trade union individually, but not calling upon the workers to join the fascist trade unions, the communists must utilize all mass movements as well as all manifestations of discontent shown by the masses in the fascist trade unions in order to form and consolidate *independent class trade unions*, while at the same time continuing their revolutionary work inside the fascist organizations;

(c) expose in the eyes of the *peasants* the policy which fascism pursues in the interests of the landlords and the kulaks, illustrating this by concrete examples from their own farm life; join the mass fascist organizations in the rural districts in order to split off the toiling peasants; organize the *agricultural proletariat* in independent trade unions which are to serve as the main lever for the whole work in the rural districts.

In fighting *against* war, the communists must prepare even now for the transformation of the imperialist war into civil war, and concentrate their forces in each country at the *vital parts of the war machine* of imperialism.

In addition to increased agitation, the communist parties must by all means in their power ensure the practical organization of *mass action* (preventing the shipping of arms and troops, hindering the execution of orders for belligerent countries, organizing demonstrations against military manoeuvres, etc.) and must *intensify political, educational work in the army and in the navy.*

The thirteenth Plenum of the ECCI calls upon all the sections of the Communist International, upon all the workers and the toilers of the world self-sacrificingly to defend the USSR against the counter-revolutionary conspiracy of the imperialists, and to defend the Chinese revolution and its Soviet power from imperialist intervention.

C. *Against social-democracy and for a united front from below*

In their fight against *social-democracy* the communists must prove to the workers that the new bankruptcy of social-democracy and the Second International was historically inevitable. While carefully exposing to the masses and refuting the hypocritical and treacherous sophistries of social-democracy, the communists must win over the social-democratic workers for active revolutionary struggle under the leadership of the communist parties.

The thirteenth Plenum of the ECCI fully approves the appeal for a united front issued by the Presidium of the ECCI, and the position of the Political Secretariat of the ECCI in the correspondence with the British Independent Labour Party. Social-democracy, which split the working class by its treachery at the time of the imperialist war and the October Revolution, has in all countries, in accordance with the directives of the Second International, refused the offers made by the communist parties for united working-class action, and sabotaged the united anti-fascist and anti-war movements created in Amsterdam and Paris, and in the face of fascism and war, strove to deepen the split in the ranks of the proletariat.

The thirteenth Plenum of the ECCI calls upon all sections of the Communist International persistently to fight for the realization of a united militant front with the social-democratic workers, in spite of and against the will of the treacherous leaders of social-democracy.

The Plenum fully approves the resolution of the Presidium of the ECCI of April 1, 1933 on the situation in Germany and the political line pursued by the Central Committee of the Communist Party of Germany, headed by Comrade Thälmann, before and at the time of the fascist *coup*. The Plenum notes the heroic Bolshevik struggle waged by the Communist Party of Germany against the fascist dictatorship. [. . .]

5

The counter-revolution of imperialist capitalism*

LEON TROTSKY

In his very pretentious, very muddled and stupid article[1] Dwight Mac-donald[2] tries to represent us as holding the view that fascism is simply a repetition of Bonapartism. A greater piece of nonsense would be hard to invent. We have analysed fascism as it developed, throughout the various stages of its development, and advanced to the forefront now one, now another of its aspects. There is an element of Bonapartism in fascism. Without this element, namely, without the raising of state power above society owing to an extreme sharpening of the class struggle, fascism would have been impossible. But we pointed out from the very beginning that it was primarily a question of Bonapartism of the epoch of imperialist decline, which is qualitatively different from Bonapartism of the epoch of bourgeois rise. At the next stage we distinguished pure Bonapartism as the prologue to a fascist regime. Because in the case of pure Bonapartism the rule of a monarch is approximated[.][3]

In postwar Italy the situation was profoundly revolutionary. The pro-letariat had every opportunity [to take power]. [The bourgeoisie at first hoped to stave off the dictatorship by means of a Bonapartist regime with Giolitti at the head. But this regime proved unstable and gave way to the fascist forces, recruited from the ranks of the petty bourgeoisie.] [It was the same with] the ministries of Bruening, Schleicher, and the presidency of Hindenburg in Germany, Pétain's government in France,[4] but they all have proved, or must prove, unstable. In the epoch of imperialist decline a pure Bonapartist Bonapartism is completely inadequate; imperialism finds it indispensable to mobilize the petty bourgeoisie and to crush the proletariat under its weight. Imperialism is capable of fulfilling this task only in case the proletariat itself reveals its inability to conquer power, while the social crisis drives the petty bourgeoisie into a condition of paroxysm.

The sharpness of the social crisis arises from this, that with today's concentration of the means of production, i.e., the monopoly of trusts, the

* Reprinted in full from the chapter 'Bonapartism, Fascism, and War', in Leon Trotsky *The Struggle against Fascism in Germany* (New York, Pathfinder Press, 1971), pp. 444–52. [The article, unfinished at Trotsky's death in July 1940, was originally printed in *Bulletin of the Opposition*, August–October, 1940.]

law of value – the market is already incapable of regulating economic relations. State intervention becomes an absolute necessity. (Inasmuch as the proletariat –) [This intervention will not solve the problems of the proletariat if the proletariat doesn't seize power and institute socialist methods of regulating the economy.]

The present war, as we have stated on more than one occasion, is a continuation of the last war. But a continuation does not signify a repetition. As a general rule, a continuation signfies a development, a deepening, a sharpening. Our policy, the policy of the revolutionary proletariat toward the second imperialist war, is a continuation of the policy elaborated during the last imperialist war, primarily under Lenin's leadership. But a continuation does not signify a repetition. In this case too, continuation signifies a development, a deepening and a sharpening.

During the last war not only the proletariat as a whole but also its vanguard and, in a certain sense, the vanguard of this vanguard, was caught unawares. The elaboration of the principles of revolutionary policy toward the war began at a time when the war was already in full blaze and the military machine exercised unlimited rule. One year after the outbreak of the war, the small revolutionary minority was still compelled to accommodate itself to a centrist majority at the Zimmerwald Conference.[5] Prior to the February Revolution and even afterwards, the revolutionary elements felt themselves to be not contenders for power but the extreme left opposition. Even Lenin relegated the socialist revolution to a more or less distant future. [In 1915 or 1916] he wrote in Switzerland: [quotation].[6] If that is how Lenin viewed the situation, then there is hardly any need of talking about the others.

This political position of the extreme left wing expressed itself most graphically on the question of the defense of the fatherland. In 1915 Lenin referred in his writings to revolutionary wars which the victorious proletariat would have to wage. But it was a question of an indefinite historical perspective and not of tomorrow's task. The attention of the revolutionary wing was centered on the question of the defense of the capitalist fatherland. The revolutionists naturally replied to this question in the negative. This was entirely correct. This purely negative answer served as the basis for propaganda and for training the cadres, but it could not win the masses who did not want a foreign conqueror. In Russia prior to the war the Bolsheviks constituted four-fifths of the proletarian vanguard, that is, of the workers participating in political life (newspapers, elections, etc.). Following the February Revolution the unlimited rule passed into the hands of defensists, the Mensheviks and the SRs. True enough, the Bolsheviks in the space of eight months conquered the overwhelming majority of the workers. But the decisive role in this conquest was not played by the refusal to defend the bourgeois fatherland but by the slogan: 'All Power to the Soviets!' And only by this revolutionary slogan! The criticism of imperialism, its militarism, the renunciation of the defense of bourgeois democracy and so on never could have won the overwhelming majority of the people to the side of the Bolsheviks. In all other belligerent countries, with the exception of Russia, the revolutionary wing toward the end of the war all [still put forward only negative slogans].

Insofar as the proletariat proves incapable at a given stage of conquering power, imperialism begins regulating economic life with its own methods; the political mechanism is the fascist party, which becomes the state power. The productive forces are in irreconcilable contradiction not only with private property but also with national boundaries. Imperialism is the very expression of this contradiction. Imperialist capitalism seeks to solve this contradiction through an extension of boundaries, seizure of new territories, and so on. The totalitarian state, subjecting all aspects of economic, political, and cultural life to finance capital, is the instrument for creating a supra-nationalist state, an imperialist empire, ruling over continents, ruling over the whole world.

All these traits of fascism we have analysed each one by itself and all of them in their totality to the extent that they became manifest or came to the forefront.

Both theoretical analysis and the rich historical experience of the last quarter of a century have demonstrated with equal force that fascism is each time the final link of a specific political cycle composed of the following: the gravest crisis of capitalist society; the growth of the radicalization of the working class; the growth of sympathy toward the working class and a yearning for change on the part of the rural and urban petty bourgeoisie; the extreme confusion of the big bourgeoisie; its cowardly and treacherous maneuvers aimed at avoiding the revolutionary climax; the exhaustion of the proletariat; growing confusion and indifference; the aggravation of the social crisis; the despair of the petty bourgeoisie, its yearning for change; the collective neurosis of the petty bourgeoisie, its readiness to believe in miracles, its readiness for violent measures; the growth of hostility towards the proletariat which has deceived its expectations. These are the premises for a swift formation of a fascist party and its victory.

It is quite self-evident that the radicalization of the working class in the United States has passed only through its initial phases, almost exclusively in the sphere of the trade-union movement (the CIO). The pre-war period, and then the war itself may temporarily interrupt this process of radicalization, especially if a considerable number of workers are absorbed into war industry. But this interruption of the process of radicalization cannot be of long duration. The second stage of radicalization will assume a more sharply expressive character. The problem of forming an independent labor party will be put on the order of the day. Our transitional demands will gain great popularity. On the other hand, the fascist, reactionary tendencies will withdraw to the background, assuming a defensive position, awaiting a more favorable moment. This is the closest perspective. No occupation is more completely unworthy than that of speculating whether or not we shall succeed in creating a powerful revolutionary vanguard party. Ahead lies a favorable perspective, providing all the justification for revolutionary activism. It is necessary to utilize the opportunities which are opening up and to build the revolutionary party.

The Second World War poses the question of change of regimes more imperiously, more urgently than did the first war. It is first and foremost a question of the political regime. The workers are aware that democracy is suffering shipwreck everywhere, and that they are threatened by fascism even in those countries where fascism is as yet nonexistent. The bourgeoisie of the democratic countries will naturally utilize this dread of fascism on the part of the workers; but, on the other hand, the bankruptcy of democracies, their collapse, their painless transformation into reactionary dictatorships compel the workers to pose before themselves the problem of power and render them responsive to the posing of the problem of power.

Reaction wields today such power as perhaps never before in the modern history of mankind. But it would be an inexcusable blunder to see only reaction. The historical process is a contradictory one. Under the cover of official reaction, profound processes are taking place among the masses, who are accumulating experience and becoming receptive to new political perspectives. The old conservative tradition of the democratic state, which was so powerful even during the era of the last imperialist war, exists today only as an extremely unstable survival. On the eve of the last war the European workers had numerically powerful parties. But on the order of the day were put reforms, partial conquests, and not at all the conquest of power.

The American working class is still without a mass labor party even today. But the objective situation and the experience accumulated by the American workers can within a very brief period of time place on the order of the day the question of the conquest of power. This perspective must be made the basis of our agitation. It is not merely a question of a position on capitalist militarism and of renouncing the defense of the bourgeois state but of directly preparing for the conquest of power and the defense of the proletarian fatherland.

May not the Stalinists turn out at the head of a new revolutionary upsurge and may they not ruin the revolution as they did in Spain and previously in China? It is of course impermissible to consider that such a possibility is excluded, for example, in France. The first wave of the revolution has often, or more correctly, always carried to the top those 'left' parties which have not managed to discredit themselves completely in the preceding period and which have an imposing political tradition behind them. Thus the February Revolution raised up the Mensheviks and SRs who were the opponents of the revolution on its very eve. Thus the German revolution in November 1918 raised to power the Social Democrats, who were the irreconcilable opponents of revolutionary uprisings.

Twelve years ago Trotsky wrote in an article published by *The New Republic*:

> There is no epoch in human history so saturated with antagonisms as ours. Under too high a tension of class and international animosities, the 'fuses' of democracy 'blow out.' Hence the short-circuits of dictatorship. Naturally the weakest 'interrupters' are the first to give way. But the force of internal and world controversies does not weaken: it grows. It is doubtful if it is destined to calm down, given that the process has so far only taken hold of the periphery of the capitalist world. Gout begins in the little finger of a hand or in the big toe, but once on the way it goes right to the heart.
>
> ('Which Way Russia?' *The New Republic*, May 22, 1929)

This was written at a time when the entire bourgeois democracy in each country believed that fascism was possible only in the backward countries which had not yet graduated from the school of democracy. The editorial board of *The New Republic*, which at that period had not yet been touched with the blessings of the GPU, accompanied Trotsky's article with one of its own. The article is so characteristic of the average American philistine that we shall quote from it the most interesting passages.

> In view of his personal misfortunes, the exiled Russian leader shows a remarkable power of detached analysis; but his detachment is that of the rigid Marxian, and seems to us to lack a realistic view of history – the very thing on which he prides himself. His notion that democracy is a fair-weather form of government, incapable of with-standing the storms of international or domestic controversy, can be supported (as he himself half admits) only by taking for your examples countries where democracy has never made more than the feeblest beginnings, and countries, moreover, in which the industrial revolution has hardly more than started.

Further on, the editorial board of *The New Republic* dismisses the instance of Kerensky's democracy in Soviet Russia and why it failed to withstand the test of class contradictions and gave way to a revolutionary perspective. The periodical sagely writes:

'Kerensky's weakness was an historic accident, which Trotsky cannot admit because there is no room in his mechanistic scheme for any such thing.'

Just like Dwight Macdonald, *The New Republic* accused the Marxists of being unable to understand history realistically owing to their orthodox

or mechanistic approach to political events. *The New Republic* was of the
opinion that fascism is the product of the backwardness of capitalism and
not its overripeness. In the opinion of that periodical which, I repeat, was
the opinion of the overwhelming majority of average democratic philistines, fascism is the lot of backward bourgeois countries. The sage editorial board did not even take the trouble of thinking about the question of
why it was the universal conviction in the nineteenth century that backward countries must develop along the road of democracy. In any case, in
the old capitalist countries, democracy came into its rights at a time when
the level of their economic development was not above but below the
economic development of modern Italy. And what is more, in that era
democracy represented the main highway of historical development which
was entered by all countries one by one, the backward ones following the
more advanced and sometimes ahead of them. Our era on the contrary is
the era of democracy's collapse, and, moreover, the collapse begins with
the weaker links but gradually extends to those which appeared strong and
impregnable. Thus the orthodox or mechanistic, that is, the Marxist
approach to events enabled us to forecast the course of developments
many years in advance. On the contrary, the realistic approach of *The
New Republic* was the approach of a blind kitten. *The New Republic*
followed up its critical attitude toward Marxism by falling under the
influence of the most revolting caricature of Marxism, namely, Stalinism.

Most of the philistines of the newest crop base their attacks on Marxism on the fact that, contrary to Marx's prognosis, fascism came instead of
socialism. Nothing is more stupid and vulgar than this criticism. Marx
demonstrated and proved that when capitalism reaches a certain level, the
only way out for society lies in the socialization of the means of production, i.e., socialism. He also demonstrated that in view of the class structure of society, the proletariat alone is capable of solving this task in an
irreconcilable revolutionary struggle against the bourgeoisie. He further
demonstrated that for the fulfillment of this task the proletariat needs a
revolutionary party. All his life Marx, and together with him and after him
Engels, and after them Lenin, waged an irreconcilable struggle against
those traits in proletarian parties, socialist parties, which obstructed the
solution of the revolutionary historical task. The irreconcilability of the
struggle waged by Marx, Engels, and Lenin against opportunism on the
one side and anarchism on the other demonstrates that they did not at all
underestimate this danger. In what did it consist? In this, that the opportunism of the summits of the working class, subject to the bourgeoisie's
influence, could obstruct, slow down, make more difficult, postpone the
fulfillment of the revolutionary task of the proletariat. It is precisely this
condition of society that we are now observing. Fascism did not at all come
'instead' of socialism. Fascism is the continuation of capitalism, an
attempt to perpetuate its existence by means of the most bestial and

monstrous measures. Capitalism obtained an opportunity to resort to fascism only because the proletariat did not accomplish the socialist revolution in time. The proletariat was paralysed in the fulfillment of its task by the opportunist parties. The only thing that can be said is that there turned out to be more obstacles, more difficulties, more stages on the road of the revolutionary development of the proletariat than was foreseen by the founders of scientific socialism. Fascism and the series of imperialist wars constitute the terrible school in which the proletariat has to free itself of petty-bourgeois traditions and superstitions; has to rid itself of opportunist, democratic, and adventurist parties; has to hammer out and train the revolutionary vanguard and in this way prepare for the solving of the task apart from which there is not and cannot be any salvation for the development of mankind.

Eastman,[7] if you please, has come to the conclusion that the concentration of the means of production in the hands of the state endangers his 'freedom' and he has therefore decided to renounce socialism. This anecdote deserves being included in the text of a history of ideology. The socialization of the means of production is the only solution to the economic problem at the given stage of mankind's development. Delay in solving this problem leads to the barbarism of fascism. All the intermediate solutions, undertaken by the bourgeoisie with the help of the petty bourgeoisie, have undergone miserable and shameful ruin. All this is absolutely uninteresting to Eastman. He noticed that his 'freedom' (freedom of muddling, freedom of indifferentism, freedom of passivity, freedom of literary dilettantism) was being threatened from various sides, and he decided immediately to apply his own measure: renounce socialism. Astonishingly enough this decision exercised no influence either on Wall Street or on the policy of the trade unions. Life went its own way just as if Max Eastman had remained a socialist. It may be set down as a general rule that the more impotent is a petty-bourgeois radical, especially in the United States, the more [firmly he clings to his freedom].

In France there is no fascism in the real sense of the term. The regime of the senile Marshal Pétain represents a senile form of Bonapartism of the epoch of imperialist decline. But this regime too proved possible only after the prolonged radicalization of the French working class, which led to the explosion of June 1936, had failed to find a revolutionary way out. The Second and Third Internationals, the reactionary charlatanism of the 'People's Fronts'[8] deceived and demoralized the working class. After five years of propaganda in favor of an alliance of democracies and of collective security, after Stalin's sudden passage into Hitler's camp, the French working class was caught unawares. The war provoked a terrible disorientation and a mood of passive defeatism, or, to put it more correctly, the indifferentism of an impasse. From this web of circumstances arose first the unprecedented military catastrophe and then the despicable Pétain regime.

Precisely because Pétain's regime is senile Bonapartism, it contains no element of stability and can be overthrown by a revolutionary mass uprising much sooner than a fascist regime.

In every discussion of political topics the question invariably flares up: shall we succeed in creating a strong party for the moment when the crisis comes? Might not fascism anticipate us? Isn't a fascist stage of development inevitable? The successes to fascism easily make people lose all perspective, lead them to forget the actual conditions which made the strengthening and the victory of fascism possible. Yet a clear understanding of these conditions is of especial importance to the workers of the United States. We may set it down as an historical law: fascism was able to conquer only in those countries where the conservative labor parties prevented the proletariat from utilizing the revolutionary situation and seizing power. In Germany, two revolutionary situations were involved: 1918–1919 and 1923–24. Even in 1929 a direct struggle for power on the part of the proletariat was still possible. In all these three cases the Social Democracy and the Comintern criminally and viciously disrupted the conquest of power and thereby placed society in an impasse. Only under these conditions and in this situation did the stormy rise of fascism and its gaining of power prove possible.

Notes

1 ['National Defense: The Case for Socialism', *Partisan Review*, July–August, 1940. – *Editor*.]

2 Dwight Macdonald, an editor of *Partisan Review* at the time, was briefly a member of the SWP in 1939–1940, but split from it under the leadership of Max Shachtman and James Burnham. He soon departed from the Shachtmanite Workers Party, became pro-anarchist for a time, and then a left-liberal.

3 [The editors of the *Bulletin of the Opposition* added a few interpolations, shown here in brackets, to complete sentences and to make the transition from one point to another, where Trotsky's dictaphone recording, and hence the manuscript, was incomplete. It should be kept in mind that these interpolations are not by Trotsky, but by the editorial board of the *Bulletin of the Opposition*. – *Editor*.]

4 Philippe Pétain (1856–1951) commanded the French at Verdun in 1916 and was made a marshal of the French army in 1918. He commanded French troops in Morocco in 1925–1926. He was minister of defense in the Doumergue government in 1934, and premier of Unoccupied France from 1940 to 1944. He was convicted of collaboration with the Nazis in 1945 and sentenced to death, commuted to life imprisonment by de Gaulle.

5 The Zimmerwald Conference was held in September 1915 on the initiative of the Italian and Swiss Socialist parties for the purpose of uniting the anti-war opposition elements of the world movement. The majority of the participants were centrists, and the resolutions failed to make a clean break with the Second International. A second conference, held at Kienthal, Switzerland, in April

1916, was more radical, but the positions taken and the composition of the participants still did not constitute the firmest basis for the formation of the Third International, according to Lenin.

6 [The English translator here added the following: 'Several citations from Lenin during that period fit Trotsky's description. We quote two:

['"It is possible, however, that five, ten and even more years will pass before the beginning of the socialist revolution." (From an article written in March, 1916, Lenin's *Collected Works*, vol. XIX, p. 45, Third Russian Edition.]

['"We, the older men, will perhaps not live long enough to see the decisive battles of the impending revolution." (Report on 1905 Revolution delivered to Swiss students, January, 1917, idem, page 357.]'

[The editors of the *Bulletin of the Opposition* inserted the latter quotation at this point in the text. – *Editor.*]

7 Max Eastman (1883–1969) was editor of *The Masses* before World War I, then editor of *The Liberator*. He was an early supporter of the Russian Left Opposition although not a member of any party. He translated several of Trotsky's books and was the first to acquaint the American public with the issues of the Trotsky–Stalin struggle. In the mid-1930s he began a retreat from Marxism, repudiating socialism in 1940. He became an anticommunist and an editor of the *Reader's Digest*.

8 The People's Front line was the right zigzag of the Comintern in 1935, that is, the policy of building coalition governments of the workers' parties and the liberal capitalist parties. This line remained in effect until the Stalin–Hitler pact on the eve of World War II in 1939.

6

*A resurgence of Bonapartism**

MIHALY VAJDA

In two European countries the fascist movement achieved its goal. The party gained power, and the dictatorship was established. In the two countries different factors motivated (or forced) the ruling bourgeoisie into handing political power over to the fascists. In accordance with their different origins, the two systems fulfilled different economic functions. But their structure – not only their political structure but their social structure too – can be regarded as essentially identical. Which class (stratum) or classes actually benefited from the fascist régime? I am in agreement with Horkheimer when he says that 'whoever does not like speaking about "capitalism" would have kept quiet about fascism too'.[1] In fact, fascism in no way restricted the bourgeoisie's economic power

---

* Reprinted in full from the chapter 'Fascism and Bonapartism', in Mihaly Vajda, *Fascism as a Mass Movement* (London, Allison & Busby, 1976) pp. 93–104.

within the factory. It did not thwart their economic interests and even helped them obtain increased satisfaction. After the downfall of the fascist régime in both countries, the fact that it had existed at all brought about a new régime which guaranteed the political rule of the haute bourgeoisie. In many respects, the fascist régime determined the nature of the new one. But this does not contradict my assertion that in the fascist system the bourgeoisie does not itself exercise political power, and that in fact it lacks a voice in the decisions of those who are ruling politically. Consequently, our understanding of the essence of fascism is helped very little by the statement that fascism is the rule of finance capital. This is only true in the sense that fascism primarily served and satisfied the interests of the haute bourgeoisie, and it carries very little conviction if it is left unexplained. This characterization of fascism is not confined to marxists alone, and can be reached from a non-marxist position too. For example, Hermann Heller writes that 'all in all, fascism cannot be considered a new form of state, it is nothing but the form of dictatorship adequate to capitalist society'.[2]

But on the other hand, we obviously cannot confine ourselves simply to a sociological description of the fascist power 'élite', or to a debate about which stratum exercises power in fascism and how it does so. We cannot simply take it for granted that fascism is evidently one of the forms of rule of the capitalist system. This is why I find Iring Fetscher's definition unsatisfactory:

> In its ideo-typical pure form, fascism is the rule of a radical minority, a minority which consists in essence of militarised and déclassé petty bourgeois, lumpenproletarian and half-educated elements, which exploits the propertied classes' fear of bolshevism and socialisation as well as the conservatives' aversion to the parliamentary system, in order to induce them to accept the seizure of power by this minority. Its objective is the destruction of political and social pluralism and the realisation of the unrestricted rule of a new 'élite', an élite which utilises any conceivable means in order to secure and extend its power, and which justifies this rule by a historical myth of a racial or some other kind.[3]

There is not much in Fetscher's description that one can object to. Everything he says is true. But since he does not raise the question of the real connections between fascism and the economic structure (although he never actually denies that fascism leaves property relations intact), he fails to give a satisfactory explanation – just as the Comintern definition (which simply restated that fascism maintains the haute bourgeoisie's economic power unbroken) failed.

The most adequate approach to the analysis of fascist dictatorship is, I think, to approach it on the basis of Marx's analysis of bonapartism in *The Eighteenth Brumaire of Louis Bonaparte*. As we have already seen,

August Thalheimer made a categorical attempt to do this. He follows
Marx's analysis of the bonapartist system step by step, in order to prove
that fascism corresponds in every respect with the notion of bonapartist
dictatorship. He writes:

> The common denominator [of bonapartism and fascism] is the open
> dictatorship of capital. Its form of appearance is characterised by the
> fact that the executive power becomes independent, that the political
> power of the bourgeoisie is destroyed and all the other social classes
> become politically subordinated to the executive power. But its social
> or class content is determined by the rule of the bourgeoisie and of
> the private proprietors in general over the working class and over all
> the other strata exploited by capital.[4]

Trotsky argued against Thalheimer and the German communist opposition, saying that only the period just preceding the fascist seizure of power
(the Brüning and Papen governments) were bonapartist. The debate
between Thalheimer and Trotsky appears to have been in many ways a
mere scholastic exercise; we cannot substitute analogies for the real analysis of a historical phenomenon, even if analogies can help in elucidating
certain problems. It can be demonstrated that both the period of the
Brüning and Papen governments and the fascist dictatorship itself corresponded in various ways with bonapartism. But would it constitute a
theoretical advance if we could actually show that one of them 'fulfilled'
Marx's definition better than the other? Is there any sense at all in trying
to determine whether fascism is a bonapartist régime or not?

From a historical perspective it may indeed seem to be a piece of
senseless hair-splitting to debate the bonapartist nature of fascism. Nevertheless, I do not agree with those who think that the problem itself is a
senseless one, as for example Angelo Tasca did when he said that 'fascism
is a post-war phenomenon, and every attempt to define it with the help of
historically "antecedent" parallels, e.g. by analogy with bonapartism,
remains unproductive and may be misleading'.[5] It is true that there are
many respects in which fascism cannot be compared to any previous
historical phenomenon. Perhaps it is more than just our moral sense
that revolts against mentioning Hitler's horrors and the rule of Louis
Bonaparte, let alone Napoleon, in the same breath. But even if it could
be proved that the two historical phenomena had nothing essentially in
common, I would still consider it undeniably valuable that some marxists
should have made the analogy between bonapartism and fascist dictatorship or the forms of rule which immediately led up to it. For by the very act
of proposing this analogy, which in itself can never supply the key to
understanding of a concrete historical phenomenon, they are accomplish-
ing a theoretical task: they are reviving one of Marx's most brilliant

analyses, the oustanding example of the analysis of political rule, political structure and economic relations as a complex.

Marx's analysis reminds our contemporaries that the theoretical examination of the actual state and characteristics of a régime must be based on an analysis of the inter-relations among all the classes and strata involved in it. Marx made a clearcut distinction between those who actually hold the reins of political rule and the classes and strata that exercise economic power. His analysis of bonapartism clearly demonstrates that the tasks of politico-sociological analysis are not exhausted simply by the examination of property relations, and that the property relations in themselves do not determine the political struc- ture of the system. *The Eighteenth Brumaire* proved to be a fertile point of departure (quite independently of whether or not it proves that fas- cism meets all the basic characteristics of bonapartism), because it drew attention to something which marxist theory as received by both social democracy and stalinism denies. This is the fact that it is possible (and was actually the case at points in history before fascism) for a political system to exist in which political rule is not exercised by the fundamental class in the given social formation, i.e. not by the class which possesses the decisive means of production. Regardless of whether fascism is bonapartism or not, we are clearly not compelled to make a theoretically untenable choice between two false alternatives: either, by looking at the unbroken and even reinforced power of monopoly capital under fascism, to assert that the fascist system was built directly on the rule of mono- poly capital, or, by examining the social origins of the stratum in power and its relation to the means of production, to deny the increased economic power of monopoly capital.

One of the most important messages of *The Eighteenth Brumaire* is that the bourgeoisie, as the leading social class, has its own very important specific feature which distinguishes it from the ruling classes of all pre- ceding societies: it does not insist on the exercise of political rule under all circumstances. In bourgeois society, the individual has been severed from the umbilical cord of the community. His place in 'civil society' in the egoistic world of economic interests, does not determine his role in the ideal sphere of the political state. In all preceding, 'naturally given' socie- ties, where 'civil society' and 'political state' were not yet separate, those who held economic power always operated as the political leaders of society, directly and (as a result of their economic position) automatically. In bourgeois society this is no longer true. The bourgeois is a bourgeois as long, but only as long, as he possesses capital, and if he does possess it he can satisfy his particular needs more or less unrestrictedly, without having to be a member of the stratum which rules the society and determines the political activity of the ideal community. For this very reason, the capitalist has little inclination to abandon his private activities and act politically, and even less to subordinate his private (i.e. bourgeois) existence to his public, political (i.e. citizen's) existence: 'the ordinary bourgeois [is] always inclined to sacrifice the general interest of his class for this or that private motive'.[6] If possible, he attends to his business and does not get involved in politics. And what is true of the individual bourgeois is essentially true also of his class. In the everyday life of civil society, the bourgeoisie does not act as a class. The class interest only comes to the fore (as that of the 'community', to which the individual bourgeois must subordinate his egoistic interests) at moments when the class is threatened. It follows from the structure and the functional mechanisms of this society, and above all from the separation between 'civil society' and 'political state', that the same holds true *mutatis mutandis* for the other classes in it too.

As long as the rule of another class prevented the bourgeoisie from freely asserting its own egoistic material interests, it was of course forced to appear as an independent political force. Until the bourgeoisie succeeded in getting rid of the feudal ruling class (as happened in France), or in forcing it into a position where it could not, in spite of its maintenance of political rule, frustrate the bourgeoisie from asserting its own material interests (as happened in Britain), it reluctantly accepted the necessity for political struggle and for the political form of existence. But as soon as the bourgeoisie could develop its material power without restrictions, political activity became a burden to it and simply obstructed its attempts to realize the opportunities it had fought so hard for. Consequently, it was sometimes prepared to abandon politics to a class or stratum which was ready to exercise it.

The first and purest historical form of this example was to be observed in France. This was no accident. Because of the resistance which it met, the French bourgeoisie fought the purest and most classical form of struggle against the feudal class. This meant that, as a class possessing real economic power, it remained essentially alone. The British bourgeoisie had already made a compromise, and only the subsequent behaviour of the French bourgeoisie made it clear that as a result of this compromise the British bourgeoisie had escaped lightly. It was only the French bourgeoisie which, by carrying its struggle through to full political victory, 'proved that the struggle to maintain its *public* interests, its own class *interests*, its *political power*, only troubled and upset it as a disturbance of private business'.[7]

In *The Eighteenth Brumaire* Marx also demonstrated that it was not only burdensome but often dangerous for the bourgeoisie to maintain its rule in pure form. The bourgeoisie could only fight feudalism if it presented its own particular interests as the general interest (and believed them to be so). But as soon as it brought about its own rule in pure form, the ideological nature of its ideals was revealed:

Instinct taught them that the republic indeed perfects their political
rule, but at the same time undermines its social foundation, since
they must now confront the subjugated classes and contend against
them without intermediation. [. . .] It was a feeling of weakness that
caused them to recoil from the pure conditions of their own class
rule, and to sigh for the less complete, less developed and consequently less dangerous forms of this rule.[8]

The question of whether or not the bourgeoisie renounces its own political
rule – and if so, in what form – always depends on the concrete, historically given class relations of the country concerned. Bonapartist dictatorship is only one (extreme) form of solution. But it is a form in which the
bourgeoisie renounces its *political* power alone, for the sake of maintaining its *social* power:

The bourgeoisie confess that their own interest dictates that they
should be rescued from the danger of governing in their own name;
that in order to restore tranquillity in the land, the bourgeois parliament must first of all be given its quietus; that in order to preserve its
social power inviolate, its political power must be broken; that the
private bourgeois can only continue to exploit the other classes and
to enjoy undisturbed property, family, religion and order on condition that their class be condemned along with the other classes to a
like political nullity; that in order to save its purse it must abandon
the crown; and that the sword which is to safeguard it must be hung
over its own head as a sword of Damocles.[9]

When Engels wrote to Marx in 1866 that 'bonapartism is after all the
real religion of the modern bourgeoisie',[10] he was already using the notion
of bonapartism in a generalized sense. His choice of words expresses
precisely the idea that the bourgeoisie is seldom able to rule alone.
Depending on the historical conditions, the bourgeoisie often shares the
exercise of political rule with other strata or classes (for example the old
feudal ruling strata) or leaves it entirely to them, as long as it has previously made sure that the latter cannot restict the growth of its economic
power. (In many cases the bourgeoisie did not even make an attempt to
seize power, as was the case in Bismarck's Germany.) Moreover, we can
nowadays see that the bourgeoisie may even accept circumstances where
political leadership is in the hands of proletarian parties (social democratic governments). I have already indicated what kind of conditions
enable it to acquiesce in this kind of situation: there must be separation
between civil society and the political state, so that even in 'normal'
circumstances political power is not exercised directly by the bourgeoisie
but by an 'independent' apparatus, which in these 'normal' circumstances
depends directly on, the bourgeoisie. It is relatively rare for the bourgeoisie

to transfer political power to a genuinely independent apparatus – that is, to a socially separate stratum which can only secure a source of livelihood by taking over executive power. This happens if a stratum exists which has somehow been driven out by 'civil society' but which, because of its origins or the economic situation of the country, cannot be reintegrated at a lower level. Louis Bonaparte's Tenth of December Society was of this nature. The existence of the Society made Louis Bonaparte a political factor in France, although he did not mean or represent anything at all in French 'civil society':

> The Tenth of December Society belonged to him, it was *his* work, his very own idea. Whatever else he appropriates is put into his hands by force of circumstances; whatever else he does the circumstances do for him, or he is content to copy from the deeds of others. [. . .]The Tenth of December Society was thus to remain the private army of Bonaparte, until he succeeded in transforming the public army into a Tenth of December Society.[11]

This kind of organization and its leader, separated as they are from bourgeois existence, have tremendous advantages over the ordinary bourgeois and also over the 'ordinary' bourgeois politician, who clearly stands in a dependent relation to the bourgeoisie itself. They have the advantage over all those who, precisely because of their functions in bourgeois life, have to preserve their 'credit'. 'Because [Bonaparte] was a bohemian, a princely lumpenproletarian, he had the advantage over any rascally bourgeois in that he could conduct the struggle meanly.[12]

Precisely because the only way for this stratum to acquire any social function at all is to take over executive power, it regards the maintenance of this power as a question of livelihood, a question of its own existence; for this very reason, it must also acquire guarantees against the bourgeoisie, just in case the bourgeoisie should no longer need it. In order to maintain his rule, the 'head' of society, Bonaparte, must grant huge advantages to his own stratum: 'alongside the actual classes of society, he is forced to create an artificial caste, for which the maintenance of his régime becomes a bread-and-butter question'.[13] The stratum which rules politically must defend itself from the bourgeoisie:

> As the executive authority which has made itself an independent power, Bonaparte feels it to be his mission to safeguard 'bourgeois order'. But the strength of this bourgeois order lies in the middle class and issues decrees in this sense. Nevertheless, he is somebody solely due to the fact that he has broken the political power of this middle class and daily breaks it anew. Consequently, he looks on himself as the adversary of the political and literary power of the middle class. But by protecting its material power, he generates its

political power anew. The cause must accordingly be kept alive; but the effect, where it manifests itself, must be done away with. But this cannot pass off without slight confusions of cause and effect, since in their interaction both lose their distinguishing features. New decrees, that obliterate the borderline. As against the bourgeoisie, Bonaparte looks on himself, at the same time, as the representative of the peasants and of the people in general, who wants to make the lower classes of the people happy within the framework of bourgeois society. New decrees, that cheat the 'true socialists' of their statecraft in advance. But above all, Bonaparte looks on himself as the chief of the Tenth of December Society, as the representative of the lumpen-proletariat to which he himself, his entourage, his government and his army belong, and whose prime consideration is to benefit itself and draw California lottery prizes from the state treasury. And he vindicates his positon as chief of the Tenth of December Society with decrees, without decrees, and despite decrees.[14]

According to Marx's analysis, the essential feature of bonapartism is the independence of executive power exercised by a statum which has no other function in 'civil society', and which is prepared if necessary to act against any class of society in the name of any other class. Nevertheless, I do not think it possible to read into his analysis the conclusion that in bourgeois society, state power and the state machinery are gradually emancipated from society. Marx analysed the gradual growth of bureaucracy from the period of absolute monarchy to the period of the parliamentary republic, and his conclusion was:

> Under the absolute monarchy, during the first revolution, and under Napoleon, bureaucracy was only the means of preparing the class rule of the bourgeoisie. Under the Restoration, under Louis Philippe and under the parliamentary republic, it was the instrument of the ruling class, however much it strove for power of its own. Only under the second Bonaparte does the state *seem* [my italics – *M.V.*] to have made itself completely independent.[15]

So this was mere appearance, for Bonaparte in fact represented a certain class: 'the state power is not suspended in mid-air. Bonaparte represents a class, and the most numerous class of French society at that, the *small peasants*'.[16] 'This class, however, can only partly be described as a class, inasmuch as its members' conditions of existence 'derive their mode of life, their interests and the culture from those of the other classes and put them in hostile contrast to the latter'.[17] But on the other hand, it is not and cannot be a class, inasmuch as 'the identity of their interests begets no unity, no national union and no political organisation'.[18] So the executive power can make itself independent only by virtue of the fact that it is held by a quasi-class unable to represent itself.

Therefore the theory[19] that Marx, repudiating the standpoint of *The Communist Manifesto*, gradually came to see the developmental trend of bourgeois society as pointing towards the growth of independence of the executive power, has no foundation in *The Eighteenth Brumaire*. It is factually false, since no such trend can actually be observed in the history of capitalism. It appears only in those periods (and *The Eighteenth Brumaire* points this out) when on the one hand the exercise of political rule has for some reason become inconvenient or even dangerous for the bourgeoisie, and on the other hand a stratum exists which has no function in 'civil society' and can only acquire a role through the exercise of executive power. But according to Marx, this power represents the interests of some class in bourgeois society even then. Marx also showed why the bourgeoisie consented to having its free movement and the free exercise of its everyday life restricted by an executive power of this kind, with its tendency to 'become independent'. The bourgeois tolerates these restrictions because otherwise he would only have the proletariat to rely on in fighting this mob:

> Instead of letting itself be intimidated by the executive power with the prospect of fresh disturbances, it ought rather to have allowed the class struggle a little elbow-room, so as to keep the exectuive power dependent on it. But it did not feel equal to the task of playing with fire.[20]

The real lesson of *The Eighteenth Brumaire*, therefore, is not that it points to some alleged tendency of the executive power to become independent. It lies in its recognition that there are cases where the bourgeoisie willingly surrenders the direct exercise of political power to other strata, and sometimes even to those which assert only the egoistic and material interests of the bourgeoisie, while considerably curtailing its civic rights. Naturally when the bourgeoisie is in power it does its best to avoid this separation from the executive power.

All this amply shows that Marx's analysis of bonapartism is well suited, down to its details, to serve as the point of departure for an analysis of fascist dictatorship. We may also conclude that Thalheimer was certainly right in his debate with Trotsky: for even if it is true that the Brüning and Papen governments existed by exploiting a class equilibrium which at that given moment seemed impossible to budge, nevertheless it was not true that, while these governments were ruling with the help of presidential decrees, executive power rested on a Hitlerite 'Tenth of December Society'. It rested on the traditional ruling strata and on the constitutional organs of coercion. But as I have already said, I think it would be unproductive to analyse this debate, and that therefore it is unnecessary to assess Thalheimer's 'bonapartist' model of fascism in detail. Griepenburg and Tjaden[21] are right when they say that the basic shortcoming of Thalheimer's theory is its rigidity. He works with prede-termined constants, and as a result he uses Marx's analysis of bonapartism to describe fascism as a phenomenon (he looks for identities and differ-ences), rather than using it as a starting-point for the exploration, with Marx's help, of the *historically specific* aspects of fascism. This accounts for the somewhat unhistorical nature of his analysis:

> In this model of politico-social evolution, both the class-constituting, socio-economic antagonism and the separation between economic reproduction and state power are in principle postulated as con-stants, as permanently present moments of bourgeois society, while the variables consist in the political dispositions of the social classes and strata. These latter determine the change in the 'totality of class relations' and discontinuously, in the specific structure and specific functions of state power.[22]

The determinants of fascism are not correlated to the basic factors of the social totality. The result is that we get an answer to the question, what is fascism? but no answer to the question, at which stage in capitalist development does the real danger of fascism, as the modern variety of bonapartism, concretely arise? If the opposition between economic repro-duction and state power is a permanent feature of bourgeois society, then fascism may arise at any time, not simply as the product of specific historical conditions. (It needs to be stressed, however, that Thalheimer came up with his theory under the immediate threat of fascism, and this explains why he emphasized the nature of fascism rather than its historical origins and possibilities.) Thalheimer's restricted viewpoint also prevents him from bringing out one of the most fundamental features of fascist bonapartism: the fact that the fascist leaders did not only have to satisfy the demands of their own private army (which was much larger than Bonaparte's) but had to make sure of much wider mass support too.

Nevertheless there are several ways in which Thalheimer's bonapartist-based analytic model of fascism is justified. The fascist seizure of power meant that the bourgeoisie parted with direct political rule and handed it over to a stratum which had been driven out of the direct reproduction of bourgeois society. The fascist masses, as I have already mentioned, con-sisted primarily of the middle classes, who felt existentially threatened; the fascist 'élite' was recruited from strata without any stable existence.[23] Furthermore, with fascism the executive power achieved an entirely independent role and entirely determined its own policies. These two interrelated aspects make it quite justified to consider fascism a form of bonapartism. Anyone who denies that these two features did in fact characterize fascist rule is simply not worth arguing with. To deny that

Hitler and Mussolini exercised their rule by annihilating even the traditional bourgeois parties and ignoring all the legal limitations is to
disregard the facts of history completely.

The question is not even whether the broad circles of the bourgeoisie
were able to influence political life under fascism, or whether they had any
institutional safeguards for the representation of their interests. The
answer is clearly in the negative. The real question is whether the *leading
personalities* in the important bourgeois circles were capable of directing
the fascist régime's policies or at least of influencing them, and to what
extent. The answer to this question is by no means so definite, although we
shall see later that it is equally a simplification, even a falsification of the
actual state of affairs to say that monopoly capital directly dictated the
fascist Führer's policies, so to speak, or that Mussolini and Hitler were
only puppets in the hands of the haute bourgeoisie which possessed
economic power. But even if we come to the conclusion that the leading
bourgeois circles were incapable of concretely determining the policies of
the fascist régime, we would still not be denying that the fascist régime's
policies in the last resort *served the interests* of the leading bourgeoisie
circles – if need be, even against the bourgeoisie itself.

Notes

1 Quoted in Wolfgang Abendroth (ed.), *Faschismus und Kapitalismus: Theorien
  über die sozialen Ursprünge und die Funktion des Faschismus* (Frankfurt/M.,
  Europäische Verlagsanstalt, 1967), p. 5.
2 Hermann Heller, *Europa und Faschismus* (Berlin and Leipzig, W. de Gruyter
  & Co., 1929), p. 123.
3 Iring Fetscher, 'Zur Kritik des sowjetmarxistischen Faschismusbegriffs', in
  Karl Marx und der Marxismus (Munich, Piper, 1967), p. 237.
4 August Thalheimer, 'Über den Faschismus', in Abendroth, op. cit., p. 28.
5 Angelo Tasca (pseud. A. Rossi), *The Rise of Italian Fascism* (London,
  Methuen, 1938), p. 338.
6 Karl Marx, 'The Eighteenth Brumaire of Louis Bonaparte', in Karl Marx,
  Selected Works (Moscow, Progress Press, 1936), p. 383.
7 Ibid., p. 396.
8 Ibid., p. 346.
9 Ibid., p. 362.
10 Letter from Engels to Marx on 13 April 1866, in *Marx–Engels Selected
   Correspondence* (Moscow, Progress Press, 1955), p. 177.
11 Marx, op. cit., pp. 371–2.
12 Ibid., p. 379.
13 Ibid., p. 420.
14 Ibid., p. 423–4.
15 Ibid., p. 414.
16 Ibid.
17 Ibid., p. 415.
18 Ibid.

19 See for example Theo Pirker, 'Vorbemerkung', in *Komintern und Faschismus. Dokumente zur Geschichte und Theorie des Faschismus* (Stuttgart, Deutsche Verlags-Anstalt, 1965), p. 21.
20 Marx, op. cit., pp. 385–6.
21 R. Griepenburg and K. H. Tjaden, 'Faschismus und Bonapartismus', in *Das Argument*, 6 (1966).
22 Ibid., p. 461.
23 See Daniel Lerner, *The Nazi Elite* (Stanford, Stanford University Press, 1951).

7

An exceptional form of the capitalist state*

NICOS POULANTZAS

In the light of the above analysis, we can now approach the problem of the fascist State provided certain factors are kept in mind:

A. The fascist State is a form of State of the *capitalist type*. In spite of everything that has been written to the contrary, it therefore has the features peculiar to the capitalist State.

B. The fascist State is a specific *form of State*, an *exceptional State* corresponding to the needs of a political crisis. Therefore:

1. It has a *different* form to the State in other social formations which belong to the same stage (the imperialist stage), but do not experience the same kind of crisis.

2. It has *features in common* with other States belonging to the imperialist stage; while it has to deal with the crisis, it has also to fulfil the functions required of it in this particular stage.

C. The fascist State is also a specific *form of regime*. Therefore:

1. It has *features in common* with other forms of regime also belonging to the form of the exceptional capitalist State, in so far as they also correspond to political crises of a similar nature in a capitalist formation, e.g. military dictatorship and Bonapartism.

2. It is *different* from these forms of regimes, in so far as it corresponds to a specific political crisis and specific class relations. The differences also depend on the period in which these forms arise. I already posed this set of problems at the beginning of the book, in analysing the *political crisis*.

* Extract from Nicos Poulantzas, *Fascism and Dictatorship: The Third International and the Problem of Fascism*, translated from the French by Judith White (London, Verso, 1979; first French edition 1970; first English edition 1974), pp. 312–19, 331–5.

Before embarking on the concrete examination of the fascist State, a few words are required about the *relevant criteria* which specify it as a form of State and a form of regime. There is no need to analyse these different criteria, which are to be understood on the basis of the distinction and the *relationship* between these two political spaces. I would simply point out that the factors for differentiating *forms* of the capitalist *State* are: (a) the relationship of the economic, the political and ideology at a given stage of the capitalist mode of production; (b) the general characteristics of the class struggle in the corresponding *period* of capitalist formations: in this instance, the general features of political crisis, leading to the exceptional State. The factors in differentiating the *forms of regime* are the concrete methods of political class struggle in a determinate *conjuncture*: in this instance, the specific political crisis to which fascism corresponds.

In the framework of a capitalist State, these factors are expressed according to a rigorously governed set of *criteria*. For the *form of State* these are:

1. The forms and modalities of State intervention in the economic and in social relations in general, and the forms and modalities of the relative autonomy of the State from the dominant classes.

2. The role, forms and inter-relationship of the State apparatus proper and the ideological State apparatuses, corresponding to modifications in the law, which is precisely what governs them.

3. The general relationship of the branches of the repressive State apparatus itself, corresponding, for the capitalist State, to the general relationship between executive and legislative.

4. The general relationship between the ideological State apparatuses.

As for the *forms of regime* occupying the political scene, the criteria are these:

1. *How far* they display the general characteristics of a form of State;

2. The specific *form* taken by these characteristics; the concrete relationships between the various branches of the State apparatus proper and between the various ideological State apparatuses, and the relations between the two when one is dominant. The political parties and class representation by party are particularly important for this.

These criteria also hold for the *exceptional State form* and for the *exceptional political regimes* dependent on this State form. I shall therefore start my analysis with a series of propositions about the *exceptional State form of the capitalist State*, and outline a theory of it. Like the other exceptional regimes (Bonapartism and military dictatorship) the fascist State belongs to this State form and displays its essential characteristics.

I shall reverse the order of presentation in this chapter, first analysing the established fascist State, then the modifications in the form of State which preceded fascism during the period of its rise. The importance of these modifications, which mark the rise of fascism, can only be seen in relation to the fascist State to which they led.

General propositions on the exceptional State

I. Forms of State intervention

The exceptional State form of the capitalist State still belongs to the *capitalist* type of State, not only in terms of State power, but also in its institutional forms; this also holds for the fascist State as an exceptional capitalist State. It has the distinguishing features of the capitalist type of State – the relative separation of the economic from the political, and the relative autonomy of the State from the dominant classes and fractions.

Because of the period and the crisis to which the exceptional State corresponds, it generally *intervenes* in the economic in a characteristic way, to adapt and adjust the system to the socialization of the productive forces. The fascist State's intervention in the economic is very important. From this point of view, it has points in common with the interventionist form of State (monopoly capitalism) of social formations not experiencing political crisis. What distinguishes it as an exceptional State is not so much the extent to which it intervenes, as the forms it uses.

The relative autonomy of the exceptional State from the dominant classes and fractions is particularly important and significant, as a result of the political crisis and the relation of forces to which it corresponds. The exceptional State needs this relative autonomy to reorganize hegemony and the power bloc, and in the context of the political crisis, supporting classes also appear quite often as social forces. The reasons for the relative autonomy of the fascist State, and the way it works, have already been stated. In the other forms of exceptional regime, this autonomy can be due to a normal or catastrophic balance of forces, which is characteristic of particular kinds of political crisis (e.g. Bonapartism).

II. Modification in the relations between the repressive apparatus and the ideological apparatuses

The exceptional State, corresponding to a reorganization of the whole State apparatus (the State system), involves radical changes in the ideological State apparatuses and in their relationship to the repressive State apparatus. The fascist State is a very good example of this.

This is a vitally important aspect, and it is no accident that the writers who talk about 'totalitarianism' make it their central theme.[1] They say that a 'totalitarian' State such as fascism is 'essentially', *innately* different from the State of 'institutional pluralism'. In the latter, there are institutions and organizations which are *autonomous* from the State on the one hand, and from the individual members of civil society on the other. These 'intermediate bodies' between State and individual are the guarantee of liberty, which is of course to be measured in terms of the autonomy of the individual from the State. Such 'autonomous', 'free' institutions supposedly includes the parties, trade unions, cultural institutions, schools, the Church, and even the various local associations, sports clubs, etc. The modern form of this ideology goes right back to Veblen, and even to Durkheim himself. Following Arendt, they continue in a series of works on 'mass society', establishing learned correlations between the propensity to totalitarianism and the absence in these 'mass societies' of these intermediary bodies between the State and the 'atoms' of society.

The totalitarian State, according to them, is characterized by the fact that every institution belongs to the State, and that all social life if brought under the State, so that there are no 'autonomous' institutions between the State and the individual.

We should pause here to recall what was said about the ideological State apparatuses. These 'institutions' are State apparatuses throughout, whatever the form of State. In other words, the difference between the fascist State (the exceptional State) and the other forms of capitalist State does not lie in the fact that in the one case the institutions belong to the State system while in the other they are independent or 'autonomous'. In fact, contrary to the all too obvious apologias of the ideologists of totalitarianism, the fascist State is akin to the other forms of the capitalist State because it is itself a *capitalist State*. Furthermore, to recall an earlier remark, the exceptional capitalist State, and in particular the fascist State, because it is a *crisis* form of the capitalist State and therefore quite specific, also reveals certain aspects of the actual functioning of the capitalist State as such – sometimes, admittedly, by contrast.

This in no way means that there are no *key differences* characteristic of the exceptional State form. They are *generally* expressed at the juridical level (that of the relation between 'public' and 'private'), by the formal attribution of a public status to the ideological apparatuses of the exceptional State.

What does this in fact mean? The differentiation between public and private status is coextensive with the relative autonomy of the ideological apparatuses within the State system. Changes in this respect in an exceptional State – especially in the fascist State – indicate the various degrees of limitation or even suppression of the relative autonomy of the ideological apparatuses: a relative autonomy they enjoy in other forms of State. This means that the whole relationship between the repressive State apparatus and the ideological State apparatuses is changed.

A. This limitation, typical of the exceptional State, stems primarily from the relations of class power and from the re-organization of hegemony which takes place in political crisis.

The relative autonomy of the ideological apparatuses in the other forms of capitalist State is due to the following factors, among others:

(a) classes or class fractions of the power bloc other than the hegemonic class or fraction hold power in them;

(b) the masses have particular ways of expressing themselves through the apparatuses (parties, unions, etc.).

In an exceptional State, the State's decisive role in reorganizing hegemony implies:

(a) a decisive limitation on the 'distribution' of power within the apparatuses;

(b) strict control of the whole of the State system by one 'branch' or one apparatus in the hands of the class or class fraction which is struggling to establish its hegemony.[2]

B. But this characteristic limitation of the relative autonomy of the ideological apparatuses in the exceptional State is also due to the *ideological crisis* which accompanies the political crisis, and therefore to the specific intervention of ideology, which concentrates and increases repression against the popular classes.

1. The first element to be stressed is that the increased role of physical repression is necessarily accompanied by a particular intervention of ideology to *legitimize* this repression. I would go further: the other forms of capitalist State have a 'constitutional' juridical arsenal to allow for the use of a broad measure of physical repression in critical situations in the class struggle, and the 'democracies' are very good at this. But such State forms often do no allow the use of ideological intervention to justify such repression, because of the relative autonomy of the ideological State apparatuses. It therefore becomes necessary to resort to the exceptional form, not so much because the established juridical rules forbid repression, but because the accompanying ideological intervention is not possible within these other forms of State.

2. This factor alone, however, does not explain this characteristic limitation of the autonomy of the ideological apparatuses in the exceptional State. It must not be forgotten that this ideological interventon becomes necessary when the dominant ideology is in crisis: the exceptional State has then to play a part itself in the actual organization of the dominant ideology. The combination of these two factors explains the limitation in question.

In other forms of State, it is in fact through the 'spokesmen of the *organic* ideology'[3] of the dominant classes, and through their ability to represent them, that the dominant ideology is 'worked out' within the ideological apparatuses, and instilled by means of these apparatuses. However, in all forms of State, the State apparatuses themselves 'secrete' *their own internal ideology.* But in those State forms not corresponding to a political and ideological crisis, this internal ideology is often perceptibly different from the dominant ideology: for example, the State 'bureaucracy', the army, the Church and the educational system all have an internal ideology of their own.

The reasons for this are:

(a) the dislocation between these apparatuses, as seats of the contradictions between various ideologies and ideological sub-systems;

(b) the contradictions within these apparatuses between (i) the *social* categories of the 'spokesmen of the organic ideology', organizing hegemony in a direct relationship of representation ('organic' in the Gramscian sense) to the hegemonic class or fraction, and (ii) those subjected to other ideologies.

This dislocation between the dominant ideology and the internal ideology of the apparatuses therefore expresses the ideological contradictions which, together with the dislocations in State power, give the ideological State apparatuses their relative autonomy.

As for the exceptional State form, the ideological and political crisis leads to the hegemonic class or fraction losing its direct links with both its political and its ideological representatives. This is where the internal ideology of the State apparatuses meets up with the dominant ideology in the formation. The 'ideological spokesmen' of the hegemonic class or fraction identify with the internal ideology of the apparatuses, excluding those of other ideologies. At the same time, the State apparatuses as a whole are subjected to this internal ideology, coinciding as it does with the dominant ideology, which itself is that of the dominant branch or State apparatus. The 'militarization' of society and of the apparatuses comes about when the army is dominant; 'bureaucratization' when the administration is dominant, and 'clericalization' when the Church is the apparatus concerned.

This particular function of the exceptional State is thus the necessary means for reorganizing ideological hegemony. But this in turn involves, to a greater or lesser extent, (i) the limitation of the relative autonomy of the ideological State apparatuses from the repressive State apparatus and (ii) the limitation of the relative autonomy of the ideological apparatus among themselves.

Even in this case, the fascist State has features in common with the other interventionist form of State, not corresponding to a political crisis. In this State form, because of the stage it belongs to, there is also both a proliferation of the role of the ideological apparatuses and a diminution of their relative autonomy, because of the overwhelming political domination of monopoly capital.

III. The displacement of the dominant branch or apparatus

The exceptional State form is therefore characterized by certain relationships between the ideological State apparatuses and the repressive State apparatus. This does not mean that the repressive State apparatus simply dominates the ideological apparatuses, contrary to the naïve idea that the exceptional State is characterized merely by increased physical repression, part of which is the subordination of the ideological apparatuses to the repressive State apparatus.

The exceptional State form is typically marked by a resurgence of organized physical repression. But the total reorganization of the State results in a new relationship between the repressive and ideological apparatuses, and it is this which is important here. In this relationship, the domination of one or the other specifies the form of *regime* of the exceptional State. In fact, depending on the relation of forces and the distribution of class power within the State system, the dominant position may belong (a) to the repressive State apparatus and one of its branches – the army in military dictatorship, the civil administration in Bonapartism, the political police in the established fascist State; (b) to an ideological State apparatus – for example the party in the first period of fascist rule, or the Church in 'clerical–military' dictatorships like the Dollfuss regime in Austria.

But it is possible to distinguish two basic common features of the exceptional State form:

1. In the other forms of capitalist State, the repressive State apparatus is dominant over the ideological State apparatuses, whether this is evident or not. It is particularly clear with the political parties, which in these forms of State are principally transmission belts, and as ideological State apparatuses are subordinate to the repressive State apparatus. In these States, where the elaboration and indoctrination of ideology operate 'normally', the *central nucleus of the State* really is dominant within the State. This is one of the reasons why the Marxist classics concentrated on analysing it.

The exceptional State form sees:

(a) the overthrow of the relation of forces within the power bloc, and the special role of social forces which, in the crisis conjuncture, is often taken over by the support classes of the State, whose ideological apparatuses are their strongest points;

(b) the new State role, outlined above, of reorganizing ideological hegemony.

In the case of the exceptional State, the reorganization of the State system *can sometimes go so far* as to let an ideological apparatus dominate the whole State system.

2. In the case of the exceptional State, even in the forms of regime dominated by a branch of the repressive apparatus, the reorganization of the whole State system has particular effects, given the new relationship between the ideological apparatuses and the State apparatus in the strict sense. The repressive and the ideological State apparatuses are distinguished from each other by their *principal aspect*, repression and ideology respectively.

In the case of the exceptional State:

(a) The reorganization of the State system may even modify the principal aspect of a branch or apparatus, as in certain examples of military dictatorship or Bonapartism, where the principal aspect (of the army or the administration respectively) becomes ideological; the political police has a similar role at a certain period of fascism. There are therefore effective *displacements* within these apparatus.

(b) Even when a branch of the repressive apparatus is dominant in an exceptional State, without going so far as to change its main aspect, its dominance is always accompanied by an upsurge in its 'secondary', ideological aspect. [. . .]⁴

General propositions on the fascist State as a form of exceptional regime

I. The established system

I shall now turn to the specific features of the fascist State as a form of regime different from other exceptional regimes such as Bonapartism and military dictatorship. The first of these is of course the 'degree' to which it possesses the characteristics mentioned above, which varies with the different exceptional regimes. But the *forms* in which the State apparatuses function and are related to each other are also important, and that is what I shall deal with now.

I. There is a particular kind of mass party within the ideological State apparatuses. The fascist State is characterized by the permanent mobilization of the masses.

II. According to the steps there are particular relationships between the fascist party and the repressive State apparatus.

Firstly, fascism is originally and essentially 'exogenous' to this apparatus. Despite the connivance between the fascist party and branches of the repressive State apparatus, the main instrument for gaining power is outside the repressive State apparatus, which is invaded 'from the outside'.

This situation persists throughout the time fascism remains in power, in the sense that there is never any fusion of the fascist party and the State apparatus. The fascist party always has a role of its own to play.

During the first period of fascist rule, the fascist party dominates the branches of the repressive State apparatus (the army, police, administration and judiciary), although major struggles still take place between the fascist party and branches of this apparatus. In the second step of fascist stabilization, the State apparatus, suitably transformed, dominates the fascist party, which is subordinated to it.

III. In this step of fascist stabilization, the dominance of the State apparatus is achieved by a reorganization of the branches of the State apparatus: one branch of the repressive State apparatus dominates the rest, and therefore the whole State system, including the ideological apparatuses. The branch in question is neither the army nor the 'administrative bureaucracy': it is the *political police*. But although the police has a special role in the exceptional State, it does not always have the dominant role. The term *political* police is used not simply to indicate the importance of political repression, but to show that the key ideological role belongs to the police branch of the fascist State apparatus.[5]

IV. The fact that the political police is dominant within the State apparatus does not mean that the relations of relative subordination and sub-dominance among the other branches of the apparatus are irrelevant. It is even possible in the case of fascism to ascribe a definite order to the subordinate branches: political police, administration, and army. The fact that the army comes below the 'bureaucratic' administration is important.

V. Fascism in power also reorganizes the relations between the ideological State apparatuses. In the first place, the relative autonomy of the apparatuses one from another, together with their relative autonomy from the repressive State apparatus, is undermined. By their very nature no rigid, continuing hierarchy is to be found among them, but it is possible to see which apparatuses dominate the establishment of the new relations, one reason for this being the forms of fascist ideology:

(a) *The fascist party*: never entirely fusing with the State, from the time it is subordinated to the State apparatus it acts as a transmission belt for subordinating the ideological apparatuses to the repressive apparatus, and as a *link* for the centralized cohesion of the ideological apparatuses it dominates. The fascist party, which previously acted as a means of controlling the State apparatus, now essentially becomes the means for the State apparatus to control the ideological apparatuses.

(b) *The family* becomes a central part of the ideological State apparatuses. In contrast with the fascist State, the role of the family in the 'normal' form of interventionist State is weaker than it was in the liberal State.

(c) *The communications and propaganda apparatus*: papers, publishing, radio etc.

Party, family and propaganda are the trinity dominating the ideological State apparatuses.

There is also a significant decline in certain of the ideological State apparatuses, in particular the educational and the religious apparatuses.

II. *The rise of fascism within the State apparatuses*

The various steps in the rise of fascism are also marked by modifications in the State form 'preceding' fascism.

I. Fascism comes to power, formally at least, *in a perfectly constitutional manner.* Hitler and Mussolini came to power 'respecting' the forms of the 'parliamentary democratic' State, and within the juridical norms which every bourgeois State has in store for critical situations of class struggle.

II. Fascism characteristically comes to power with the collusion of the State apparatus. Although the fascist phenomenon is strictly speaking exogenous to the repressive State apparatus, with the beginnings of the rise of fascism it is able to penetrate and take over this apparatus from the outside, and at the point of no return, it neutralizes the branches or sectors still hostile to it. Fascism would never have come to power without decisive help from the repressive State apparatus in the struggle against the masses. Contrary to what many social democrats say, it is quite incorrect to speak of *three forces* in struggle during the rise of fascism: the fascist camp, the State, and the anti-fascist camp.

The specific feature of fascism is that the kind of crisis to which it corresponds allows it first to neutralize the divisions it encounters in the repressive State apparatus, and then to come to power 'constitutionally'. The neutralization is mainly possible because the masses have already experienced a series of defeats when the rise of fascism begins, and when it comes to power, fascism has already won the support of, or at least neutralized, the power bloc as a whole.

III. It is useful to recall the dislocation between *formal power* and *real power* in the State throughout the rise of fascism.

Its characteristics are the parliamentary crisis resulting from the crisis of party representation; the instability of the government, resulting from the instability and lack of hegemony; the duplication of the political parties by parallel power networks, varying from pressure groups to private militia; the resurgence of the role of the 'executive' and the repressive State apparatus, and the increasingly important role of the police; the deterioration of the juridical system ('order') and the direct infiltration of the judiciary by fascism.

What becomes apparent is that the dislocation between formal and real power represents a *dismembering*, but not as has often been claimed a 'disintegration' of the State apparatus.

It is a dismembering in the sense that the relations between branches and apparatuses no longer work in the same way as in the State form 'preceding' fascism. They often undergo radical change, corresponding to a modification in the relation of forces, and due among other things to the instability or lack of hegemony. Internal contradictions and frictions among the apparatuses increase, as a result of the political disorganization of the power alliance. This often takes the form of splits between the top ranks and the lower levels of a branch or apparatus. The reorganization of these relations therefore only seems possible through a new system, to be established through the 'exogenous' factor, fascism.

The State apparatus is however far from disintegrating, as it would do if fascism was an 'emergency' reaction to a revolutionary situation or to open civil war, as the Comintern believed in the German case. The repressive State apparatus does seem to lose some of its monopoly of legitimate violence to the private militia during the rise of fascism. But it is only other armed organizations of the power bloc which gain, and in any case the collusion of the State apparatus and the militia should not be forgotten – the militia were armed by the State. What does take place in this process is a transfer or delegation of functions, further legitimized by the judiciary.

Notes

1 This is particularly the case with Hannah Arendt, *The Origins of Totalitarianism* (New York, Harcourt Brace, 1973); W. Kornhauser, *The Politics of Mass Society* (Glencoe, Ill., Free Press, 1959); Carl Friedrich and Zbigniew Brzezinsky, *Totalitarian Dictatorship and Autocracy* (Cambridge, MA., Harvard University Press, 1956), etc.
2 There is an apparently paradoxical feature here. The exceptional State is characterized both by *increased* autonomy from the hegemonic class or fraction, and by a limitation of the relative autonomy of the ideological State apparatuses. The paradox was noted by Marx in his work on Bonapartism: the greater the relative autonomy of the State from the hegemonic class or class fraction, the stronger is its internal 'centralization'. But the paradox is only superficial: such relative autonomy from the hegemonic class or fraction is necessary precisely so that the State can establish its hegemony, by reorganizing and consolidating the power bloc. In this conjuncture of crisis, this implies the restriction and radical control of the power 'game' which was previously sanctioned by the relative autonomy of the ideological State apparatuses. The

class contradictions within the exceptional State, contradictions which it is in fact based on, take different forms.

3 Particular care should be taken with the use of the term 'intellectuals', given the ideological connotations of its common use. This is why I prefer to use the more limited term of 'ideological spokesmen'.

4 When the Comintern referred to *State apparatuses* in the case of fascism, it generally only meant increased 'physical repression' or 'open terrorism' (Dimitrov). Fascism is therefore primarily defined, at the level of the apparatuses, in a *negative* way: *things have changed*, because now there is more repression. Dimitrov quotes Stalin, for whom 'the bourgeoisie is no longer in a condition to exercise power by the old parliamentary means or by the methods of bourgeois democracy, and is therefore obliged to resort to terrorist methods of government'. The Comintern certainly insisted continually on the *ideological role* of fascism. Clara Zetkin pointed out that only social democrats define fascism as 'violence' alone. It is, however, very typical that even where the Comintern emphasized the ideological role of fascism, *it rarely accompanied its analysis of 'fascist ideology' with a concrete study of the ideological apparatus*. In the official documents at least there are at best a few scattered remarks, mainly about the role of the Church. The only point noted is the 'attitude' of the 'members' of these apparatuses towards fascism.

5 The role of the 'political police' cannot be understood without analysing the reorganization of the whole State system and the displacement of functions within it. The Comintern did not always pay attention to this factor, generally limiting itself to analysing the role of the *army*, and so often confusing military dictatorship and fascism. The same is true of Trotsky: 'To be sure, fascism, as the Italian example shows, leads in the end to a military–bureaucratic dictatorship of the Bonapartist type.' (*The Struggle against Fascism in Germany*, New York, Pathfinder Press, 1971, p. 278.) *The only exception was Gramsci*, who, with his concept of the ideological State apparatus, was able to point to the problem:

> In the period up to Napoleon III, the regular military forces or soldiers of the line were a decisive element in the advent of Caesarism, and this came about through quite precise coups d'état, through military actions, etc. Modern political technique became totally transformed [. . .] after the expansion of parliamentarism and of the associative systems of union and party, and the growth in the formation of vast State and 'private' bureaucracies [. . .] and after the transformations which took place in the organization of the forces of order in the wide sense – i.e. not only the public service designed for the repression of crime, but the totality of forces organized by the State and by private individuals to safeguard the political and economic domination of the ruling classes. In this sense, entire 'political' parties and other organizations – economic or otherwise – must be considered as organs of political order, of an investigational and preventive character. (*Prison Notebooks*, London, Lawrence and Wishart, 1971, pp. 220–1.)

THE PRODUCT OF A CRISIS
OF MODERNIZATION

8

Extremism of the centre*

SEYMOUR MARTIN LIPSET

'Fascism' and the middle class

The thesis that fascism is basically a middle-class movement representing a
protest against both capitalism *and* socialism, big business *and* big unions,
is far from original. Many analysts have suggested it ever since fascism and
Nazism first appeared on the scene. Nearly twenty-five years ago, the
economist David Saposs stated it well:

> Fascism [. . .] [is] the extreme expression of middle-classism or
> populism. [. . .]The basic ideology of the middle class is populism.
> [. . .] Their ideal was an independent small property-owning class
> consisting of merchants, mechanics, and farmers. This element [. . .]
> now designated as middle class, sponsored a system of private prop-
> erty, profit, and competition on an entirely different basis from that
> conceived by capitalism. [. . .] From its very inception it opposed 'big
> business' or what has now become known as capitalism.
>
> Since the war the death knell of liberalism and individualism has
> been vociferously, albeit justly sounded. But since liberalism and
> individualism are of middle-class origin, it has been taken for granted
> that this class has also been eliminated as an effective social force. As
> a matter of fact, populism is now as formidable a force as it has ever
> been. And the middle class is more vigorously assertive than ever.
> [. . .][1]

And although some have attributed the lower middle-class support for
Nazism to the specific economic difficulties of the 1930s, the political
scientist, Harold Lasswell, writing in the depths of the Depression, suggested that middle-class extremism flowed from trends inherent in capitalist industrial society which would continue to affect the middle class
even if its economic position improved.

> Insofar as Hitlerism is a desperation reaction of the lower middle
> classes, it continues a movement which began during the closing

* Extract from '"Fascism" – Left, Right and Centre', in S. M. Lipset, *Political Man*
(expanded edtion, Baltimore, Johns Hopkins University Press, 1981; London, Heinemann,
1983), pp. 131–7.

years of the nineteenth century. Materially speaking, it is not necessary to assume that the small shopkeepers, teachers, preachers, lawyers, doctors, farmers and craftsmen were worse off at the end than
they had been in the middle of the century. Psychologically speaking,
however, the lower middle class was increasingly overshadowed by the
workers and the upper bourgeoisie, whose unions, cartels and parties
took the center of the stage. The psychological impoverishment of the
lower middle class precipitated emotional insecurities within the
personalities of its members, thus fertilizing the ground for the
various movements of mass protest through which the middle classes
might revenge themselves.[2]

As the relative position of the middle class declined and its resentments
against on-going social and economic trends continued, its 'liberal' ideology – the support of individual rights against large-scale power – changed
from that of a revolutionary class to that of a reactionary class. Once
liberal doctrines had supported the *bourgeoisie* in their fight against the
remnants of the feudal and monarchical order, and against the limitations
demanded by mercantilist rulers and the Church. A liberal ideology
opposed to Throne and Altar and favoring a limited state emerged. This
ideology was not only revolutionary in political terms; it fulfilled some of
the functional requirements for efficient industrialization. As Max Weber
pointed out, the development of the capitalist system (which in his analysis
coincides with industrialization) necessitated the abolition of artificial
internal boundaries, the creation of an open international market, the
establishment of law and order, and relative international peace.[3]

But the aspirations and ideology which underlay eighteenth- and nineteenth-century liberalism and populism have a different meaning and serve
a different function in the advanced industrial societies of the twentieth
century. Resisting large-scale organizations and the growth of state authority challenges some of the fundamental characteristics of our present
society, since large industry and a strong and legitimate labor movement
are necessary for a stable, modernized social structure, and government
regulation and heavy taxes seem an inevitable concomitant. To be against
business bureaucracies, trade-unions, and state regulation is both unrea-
listic and to some degree irrational. As Talcott Parsons has put it, the 'new
negative orientation to certain primary aspects of the maturing modern
social order has above all centered in the symbol of "capitalism". [. . .]
The reaction against the "ideology" of the rationalization of society is the
principal aspect at least of the ideology of fascism."[4]

While continuing conflict between management and labor is an integral
part of large-scale industrialism, the small businessman's desire to retain
an important place for himself and his social values is 'reactionary' – not
in the Marxist sense of slowing down the wheels of revolution, but from

the perspective of the inherent trends of a modern industrial society. Sometimes the efforts of the small business stratum to resist or reverse the process take the form of democratic liberal movements, like the British Liberal party, the French Radicals, or the American Taft Republicans. Such movements have failed to stop the trends which their adherents oppose, and as another sociologist, Martin Trow, recently noted: 'The tendencies which small businessmen fear – of concentration and centralization – proceed without interruption in depression, war and prosperity, and irrespective of what party is in power; thus they are *always* disaffected. [. . .]'[5] It is not surprising, therefore, that under certain conditions small businessmen turn to extremist political movements, either fascism or anti-parliamentary populism, which in one way or another express contempt for parliamentary democracy. These movements answer some of the same needs as the more conventional liberal parties; they are an outlet for the stratification strains of the middle class in a mature industrial order. But while liberalism attempts to cope with the problems by legitimate social changes and 'reforms' ('reforms' which would, to be sure, reverse the modernization process), fascism and populism propose to solve the problems by taking over the state and running it in a way which will restore the old middle classes' economic security and high standing in society, and at the same time reduce the power and status of big capital and big labor.

The appeal of extremist movements may also be a response by different strata of the population to the social effects of industrialization at different stages of its development. These variations are set in sharp relief by a comparison of the organized threats to the democratic process in societies at various stages of industrialization. As I have already shown, working-class extremism, whether Communist, anarchist, revolutionary socialist, or Peronist, is most commonly found in societies undergoing rapid industrialization, or in those where the process of industrialization did not result in a predominantly industrial society, like the Latin countries of southern Europe. Middle-class extremism occurs in countries characterized by both large-scale capitalism and a powerful labor movement. Right-wing extremism is most common in less developed economies, in which the traditional conservative forces linked to Throne and Altar remain strong. Since some countries, like France, Italy, or Weimar Germany, have possessed strata in all three sets of circumstances, all three types of extremist politics sometimes exist in the same country. Only the well-to-do, highly industrialized and urbanized nations seem immune to the virus, but even in the United States and Canada there is evidence that the self-employed are somewhat disaffected.

The different political reactions of similar strata at different points in the industrialization process are clearly delineated by a comparison of the politics of certain Latin-American countries with those of Western Europe. The more well-to-do Latin-American countries today resemble Europe in the nineteenth century; they are experiencing industrial growth while their working classes are still relatively unorganized into trade-unions and political parties, and reservoirs of traditional conservatism still exist in their rural populations. The growing middle class in these countries, like its nineteenth-century European counterpart, supports a democratic society by attempting to reduce the influence of the anti-capitalist traditionalists and the arbitrary power of the military.[6] To the extent that there is a social base at this stage of economic development for extremist politics, it lies not in the middle classes but in the growing, still unorganized working classes who are suffering from the tensions inherent in rapid industrialization. These workers have provided the primary base of support for the only large-scale 'fascist' movements in Latin America – those of Peron in the Argentine and Vargas in Brazil. These movements, like the Communist ones with which they have sometimes been allied, appeal to the 'displaced masses' of newly industrializing countries.

The real question to answer is: which strata are most 'displaced' in each country? In some, it is the new working class, or the working class which was never integrated in the total society, economically or politically; in others, it is the small businessmen and other relatively independent entrepreneurs (small farm owners, provincial lawyers) who feel oppressed by the growing power and status of unionized workers and by large-scale corporative and governmental bureaucracies. In still others, it is the conservative and traditionalist elements who seek to preserve the old society from the values of socialism and liberalism. Fascist ideology in Italy, for example, arose out of an opportunistic movement which sought at various times to appeal to all three groups, and remained sufficiently amorphous to permit appeals to widely different strata, depending on national variations as to who were most 'displaced'.[7] Since fascist politicians have been extremely opportunistic in their efforts to secure support, such movements have often encompassed groups with conflicting interests and values, even when they primarily expressed the needs of one stratum. Hitler, a centrist extremist, won backing from conservatives who hoped to use the Nazis against the Marxist left. And conservative extremists like Franco have often been able to retain centrists among their followers without giving them control of the movement.

In the previous chapter on working-class authoritarianism I tried to specify some of the other conditions which dispose different groups and individuals to accept more readily an extremist and demonological view of the world. The thesis presented there suggested that a low level of sophistication and a high degree of insecurity predispose an individual toward an extremist view of politics. Lack of sophistication is largely a product of little education and isolation from varied experiences. On these grounds, the most authoritarian segments of the middle strata should be found among the small entrepreneurs who live in small communities or on farms.

These people receive relatively little formal education as compared with those in other middle-class positions; and living in rural areas or small towns usually means isolation from heterogeneous values and groups. By the same token, one would expect more middle-class extremism among the self-employed, whether rural or urban, than among white-collar workers, executives, and professionals. [. . .]

Notes

1 David J. Saposs, 'The Role of the Middle Class in Social Development: Fascism, Populism, Communism, Socialism', in *Economic Essays in Honor of Wesley Clair Mitchell* (New York, Columbia University Press, 1935), pp. 395, 397, 400. An even earlier analysis by André Siegfried, based on a detailed ecological study of voting patterns in part of France from 1871 to 1912, suggested that the petty bourgeoisie who had been considered the classic source of French democratic ideology were becoming the principal recruiting grounds for extremist movements. Siegfried pointed out that though they are

> by nature egalitarian, democratic, and envious [. . .] they are fearful above all of new economic conditions which threatened to eliminate them, crushed between the aggressive capitalism of the great companies and the increasing rise of the working people. They place great hopes in the Republic, and they do not cease being republican or egalitarian. But they are in that state of discontent, from which the Boulangisms marshal their forces, in which reactionary demagogues see the best ground in which to agitate, and in which is born passionate resistance to certain democratic reforms. André Siegfried, *Tableau politique de la France de l'ouest sous la troisième république* (Paris, Librairie Armand Colin, 1913), p. 413.

2 Harold Lasswell, 'The Psychology of Hitlerism', *The Political Quarterly*, 4 (1933), p. 374.
3 See also Karl Polanyi, *The Great Transformation* (New York, Farrar and Rinehart, 1944).
4 Talcott Parsons, 'Some Sociological Aspects of the Fascist Movement', in his *Essays in Sociological Theory* (Glencoe, The Free Press, 1954), pp. 133–4. Marx himself pointed out that 'the small manufacturer, the small merchant, the artisan, the peasant, all fight against the [big] bourgeois, in order to protect their position as a middle class from being destroyed. They are, however, not revolutionary, but conservative. Even more, they are reactionary, they look for a way to reverse the path of history,' quoted in S. S. Nilson, 'Wahlsoziologische Probleme des Nationalsozialismus', *Zeitschrift für die Gesamte Staatswissenschaft*, 110 (1954), p. 295.
5 Martin A. Trow, 'Small Businessmen, Political Tolerance, and Support for McCarthy', *American Journal of Sociology*, 64 (1958), pp. 279–80.
6 For an analysis of the political role of the rapidly growing Latin-American middle classes see John J. Johnson, *Political Change in Latin America – the Emergence of the Middle Sectors* (Stanford, Stanford University Press, 1958). The different political propensities of a social group at successive stages of industrialization are indicated by James Bryce's comment in 1912 that 'the

absence of that class of small landowners which is the soundest and most stable element in the United States and in Switzerland and is equally stable, if less politically trained, in France and parts of Germany, is a grave misfortune for South and Central America'. This may have been true in an early period, before the impact of large-scale organization of the farms meant economic competition for small farmers and added them to the rank of the potential supporters of fascism, as the data on Germany and other countries discussed here show. See James Bryce, *South America: Observations and Impressions* (New York, Macmillan, 1912), p. 533.

7 A comparison of the European middle class and the Argentine working class, which argues that each is most 'displaced' in its respective environment, is contained in Gino Germani, *Integración política de las masas y la totalitarismo* (Buenos Aires, Colegio Libre de Estudios Superiores, 1956). See also his *Estructura social de la Argentina* (Buenos Aires, Raigal, 1955).

9

*A metapolitical counter-revolution**

ERNST NOLTE

Fascism has been defined on three levels. On the first level it was examined as an internal political phenomenon and described as 'anti-Marxism' seeking to destroy the enemy by the development of a radically opposed yet related ideology and the application of nearly identical, although typically transformed methods; always, however, within the unyielding framework of national self-assertion and autonomy. This definition is valid for all forms of fascism.[1]

The second definition, which describes fascism as the 'life-and-death struggle of the sovereign, martial, inwardly antagonistic group', no longer looks at it as a manifestation within politics, but sees in it the natural foundation of politics itself brought to light and to self-consciousness. This definition could only be unequivocally demonstrated by the radical–fascist form and could be adequately illustrated within the context of this derivation.

On the third level – the least accessible and the most fundamental – fascism was termed 'resistance to transcendence'. This definition could be derived from fascism's oldest as well as its most recent forms: it describes fascism as a metapolitical phenomenon. It can be neither illustrated by historical details nor demonstrated by simple considerations. It requires a

* Extract from E. Nolte, *Three Faces of Fascism* (London, Weidenfeld & Nicolson, 1965), pp. 429–30, 433–4, 450–4.

new departure in thought if it is not to remain a mere suggestion in the semiobscurity of approximate insight.

The historical section of this analysis was completed with the definition of fascism on internal and external political levels; the third level has hardly been touched, let alone demarcated. To grasp the phenomenon in its entirety, a final step must be taken and the nature of fascism explored in purely philosophical terms, even if only in outline and despite the danger that the object may seem to disappear for a time and that the striving for abstraction may mean sacrificing the support of demonstrable evidence. Nevertheless, this abstraction is no airy speculation. It is the means of probing to the hidden foundations of the structure. For in these foundations are situated all the complexity, all the tensions, of the edifice. It is not a featureless, uniform basis: on the contrary, it has its own characteristic measurements and proportions, and it is these which this method of abstraction seeks to uncover.

It becomes clear that this third approach is not simply an appendage which could just as well be left out when it is realized that the three definitions are something more than unconnected links in a random pile of associations. From certain aspects the first definition already contains the second, and a concept as central as that of ideology in turn requires the context of the second definition in order to achieve final clarification. The second definition for its part is irresistibly propelled toward the third, since politics itself is not a political fact and can only be manifested as such when set off against a foil whose nature differs from its own. [. . .]

In summing up the following definitions may be given:

Theoretical transcendence may be taken to mean the reaching out of the mind beyond what exists and what can exist toward an absolute whole; in a broader sense this may be applied to all that goes beyond, that releases man from the confines of the everyday world and which, as an 'awareness of the horizon', makes it possible for him to experience the world as a whole.

Practical transcendence can be taken to mean the social process, even its early stages, which continually widens human relationships, thereby rendering them in general more subtle and more abstract – the process which disengages the individual from traditional ties and increases the power of the group until it finally assails even the primordial forces of nature and history. However, since it is only possible to experience it as transcendence when it reaches its universal stage, the concept is usually limited to this stage. As a synonym the term 'abstraction of life' can be used, as against 'abstraction of thought' for theoretical transcendence.

A phenomenon will be called transcendental in which transcendence achieves dominant form, or which adopts a specific relationship to it. But (with an ambivalence already present in Kant) a method of observation will also be called transcendental when it seeks to uncover the transcendental nature of an object which in the case of a political phenomenon may be called 'metapolitical'. [. . .]

Typical of the transcendental nature of bourgeois society is that within it practical transcendence has developed to an undreamed-of-efficacy, without supplanting the traditional forms of theoretical transcendence. The politico-sociological aspect (which is superficial when isolated) may be formulated as follows:

Bourgeois society is that form of society in which the leading class performs its task of establishing the technical and economic unity of the world, and emancipating all men for participation in this undertaking, in ever new political and intellectual compromises with the hitherto ruling powers: it is the society of synthesis. Hence in bourgeois society the historically new and specific – that unprecedented expansion of the practical scope of mankind and the revolutionary change in the status of the individual and all groups within society as a whole which is summarily known as 'industrialization' – is proceeding almost clandestinely and without the consent of considerable sections of its own intellectual stratum, whose spiritual home is after all theoretical transcendence, however arbitrarily and undogmatically they may interpret it.

The thesis that when threatened this stratum ultimately aligns itself with bourgeois society and *its* class and that its thinking is therefore dependent on its environment, is, although generally speaking correct, nevertheless remarkably naïve. For its relative (and in some cases absolute) disengagement is precisely what is so astonishing, so singular, and so much in need of explanation. Bourgeois society gave birth to practical transcendence, at the same time endowing it with a guilty conscience. Its self-consciousness is only precariously derived from the contest of a plethora of modes of thought of which the most extreme are a utopian reaching into the future, or a glorifying emphasis on certain typical features of the past. This character of bourgeois society is without doubt associated with the fact that within the state private entrepreneurs have initiated the movement of this society and kept it going: but presumably it could also be 'socialistically' organized, without sacrificing its transcendental nature, provided the starting point was abundance and not want, and that power did not fall into the hands of dogmatists. For bourgeois society did not remain unchanged in its structure; within its own framework it produced that new class, the 'technical intelligentsia' which Marx had completely ignored and which combined on various levels with the older classes, turning out to be the most productive and expansive group within this structure. It is advisable, therefore, to abandon the narrow term 'bourgeois society' and to speak instead of 'liberal society'.

Liberal society is a society of abundance – all forms of theoretical transcendence can develop independently, although not without being affected externally; a self-critical society – the attainment of practical transcendence remains subject to criticism; an uncertain society – it is continually subject to self-doubts.

Kant's and Hegel's ideas show how unquestionably the early self-image of this society is rooted in philosophy; Marx and Nietzsche mark the extremes of this self-doubting – which is, of course, a product of their philosophical detachment. For the obvious possibility of a nontranscendental yet advantageous subordination of individuals in the social process – the basic supposition of classical political economy – is rejected by both with equal fervor. Their antithetical solutions were adopted by social structures which are transcendentally distinct from liberal society. But Max Weber's work demonstrates that this society need not necessarily be driven in directions where it will retain mere fragments of its uncurtailed self.

Bolshevism achieved power in Russia in defiance of the acknowledged premises of the Marxist doctrine, and it modeled itself on the master's more esoteric expectations for a short time only. Nevertheless, it is to some extent entitled to invoke Marx as its authority.

Lenin found it difficult to forsake the orthodox assumption that what was really on the agenda was the revolution of the Western European proletariat, and that his own enterprise was historically premature. At first he was still convinced that the functions of power-wielding were by that time so simplified that they were open 'to every nonilliterate',[2] and that the age of nonrule was hence rapidly approaching: 'Under socialism *all* will rule in turn and quickly get used to the fact that no one rules.'[3]

But it was not long before the Marxist postulates were replaced, both in practical measures and a number of theoretical utterances, by a complete mobilization, directed by a single will, of the cluster of races that is Russia in a grim struggle for existence. He realized it was not a matter of setting mankind an example of a higher and better way of life – the crossroad at which the country now stood was more commonplace, more ruthless: 'Go under, or forge full steam ahead. That is the question put by history,'[4] It was a matter of 'catching up', of struggling up out of backwardness, lack of culture, want, and poverty in the midst of a hostile world. In their overwhelming simplicity and conviction, a great number of utterances from his latest period leave no doubt whatever that this more modest interpretation represents Lenin's final insight rather than this or that bombastic pronouncement about the victory of socialism over capitalism.[5]

Thus the 'day-to-day problems of the economy' became 'the most important affairs of state'.[6] It is easier to grasp the nature of bolshevism from any front page of any Soviet daily newspaper than from the most shocking reports of famine and barbarism. Famine and barbarism have always existed; but never since the existence of a bourgeois society and of newspapers had the headlines dealt with production records, reports on working methods, and appeals for increased productivity. Bolshevism signifies the dominating emergence of the element that had remained half-hidden in bourgeois society: it is the most unequivocal affirmation of material production and at the same time of practical transcendence. Society[7] thereby loses its spiritual wealth and the spur of self-criticism, and acquires an unshakable complacency and a hitherto unknown enthusiasm in its sense of historical necessity.

But in this case all that remains, if anything, of Marx's own special and personal concepts, which in his eyes alone justify the unique quality of practical transcendence, is a propagandistic semblance. As a result, bolshevism's battle with the orthodox Marxists in its own ranks is among the most tragic and moving chapters of the history of our time. And yet the Soviet Union has conformed to Marxist thought insofar as it has always regarded the emancipation of its own peoples (that is, their adaptation to the exigencies of industrial society) in terms of a higher world process. True, the concept of 'world revolution' has led more than any other to the defeats of bolshevism in its confrontation with developed bourgeois society; at the same time, it constitutes a hallmark of world-historical distinction, since it is evidence of a relationship not only to a selfishly interpreted 'industrial production' but also to the total process of practical transcendence. For this very reason the term 'development dictatorship' is inadequate as applied to the Soviet Union and, despite all structural similarities, the difference as against fascism is fundamental. The fact that, alone among non-Western powers, the Soviet Union could complete its industrialization[8] on the strength of its own initiative and to a large extent under its own steam; that, in spite of the known harshness of its methods of government, it enjoys what often seems a mysterious prestige among the underdeveloped nations; that it was the first state to succeed in penetrating outer space – these are all closely related facts which become intelligible when seen against a background of transcendental definition.

It has now become evident what fascism actually is. It is not that resistance to practical transcendence which is more or less common to all conservative movements. It was only when theoretical transcendence, from which that resistance originally emanated, was likewise denied that fascism made its appearance. Thus fascism is at the same time resistance to practical transcendence and struggle against theoretical transcendence. But this struggle must needs be concealed, since the original motivations can never be entirely dispensed with. And insofar as practical transcendence from its most superficial aspect is nothing but the possibility of concentration of power, fascism pursues its resistance to transcendence from within that transcendence and at times in the clear consciousness of a struggle for world hegemony. That is the transcendental expression of the sociological fact that fascism has at its command forces which are born of the emancipation process and then turn against their own origin. If it may be called the despair of the[9] feudal section of bourgeois society for its traditions, and the bourgeois element's betrayal of its revolution, now it is clear what this tradition and this revolution actually are. Fascism represents the second and gravest crisis of liberal society, since it achieves power on its own soil, and in its radical form is the most complete and effective denial of that society.

It is precisely in this broadest of all perspectives that the observer cannot withhold from fascism that 'sympathy' of which we have spoken. This sympathy is directed not toward persons or deeds, but toward the perplexity underlying the colossal attempt to overcome that perplexity, which is the most universal characteristic of an era whose end cannot be foreseen. For transcendence, when properly understood, is infinitely remote from the harmlessness of safe 'cultural progress'; it is not the couch of the finite human being, but in some mysterious unity his throne and his cross.

Nevertheless, fascism as a metapolitical phenomenon still serves as a means of understanding the world today: only when liberal society, after steadfast and serious reflection, accepts practical transcendence as its own although no longer exclusive product; when theoretical transcendence escapes from its ancient political entanglements into genuine freedom; when Communist society looks at itself and its past with realistic but not cynical eyes and ceases to evade either one; when the love of individuality and barriers no longer assumes political form, and thought has become a friend of man – only then can man be said to have finally crossed the border into a postfascist era.

Notes

1 For the Action Française, however, only inasmuch as, in opposing the republic, it was combating the socialist revolution which allegedly was bound to arise out of the democratic soil.
2 Lenin, 'Staat und Revolution', *Ausgewählte Werke*, II, (Berlin, 1955), p. 190.
3 Ibid., p. 250.
4 Lenin, 'Die drohende Katastrophe und wie man sie bekämpfen soll', ibid., p. 130.
5 E.g., Lenin, 'Über die Naturalsteuer', ibid., p. 830: '. . . it is our task to learn state capitalism from the Germans, to adopt it with all our might, to shrink from no dictatorial methods to hasten this transferring of Western culture to barbaric Russia, without hesitating to use barbaric fighting methods against barbarism'.
   'But why do we commit stupidities? That is easy to understand. First, we are a backward country; second, education in our country is minimal; third, we receive no assistance. Not a single civilized state assists us. On the contrary, they are all working against us' ('Fünf Jahre russische Revolution', ibid., pp. 973 f.).
   'Not even Marx thought of writing a single word about it [the state capitalism which occurs under communism] and he died without leaving behind a

single exact quotation or any irrefutable evidence. So now we have to try and help ourselves' ('Politischer Bericht des ZK auf dem XI. Parteitag', ibid., p. 926; cf. also p. 995).

6 Lenin, 'Die nächsten Aufgaben der Sowjetmacht', ibid., p. 377.

7 Here 'society' means not the totality of its members but the leading group.

8 'Industrialization' is also meant here as a total process and hence distinguished from feudal Japan's purely technical adoption of industrial forms of production.

9 It is no doubt clear from the foregoing that here the definite article is used not collectively but hypothetically.

10

*A revolt against modern civilization**

WOLFGANG SAUER

[. . .] Thus, the attempt to write the history of Nazism confronts the historian with an apparently unsolvable dilemma and raises the question of what historical understanding and historical objectivity may mean in the face of Nazism. One of the merits of the totalitarianism theory was that it took care of this condition; from this point of view, one might be tempted to define it as a scholarly formulation of our lack of understanding.

Is there a better way to conceal our weakness? Among the established concepts one remains: fascism. To be sure, the theory of fascism has also suffered severely from both the politics of and the historical studies on Nazism. This concerned, however, the Marxist–Leninist interpretation of fascism, and it may be worthwhile to ask if this interpretation is the only possible one. Attempts have indeed been made recently to repair the damaged tool for use. Some outstanding examples are Seymour Lipset's *Political Man*, which contains a comprehensive study of fascism on the basis of election analyses; Iring Fetscher's article on *Faschismus und Nationalsozialismus*, in which the author explicitly aims at a refutation of the Marxist concept of fascism; Eugen Weber's works on the *Action Française* and the European Right; and Ernst Nolte's volume *Der Faschismus in seiner Epoche* of which an English translation has meanwhile appeared. Mention must also be made in this context of Arthur Schweitzer's *Big Business in the Third Reich* in which the author attempts, unsuccessfully, I believe, to fuse elements of Max Weber's and Marxist theories.[1]

* Extract from Wolfgang Sauer, 'National Socialism: Totalitarianism or Fascism?', *American Historical Review*, 73(2) (Dec.), 1967, pp. 408–11, 412–22.

These works constitute, as a whole and despite differences in approach and position, the first serious attempt to develop a workable, non-Marxist concept of fascism. Their results are less conclusive regarding the relationship between fascism and totalitarianism; this issue needs further clarification. A shift in emphasis toward an interpretation in terms of fascism is, nevertheless, unmistakable. In this context it is notable that works like William S. Allen's study of Nazi rule in a northern German town, Schweitzer's study, and Alan S. Milward's brilliant book on *The German Economy at War*[2] show a disposition of historians to turn to the neglected topics of Nazi history. In the case of Schweitzer the turn is obviously related to the fascism approach; his book continues the earlier analysis of Neumann. Allen and Milward, by contrast, seem to have chosen their subjects without major theoretical considerations.[3] But whatever the reasons for this turn, the tendency expressed in all of these works seems to be the most characteristic development in recent studies of Nazism.

Leaving aside the mainly empirical studies of Allen and Milward, we may ask what image of fascism emerges from these works. A summary is naturally difficult in view of the differences in individual positions, and yet there are two closely related points of agreement. First, the authors agree that fascism is not, as the Marxist interpretation holds, merely a manipulation by monopoly capitalists: it is a mass movement with a character and aim of its own, indicating a major crisis in liberal democracy and capitalism. Whether or not this crisis is temporary remains controversial. Second, it is now established beyond doubt that the lower middle classes, both rural and urban, were at least one of the major social components of fascist movements.

There are also many divergences and discrepancies, however. Some confusion exists regarding the distinction between fascist movements and fascist regimes. Fetscher's analysis shows that fascist movements can ally, in view of their basic opportunism, with a wide variety of other groups; Schweitzer has exemplified this in the case of Nazism.[4] Consequently, there may be a marked difference between the original, relatively homogeneous fascist movements prior to the seizure of power and what emerges as fascist regimes after that event. This leads to the equally important problem of the relationships between fascist movements and their allies. For example, Lipset's interesting definition of fascism as the extremism of the liberal Center, in contrast to Right-wing extremism and Left-wing extremism (Communism), does not sufficiently explain why fascist regimes were frequently built on alliances with conservatives while alliances with Communists never materialized. Which social groups, then, were likely to become allies of fascist movements, and what functional role did these alliances play in the structure of the individual fascist regimes?

Other questions concern the social composition and the revolutionary aims of the movements. On the first question, most authors limit their analysis to the lower middle class and the problems of its definition. This is, indeed, an important issue since the concept of the lower middle class still needs clarification, both in itself and in relation to the varieties of fascist supporters. Historical evidence shows that support of fascism may not be confined to the classical elements of the lower middle class (*Mittelstand* – peasants, artisans, small businessmen, and so forth), but may extend to a wide variety of groups in the large field between the workers on the one hand and big business, the aristocracy, and the top levels of bureaucracy on the other. This evidence agrees, interestingly enough, with Leo Baeck's statement that it was among the workers, the aristocracy, and the upper strata of the civil servants that the Jews found strongest support against persecution in Germany.[5] [. . .]

The control fascist regimes achieved over the dynamism of their movements creates doubts concerning the revolutionary character of fascist movements. There is virtual agreement among scholars that fascist movements contained, contrary to the Marxist thesis, a true revolutionary potential. This seems to conflict, however, with the noted opportunism of these movements. Rudolf Heberle's well-known study on the Schleswig-Holstein peasants, recently republished in its unabridged German form,[6] first revealed this point, and Lipset has now been able to generalize Heberle's results. A look at the fascist regimes in operation, moreover, would show that, whatever the revolutionary potential of the movements, the revolutionary results were meager.

How can this problem be resolved? May an answer be found by setting fascism in a wider historical framework? This is the way Nolte approaches his subject, but his answer is suggestive rather than conclusive. He advances the thesis that fascism was a revolt against the universal process of secularization, democratization, and international integration in the modern era. When this process reached its critical stage in the period of the two world wars, those elements in the culture that were doomed to perish revolted, according to Nolte, with increasing radicalism and decreasing rationality, or, in national terms, from the French *Action Française* through Italian Fascism to German National Socialism. On the last, most radical stage, fascism turned, Nolte argues, into a resistance against what he calls the 'transcendence'. He does not succeed, however, in clarifying this point sufficiently.

Nolte's thesis is not new in terms of facts. Its originality lies in assigning a metaphysical dimension to the fascist revolt and definitely attaching this revolt to a historical period. Fascism, Nolte suggests, is dead. This is, on the one hand, a more optimistic variation of the totalitarianism analysis; on the other hand, he tries to ascribe a historical meaning to fascism, which would provide a starting point for historical understanding. Much of this remains abstract and vague, however – mere *Ideengeschichte*. If the modernization process was universal, was fascist revolt also universal? If so, why does Nolte deal only with France, Italy, and Germany? If not, why did the fascist revolt occur only in these (and some other) countries? And what was the cause for differentiation? Why was this revolt most radical in Germany? Or, to put the question in a sociological rather than a national form, which social groups provided the mass basis of fascism, and why were just these groups antimodernist in their orientation? Why did the antimodernist fascist revolt frequently foster industrialization? And, finally, what exactly does 'transcendence' mean, and by which concrete means did the fascist resistance against it manifest itself?

Nolte's neglect of these questions can be attributed primarily to his method, which he calls 'phenomenological' and which he conceives as an attempt to return to G. W. F. Hegel's integration of philosophy and history.[7] This attempt is, however, problematical. Hegel's striking success in synthesizing philosophy and history depended on his dialectical 'logic'; Nolte's method is not dialectical. Nor does Nolte develop an alternative. He has not succeeded, therefore, in invalidating Leopold von Ranke's argument against Hegel that philosophy in itself does not produce a method for the analysis and organization of empirical facts. Philosophy alone was, indeed, not sufficient for Nolte; his phenomenological method turns out, under scrutiny, to be essentially Dilthey's good, old method of empathy, supplemented by some fragmentary social-scientific concepts formed *ad hoc* to satisfy immediate needs.

To be sure, Nolte makes this method operative by confining his study mainly to an interpretaton of the ideas of the fascist leaders – Charles Maurras, Mussolini, Hitler – and he achieves much in this way, especially with regard to psychological and ideological analysis. Such a biographical approach is too narrow, however, to support Nolte's generalizations. What is true of the fascist leaders is not necessarily true of the masses of their followers. Their attitudes and motivation can be recognized only by a social analysis that includes economic factors. Nolte would perhaps respond to such a suggestion with as much contempt as he shows for the use of the concept of industrialization.[8] What does his concept of 'practical transcendence' mean, however, if not that economic factors have adopted in modern societies a significance that transcends their 'materialistic' meaning? And if this is true, how can we expect to gain meaningful results about modern societies without taking these factors into account? Nolte's method, in fact, seems to conflict heavily with his concept of 'practical transcendence'.

This must raise some doubts about the origin of Nolte's thesis of fascism as an antimodernist revolt. Indeed, he seems to have obtained his thesis, not through his biographical analyses, but rather through an analysis of Maurras's ideas. Nolte's decision, not too plausible at first glance, to raise the *Action Française* to a prominent position in the history of the origins of fascism, has, actually, methodological rather than historical reasons. The

Action Française is important to Nolte because Maurras succeeded in building an intellectual bridge between the counterrevolutionary tradition and fascism, thereby establishing a unified concept of antimodernism that Nolte found apparently suggestive as an analytical concept for his own study. His chapter on the *Action Française* is, thus, actually a part of his methodological introduction.

The conclusion that Nolte arrived at his thesis in a methodologically irregular way does not necessarily imply that the thesis is wrong. It does imply, however, that he has not proven his case. Fascism and counter-revolution are actually different social phenomena, the latter being the earlier position of a part of what has been defined here as the allies of fascism. Fascism had its own independent antecedents: pseudo revolutionaries like Father Jahn and the anti-Semites of the 1880s and 1890s (as examples in Germany).[9] To be sure, counterrevolution showed a combination of revolutionary and reactionary elements similar to fascism, but it was a revolution from above while fascism is a revolution from below. The discussion of Maurras by Nolte explains, therefore, the possibility of the fascist-conservative alliance, but it does not explain fascism. Nor does Nolte provide a satisfying answer to the question of the origins of fascism, especially in the German case. Nolte's chapters on pre-1914 Germany and Austria are in fact among the weakest in his book, though this is owing partly to Nolte's general weakness in historical knowledge.

These criticisms do not, however, detract from the value of the book, which is a major step forward in the study of fascism. If verified, Nolte's hypothesis can offer, for example, an explanation for the fascist tendencies in the military; its metaphysical implications might, in addition, open a way to understand certain aspects in the relationship between the churches and fascism. Nolte might indeed have achieved his aim of developing a comprehensive theory of fascism had it not been for his mistaken conception of the relationship of philosophy and history and his refusal to consider the socio-economic aspects of the problem.

The task is, then, to provide the non-Marxist theory of fascism with a socio-economic dimension; more precisely, the task is to bring the earlier attempts of this kind up to date. Some contributors to the discussion in the 1930s have already laid important foundations for a socio-economic theory of fascism.[10] We have only to adjust these foundations to today's advanced stage of practical experience, historical research, and theoretical thought. With regard to theory the most important recent contribution probably comes from economic historians who have worked out, on the basis of the experiences of both the Great Depression and the underdeveloped countries, a non-Marxist concept of economic development that is highly suggestive to the analysis of fascism.

The attempt to use this concept for the interpretation of fascism poses, of course, certain problems. The Marxist trap of economic determinism is but a minor difficulty. Apart from the fact that the difference between causes and conditions in social developments has meanwhile become sufficiently familiar to social scientists, it must also be stressed that the main purpose in using, here, an economic theory for a historical analysis is merely a heuristic one. In addition, the 'theory of economic growth' is, in the last analysis, not strictly an economic theory. It is rather a historical synthesis of the process of industrialization on the basis of a socio-economic analysis. Consequently, it already implies that the relationship between social and economic factors is a reversible one. In applying this theory to the interpretation of fascism, we merely shift the perspective without abandoning reversibility.

A more important problem arises because we have to face, as usual, several conflicting formulations of that theory. Only those formulations that focus on continental European conditions, however, are useful to the analysis of fascism. This reduces the number of alternatives to two: the models of Alexander Gerschenkron and W. W. Rostow.[11] If we analyze the results of these two theories with regard to the social context of industrialization, we find that they are complementary. Gerschenkron's theory of 'relative backwardness' provides a model of historical differentiation missing in Rostow's 'stage' theory, and the latter offers a model for periodization not developed by Gerschenkron.

The critical problem is the development of a model for the advanced period of the industrialization process. Gerschenkron's model of relative backwardness cannot be directly extended to it since it deals with the starting conditions, while Rostow's definition as a stage of 'high mass consumption' is still unsatisfactory.[12] Rostow hits, certainly, the essential point: that industry, if it exceeds a certain limit of growth, must turn to mass production. He is also aware that private mass consumption is not the only possible response. Rostow's idea, however, that societies on the stage of mass production have a choice between high mass consumption and national political expansion (or, between private mass consumption and mass consumption by the state), does not entirely agree with the historical evidence. There is certainly an element of choice in the situation; yet it may well be that there are also contraints working against a choice. They may be owing to the consequences of relative backwardness, or to differential national developments and resulting international tensions and crises such as war. Rostow neglects the impact of national economic growth on international relations and vice versa; this seems to be, in fact, the major weakness of his theory. If we analyze twentieth-century history from this point of view, we do indeed find a period of world crises (World War I, the Great Depression, World War II) spreading between Rostow's stages of industrial maturity and high mass consumption.

In terms of a theory of economic growth revised in this way, fascism can be defined as a revolt of those who lost – directly or indirectly, temporarily or permanently – by industrialization. Fascism is a revolt of the *déclassés*. The workers and industrialists do not fall under this definition; it applies mainly to most of the lower middle class as defined above. They indeed suffered, or feared they would suffer, from industrialization – peasants who opposed the urbanizing aspects of industrialism; small businessmen and those engaged in the traditional crafts and trades that opposed mechanization or concentration; white-collar workers (at least as long as they felt the loss of economic independence); lower levels of the professions, especially the teaching profession, which opposed changing social values; and so forth. Also the military joins here, with opposition against the industrialization of war, which tended to destroy traditional modes of warfare and which by its increasing destructiveness intensified pacifism and antimilitarism. On the other hand, groups like the aristocracy, the large landlords, the higher bureaucrats, and so on, who lost also by industrialization, generally did not turn to fascism. In continuing the counter-revolutionary position, they defended hierarchical society and abhorred, therefore, the egalitarian elements in fascism. In exact distinction, then, fascist movements represented the reaction of the lower-class losers, while the upper-class losers tended to react in a nonfascist way, but were potential allies of fascist regimes.

Such an analysis seems to be a way of explaining the intriguing paradox of a revolutionary mass movement whose goals were antirevolutionary in the classical sense. As a movement of losers, it turned against technological progress and economic growth; it tried to stop or even to reverse the trend toward industrialization and to return to the earlier, 'natural' ways of life. In this respect the movement was reactionary, but, as a movement of the lower classes, its means were necessarily revolutionary. In defining fascism as a revolt of losers, we can also understand better both fascist atavism and fascist opportunism. Since the process of industrialization as a whole is irresistible, the existence of civilization is inextricably bound to it. Fascist revolt against industrialization must, therefore, eventually turn against civilization too. This was most evident in Germany, where Nazism developed into full-fledged neobarbarism, but it is also true of the other fascist movements, though for various reasons neobarbarism remained, there, more or less underdeveloped. Such a definition of fascism as a neobarbaric revolt against civilization seems to describe in more concrete terms what Nolte calls the resistance against the 'transcendence'.

The same condition led to fascist opportunism. Since fascists acted, as losers, essentially from a position of weakness, they were compelled, in spite of their tendency toward violence, to compromise with their environment, even with their industrial enemy. This accounts for the contradiction that fascist regimes often fostered industrialization and yet insisted, ultimately, upon setting the clock back. The dialectic that resulted from this condition led eventually to a point at which the movement assumed suicidal proportions. Industrialization was sought in order to destroy industrial society, but since there was no alternative to industrial society, the fascist regime must eventually destroy itself. This was the situation of Nazism. The Nazis built an industrial machinery to murder the Jews, but once in operation the machine would have had to continue and would have ruined, indirectly at least, first the remnants of civilized society and then the fascist regime. Industrialization of mass murder was, thus, the only logical answer Nazism had to the problems of industrial society.

The analysis of fascism in terms of economic growth also offers a way to define more precisely the fallacy in the Marxist–Leninist concept of fascism. The fallacy lies in that Marxism blurs the distinction between early commercial and late industrial capitalism. Fascism indicated a conflict within capitalism, between traditional forms of commercialism and the modern form of industrialism. The fact that the former had survived in the twentieth century only on the lower levels of the middle classes accounted for the social locus of fascism. It is true, therefore, that fascism was capitalist by nature; it is not true that it was industrial. It is also true that fascist regimes often were manipulated in varying ways and degrees, but the share of industrialists in manipulation was rather small. Fetscher shows convincingly that the share was indeed larger in industrially underdeveloped Italy than it was in industrially advanced Germany.

On the other hand, the difference between fascism and Bolshevism appears, in light of this analysis, more fundamental than the totalitarianism analysis would admit. Neither V. I. Lenin nor Joseph Stalin wished to turn the clock back; they not merely wished to move ahead, but they wished to jump ahead. The Bolshevik revolution had many elements of a development revolution not unlike those now under way in the underdeveloped countries. One of the striking differences between the two systems appears in the role of the leaders. The social and political order of Bolshevism is relatively independent from the leadership; it is, so to speak, more objective. Fascist regimes, by contrast, are almost identical with their leaders; no fascist regime has so far survived its leader. This is why Bullock's interpretation of Hitler in terms of traditional tyranny has some bearing. The limits of this approach would become evident, I believe, if scholars could be persuaded to balance their interest in Hitler's secret utterances and political and military scheming by also stressing his role as a public speaker. The Nazi mass rallies with their immediate, ecstatic communication between leader and followers were, indeed, what might be called a momentary materialization of the Nazi utopia, at least so far as the 'Nordic race' was concerned.[13]

Finally, it is plain from an analysis in terms of economic growth that the degree of radicalization must somehow be related to the degree of industrialization. The more highly industrialized a society, the more violent the reaction of the losers. Thus Germany stood at the top, Italy lagged behind, and Spain and others were at the bottom. In Germany, fascism gained sufficient momentum to oust its allies. By the dismissal of Schacht, Werner von Blomberg, Werner von Fritsch, and Konstantin von Neurath in 1937–1938, the Nazis assumed control over the economy, the army, and the diplomacy, those exact three positions that their conservative allies of January 30, 1933, had deemed it most important to maintain.[14] In Italy a fairly stable balance was sustained between the movement and its various allies until the latter, relying on the monarchy and assisted by Fascism's defeat in war, finally ousted the Fascists. In Spain, a borderline case, the allies assumed control from the outset and never abandoned it. Similar observations can be made with the many cases of pre-, proto-, and pseudofascist regimes in Central, Eastern, and Southeastern Europe.

The thesis of the parallel growth of industrialization and fascist radicalization seems to conflict, however, with the evidence of some highly industrialized societies such as France and England where fascist opposition never gained much momentum. The problem can be solved only by adding a broader historical analysis involving the specific national, social, and cultural traditions that industrialization encountered in individual societies. It is perhaps not accidental that the industrialization process ran relatively smoothly in West European nations whose political rise concurred with the rise of modern civilization since the late Middle Ages. Fascist opposition, by contrast, was strongest in the Mediterranean and Central European regions where the premodern traditions of the ancient Roman and the medieval German and Turkish Empires persisted. The religious division between Protestantism and Catholicism may also have some relevance: one remembers both Max Weber's thesis on the correlation of Protestantism and capitalism and the recent controversy on the attitude of Pope Pius XII toward Fascism and Nazism. In other words, fascism emerged where pre-industrial traditions were both strongest and most alien to industrialism and, hence, where the rise of the latter caused a major break with the past and substantial losses to the nonindustrial classes.

This definition is still incomplete, however, since it does not tell why fascism emerged rather simultaneously throughout Europe though the countries affected were on different levels of economic growth. We face here the question of the 'epoch' of fascism, raised but not answered by Nolte. The general conditions of fascism as defined above existed after all, earlier. In Germany, for example, lower-middle-class opposition against industrialization had already emerged in the mid-nineteenth century and accompanied economic growth in varying degrees through all its stages.[15] Why did it not turn into fascism prior to 1914, though it did so on parallel stages of growth in Italy and Spain after the First World War? At this point the importance of the military element for the analysis of fascism becomes apparent again: Only after total war had militarized European societies and had created large military interests were the conditions required for fascism complete.[16] The First World War had tremendously strengthened industrialization in technical terms, but it had diverted it from production to destruction. After the war the victorious nations of the West managed, on the whole, to stabilize industrial society and to return to production, but the defeated nations and those industrially underdeveloped found it extremely difficult to follow the same course. When they met with economic crises, many of them abandoned whatever advance they had made toward democracy and turned to fascism.

This breakdown occurred roughly along the social and cultural lines defined above. If we examine the geographical distribution of fascist regimes in Europe between the two world wars, we find that they emerged mainly in three areas: the Mediterranean coast; the regions of Central, Eastern, and Southeastern Europe; and Germany. In the first area, the original and highly developed Mediterranean urban and commercial civilization that reached back to antiquity faced destruction by the invasion of industrialism as released or accelerated by World War I. Defeat, either imagined as in the case of Italy or real as in the case of Spain at the hands of Abd-el-Krim at Anual in 1921, played an additional role. In the second area, an old feudal civilization struggled with the problems arising out of sudden liberation from Habsburg or tsarist dominations as well as from competition with both Western industrialism and Eastern Bolshevism. Both regions were predominantly Catholic. In the third area, a technologically fully developed industrial society clashed violently with the stubborn resistance of surviving remnants of pre-industrial forms of society over who was to pay for defeat and economic crises. Catholicism played, here, a dual and partly contradictory role. On the one hand, it seems to have influenced indirectly Nazism as such top Nazi leaders as Hitler, Himmler, and Goebbels were Catholic by origin, and the Vatican was quick to compromise with the Hitler regime. On the other hand, the vast majority of the Catholic population was relatively immune to Nazi temptations. Significantly enough, Protestantism also split, though along somewhat different lines.

These differentiations suggest a division into three subtypes of fascism: the Mediterranean as the 'original' one; the various and not too long-lived regimes in Central, Eastern, and Southeastern Europe as a mixed, or not full-fledged, variation; and German Nazism as a special form.

The 'epoch' of fascism starts, thus, with the aftermath of the First World War, but when does it end? Eugen Weber and Lipset agree with many scholars who believe that there is no epoch of fascism, that fascism is a general condition of modern society contingent upon crises in liberal democracy.[17] This is certainly indisputable as far as fascist attitudes and movements are concerned; it is quite another problem, however, whether fascist regimes will emerge again. This emergence seems unlikely for two reasons. First, the socio-economic development in the highly industrialized societies of the West generally rules out the re-emergence of the historical condition of fascism – a disarrangement of society in which the rise of large masses of *déclassés* coincides with the rise of a sizable group of military desperadoes. There are no longer economic losers of industrialization, at least not on a mass scale, and Charles de Gaulle's victory over the rebellious French military shows that military desperadoes alone will not get very far.[18] In addition, the horrible experience of neobarbarism puts a heavy burden on all attempts at imitation. If the success of fascism under modern, Western conditions is unlikely, there remain, theoretically, the underdeveloped countries as possible breeding grounds of fascism. Yet it is doubtful whether opposition against industrialization will assume there the form of fascism since these countries lack the specific traditions of the ancient and medieval civilizations that conditioned the anti-modernist revolt in Europe. The second reason working against fascist regimes is, thus, that fascism is inseparable from its Central and South European conditions; it is, in fact, one of the products of the dialectical movement of European civilization. [. . .]

Notes

1 Seymour M. Lipset, *Political Man* (New York, Doubleday, 1960), Chap. v; Iring Fetshcer, 'Faschismus und Nationalsozialismus: Zur Kritik des sowjet-marxistischen Faschismusbegriffs', *Politische Vierteljahrsschrift*, III (Mar. 1962), 42–63; Eugen Weber, *Action Française* (Stanford, CA., Stanford University Press, 1962); *The European Right: A Historical Profile*, Hans Rogger and Eugen Weber (eds) (Berkeley, CA., University of California Press, 1964); Eugen Weber, *Varieties of Fascism* (Princeton, NJ, Van Nostrand, 1964); Ernst Nolte, *Der Faschismus in seiner Epoche* (Munich, Piper, 1963), tr. as *Three Faces of Fascism* (New York, 1966); Arthur Schweitzer, *Big Business in the Third Reich* (Bloomington, IND., Indiana University Press, 1964).

2 William S. Allen, *The Nazi Seizure of Power: The Experience of a Single German Town, 1930–1935* (Chicago, Quadrangle, 1965); Alan S. Milward, *The German Economy at War* (London, Athlone Press, 1965). Since the completion of this article in May 1966, further studies have been published confirming this trend and covering many of the hitherto neglected subjects.

3 Allen tends, in fact, to use the totalitarianism concept, but his results disprove largely his thesis that Nazi rule led to an 'atomization' of society. (See, e.g., Allen, *Nazi Seizure of Power*, op. cit. p. 278.)

4 Schweitzer, *Big Business*, op. cit., distinguishes two periods in the Nazi rule: 'partial Fascism' with alliances between fascism and other groups until 1936 and 'full Fascism' after this date. The thesis is basically correct, though Schweitzer is too rigid on several points. (Cf. Carl Landauer's criticism, *Journal of Economic History*, XXV (1965), pp. 293–95.)

5 *Das Dritte Reich und die Juden*, Leon Poliakov and Josef Wulf (eds) (Berlin, Arani, 1955), p. 439.

6 Rudolf Heberle, *Landbevölkerung und Nationalsozialismus: Eine soziologische Untersuchung der politischen Willensbildung in Schleswig-Holstein 1918 bis 1932* (Stuttgart, Deutsche Verlags-Anstalt, 1963), tr. as *From Democracy to Nazism: A Regional Case Study on Political Parties in Germany* (Baton Rouge, LA., 1945).

7 Nolte, *Der Faschismus*, op. cit., pp. 516–17.

8 Ibid., p. 541.

9 The German anti-Semitic movement around 1900 has attracted, understandably enough, much attention in recent years. It is important to note, however, that it was only a part of a broader trend that extended to France (the Dreyfus affair, Edouard Drumont) and Austria (Karl Lueger and the Christian-Social party). As a whole, it has not yet been sufficiently investigated; Nolte (*Der Faschismus*) and Weber (*Action Française*) focus on France while Peter G. J. Pulzer, *The Rise of Political Anti-Semitism in Germany and Austria* (New York, Wiley, 1964), disregards France.

10 Harold D. Lasswell, 'The Psychology of Hitlerism', *Political Quarterly* 4, (1933), pp. 373–84; David J. Saposs, 'The Role of the Middle Class in Social Development: Fascism, Populism, Communism, Socialism', in *Economic Essays in Honor of Wesley Clair Mitchell, Presented to Him by His Former Students on the Occasion of His 60th Birthday* (New York, Columbia University Press, 1935); Talcott Parsons, 'Some Sociological Aspects of the Fascist Movement', (1941), reprinted in Talcott Parsons, *Essays in Sociological Theory* (Glencoe, Ill., Free Press, 1954).

11 Alexander Gerschenkron, *Economic Backwardness in Historical Perspective* (Cambridge, MA., Belknap Press of Harvard University, 1962), esp. pp. 1–51, 353–64; W. W. Rostow, *The Stages of Economic Growth* (Cambridge, Cambridge University Press, 1959); *The Economics of Take-off into Sustained Growth*, W. W. Rostow (ed.) (London, Macmillan, St. Martin's Press, 1963). Cf. the review by Henry Rosovsky, 'The Take-off into Sustained Controversy', *Journal of Economic History*, XXV (1965), pp. 271–5.

12 Rosovsky, 'The Take-off', pp. 274–5, proposes to replace the concept of 'stage' by that of the 'long swing'. This might, however, deprive the concept of growth of its meaning and would necessitate, therefore, a decision on whether the idea of growth should be abandoned altogether or whether the idea of swing must be adjusted to that of growth. In the latter case, the concept of stage might prove indispensable as a complement.

13 This is one of the reasons why the lack of a collection of Hitler's speeches, as complete as technically possible, is one of the most serious obstacles to a successful study of Nazism. Such a collection is indispensable not only for a biography of Hitler (How can we expect to understand a man whose political career was built to such an extent on success as a public speaker if we have no means to analyze him in this role?), but still more for the analysis of the Nazi ideology. Only if we approach the Nazi ideology through a dynamic analysis will we be able to solve the methodological dilemma of dealing rationally with Nazi irrationalism and with whether the Nazi ideology had substance or was merely a tactical function. To this effect we must follow the course of Hitler's thought an its response to the successive political changes, and this can be done only by following him through his speeches.

14 The focus of present studies on the spectacular Blomberg-Fritsch affair has

blurred the comprehensive character and the importance of the change in 1937–1938.

15 Already Marx observed the antimodernist attitude of the petty bourgeoisie, though he partly misinterpreted it. The anti-Semitic movement at the end of the century was indicative of the growing radicalization of lower-middle-class opposition. (See Hans Rosenberg, *Grosse Depression und Bismarckzeit* [Berlin, 1966]; for France, see André Siegfried, *Tableau politique de la France de l'ouest sous la troisième république* [Paris, 1913], p. 413; cf. Lipset, *Political Man*, op. cit. pp. 131–2.)

16 The *Vaterlandspartei*, organized in 1917 by military and agrarian groups (Alfred von Tirpitz; Wolfgang Kapp) in Germany to support imperialist warfare, was, significantly enough, the first prefascist mass movement. The foundation of the Nazi party later followed the same pattern: Hitler acted originally as an agent of the Munich headquarters of the *Reichswehr*. In addition, Anton Drexler, the founder of the first nucleus of the Nazi party, was a member of the *Vaterlandspartei*. Both the *Reichswehr* officers in Munich and Drexler aimed at overcoming what they felt was the major shortcoming of the *Vaterlandspartei*: it had no appeal to the workers. (Among recent accounts, see Günther Franz-Willing, *Die Hitlerbewegung* (Hamburg, 1962), p. I.)

17 Weber, *Varieties of Fascism*, op. cit., p. 3; Lipset, *Political Man*, op. cit., Chapter v.

18 It would be different in case of large-scale war which might, of course, drastically change present social conditions.

THE EMERGENCE OF A
NEW CONSENSUS

11

A *modernizing dictatorship**

A. JAMES GREGOR

Henry Ashby Turner's recent suggestions[1] concerning the analysis of fascism in terms of its relationship to the processes we have come to understand as 'modernization' are too important and interesting to pass without critical comment. So much of what Turner says is persuasive that we run the risk of uncritically accepting what might be the chaff of his discussion along with its welcome substance.

There are at least two types of reservations with respect to Turner's account. One type turns on the general thesis he entertains; the second deals with the specifics of his argument.

I

Turner suggests that, given the 'erosion of theories of totalitarianism', we find ourselves without a 'suitable concept' for characterizing those 'inter-war authoritarian movements and regimes' that are generally identified as 'fascist'. He indicates that the theory of modernization might afford the absent 'suitable concept' or 'frame of reference' requisite to a more compelling analysis of the complex phenomena with which we are concerned.

While the theory of totalitarianism has regrettably given evidence of vagueness and conceptual porosity, the theory of modernization is, unfortunately, hardly less imprecise and ambiguous. Exponents of modernization have used the concept in any number of perplexing, inclusive, vague, complex, and sometimes mutually exclusive ways. Some theoreticians speak of modernization as an organic or holistic process, involving an array of social, economic, cultural, attitudinal, and political manifestations in a complex interaction.[2] Others seem to focus, more specifically, on economic development and growth as critical or determinant variables – with social, cultural, political, and psychological variables as contingent, dependent, or epiphenomenal effects.[3] The theory of modernization may (or may not) have more immediate common currency than the theory of totalitarianism, but it would be hard to make a case for its

* Extract from A. J. Gregor, 'Fascism and Modernization: Some Addenda', *World Politics*, 26 (1974), pp. 370–84.

being any more precise or providing greater leverage on analysis, explanation, or prediction.

Turner himself conceives of modernization as being a complex process
'involving industrialization, urbanization, secularization, and rationalization'.[4] Objective indices can perhaps be provided for two of the four
defining properties of modernization: industrialization and urbanization.
Overall, sectoral, and subsectoral rates of growth can, in principle, be
plotted for industrialization. We can, in principle, discover some measures
of aggregate output, output per man, and output per man-hour for industrial production. We can, in principle, provide some reasonably accurate
figures for population flow and some measures of urbanization. It is hard
to say, however, what we might use to measure secularization and rationalization. Most judgments must remain impressionistic and intuitive.

In order to obtain purchase on a vague and somewhat fugitive notion –
fascism – we are asked to invoke what appear to be the equally vague and
mercurial notions associated with modernization. If some of the central
notions entailed by the latter concept have, at best, indeterminate reference, it becomes very difficult to know when we have made defensible
ascriptions of modernizing or anti-modernizing to any complex political
movement.

As a case in point, Turner seems to argue that even anti-modernizing
regimes might suffer some measure of industrial growth (and attendant
urbanization) because of their fascination with industrial products. That
fascists might have had a 'positive attitude toward the products of modern
industry', we are informed, 'should not necessarily be equated with
approval of the larger process of modernization'.[5]

We can only be puzzled. Fascists can, apparently, foster or suffer industrialization – one of the four constituent components of modernization –
while rejecting the 'larger process of modernization'. What this seems to
mean is that, in fact, fascists really want to de-urbanize and de-industrialize,
but somehow entertain a need and desire for the products of industry. This
generates an air of paradox.

Turner seems to be saying that fascists actually do not wish to
industrialize, urbanize, secularize, or rationalize. They are *intentionally*
anti-modern, and harken back to some pre-modern ideal. Fascists, it
would seem, 'implemented many modernizing policies . . . only as the
means to anti-modernist ends'.[6] Much of Turner's argument thus pertains
to what fascist *intentions* might have been – which, in turn, would require
a reasonably competent and objective catalogue of fascist doctrinal
commitments.

What Turner's argument requires is an adequate rehearsal of fascist
intentions. In neither the National Socialist nor the Italian Fascist case
does Turner provide what is critical to his discussion. The weaknesses in
his argument can be made more transparent by considering specifically the

intentions of the Italian Fascists. As Turner insists, the 'central question' around which his discussion gravitates is 'what [fascist] leadership cadres wanted to do with their societies. [. . .]'[7] Did they really aspire to a restoration of a pre-modern social, political, and economic system?

II

The discussion of some of the general disabilities of Turner's argument has led us to a consideration of some of his specific claims. Can it be plausibly argued that Italian Fascists sought to recreate a utopian 'ancient Rome'? Were their explicit intentions anachronistic and reactionary? Turner is disposed to leave these questions open – but they are clearly not as open as he seems to suggest.

The most striking feature of discussions of this sort is the apparent indisposition of discussants to catalogue Fascist commitments as the Fascists themselves articulated them. In his account, for example, Turner does allude to some National Socialist literature, but he does not make a single direct reference to primary Fascist literature. We are, rather, treated to a recital of a collection of folk sayings about Fascist ideals and intentions. We are told that the Fascists aspired to a 'revived Roman Empire', and that Mussolini intended to 'ruralize' Italy. Moreover, Fascists entertained a reactionary 'martial . . . ideal'.[8] All of which suggests to Turner that Fascism might have been a 'utopian anti-modernism'.

Almost everything we know of the original Fascist movement as it collected around Mussolini in 1919 indicates, in fact, that it could not be persuasively characterized as anti-modern – unless the notion of modernization is used in a totally idiosyncratic fashion. The principal constituents that entered into the coalition that became Fascism – Futurism, Italian Nationalism, and Revolutionary National Syndicalism – seem to have all been clearly modernizing in intention. They advocated an industrialized Italy, with flourishing urban centers, secular political control of community life (sometimes with due regard for traditional religious values), and a rationalized bureaucratic (if anti-parliamentarian) infrastructure to govern the peninsula effectively. All three political movements dated from the pre-war period and all three seem clearly to have been committed to the modernization of Italy.

Futurism, for its part, was the product of the brain of F. T. Marinetti – and whatever else it was, Futurism seems to have been a modernizing movement. In the *Futurist Manifesto* of 1909, Marinetti proclaimed, for instance, that the 'magnificence of the world has been enriched with a new beauty: the beauty of speed. [. . .]' Marinetti was giving voice to what he conceived to be a new secular 'religiosity' – a devotion to mechanization.[9] Marinetti, in fact, advocated an 'identification of man with machine', a new humanity metered to the measure of machinery.[10] So intense were Futurist sentiments that Futurists formed a 'Society for the Protection of Machines' – machines which, they argued, have 'enriched life [. . .] destroyed distance and bridged space and enhanced the very tenor of life'. Machines, to Futurists, were 'concentrated power, inexorable precision, constancy and sincerity [!]'. The Futurists, furthermore, were the advocates of cities that would be 'geometrized [. . .] [fashioned in] cement, steel, crystal' – and filled with 'machines, machines, machines, machines'. They admonished Italians to 'love and protect machines'.[11] They aspired to create an Italy controlled by a technocracy, characterized by vast industrial complexes, modern communications systems, and urban developments.[12] In James Joll's judgment, some of the main themes of the Futurist movement included an

> intense excitement about the prospects of the new century that was just beginning, an awareness of the beauty of machines which could replace the more traditional objects of aesthetic satisfaction, and a realization of the heightening of experience which new sensations of speed and mechanical power could give.[13]

The Futurists seem to have been modernizers, and as modernizers they were among the first leadership cadres of the nascent Fascist movement. Marinetti and his immediate followers were in attendance at the founding meeting of the movement in San Sepolcro in 1919. Futurism, in effect, made up one of the currents that constituted the subsequent flood tide of Fascism.

Another current which was to contribute to that tide was the Nationalism of Enrico Corradini. Whatever else Corradini's Nationalism was, it seems to have been clearly modernizing in intention. As early as 1910 Corradini identified Italy as a 'proletarian' nation suffering economic retardation; by 1914 he explicitly argued that the fortunes of all Italians, whether characterized as 'proletarian' or 'bourgeois', were inextricably bound up in the *quantity and quality of national production*. Italy was 'economically retarded', its industrialization 'impeded' by constraints imposed by foreign 'imperialisms' and archaic traditions. 'Nationalism', Corradini insisted, 'rests on the principle of production, which precedes and transcends that of distribution. [. . .][14] The only way open for Italy to attain her 'rightful place' in the community of nations was to undertake a program of accelerated economic development. Italy was at the 'very commencement' of her curve of economic growth. What was required was a marshalling, rationalization, and disciplining of human and natural resources to the tasks such a process would inevitably entail.[15] Sacrifice and discipline were advocated as cardinal virtues for a nation of 'producers'. The 'maximization of production' became a critical instrumental consideration in the program of making Italy a 'major world power'. For the Nationalists, 'production' constituted the 'central dynamic of modern civilization, the central dynamic that provides for the future of modern nations'. The organization of modern nations should be calculated to afford 'maximum efficiency' to productive processes.[16] By 1916 Corradini made the issue of Italian industrial development central to his arguments. The war, he insisted, had forced the expansion and acceleration of Italian industrial growth. He spoke of an 'intelligent political policy' of maximizing capital accumulation, a rationalization of financial institutions, and a mobilization of the labor force in pursuit of an organized policy of growth. Corradini reiterated with tedious regularity that the critical elements determining the future of modern nations were those identified with 'industrial production'. 'Producers', whether the entrepreneurial bourgeoisie or the workers, constituted for Corradini the 'true aristocracy of our epoch', and productive expansion and the extension of markets constituted critical instrumental ends in the service of the nation. To achieve those ends, Corradini advocated the regular accumulation of investment capital, the substitution of an efficient bureaucracy composed of technocrats for a parliament composed of ineffectual lawyers. Such reforms would facilitate economic maturation and expansion.[17] These themes remained constant throughout the period that marked the transition between the termination of the First World War and the advent of Fascism. By 1923 Nationalism and its modernizing fervor had been absorbed by Fascism, and in 1924 Corradini could dedicate the volume that contained his collected speeches to 'Benito Mussolini, the Duce of Victorious Italy'.

If both Futurism and Nationalism, two of the three principal constituents of victorious Fascism, could be characterized as 'modernizing' in intention, no less could be said of National Syndicalism, the radical syndicalism that survived the war under Mussolini's leadership and provided the rationale for Fascism's specific economic and social policies.

As early as August 1918 Mussolini had changed the subtitle of his newspaper from that of a 'Socialist Daily' to 'A Daily of Combatants and *Producers*'. This signaled a shift from what he was later to characterize as 'destructive' to 'constructive' socialism. Mussolini began to speak of '*productive* classes' rather than classes of the oppressed and classes of the oppressors. He spoke of a 'coincidence of interests' that united the Italian proletariat and the Italian productive bourgeoisie in a rationalized national program of economic development.[18] By the end of the war, Mussolini spoke of the tasks that faced the nation in terms of an 'economic renovation' that included an 'association of energies' to 'resolve the problem of increased production'.[19] By 1919 he was calling his socialism a 'socialism' preoccupied with 'production', a 'productivistic socialism'.[20]

At the meeting at which Fascism was founded, Mussolini maintained that Italy was a 'proletarian' nation, disadvantaged in the competition with 'rich' or 'plutocratic' nations. He insisted that whatever policies

Fascism advanced, two considerations must remain central to its concerns: the reality of the nation and the *exigencies of production*. Mussolini stressed that the 'capstone' of Fascist policies would be the 'maximizing of production'. Under no circumstances should production be limited or 'prejudiced'.[21] In July 1919 Mussolini emphasized that the programmatic formula of Fascism was 'the maximization of production' to which variable pragmatic tactics would be tailored.[22]

When revolutionary socialists seized industrial plants throughout Northern Italy, Mussolini indicated that Fascism was prepared to support the enterprise only if the workers could insure the maintenance of productive levels. Mussolini insisted that the Fascists consider problems only in terms of 'productivity'.[23] In 1920 the Fascists published their 'Postulates for a Fascist Program' in which they identified their interest in the 'maximization of production and well-being'.[24]

By the time of Mussolini's accession to power, Fascism had given clear evidence of its commitment to industrialization and modernization of the economy. Not only were the Futurists, Nationalists, and National Syndicalists agreed that the maximization of production was the first order of business, but all were advocates of urban development, the rationalization of financial institutions, the reorganization of the bureaucracy on the basis of technical competence, the abolition of 'traditional' and nonfunctional agencies, the expansion of road, rail, waterways, and telephonic communications systems, the modernization and secular control of the educational system, and the reduction of illiteracy.

The advent of Fascism brought with it the first efforts at theoretical interpretation. When Luigi Salvatorelli suggested that Fascism might be conceived as a product of 'petty bourgeois humanistic' dispositions, Giovanni Ansaldo was quick to remind him that not 'humanism' but *'industrial development'* constituted the preoccupation of the cadres of Fascism. Ansaldo reminded his readers that it was 'the apotheosis of industrial development' which animated the Fascists – and that such a concern was calculated to warm the hearts of the Milanese *'technical* petty bourgeoisie'. Fascism, Ansaldo insisted, resonated with the interests of the 'Italian petty bourgeoisie *obsessed with modernity'*.[25]

It seems fairly clear that by 1923 Fascism could be – and was by a considerable number of contemporaries – recognized as a modernizing and industrializing movement. In the opinion of Ludovico Garruccio, those representatives of the 'traditional' or 'anti-modern' sectors of Italian society that were attracted to Fascism were quickly domesticated, or else purged in the service of 'developmental' and 'modernizing' Fascism.[26]

Mussolini piloting his own aircraft and tooling through the Italian hills in his red sports car were public displays of this modernizing temper. The public policies of introducing the work ethic among civil servants, of insistence that the trains run on time, and plans for the development of a modern road system were the first overt indications of the character of Fascism's modernizing dispositions.

Immediately after accession to power, Fascism's domestic policy was largely governed by the efforts to rationalize and improve both the infrastructural bureaucracy and the productive plant. In 1924 Sergio Panunzio, one of the principal ideologues of Fascism, characterized Fascist policy as a 'means [to] the production of national wealth', a concern for the efficient and rationalized reorganization of the productive forces of the nation.[27] Fascism continued to characterize itself in this way throughout the Fascist period. By 1930 Nazareno Mezzetti could identify the 'principle of defense and development of production' as the central concern of Fascist economic policy.[28] Gioacchino Volpe, the official historian of Fascism, identified Fascist policy as a calculated effort to 'break away from the plutocratic nations [and] the development of the forces of internal production. [. . .]'[29] Volpe regularly alluded to Fascism's role in providing a 'massive impulse' to economic development.[30]

All of this, conjoined with the Fascist programs of urban redevelopment and expansion that made Rome, Milan, Turin, and Genoa heavily populated modern industrial and commercial centers, suggests that Fascism could hardly be conceived as a 'utopian anti-modernism' in intention. Considering the long struggle for secular political control of all facets of public life (coupled with the political accommodations necessitated by the presence of organized Catholicism in Italian life), it is hard not to read in Fascist intentions and performance the efforts of a modernizing movement.

When one reviews the economic performance of Italy during the Fascist period, it becomes fairly obvious that Italy enjoyed a steady rate of industrialization and economic modernization. If Fascism was 'antimodern' in intention, then the Fascists apparently were unsuccessful in impeding the modernization of the economy they controlled. With a base index of 100 in 1922, the aggregate indices of industrial production in Italy had risen to 182.2 by 1934. The metallurgical, building, textile, and hydroelectric generating industries all showed significant advances.[31] The rates of growth remained relatively constant, and the economic and industrial performance of Fascist Italy compared favorably with the economic and industrial performances of more resource-favored advanced industrial states. By 1938, using 1913 as a base, the index of aggregate volume of output for Italy had risen to 153.8, which compared more than favorably with that of France (109.4), and Germany (149.9). Again using 1913 as a base, the aggregate index for output per man in 1938 stood at 145.2 for Italy, 136.5 for France, 122.4 for Germany, 143.6 for the United Kingdom, and 136.0 for the United States; the aggregate index for output per manhour stood at 191.1 for Italy, at 178.5 for France, 137.1 for Germany, and 167.9 for the United Kingdom.[32] All of this seems to imply rationalization and increasing role specificity among the labor force and functional entrepreneurs.

In point of fact, analysts like A. F. K. Organski and Charles F. Delzell are wrong when they suggest that the Fascists 'severely repressed' economic development, and that the rate of economic development in Italy 'slowed down in the 'twenties and virtually came to a halt in the 'thirties'.[33] The fact is that between 1922 and 1938 Fascist Italy had become (both in terms of industrial growth and the modernization of agriculture) an economically mature society. In the opinion of Roland Sarti, Italy's post-war 'economic miracle' would have been impossible without the developments of the antecedent Fascist period.[34] That judgment is shared by the most unlikely commentators.

In effect, there is very little either in the explicit intentions of Fascist ideologues or in Fascist performance that would suggest that Italian Fascism belonged to the class of anti-modern utopian movements. Mussolini's appeal to ancient glories, his effort to paramilitarize Italian society, and his advocacy of martial virtues do not an 'anti-modern utopian' make. Modernizing Japan, Maoist China, and the Soviet Union all have regularly appealed to the ancient glories of their peoples in order to mobilize their energies for the efforts required in industrialization and modernization. Each of them, immediately or ultimately, has perceived the benefits of paramilitarization and the organization of 'work brigades', 'wars' of production, and 'battles' for meeting quotas. All of them, in some way or another, have invoked 'martial virtues' in the effort to mobilize and control the energies necessary for their enterprise.

No matter what can be said of National Socialism in Germany it would appear that Italian Fascism was an exemplar of the class of contemporary mass-mobilizing and modernizing dictatorships operating under single-party auspices.

However one chooses to interpret the available evidence, it is clear that the comparative study of mass-mobilizing movements of the twentieth century is facing critical problems of typology and classification. If Italian Fascism was, in fact, a mass-mobilizing developmental dictatorship under single-party auspices, how can one rigorously distinguish it from Stalinism, or Maoism, or, for that matter, Castroism? Fascists, as early as the twenties, maintained that there were substantial similarities between themselves and the political system developing in the Soviet Union. In 1925 Sergio Panunzio argued that 'Fascism and Bolshevism are phenomena that share critical similarities.'[35] In the more elaborate discussions of the thirties, Fascists argued that the anarcho-syndicalist and anti-statist ideas of Lenin had eroded under the weight of Stalinist practice, and what resulted was a 'political formula that galvanizes the Russian people in the service of industrial development – to nationalist purpose',[36] a political formula that 'transformed Marxist-Leninist principles into their "contraries", that is to say, the ideas that provide the shape and substance of the Fascism of Mussolini'.[37]

Among Marxists, Leon Trotsky spoke of the symmetry between Fascism and Stalinism – a 'deadly similarity' in many of their features.[38] After the Second World War, Bruno Rizzi could only lament that 'that which Fascism consciously sought, [the Soviet Union] involuntarily constructed'.[39]

If one takes these suggestions seriously, they indicate that we are confronted with a typological and classificatory problem of staggering complexity. Is Italian Fascism a member of the class of mass-mobilizing developmental dictatorships under single-party auspices that includes Stalinism, Maoism, and Castroism, as well as an indeterminate number of related political systems? If so, does that make Stalin, Mao and/or Castro fascists? If it does, does such a notion 'strain language well beyond its breaking point', as Peter Wiles suggests?[40]

If we do not wish to strain ordinary language unduly, might the concept 'totalitarianism' serve some purpose? But if such a strategy suggests itself, are we not back where we started? Might not the notion of modernization be effectively incorporated into the classificational system suggested in the works devoted to totalitarianism?

Even if we grant this possibility, we have as yet no suggestion as to how one might characterize the specific subspecific differentiae that distinguish the species or subspecies of such an inclusive class. Do manifest or latent functions of the various political systems differentiate between them? Do they distinguish themselves in terms of their ideological commitments, the class provenience of their leadership or their membership, the economic conditions under which they manifest themselves, or their real and pretended treatment of capitalist institutions and capitalists?

There are very few serious treatments of these issues in the literature. We continue to use the generic term 'fascist' to cover a wide diversity of significantly different social and political movements and extant and/or extinct political systems. Whether we continue to employ the term 'fascist' in such fashion, or whether we subsume such movements and regimes under the more omnibus 'totalitarian', or allude to the more inclusive class as 'fascistic'[41] is a matter of little *cognitive* significance – as long as we understand that we have not yet begun the serious analytic and classificatory task of defining the critical concepts that we wish to employ for the purpose of identifying significant features within our universe of inquiry. Until we satisfy some of these analytic obligations, we can hardly expect to *describe* effectively some of the most important political phenomena of the twentieth century, much less *isolate recurrent regularities* that might permit us to *generalize* over them. If we cannot effectively describe or generalize, it is doubtful that we can hope to articulate compelling theories which might explain them.

Notes

1 Henry A. Turner, Jr., 'Fascism and Modernization', *World Politics*, XXIV (July 1972), pp. 547–64.
2 Cf. Cyril E. Black, *The Dynamics of Modernization* (New York, 1967), particularly chap. 1; Guy Hunter, *Modernizing Peasant Societies* (New York, 1969); David E. Apter, *The Politics of Modernization* (Chicago, 1965).
3 Cf. Irving L. Horowitz, *Three Worlds of Development* (New York, 1966); Walt W. Rostow, *The Stages of Economic Growth* (New York, 1960); Robert T. Holt and John E. Turner, *The Political Basis of Economic Development* (Princeton, 1966); A. F. K. Organski, 'Fascism and Modernization', in S. J. Woolf, ed., *The Nature of Fascism* (New York, 1969).
4 Turner op. cit., p. 548.
5 Ibid., p. 556.
6 Ibid., p. 562.
7 Ibid., p. 550.
8 Ibid., p. 555f.
9 Filippo T. Marinetti, 'Fondazione e Manifesto del Futurismo', and 'La nuova religione-morale della velocità', in *Teoria e invenzione futurista* (Verona, 1968), pp. 10, IIIff.
10 Ibid., 'L'uomo moltiplicato e il regno della macchina', p. 255ff.
11 'Per una Società di Protezione delle Macchine', in Luigi Scrivo, ed., *Sintesi del futurismo: storia e documenti* (Rome, 1968), p. 186f.
12 Marinetti op. cit., 'Al di là del Comunismo', p. 419f.
13 James Joll, *Three Intellectuals in Politics* (New York, 1960), p. 135.
14 Enrico Corradini, 'Nazionalismo e socialismo', in *Discorsi Politici* (Florence, 1924), pp. 214–29.
15 Ibid., 'Le nazioni proletarie e il nazionalismo', p. 180ff; 'Nazionalismo e democrazia', p. 161; 'Per la guerra d'Italia', p. 302; and 'Commemorazione dei soldati morti in battaglia', p. 314.
16 Ibid., 'Diritti e doveri nazionali dei produttori', pp. 341, 354f.
17 Ibid., 'Politica ed economia della Nazione e delle classi', pp. 376f, 388f.
18 Benito Mussolini, '"Tu quoque," Jouhaux?' *Opera Omnia* (Florence, 1953), XI, p. 357f.
19 Ibid., XII, 'Il sindacalismo nazionale: per rinascere!', pp. 11–14.
20 Ibid., 'Nel mondo sindacale italiano: rettifiche di tiro', p. 250.
21 Ibid., 'Atto di nascita del fascismo', pp. 325, 327; and 'La politica nazionale: primo squillo', p. 223.
22 Ibid., XIII, 'Per l'intesa e per l'azione: fra gli interventisi di sinistra', p. 254.
23 Ibid., XV, 'Discorso di Cremona', p. 186.
24 'Per una economia di massima produzione', Postulati del programma fascista (May 1920), in Renzo De Felice, *Mussolini il rivoluzionario* (Turin, 1965), p. 747.
25 Giovanni Ansaldo, 'Il fascismo e la piccola borghesia tecnica', in Costanzo Casucci, ed., *Il fascismo* (Bologna, 1961), pp. 208, 210; emphasis added.
26 Ludovico Garruccio, *L'industrializzazione tra nazionalismo e rivoluzione* (Bologna, 1969), p. 105f.
27 Cf. Sergio Panunzio, *Che cosa è il fascismo?* (Milan, 1924), p. 24.
28 Nazareno Mezzetti, *Mussolini e la questione sociale* (Rome, 1931), p. 27.
29 Gioacchino Volpe, *History of the Fascist Movement* (Rome, 1936), p. 48.
30 Cf. Volpe, *Lo sviluppo storico del fascismo* (Rome, 1928), *passim*.

31 Cf. William Welk, *Fascist Economic Policy* (Cambridge, 1938), pp. 191–205;
    Antonio S. Benni, 'Lo sviluppo industriale dell'Italia fascista', in Tomaso
    Sillani, ed., *Lo Stato Mussoliniano* (Rome, 1930), pp. 97–105, updated as
    'The Industrial Growth of Fascist Italy', in T. Sillani, ed., *What is Fascism
    and Why?* (New York, 1931), pp. 281–9.

32 Angus Maddison, *Economic Growth in the West* (New York, 1964), Appen-
    dices A, E, H, I.

33 Organski op. cit., pp. 37ff. Cf. Charles F. Delzell, *Mediterranean Fascism,
    1919–1945* (New York, 1970), p. 138.

34 Roland Sarti, *Fascism and the Industrial Leadership in Italy, 1919–1940*
    (Berkeley, 1971), p. 122f. Cf. Garruccio, op. cit., p. 140.

35 Sergio Panunzio, *Lo stato fascista* (Bologna, 1925), p. 145ff.

36 Agostino Nasti, 'L'Italia, il bolcevismo, la Russia', *Critica Fascista*, xv (March
    15, 1937), p. 162.

37 Tomaso Napolitano, 'Il "fascismo" di Stalin ovvero l'U.R.S.S. e noi', *Critica
    Fascista* xv (October 1, 1937), p. 397.

38 Leon Trotsky, *The Revolution Betrayed* (New York, 1937), p. 278.

39 Bruno Rizzi, *Le lezioni dello Stalinismo* (Rome, 1962), p. 38.

40 Peter Wiles, 'Comment on Tucker's "Movement-Regimes"', *American Politi-
    cal Science Review*, LV (June 1961), p. 293.

41 In my *The Fascist Persuasion in Radical Politics* (Princeton, 1974), I have used
    the terms 'fascist' and 'fascistic' to cover the entire class of mass-mobilizing,
    developmental dictatorships under single-party auspices with the conviction
    that this use will outrage most of my colleagues. I am hopeful that such usage
    will also provoke my colleagues to reconsider some intuitive and common-
    sensical ordinary language classifications that suggest that the terms 'fascist'
    and 'Marxist' refer to mutually exclusive classes.

12

A politico-cultural revolution*

GEORGE L. MOSSE

In our century two revolutionary movements have made their mark upon
Europe: that originally springing from Marxism, and the fascist revolution. The various forms of Marxism have occupied historians and political
scientists for many decades, and only now is the study of fascism catching
up. Even so, because of the war and the fascist record in power, fascism
has remained synonymous with oppression and domination; it is alleged
that it was without ideas of its own, but merely a reaction against other
more progressive movements such as liberalism, or socialism. Scholarship

* Extract from 'Towards a General Theory of Fascism', in G. L. Mosse, *International
Fascism: New Thoughts and New Approaches* (New York, Howard Fertig, 1979), pp.
1–6, 15–17, 25–7, 36–41.

concerning fascism has been singularly vulnerable to subjective viewpoints and more often than not has consequently been used to fight contemporary polemical battles.

In a justified reaction against the fascist stereotype, recent scholarship has been suspicious of general theories of fascism. As many local and regional studies show, on one level it may have presented a kaleidoscope of contradictory attitudes – nevertheless, these attitudes were based upon common assumptions. To be sure, any general theory of fascism must be no more than a hypothesis which fits most of the facts. We shall attempt to bring together some of the principal building blocks for such a general theory – there seem to be enough of them to construct at least a provisional dwelling. Germany and Italy will dominate the discussion, as the experience of European fascism was largely dominated by Italian fascism and German National Socialism. The word 'fascism' will be used without qualification when both these movements are meant. From time to time we shall also refer to various other fascisms in Europe, but only specifically or as subsidiary examples.

We can best develop a general theory of fascism through a critique of past attempts to accomplish this task. Some historians have seen an integral connection between bolshevism and fascism. Both were totalitarian regimes and, as such, dictatorships based upon the exlusive claim to leadership by one political party.[1] Although such an equation was often politically motivated, it was not, as its opponents claimed, merely a child of the cold war.

Both movements were based on the ideal, however distorted, of popular sovereignty. This meant rejection of parliamentary government and representative institutions on behalf of a democracy of the masses in which the people directly governed themselves. The leader symbolized the people, he expressed the 'general will' – but such a democracy meant that, instead of representative assemblies, a new secular religion mediated between people and leaders, providing, at the same time, an instrument of social control over the masses. It was expressed on the public level through official ceremonies, festivals, and not least, imagery, and on a private level through control over all aspects of life by the dictates of the single political party. This system was common in various degrees to fascist and bolshevist movements.

The danger inherent in subsuming both systems under the concept of totalitarianism is that it may serve to disguise real differences, not only between bolshevism and fascism, but also among the different forms of fascism. Moreover, the contention that these theories really compare fascism not with Lenin's bolshevism but with Stalinism seems fully justified. Indeed, totalitarianism as a static concept often veils the development of both fascism and bolshevism. In Soviet Russia, for example, the kind of public ceremonies and festivals which mark the fascist political style were tried early in the regime but then dropped, and not resumed until after the Second World War, when they came to fulfil the same functions as they had earlier for fascism. In 1966 *Pravda* wrote that rallies, ceremonial processions, speeches and concerts gave emotional strength to the political commitment of the people.[2] Fascism, too, did not remain static, although even some critics of totalitarian theory apparently see it as unchanging. There is, for example, a difference between fascism as a political movement and as a government in power.

Theories of totalitarianism have placed undue emphasis upon the supposedly monolithic leadership cult. Here again, this was introduced into the Soviet Union by Stalin and not Lenin. Even within fascism the cult of the leader varied: Piero Melograni tells us here how the cult of 'Il Duce' and fascism were not identical, and that it was 'Mussolinianism' which won the people's allegiance. In Germany there is no discernible difference between Hitlerism and National Socialism.

More serious is the contention, common to most theories of totalitarianism, that the leader manipulates the masses through propaganda and terror: that free volition is incompatible with totalitarian practice.[3] The term propoganda, always used in this context, leads to a misunderstanding of the fascist cults and their essentially organic and religious nature. In times of crisis they provided many millions of people with a more meaningful involvement than representative parliamentary government – largely because they were not themselves a new phenomenon, but were instead based upon an older and still lively tradition of popular democracy which had always opposed European parliaments.

Even the widespread notion that fascism ruled through terror must be modified. Rather, it was built upon a fragile consensus. Tangible successes, the ability to compromise and to go slow, combined with the responsive chord struck by fascist culture, integrated Italians and Germans into this consensus, which undoubtedly was more solid in Germany than Italy. Hitler, after all, shared a volkish faith with his fellow Germans, and his tangible successes in domestic and foreign policy were much more spectacular than Mussolini's achievements.

Terror increased with the continued survival of the regimes, for disillusionment with fascism in power could easily lead to unrest. By the time many earlier supporters woke up to fascist reality it was too late to resist, except by martyrdom. Mass popular consensus during the first years of fascism allowed it to develop an effective secret police – outside and above regular channels and procedures[4] – as well as the special courts needed to reinforce its actions. This was easier in the Soviet Union since the revolution had destroyed the old legal framework; while in Germany and Italy, traditional safeguards paradoxically continued to exist and even to be used side by side with arbitrary action. In Germany, judges freed some concentration camp inmates as late as 1936.

Terror must not then be treated as a static concept, but as something which develops in intensity. Not only must historical development be taken into account, but also the existence and extent of a consensus, which, although differing in scope in the three so-called totalitarian nations, did exist at some time in each of them.

Despite all these caveats, both bolshevists and fascists reached back into the antiparliamentary and antipluralistic traditions of the nineteenth century in order to face the collapse of social, economic and political structures in their nations during and after the First World War. Totalitarianism was new only as a form of legitimate government: it derived from a long tradition; otherwise it would not have received such immediate mass support. Beginning its modern history with the French Revolution, that tradition continued to inform both the nationalism and the quest for social justice of the nineteenth century. Even if Jacob Talmon's concept of 'totalitarian democracy' rests, as some have claimed, upon a misreading of the Enlightenment,[5] men like Robespierre and Saint-Just shared in such misconceptions. Rousseau's 'general will', his exaltation of 'the people', was bent by the Jacobins into a dictatorship in which the people worshipped themselves through public festivals and symbols (such as the goddess of reason), where religious enthusiasm was transferred to civic rites.[6]

The distinction between private and public life was eradicated, just as totalitarian regimes would later attempt to abolish such differences. Public allegiance, through active participation in the national cults, was the road to survival, and as, for example, the Jacobins used dress as an outward sign of true inner allegiance (the revolutionary cap and trousers instead of breeches), so fascists and bolshevists integrated various uniforms into their systems. Nationalist movements during the nineteenth century carried on these traditions, even if at times they attempted to compromise with liberal values. The workers' movement, though most of it was in fact wedded to parliamentary democracy, stressed outward symbols of unity (as in the serried ranks and Sunday dress of May Day parades), massed flags, and the clenched fist salute. Italy was less influenced by this legacy, but it also played a part in the fight for national unity. At the turn of the century, the radical left and the radical right were apt to demand control of the whole man and not just a political piece of him.

Bolshevism and fascism attempted to mobilize the masses, to substitute modern mass politics for pluralistic and parliamentary government. Indeed, parliamentary government found it difficult to cope with the crises of the post-war world and abdicated without a struggle, not only in Germany and Italy, but also in Portugal and, where it had existed immediately after the war, in the nations of Eastern Europe. The fascists helped the demise of parliamentary government, but that it succumbed so readily points to deep inherent structural and ideological problems – though, indeed, few representative governments have withstood the pressures of modern economic, political and social crises, especially when these coincided with defeat in war and unsatisfied national aspirations.[7] Wherever inter-war totalitarian governments came to power they merely toppled regimes ripe for the plucking; this holds good for Russia as well as for Germany and Italy. But unlike bolshevism, fascism never had to fight a civil war on its road to power: Mussolini marched on Rome in the comfort of a railway carriage, and Hitler simply presented himself to the German President. Certainly representative government and liberal politics allowed individual freedom to breathe, but totalitarianism cannot be condemned without taking the collapse of existing parliaments and social structures into account. We must not look at a historical movement mainly from the viewpoint of our political predilections, lest we falsify historical necessity.

If some historians have used the model of totalitarianism in order to analyse fascism, others, and they are in the majority, have used the model of the 'good revolution'.[8] The French, American, and especially the Russian Revolutions, so it is said, led to the progress of mankind, while fascism was an attempt to stop the clock, to maintain old privilege against the demands of the new classes as represented by the proletariat. In reality, fascism was itself a revolution, seizing power by using twentieth-century methods of communication and control, and replacing an old with a new elite. (In this sense, National Socialism brought about a more fundamental change than Italian fascism, where new and traditional elites coexisted to a greater extent.) Economic policy was subordinated to the political goals of fascism, but in Germany, at least, this did not preclude nationalization (for example, the so-called 'Hermann Goering Steel Works'). By and large, however, fascism worked hand in hand with the larger industrial enterprises.

Yet one-sided emphasis upon economic factors or upon the proletariat obscures our view of the revolutionary side of fascism. Fascism condemned the French Revolution and yet, at least in its beginnings, was a direct descendant of the Jacobin political style[9] Above all, the fascist revolution saw itself as a 'Third Force' rejecting both 'materialistic marxism' and 'finance capitalism' in the name of an idealism intended to transcend the unpalatable capitalist and materialist present. This was the revolutionary tradition within which fascism worked, but it was not alone in such an aim; in the post-war world, many left-wing intellectuals rejected both Marxist orthodoxy and capitalism. Unlike the fascists, however, they sought to transcend both by emphasis on the triumphant goodness of man once capitalism was abolished. [. . .]

Fascism retreated instead into the nationalist mystique. The crucial role which the war experience played in National Socialism is well enough known. The war was 'a lovely dream' and a 'miracle of achievement', as one Nazi children's book put it. Any death in war was a hero's death and thus the true fulfilment of life.[10] There was no doubt here about the 'greatness and necessity of war'.[11] In Mussolini's hands, this myth had even greater force because of the absence of a truly coherent volkish ideology in Italy. The fascist struggle was a continuation of the war experience. But here, as in Germany, the glorification of struggle was linked to wartime camaraderie and put forward as an example to end class divisions within the nation. 'Not class war but class solidarity' reigned in face of death, wrote an Italian socialist in the last months of the war: it was not a conflict among potentates or capitalists but a necessity in defence of the people. Historical materialism was dead.[12]

The *élan* of the battlefield was transformed into activism at home. The *fasci* and the German storm troopers regarded their post-war world as an enemy which as patriotic shock troops they must destroy. Indeed, the leaders of these formations were in large part former front-line officers: Roehm, the head of the SA; Codreanu, founder of the Iron Guard; De Bono in Italy and Szalasi in Hungary – to give only a few examples. But this activism was tamed by the 'magic' of the leadership of which Gustav Le Bon had written towards the end of the nineteenth century. Among the returned veterans it was even more easily controllable, for they desperately sought comradeship and leadership, not only because of the war experience, but also to counteract their sense of isolation within a nation which had not lived up to their expectations.

The revolutionary tradition of the 'Third Force' contained legendary ingredients essential to this taming process: stress upon the national past and the mystical community of the nation, emphasis upon that middle-class respectability which proved essential for political success. The 'cult element' to which we have referred earlier gave it direction by channelling attention towards the eternal verities which must never be forgotten. Activism there must be, enthusiasm was essential, but it had to focus upon the leader who would direct it into the proper 'eternal' channels.

The liturgical element must be mentioned again, for the 'eternal verities' were purveyed and reinforced through the endless repetition of slogans, choruses, symbols and participation in mass ceremony. These are the techniques which went into the taming of the revolution and which made fascism a new religion with rites long familiar through centuries of religious observance. Fascist mass meetings seemed something new, but in reality contained predominantly traditional elements in technique as well as in ideology.

To be sure, this process did not always work. The youthful enthusiasm which reigned at the outset of the movement was apt to be disappointed with its course. Italy, where fascism lasted longest, provides the best example, for the danger point came with the second fascist generation. There the young men of the 'class of 35' wanted to return to the beginnings of the movement, to its activism and its war on alienation – in short, to construct the fascist utopia. By 1936 they had formed a resistance movement within Italian fascism which stressed that 'open-endedness' the revolution had at first seemed to promise: to go to 'the limits of fascism where all possibilities are open'.[13] Similar signs can be discerned as Nazism developed, but here the SS managed to capture the activist spirit. Had it not been for the war, Hitler might well have had difficulty with the SS, which thought of itself as an activist and spartan elite. But then fascism never had a chance to grow old except in Italy: given the ingredients which went into the revolution, old age might have presented the movement with a severe crisis.

But in the last resort taming was always combined with activism, traditionalism inevitably went hand in hand with a nostalgic revolution. Both Hitler and Mussolini disliked drawing up party programmes, for this smacked of 'dogmatism'. Fascism stressed 'movement' – Hitler called his party a 'Bewegung', and Mussolini for some time favored Marinetti's futurism as an artistic and literary form which stressed both movement and struggle. All European fascism gave the impression that the movement was open-ended, a continuous Nietzschean ecstasy. But in reality definite limits were provided to this activism by the emphasis upon nationalism, sometimes racism, and the longing for a restoration of traditional morality. The only variety of fascism of which this is not wholly true is to be found among the intellectuals in France. There a man like Drieu La Rochelle continued to exalt the 'provisional', the idea that all existing reality can be destroyed in one moment.[14] Elsewhere that reality was 'eternal', and activism was directed into destroying the existing order so that the eternal verity of *Volk* or nation could triumph, and with it the restoration of traditional morality. [. . .]

Within its basic presuppositions of revolution, nationalism and the war experience, fascism contained two rhythms: the amoeba-like absorption of ideas from the mainstream of popular thought and culture, countered by the urge towards activism and its taming. Both were set within the nationalist myth, and the whole gave the proper attitude towards life. Fascism attempted to cater to everything held dear, to give new meaning to daily routine and to offer salvation without risk. The fact that Adolf Hitler shared in popular tastes and longings, that in this sense he was a man of the people, is one vital ingredient of his success. Mussolini entertained intellectual pretensions which Hitler never claimed, nor did he share the tastes of the people, perhaps because in Italy, popular culture was diversified in a nation with stronger regional traditions and ties than in Germany.

The frequent contention that fascist culture diverged from the mainstream of European culture cannot be upheld. On the contrary, it absorbed most of what had proved to have the greatest mass appeal in the past. In fact, it positioned itself much more in this mainstream than socialism, which tried to educate and elevate the tastes of the worker. Fascism made no such attempt: it accepted the common man's preferences and went on to direct them to its own ends. Moreover, the lack of original ideas was not a disadvantage, as many historians have implied: far from that, originality does not lead to success in an age of democratic mass politics. The synthesis which fascism attempted between activism and order, revolution and the absorption of past traditions, proved singularly successful. To be sure, Marxism, conservatism and liberalism made original contributions to European thought. But then they underwent a long period of gestation, and by the time they became politically important movements, they had founded their own traditions. Fascism had no time to create a tradition for itself: like Hitler, it was in a hurry, confronted with an old order which seemed about to fall. Those who did not strike at once were sure to be overtaken by other radicals of the left or right.

Yet fascism would never have worked without the tangible successes achieved by fascist regimes; social and economic factors are not to be ignored. But the pre-eminence of the cultural factors already discussed is certainly the other half of the dialectic, and without them the ways in which the men and women of those times were motivated cannot be properly understood.

What, then, of the fascist utopia? It was certainly a part of the fascist myth. The fairy tale would come true once the enemies had been defeated. The happy ending was assured, but first men must 'overcome' – the mystical ingredient of National Socialism was strong here; and in Italy the ideal of continuing the wartime sacrifice was stressed. The happy end would bring about the 'new Rome' or the Third German Empire, infused with middle-class virtues: a combination of the ancient past and the nineteenth-century bourgeois ideal. The new fascist man would usher in this Utopia – and he already existed, exemplified by the Führer and the Duce. Eventually, it was implied, all Germans or Italians would approach their example.

The new fascist man provided the stereotype for all fascist movements. He was, naturally, masculine: fascism represented itself as a society of males, a result of the struggle for national unity which had created fellow-ships such as 'Young Italy', or the German fraternities and gymnastic societies. Moreover, the cult of masculinity of the *fin de siècle*, which Nietzsche himself so well exemplified, contributed its influence. More immediately, a male society continued into the peace the wartime camar-aderie of the trenches: that myth of the war experience so important in all fascism. The masculine ideal did not remain abstract, but was personified in ideals of male strength and beauty.

Such an ideal my be vague, as in a children's book where the Duce is described as being as beautiful as the sun, as good as the light and as strong as the hurricane.[15] It is less vague in sculptures of the Duce as a Renaissance prince or, more often, as the Emperor Augustus. In addition, the innumerable pictures of the Duce harvesting, running, boxing – often bare-chested – portrayed the image of a strong and invulnerable masculinity. Yet such stereotypes were not all-pervasive; they were absent even at such events as the exhibition honouring the 10th anniversary of the March on Rome (1933).[16] The inner characteristics of this new man were more clearly defined: athletic, persevering, filled with self-denial and the spirit of sacrifice. At the same time, the new fascist man must be energetic, courageous and laconic.[17] The ideal fascist was the very opposite of muddle-headed, talkative, intellectualizing liberals and socialists – the exhausted, tired old men of the old order. Italian fascism's dream of an age-old masculine ideal has not indeed vanished from our own time. [. . .]

The building blocks for a general theory of fascism now seem to lie before us. Fascism was everywhere an 'attitude towards life', based upon a national mystique which might vary from nation to nation. It was also a revolution attempting to find a 'Third Way' between Marxism and capitalism, but still seeking to escape concrete economic and social change by a retreat into ideology: the 'revolution of the spirit' of which Mussolini spoke; or Hitler's 'German revolution'. However, it encouraged activism, the fight against the existing order of things. Both in Germany and Italy fascism's chance at power came during conditions of near civil war. But this activism had to be tamed, fascism had to become respectable: for activism was in conflict with the bourgeois desire for law and order, with those middle-class virtues which fascism promised to protect against the dissolving spirit of modernity. It also clashed with the desires of a head of state who represented the old order and who could not be ignored. While Hitler was freed from this constraint by President von Hindenburg's death in 1934, Mussolini always had to report to King Victor Emmanuel. The result was that activism had to exist side by side with the effort to tame it. This was one of the chief problems faced by Hitler and Mussolini before their rise to power and in the early years of their rule.

Fascism could create a consensus because it annexed and focused those hopes and longings which informed diverse political and intellectual movements of the previous century. Like a scavenger, fascism scooped up scraps of romanticism, liberalism, the new technology and even socialism, to say nothing of a wide variety of other movements lingering from the nineteenth into the twentieth century. But it threw over all these the mantle of a community conceived as sharing a national past, present and future – a community which was not enforced but 'natural', 'genuine', and with its own organic strength and life, analogous to nature. The tree became the favorite symbol, but the native landscape or the ruins of the past were also singled out as exemplifying on one level the national community, a human collectivity represented by the fascist party.

Support of fascism was not built merely upon appeal to vested interests. Social and economic factors proved crucial in the collapse after the First

World War, and in the Great Depression the social and economic successes of fascism gave body to fascist theories. But, and this seems equally crucial, political choices are determined by people's actual perception of their situation, their hopes and longings, the utopia towards which they strive. The fascist 'attitude towards life' was suffused by cultural factors through which, as we have attempted to show, the movement presented itself: it was the only mass movement between the wars which could claim to have a largely cross-class following.

In the end, the fascist dream turned out to be a nightmare. It is not likely that Europe will repeat the fascist or the National-Socialist experience. The fragments of our Western cultural and ideological past which fascism used for its own purposes still lie ready to be formed into a new synthesis, even if in a different way. Most ominously, nationalism, the basic force which made fascism possible in the first place, not only remains, but is growing in strength – still the principal integrative force among peoples and nations. Those ideals of mass politics upon which fascism built its political style are very much alive, ready to absorb and exploit the appropriate myths. The danger of some kind of authoritarianism is always present, however changed from earlier forms or from its present worldwide manifestations. [. . .]

Speculations about the future depend upon an accurate analysis of the past. This essay is meant to provide a general framework for a discussion of fascism, in the hope of leading us closer to that historical reality without which we cannot understand the past or the present.

Notes

1 The best recent discussion of fascism and totalitarian doctrine is Karl Dietrich Bracher, *Zeitgeschichtliche Kontroversen, um Faschismus, Totalitarismus, Demokratie* (Munich, Piper, 1976).
2 Aryeh L. Unger, *The Totalitarian Party, Party and People in Nazi Germany and Soviet Russia* (Cambridge, Cambridge University Press, 1934), pp. 189, 202.
3 Ibid., 1, p. 264.
4 Cf. George L. Mosse (ed.), *Police Forces in History* (London and Beverley Hills, Sage Publications, 1975).
5 J. L. Talmon, *The Rise of Totalitarian Democracy* (Boston, Beacon Press, 1952); and the criticism in Peter Gay, *The Party of Humanity* (New York, W. W. Norton, 1964), pp. 179–81.
6 Mona Ozouf, *La Fête révolutionnaire 1789–1799* (Paris, Gallimard, 1976), p. 22.
7 For a more thorough discussion of the point see George L. Mosse, *The Nationalization of the Masses* (New York, Howard Fertig, 1975) and the unjustly forgotten Harold J. Laski, *Reflections on the Revolution of our Time* (New York, Allen & Unwin, 1943), not for his analysis of fascism but on the weakness of parliamentary government.
8 The term 'good revolution' is Karl Dietrich Bracher's, op. cit., p. 68.

9 Renzo De Felice, *Fascism* (New Brunswick, New Jersey, Transaction Books, 1976), p. 24.

10 Peter Hasubeck, *Das Deutsche Lesebuch in der Zeit des Nationalsozialismus* (Hannover, 1972), pp. 77, 79.

11 Ernst Jünger, Vorwort, *Das Antlitz des Weltkrieges*, ed. Ernst Jünger (Berlin, 1930).

12 Aldo Marinelli, quoted in Emilio Gentile, *Le Origini dell' Ideologia Fascista* (Bari, Laterza, 1974), p. 92.

13 Ruggero Zangrandi, *Il lungo viaggio attraverso il fascismo* (Milan, Garzanti, 1948); for a recent discussion of this revolt of youth see Michael Ledeen, *Universal Fascism* (New York, 1972).

14 Drieu La Rochelle, *Socialisme Fasciste* (Paris, Gallimard, 1943), p. 72.

15 Schkem Gremigni, *Duce d'Italia* (Milan, Istituto di Propaganda d'Arte e Cultura, 1927), p. 116.

16 E.g., *Ausstellung der Faschistischen Revolution, erste Zehnjahrfeier des Marsches auf Rom* (1933). Typically enough, the official poster for the exhibition featured soldiers from the First World War.

17 Donino Roncará, *Saggi sull' Educazione Fascista* (Bologna, 1938), p. 61.

13

*A form of revolutionary ultra-nationalism**

STANLEY G. PAYNE

The common characteristics of fascist movements were grounded in specific philosophical and moral beliefs, a new orientation in political culture and ideology, generally common political goals, a distinctive set of negations, common aspects of style, and somewhat novel modes of organization – always with notable differences in the specific character of these new forms and ideas among the various movements. To arrive at a criterial definition applicable to all the inter-war fascist movements *sensu stricto*, it becomes necessary therefore to identify common points of ideology and goals, the fascist negations, and also special common features of style and organization.[1] The descriptive typology in table 13.1 is suggested merely as an analytic device for purposes of comparative analysis and definition. It does not propose to establish a rigidly reified category but a wide-spectrum description that can identify a variety of differing allegedly fascist movements while still setting them apart as a group from other kinds of revolutionary or nationalist movements. Individual movements might

* Extract from the Introduction to S. G. Payne, *A History of Fascism, 1914–1945*, (Madison, Wisconsin, The University of Wisconsin Press, 1996; London, UCL Press, 1996), pp. 6–14.

Table 13.1 Typological description of fascism

A. Ideology and Goals:
    Espousal of an idealist, vitalist, and voluntaristic philosophy, normally
    involving the attempt to realize a new modern, self-determined, and secular
    culture
    Creation of a new nationalist authoritarian state not based on traditional
    principles or models
    Organization of a new highly regulated, multiclass, integrated national
    economic structure, whether called national corporatist, national socialist,
    or national syndicalist.
    Positive evaluation and use of, or willingness to use, violence and war
    The goal of empire, expansion, or a radical change in the nation's
    relationship with other powers.

B. The Fascist Negations:
    Antiliberalism
    Anticommunism
    Anticonservatism (though with the understanding that fascist groups were
    willing to undertake temporary alliances with other sectors, most commonly
    with the right)

C. Style and Organization:
    Attempted mass mobilization with militarization of political relationships
    and style and with the goal of a mass party militia
    Emphasis on aesthetic structure of meetings, symbols, and political liturgy,
    stressing emotional and mystical aspects
    Extreme stress on the masculine principle and male dominance, while
    espousing a strongly organic view of society
    Exaltation of youth above other phases of life, emphasizing the conflict of
    generations, at least in effecting the initial political transformation
    Specific tendency toward an authoritarian, charismatic, personal style of
    command, whether or not the command is to some degree initially elective

then be understood to have also possessed further doctrines, characteristics, and goals of major importance to them that did not necessarily contradict the common features but were added to them or went beyond them. Similarly, an individual movement might differ somewhat with regard to one or two individual criteria but nonetheless conform generally to the overall description or ideal type.

The term *fascist* is used not merely for the sake of convention but because the Italian movement was the first significant force to exhibit those characteristics as a new type and was for a long time the most influential. It constituted the type whose ideas and goals were the most readily generalized, particularly when contrasted with racial National Socialism.

It has often been held that fascism had no coherent doctrine or ideology, since there was no single canonical or seminal source and since major aspects of fascist ideas were contradictory and nonrationalist. Yet fascist movements did possess basic philosophies that were eclectic in character and in fact, as Roger Eatwell has pointed out, represented a kind of synthesis of concepts from varied sources.[2] Griffin reminds us that all ideology contains basic contradictions and nonrational or irrational elements, usually tending toward utopias that cannot ever be realized in practice. Fascist ideology was more eclectic and nonrational than some others, but these qualities did not prevent its birth and limited development.[3]

The extreme nationalism of each fascist movement inevitably produced certain distinct or idiosyncratic features in each group, so that every fascist organization tended to differ more from its fellows in other countries than, for example, any given Communist party in comparison with other Communist groups. Different national emphases did not, however, blur a common physiognomy based on the common fascist beliefs and values.

Fascist ideology, unlike that of most of the right, was in most cases secular but, unlike the ideology of the left and to some extent of liberals, was based on vitalism and idealism and the rejction of economic determinism, whether of Manchester or Marx. The goal of metaphysical idealism and vitalism was the creation of a new man, a new style of culture that achieved both physical and artistic excellence and that prized courage, daring, and the overcoming of previously established limits in the growth of a superior new culture which engaged the whole man. Fascism was not, however, nihilistic, as many critics charged. Rather, it rejected many established values – whether of left, right, or center – and was willing to engage in acts of wholesale destruction, sometimes involving the most ghastly mass murder, as 'creative destruction' to usher in a new utopia of its making, just as Communists murdered millions in the name of an egalitarian utopia.

Fascist ideas have often been said to stem from opposition to the Enlightenment or the 'ideas of 1789', when in fact they were a direct by-product of aspects of the Enlightenment, derived specifically from the modern, secular, Promethean concepts of the eighteenth century. The essential divergence of fascist ideas from certain aspects of modern culture lay more precisely in the fascist rejection of rationalism, materialism, and egalitarianism – replaced by philosophical vitalism and idealism and the metaphysics of the will, all of which are also intrinsically modern. Fascists aspired to recover what they considered the true sense of the natural and of human nature (themselves originally eighteenth-century concepts) in opposition to the reductionist culture of modern materialism and prudential egotism.

Fascists strongly reflected the preoccupation with decadence in society and culture that had been growing since the mid-nineteenth century. They believed that decadence could only be overcome through a revolutionary new culture led by new elites, who would replace the old elites of liberalism and conservatism and of the left.

The free man of developed will and determination would be self-assertive like few before him, but he would also be able to transvalue and go beyond himself and would not hesitate to sacrifice himself for the sake of those ideals. Such modern formulations rejected nineteenth-century materialism but did not represent anything that could be called a reversion to the traditional moral and spiritual values of the Western world before the eighteenth century. They represented a specific effort to achieve a modern, normally atheistic or agnostic form of transcendence and not, in Nolte's words, any 'resistance to transcendence'. Griffin has aptly observed that fascist doctrine encouraged self-assertion and self-transcendence at the same time.

One key modality in which fascist movements seemed to parallel certain religious groups was the projection of a sense of messianic mission, typical of utopian revolutionary movements. Each had the goal of realizing a new status and mode of being for its nation, but the fascist ambitions typically paralleled those of other secular revolutionary movements in functioning within an immanent, this-worldly framework, rather than the other-worldly transcendance of religious groups.

Fundamental to fascism was the effort to create a new 'civic religion' of the movement and of its structure as a state. This would build a system of all-encompassing myths that would incorporate both the fascist elite and their followers and would bind together the nation in a new common faith and loyalty. Such civic religion would displace preceding structures of belief and relegate supernatural religion to a secondary role, or to none at all.

This orientation has sometimes been called political religion, but, though there were specific examples of religious or would-be 'Christian fascists', fascism basically presupposed a post-Christian, postreligious, secular, and immanent frame of reference. Its own myth of secular transcendance could earn adherents only in the absence or weakness of traditional concepts of spiritual and otherworldly transcendence, for fascism sought to re-create nonrationalist myth structures for those who had lost or rejected a traditional mythic framework. Ideologically and politically, fascism could be successful only to the extent that such a situation existed.

Fascists were even more vague about the shape of their ultimate utopia than were members of most other revolutionary groups, because their reliance on vitalism and dynamism produced a mode of 'permanent revolution' that almost by definition could take no simple, clear final form. They sought nothing so seemingly clear-cut as the classless society of Marxists or the stateless society of anarchists but rather an expansive nationalism built of dynamic tension ever seeking new expression. This generated an inherent irrationality that was itself one of the greatest handicaps, if not the greatest, that fascist movements had to overcome.

Much of the confusion surrounding interpretation of the fascist movements stems from the fact that only in a very few instances did they succeed in passing to the stage of governmental participation and only in the case of Germany did a regime in power succeed in carrying out the broader implications of a fascist doctrine, and even then incompletely. It is thus difficult to generalize about fascist systems or the fascist doctrine of the state, since even the Italian variant was seriously compromised. All that can be established with clarity is that fascist aspirations concerning the state were not limited to traditional models such as monarchy, mere personal dictatorship, or even corporatism but posited a radical new secular system, authoritarian and normally republican. Yet to specify the full aim of totalitarianism, as has Nolte, seems unwarranted, for, unlike Leninism, fascist movements never projected a state doctrine with sufficient centralization and bureaucratization to make possible complete totalitarianism. In its original Italian meaning, the sense of the term was more circumscribed. [. . .]

Least clear within fascist ideology was the issue of economic structure and goals, but in fact all fascist movements generally agreed on a basic orientation toward economics. This subordinated economic issues to the state and to the greater well-being of the nation, while retaining the basic principle of private property, held inherent to the freedom and spontaneity of the individual personality, as well as certain natural instincts of competitiveness. Most fascist movements espoused corporatism, beginning with the Italian prototype, but the most radical and developed form of fascism, German National Socialism, explicitly rejected formal corporatism (in part because of the pluralism inherent in it). The frequent contention of Marxist writers that the aim of fascist movements was to prevent economic changes in class relationships is not borne out by the movements themselves, but since no fascist movement ever fully completed the elaboration of a fascist economic system, the point remains theoretical. What fascist movements had in common was the aim of a new functional relationship for the social and economic systems, eliminating the autonomy (or, in some proposals, the existence) of large-scale capitalism and major industry, altering the nature of social status, and creating a new communal or reciprocal productive relationship through new priorities, ideals, and extensive governmental control and regulation. The goal of accelerated economic modernization was often espoused, though in some movements this aspect was muted.

Equally if not more important was the positive evaluation of violence and struggle in fascist doctrine. All revolutionary mass movements have initiated and practiced violence to a greater or lesser degree, and it is probably impossible to carry violence to greater lengths than have some Leninist regimes, practitioners of, in the words of one Old Bolshevik, 'infinite compulsion'. The only unique feature of the fascist relationship to violence was the theoretical evaluation by many fascist movements that violence possessed a certain positive and therapeutic value in and of itself, that a certain amount of continuing violent struggle, along the lines of Sorelianism and extreme Social Darwinism, was necessary for the health of national society.

Fascism is usually said to have been expansionist and imperialist by definition, but this is not clear from a reading of diverse fascist programs. Most were indeed imperialist, but all types of political movements and systems have produced imperialist policies, while several fascist movements had little interest in or even rejected new imperial ambitions. Those which appeared in satisifed national or imperialist states were generally defensive rather than aggressive. All, however, sought a new order in foreign affairs, a new relationship or set of alliances with respect to contemporary states and forces, and a new status for their nations in Europe and the world. Some were frankly oriented toward war, while others merely prized military values but projected no plans for aggression abroad. The latter sometimes sought a place of cultural hegemony or other nonmilitary forms of leadership.

Though fascism generally represented the most extreme form of modern European nationalism, fascist ideology was not necessarily racist in the Nazi sense of mystical, intra-European Nordic racism, nor even necessarily anti-Semitic. Fascist nationalists were all racists only in the general sense of considering blacks or non-Europeans inferior, but they could not espouse Germanicism because most of the movements were not Germanic. Similarly, the Italian and most western European movements were not initially – or in some cases ever – particularly anti-Jewish. All fascist movements were nontheless highly ethnicist as well as extremely nationalist, and thus they held the potential for espousing doctrines of inherent collective superiority for their nations that could form a functional parallel to categorical racism.

The nature of the fascist negations is clear enough. As 'latecomers' (in Linz's phrase), the post-World War I radical nationalist movements that we call fascist had to open new political and ideological space for themselves, and they were unique in their hostility to all the main currents, left, right, and center. This was complicated, however, by the need to find allies in the drive for power. Since such movements emerged mostly in countries with established parliamentary systems and sometimes relied disproportionately on the middle classes, there was no question of their coming to power through coups d'état or revolutionary civil wars, as have Leninist regimes. Though Fascists in Italy established a short-lived tactical alliance with the right center and in Portugal with the anarchist left, their most common allies lay on the right, particularly on the radical authoritarian right, and Italian Fascism as a fully coherent entity became partly defined by its merger with one of the most radical of all right authoritarian movements in Europe, the Italian Nationalist Association (ANI). Such alliances sometimes necessitated tactical, structural, and programmatic concessions. The only two fascist leaders who actually rose to power, Hitler and Mussolini, began their governments as multiparty coalitions, and Mussolini, despite the subsequent creation of a one-party state, never fully escaped the pluralist compromise with which he had begun. Moreover, since the doctrines of the authoritarian right were usually more precise, clear, and articulate – and often more practical – than those of the fascists, the capacity of the former for ideological and programmatic influence was considerable. Nonetheless, the ideas and goals of fascists differed in fundamental respects from those of the new authoritarian right, and the intention to transcend right-wing conservatism was firmly held, though not always clearly realized in practice.

Most fascist movements did not achieve true mass mobilization, but it was nonetheless characteristic that such was their goal, for they always sought to transcend the elitist parliamentary cliquishness of poorly mobilized liberal groups or the sectarian exclusiveness and reliance on elite manipulation often found in the authoritarian right. Together with the drive for mass mobilization went one of the most characteristic features of fascism, its attempt to militarize politics to an unprecedented degree. This was done by making militia groups central to the movement's organization and by using military insignia and terminology in reenforcing the sense of nationalism and constant struggle. Party militia were not invented by fascists but by nineteenth-century liberals (in countries such as Spain and Portugal) and later by the extreme left and radical right (such as Action Française). In inter-war Spain the predominant 'shirt movements' practicing violence were those of the revolutionary left. The initial wave of central European fascism, however, was disproportionately based on World War I veterans and their military ethos. In general, the party militia played a greater role and were developed to a greater extent among fascists than among leftist groups or the radical right.

The novel atmosphere of fascist meetings struck many observers during the 1920s and 1930s. All mass movements employ symbols and various emotive effects, and it might be difficult to establish that the symbolic structure of fascist meetings was entirely different from that of other revolutionary groups. What seemed clearly distinct, however, was the great emphasis on meetings, marches, visual symbols, and ceremonial or liturgical rituals, given a centrality and function in fascist activity which went beyond that found in the left revolutionary movements. The goal was to envelop the participant in a mystique and community of ritual that appealed to the aesthetic and the spiritual sense as well as the political.

This has aptly been called theatrical politics, but it went beyond mere spectacle toward the creation of a normative aesthetics, a cult of artistic and political beauty that built upon the broad diffusion of aesthetic forms and concepts in much of nineteenth-century society to create a 'politics of beauty' and a new visual framework for public life. More than any other new force of the early twentieth century, fascism responded to the contemporary era as above all a 'visual age' to be dominated by a visual culture. This relied on stereotypes of form and beauty drawn from neo-classical concepts as well as key modern images of the nineteenth and early twentieth centuries. Standard motifs included the representation of male and female bodies as the epitome of the real and the natural, almost always in poses that emphasized the dynamic and muscular, even though normally balanced by a posture of discipline and self-control.[4]

Another fundamental characteristic was extreme insistence on what is now termed male chauvinism and the tendency to exaggerate the masculine principle in almost every aspect of activity. All political forces in the era of fascism were overwhelmingly led by and made up of men, and those that paid lip service to women's equality in fact seem to have had little interest in it. Only fascists, however, made a perpetual fetish of the virility of their movement and its program and style, stemming do doubt from the fascist militarization of politics and need for constant struggle. Like that of many rightist and also some leftist groups, the fascist notion of society was organic and always made a place for women, but in that relationship the rights of the male were to enjoy predominance.[5] Griffin has termed this fascist reality a 'radical misogyny or flight from the feminine, manifesting itself in a pathological fear of being engulfed by anything in external reality associated with softness, with dissolution, or the uncontrollable'.[6] No other kind of movement expressed such complete horror at the slightest suggestion of androgyny.

Nearly all revolutionary movements make a special appeal to young people and are disproportionately based on young activists. By the 1920s even moderate parliamentary parties had begun to form their own young people's sections. Fascist exaltation of youth was unique, however, in that it not only made a special appeal to them but also exalted youth over all other generations, without exception, and to a greater degree than any other force based itself on generational conflict. This no doubt stemmed in part from the lateness of fascism and the identification of the established forces, including much of the left, with leaders and members from the older, pre-war generation. It also stemmed in part from the organic concept of the nation and of youth as its new life force, and from the predominance of youth in struggle and militarization. The fascist cult of daring, action, and the will to a new ideal was inherently attuned to youth, who could respond in a way impossible for older, feebler, and more experienced and prudent, or more materialistic, audiences.

Finally, we can agree with Gaetano Mosca, Vilfredo Pareto, and Roberto Michels that nearly all parties and movements depend on elites and leadership but some recognize the fact more explicitly and carry it to greater lengths. The most unique feature of fascism in this regard was the way in which it combined populism and elitism. The appeal to the entire people and nation, together with the attempt to incorporate the masses in both structure and myth, was accompanied by a strong formal emphasis on the role and function of an elite, which was held to be both uniquely fascist and indispensable to any achievement.

Strong authoritarian leadership and the cult of the leader's personality are obviously in no way restricted to fascist movements. Most of them began on the basis of elective leadership – elected at least by the party elite – and this was true even of the National Socialists. There was nonetheless a general tendency to exalt leadership, hierarchy, and subordination, so that all fascist movements came to espouse variants of a *Führerprinzip*, deferring to the creative function of leadership more than to prior ideology or a bureaucratized party line.

If these fundamental characteristics are to be synthesized into a more succinct definition, fascism may be defined as 'a form of revolutionary ultra-nationalism for national rebirth that is based on a primarily vitalist philosophy, is structured on extreme elitism, mass mobilization, and the *Führerprinzip*, positively values violence as end as well as means and tends to normatize war and/or the military virtues'.[7]

Notes

1 The idea of a tripartite definition was first suggested to me by Juan J. Linz at a conference in Bergen, Norway, in June 1974. The specific content is my own.
2 R. Eatwell, 'Towards a New Model of Generic Fascism', *Journal of Theoretical Politics*, 4(1) (April 1992), pp. 1–68; R. Eatwell, 'Fascism', in *Contemporary Political Ideologies*, ed. R. Eatwell and A. Wright (London, Pinter, 1993), pp. 169–91.
3 R. Griffin, *The Nature of Fascism* (London, Pinter, 1991), pp. 26–7.
4 Here I am drawing particularly on George L. Mosse's unpublished paper 'Fascist Aesthetics and Society: Some Considerations' (1993).
5 The term *organic* will be used in this study in a general sense to refer to concepts of society in which its various sectors are held to bear a structured relationship to each other that serves to define and delimit their roles and rights, taking precedence over the identities and rights of individuals.
6 R. Griffin, *Nature of Fascism*, op. cit., p. 198.
7 A different but noncontradictory and partially parallel approach may be found in Eatwell's 'Towards a New Model of Generic Fascism'.

CAUSAL FACTORS IN THE RISE OF FASCISM

Presentation

The question of the causes of fascism is intimately bound up with its definition. In fact some of the major attempts at defining fascism in the past turn out on closer inspection to be little more than schematized versions of causal explanations. This is true of most Marxist definitions, which amount to variations on the theme of how fascism arises from the structural dysfunction of capitalism as an economic, social, and political system, and from the subsequent crisis experienced by at least one section of the 'hegemonic' (ruling) classes, or by the liberal state that represents their interests in 'normal' times. For example, the Comintern declaration of 1933 (Reading 4) sounds at first like that rarity of rarities, a single-sentence definition of fascism – 'the open, terrorist dictatorship of the most reactionary, most chauvinist and most imperialist elements of finance capital'. But, as the ensuing paragraphs demonstrate, it actually tells us nothing about what fascism is at a surface level, i.e. its typical ideology, organizations, and institutions. Instead, the diagnosis of the situation created by Hitler's conquest of state power assumes that it is understandable exclusively in terms of Nazism's alleged 'real' purpose, namely to stave off the revolutionary overthrow of the capitalist system by the proletariat, and in doing so resolve the crisis of that system which forced it to usurp its management from liberalism in the first place.

A particular weakness of definitions of fascism based on the premise that it is no more than a mask for forces of oppression which do not openly declare themselves (e.g. big business, monopoly capital, imperialism, the state) is that they tend to be unconcerned with providing criteria for recognizing it on the basis of its salient characteristics as an empirical reality, or for distinguishing a fascist dictatorial regime of the right from a non-fascist one. The only litmus test implied by the Comintern analysis, for example, is establishing whether or not a 'putative' fascist regime (movements are not even considered) employs terror in order to defend the interests of finance capital, something which can only be inferred since fascism's stated goals will be quite different. The same weakness is inherent in definitions based on the assumption that fascism is a side-product or epiphenomenon of another basic historical process, such as nation-building, the process of modernization, or the growth in 'transcendence', in which case its basic causes are traced to dysfunctions in an allegedly 'normal' transition from traditional society to nationhood, modernity, or 'human emancipation'. Whether fascism is attributed to a crisis within capitalism or within modernization, there is no obvious discriminating criterion built into either approach to prevent fascism being identified with any authoritarian regime which crushes revolutionary socialism and suppresses political and cultural pluralism without abolishing capitalism. This yardstick applies to so many repressive states in the twentieth century that the term 'fascism' undergoes massive 'inflation'.[1]

The 'new consensus' (see Introduction, pages 13–15) implies a more complex causality altogether. If 'fascism is a genus of modern revolutionary "mass" politics' which is 'extremely heterogeneous in its social support'[2] then its causes will be as complex as those of any modern revolution. As historians have made abundantly clear in the case of the French Revolution, this means applying a multi-causal analysis which takes a whole range of factors (social, economic, ideological, cultural, etc.) into account, as well as short-term, medium-term, and long-term processes. Parallels with Europe's '1848 Revolutions' are also striking, since each fascism will have causes and features peculiar to the national context where it arises, making generalization hazardous and calling into question the idea that all the putative fascisms are actually variants of the 'same' revolution. Important consequences flow also from the premise accepted by the new consensus that fascist movements and regimes are attempts to realize strategies and policies derived from a particular genus of ideology, namely one with the 'core myth that a period of perceived national decline and decadence is giving way to one of rebirth and renewal in a post-liberal new order'. Not only does this allow fascist movements and regimes to be distinguished from authoritarian conservative or restorationist ones, which by definition lack any genuinely *revolutionary populist* assault on the status quo even if they are equally hostile to liberalism and socialism, but it suggests that on one level what produces fascism is inextricably bound up with what shapes the peculiar ideological convictions which drive it in any one instance. In other words, any comprehensive causal analysis of generic fascism must take account of the socio-cultural influences which foster its core myths and the psychological predispositions which underpin them, as well as the role played by economics, social structures, institutions, and outstanding personalities in giving rise to individual instances of the genus, factors which are the stock-in-trade of conventional historians.

Clearly this is an enormous subject in its own right. Every level of causation, whether cultural, political, socio-economic, institutional, ideological, and psychological, is not only extraordinarily intricate, but is embedded within academic specialisms on which the amount of published research just in English is vast, and often contains only pockets of fragile consensus on key areas (this is particularly true of theories relating to ideology and psychology, all of which are highly contentious). Nevertheless, for the purposes of this Reader it is hopefully useful at least to give a hint of the way scholars within various disciplines of the human sciences have made significant contributions to understanding different causal factors which, when treated as complementary rather than conflicting, cumulatively build into an explanatory model of fascism entirely compatible with approaching it as a revolutionary form of populist ultra-nationalism driven by a central obsession with decadence and renewal in all spheres of the life of 'the people'.

The first piece (Reading 14), the briefest of extracts from a chapter of impressive depth and breadth written by Zeev Sternhell, establishes one precondition for the rise of fascism, namely the intellectual crisis of the 1890s ('*fin-de-siècle*') in which many of Europe's foremost intellectuals and artists called into question the validity and health of prevailing values as the basis for sustaining Western civilization.

Despite, and in some respects because of, the rampant material and technological dynamism of an age identified with the growing self-confidence of the bourgeoisie, there was a generalized sense within the intelligentsia that the 'West' had lost its way spiritually, a sentiment which either expressed itself in 'cultural pessimism' and a sense of inexorable decline ('decadence'), or in a plethora of visionary schemes for its renewal. It was in this hot-house climate of what is sometimes called 'the revolt against positivism' (though it might more usefully be conceived as 'the revolt against decadence') that vigorous new species of nationalism evolved far removed from both its liberal and ultra-conservative varieties. It was a nationalism at the heart of which was the promise of regeneration and rejuvenation of the 'whole people', a myth central to what would later become fascism. Though Sternhell is idiosyncratic in his insistence that Nazism is not to be treated as a permutation of fascism, and that it was France rather than Italy where fascism first burgeoned as a new ideological synthesis, there is no questioning the major service he has performed to fascist studies by exhaustively analysing the emergence of what could be called a 'nomic crisis' (crisis of values and meaning) and its concomitant, a 'palingenetic' mentality (preoccupation with renewal), in European culture at the end of the nineteenth century, and by showing how the prevalence of that mentality was a precondition to an 'organic nationalism' becoming fused with 'anti-Marxist social-ism' to produce fascism, or at least one of its main varieties.[3]

Juan Linz provides other pieces of the causal jigsaw in the section of his chapter on 'totalitarian and authoritarian regimes' which places fascism in the context of 'authoritarian regimes using mass-mobilization' (Reading 15). Its value lies both in the emphasis on seeing fascism as the by-product of a generalized crisis of democracy provoked by the First World War, and in the theory of generic fascism which he offers, which should hopefully now be familiar territory to those who have studied the texts in Section II. The passage opens with a sketch-map outlining the extremely uneven way the long-term process of democratization challenged the individual parts of the *ancien régime* in Europe. This led in the case of some nation–states to stable liberal systems, but in others to societies where the democratization of state institutions and the population at large was too shallow and flawed to resist the structural crises triggered by the First World War and its aftermath. However, the degree of liberalism which *had* been achieved precluded the installation of crude military or totalitarian dictatorships on Latin American or African lines, since every authoritarian regime which attempted to solve the state crisis had to maintain at least the illusion of populist consensus (e.g. through plebiscites and the creation of a mass single party).

Linz treats fascism on a par with Leninism as far as its revolutionary dynamic is concerned, while in other respects it is its mirror image: the solution which it offered to the crisis of European societies resulting from the First World War was a radically anti-internationalist, anti-liberal, anti-communist, anti-rational form of politics which sought to create a new form of democracy based on the identifica-tion of the leader with the 'people' (conceived emphatically in the sense of the national community rather than class). In considering Fascism as the first successful example of this new type of politics, Linz stresses the role played in preparing the ground both by the manifestations in Italy of the 'revolt against positivism' such as the Futurists (thus corroborating Sternhell's emphasis on its importance to the origins of fascism), and by the particularly acute structural crisis experienced by Italy at the end of the war. He also emphasizes that once the Third Reich was established it became necessary to find another explanation for fascism other than peculiarities of Italian history or economic development, thus highlighting the point at which 'generic fascism' became such a vital but contentious issue for academics (as this Reader testifies over six decades later!). Linz is particularly unimpressed by Marxist theories of fascism, especially the notion that fascists were mere puppets of capitalism, though he is willing to concede that, in practice, fascism did indeed operate in a counter-revolutionary spirit, and depended on the perceived threat of Communism to rally a cadre of paramilitary activists and a mass base.

Linz's own reflections on the nature of fascism can be seen as foreshadowing Payne's 1980 model (see Reading 13), and partially adumbrating the 'new consensus' some twenty years before it crystallized. Its crucial assumptions are that: (a) fascism is to be treated first and foremost not as a regime, but as an ideology which finds its natural expression in a political movement; (b) the fascist negations are crucial to its appeal, and are to be explained as the result of fascism being a late-comer, and thus finding political space[4] extensively occupied by existing ideologies, which forced it to define itself in terms of what it was against; (c) the fascist negatives are also the corollary of the fervent ultra-nationalism which is central to fascism's mythic appeal; (d) the positive appeal of fascism lies precisely in its celebration of the 'national community' and what mythically constitutes it: e.g. work, the paternalistic state, the peasant, the artisan, the soldier; (e) fascism developed a new form of organization based on the movement rather than the party, and demanded a far higher level of activism and enthusiasm from its members than conventional political parties; (f) this new activism was in turn underpinned by a ritual, spectacular style of politics which encouraged mass participation and enthusiasm. As for what regimes fit this model (which Linz specifically refers to as an ideal type[5]), he sees one example in the 'national socialism' of Gregor Strasser, the 'left wing' of Nazism, but not the radically racist 'Hitlerism'. This is an interesting half-way house between the positions adopted by Sternhell, who dismisses Nazism's fascist credentials, and Payne, who accepts them. Linz goes on to show how objective conditions prevented fascism from coming to power elsewhere, though, as in Spain, where the Falange was absorbed by Franco's conservative regime, it might contribute a (pseudo-)populist ingredient to authoritarianism.

Since the Strasserite faction was effectively wiped out in the Röhm Purge of 1934, it would seem that in Linz's eyes only Mussolini's Fascism corresponds to his category of 'fascist-mobilizational authoritarian regimes', for the Third Reich overall does not, while it is unclear which others do.[6] This is symptomatic of a perennial problem in fascist studies, namely, how to generalize from the particular when the particular is so idiosyncratic. Rather like Poulantzas (Reading 7), Linz seems to have extrapolated from one particular putative fascist regime (this time Fascism itself) a theory of generic fascism which, tautologically, only applies to the regime it was abstracted from in the first place.

Whereas Sternhell concentrates on the long-term cultural roots of the fascist bid to overcome decadence so as to create a new nation, a new civilization, a new man, 'Linz reminds us of the crucial role played by the First World War in precipitating the generalized crisis in Western societies which opened up the political space which fascism could fill as a revolutionary new force in politics even as a late-comer. Both accept fascism had an ideology, yet for Sternhell the key components are (organic) nationalism combined with (anti-Marxist) socialism, while for Linz, as his extensive essay on comparative fascist studies in Laqueur's *Fascism: A Reader's Guide*[7] makes even clearer, it revolved around negations and a revolutionary form of nationalism. However, he does not attempt to go into what constituted the contents of that nationalism. This is consistent with the stress which he places on fascism's innovative style of politics: it is still being defined primarily in terms of how it operated as a movement and regime, not as a distinctive genus of ideology with numerous permutations.

Roger Eatwell tackles the issue from an entirely different angle (Reading 16), reflecting the way by the 1990s fascist studies was at last able to move away from 'exogenous' interpretations of fascism (which explain it in terms of extrinsic factors such as capitalism, nation-building, or modernization) to 'endogenous' ones (based on an analysis of its internal dynamics). The first part of his article (omitted here) is a survey of the main strategies which have been adopted by academics to explain the nature of fascism, and a critique of their various shortcomings. His premise, still a provocative one in the early 1990s, is that fascism is to be approached in the first instance as a distinctive ideology. This ideology he sees as definable in terms not of a simple formula, but of a cluster of core axioms which in practice assume a wide range of different formulations and rationalizations reflecting the highly variegated national, cultural, and historical contexts in which individual ideologies live or movements arise. Indeed, what emerges from his analysis is that a major feature of fascism taken generically has been its readiness to synthesize ideas and theories appropriated from a wide range of (originally non-fascist) contexts, and just how flexible it has been in adapting to the changing conditions in which it challenges the existing order (an especially important feature when considering contrasts between inter-war and post-war fascism). This mercurial, chameleon, scavenger quality is partly a consequence of being (as Linz stressed) a late-comer on a European scene already saturated with rival value systems and political theories. This has forced it to beg, borrow, and steal its own doctrinal contents. It is also attributable to the fact that as a force which celebrates the active, vitalistic, and the mythic in human life and history, fascism tends to post-rationalize existing predispositions with little sense of scholarly nicety or rigour (which is not to say that vast numbers of well-educated academics and intellectuals were not directly involved in those rationalizations).

The core axioms of fascism identified by Eatwell are the familiar ones of the new consensus: the decadence of the existing nation's political and social system and of Western civilization as a whole; the need to regenerate society and thereby civilization by creating a 'new man';[8] the importance of carrying out this revitalizing mission within the framework of the nation, whether conceived as the historical nation–state or the race; the concomitant need to create an alternative socio-economic system to the one based on global or *laissez-faire* capitalism but without abolishing private property as such: the corporatist experiments of Fascism, the large-scale state intervention in the economy under Nazism, and the mass organizations spawned by both regimes are symptomatic of the bid to create a radical alternative to both liberalism and communism. The composite fascist minimum which these axioms constitute when taken together is 'a form of thought which preaches the need for social rebirth in order to forge a *holistic-national radical Third Way*'.[9] This is profoundly compatible both with my concept of 'palingenetic ultra-nationalism' (see Reading 2) and with Payne's tripartite 'typological description' and the single-sentence definition that flows from it: 'a form of revolutionary ultra-nationalism for national rebirth' (see Reading 13). It significantly parts company from Sternhell, though, both by accepting Nazism as a fully fledged form of fascism, and by rejecting the formula 'nationalism plus socialism' as encapsulating the essential matrix of its ideology.

To understand why Eatwell in fact rejects this or any other particularized formulation of the fascist minimum is to realize the originality of his approach. He suggests that fascism's anti-conservative bid to regenerate the political, social, cultural, and economic life of the whole nation to the point of actually 'remaking man' can be expressed in a wide range of theoretical rationalizations and concrete policies. These are formulated in an activistic (non-intellectual, non-theoretical) spirit of synthesis, or more precisely, of a process called 'syncretism', which welds together elements taken from diverse and often conflicting bodies of pre-fascist thought (ideologies, philosophies, social theories, religious principles, prejudices, etc.), within a spectrum of possible theoretical positions which could correspond to the same core belief. Eatwell suggests these varying formulations can be mapped out under three headings: natural history, geopolitics, and political economy. Thus 'socialism plus nationalism', at least in the fairly specific way in which Sternhell conceives the combination, represents only one of the many possible positions within the spectrum, and hence is not valid for all fascisms at any time, for it is perfectly possible for a right-wing, anti-socialist project of national renewal to be adopted which is still fascist, no matter how 'biologically racist' it is.[10]

The ability to spot the hub of fascism's core principles despite major variations in the ideological spokes which constitute any one of its particular 'wheels' is particularly important when considering the less researched putative fascisms (e.g. in Brazil or South Africa), or monitoring how fascism has adapted to the very different historical climate of post-war Europe. Thus corporatist economics or imperial expansion may be a common theme of fascism in the inter-war period, but would be aberrant in the 1990s, whereas the contemporary world is far more conducive to ecological, pan-European, and international variants of fascism, some of which happily advertise themselves on the post-modern Internet or assimilate elements of Heavy Metal rock culture in ways which would have been literally inconceivable to inter-war fascists, and probably anathema to most. Adopting Eatwell's 'spectral–syncretic' model also means that many features of fascist style and organization, such as the leader cult, paramilitarism, or mass rallies, can be recognized as being contingent on the particular conditions of Europe after the First World War rather than being definitional traits – a point particularly pertinent to Payne's definition which is cluttered with elements derived from a specifically inter-war historical climate (see Reading 13).

If Eatwell's article throws welcome light on the extraordinary variety of ideo-logical subspecies generated by the single genus fascism, what it does not present is a model which explains why an intrinsically variegated political vision of national renewal should achieve significant transclass support, and in some cases even a mass following, precisely in the inter-war period when liberal democracy was in crisis.[11] This vital component of a multi-causal analysis of fascism is provided by Platt's chapter on the socio-psychological dynamics of revolutionary movements (Reading 17). The section which precedes the extract reproduced here opens with a critique of established attempts to explain revolutions in sociological, psychological, and psychohistorical terms which ignore the subjectivities of those who take part in revolutions and choose instead to explain their motivation as the product of simplistic categories such as 'class' – Lipset's 'middle-class thesis' of Nazism is cited as a blatant example – or a particular psychological type (e.g. the 'authoritarian personality').[12] As a result a revolution comes to be treated mono-causally as if it involved a homogeneous ideology which inspires the idealism of activists representing a single, unified social or psychological grouping. The trouble is that all hard data relating to the ideology and sociology of revolutionary move-ments points instead to a situation of extreme heterogeneity.[13] In support of his argument Platt cites evidence relating to the social composition both of the two sides in the English Civil War and, more significant in the context of this Reader, of support for Nazism.[14]

Since 'categorical analysis' fails to explain revolutionary behaviour, Platt sets about providing an alternative explanatory framework. The key to his model is the actual language used by revolutionaries and their supporters, which he treats not as a causal factor in itself, but rather as the expression of the realm of subjective meaning experienced by the participants. It is language which enables the sharing and transmission of values, thus forming an ideology which makes sense of people's lives and binds them together in an affective community (a community of emotion and experience) which transcends the myriad differences which exist between them on other socio-economic and experiential levels. When an ideology fails to make sense of everyday experience because of the impact of large-scale and profound socio-political upheavals, this inevitably gives rise to what Platt terms a 'sense-making crisis'. At this point an ideology which effectively offers an alternative sense-making interpretation can suddenly acquire significant affective support, not because of the social or psychological homogeneity of the converts to it, but because it offers a solution to a breakdown of meaning which is a communal experience, even if it affects every supporter in a uniquely personal way. It is thus ideology which creates the illusion of a unified community, not the social or psychological categories to which the members of that community belong. In practice a revolutionary ideology will itself contain numerous 'subfeatures', and different supporters of the new cause will be drawn by different combinations of the subfeatures, even if the subjective experience is that they all belong to the same movement.

Though Platt's central concern is the psycho-dynamics of generic revolution rather than of generic fascism, his theory acquires considerable suggestive power in the context of the new consensus. This has defined the ideological core as a combination of ultra-nationalism and rebirth myth which offers a 'total' solution to the perceived decadence and crisis of the nation. The inter-war crises of liberal democracies in Europeanized societies occurred after a century in which local varieties of populist nationalism had grown relentlessly. Their implicit illiberalism had then been fanned (even in liberal countries) by a World War of unprecedented ferocity and destructiveness between 1914 and 1918, and exacerbated in many states by the fear that bolshevism would succeed in its bid to launch an international, and hence nation-threatening, proletarian revolution after 1917. It was precisely in societies in which democracy had been strong enough to undermine conservative traditionalism but too weak to stem the tide of illiberal nationalism (e.g. Germany, Romania, Hungary) where the crises brought about the rise of fascism. In such countries fascism thus fed symbiotically off democracy's sense-making crisis by offering a new mythic framework of values at the heart of which was the image of the nation's Phoenix-like rise from the ashes of the old order. No matter how idiosyncratically constituted, each individual conversion to the fascist cause could thus be experienced psychologically as a magic moment of direct participation in the imminent rebirth of the nation.

Platt provides an elegant model of the psychohistorical dynamics behind mass support to a revolutionary cause. He does not, however, set out to reconstruct the precise emotional syndrome or psychological process involved in becoming a fascist. At this point the extract from Theweleit takes on a particular significance (Reading 18). His two-volume *Male Fantasies* offers a model of the psycho-dynamics of fascism which is impressive in the density of methodological self-consciousness and in the wealth of evidence he has accumulated to document his central thesis. Unfortunately, even if Theweleit's approach generates a profusion of fascinating information and insights, it is open to the charge of being precisely what Platt has called a 'categorical analysis'. In other words, it is simplistic and reductionist, being based mainly on an elaborate extrapolation from a close study of the writings of a handful of members of the Freikorps, the paramilitary volunteer movement of fanatical ultra-nationalists which spontaneously sprang up to fight communists and other perceived enemies of the *Volk* after Germany's defeat in the First World War. This small group of hyper-patriots, many of whom subsequently converted to the NSDAP – notably Ernst von Salomon, famous writer of militaristic fiction,[15] and Rudolf Höss, the future commandant of Auschwitz labour and exter-mination camp – is taken as paradigmatic, not just of Nazis, but of fascists in general, thus further compounding the reductionism of heterogeneity to homogeneity.

Despite the considerable methodological flaw implicit in Theweleit's mono-causal approach to fascism, his investigation is still extremely valuable once it is taken as a meticulously argued and documented case-study in the complex psychological process involved in the conversion to palingenetic ultra-nationalism of one social group who went on to become some of the most violent activists of early Nazism. Using a conceptual framework too elaborate to be summarized here, he argues that the adult personality of each Freikorps member bore the traces of an early trauma which had severely interfered with his 'individuation', the process which leads to a healthy relationship with external reality and fellow human beings in general. In psychodynamic terms he was not yet fully born, and hence suffered from a hypertrophied (over-developed) masculine principle which manifested itself in a chronic fear of being engulfed by chaos, weakness, and dirt.

As Theweleit demonstrates through a detailed study of his subject group's own written testimony, this fear was projected in the first instance onto women, producing an intense misogyny, and then by extension onto anything which threatened the neurotic need for a clearly demarcated and delimited territory which had become subjectively identified with the nation. (The analysis is brought alive with an abundance of striking illustrations throughout, though the plates which accompanied the extract reproduced here have been omitted.) This man-ifested itself in a pathological hatred of Jews, 'Reds', homosexuals, the undiffer-entiated crowd or masses, the racially 'abnormal' or 'inferior', and any type of human being experienced as 'liminal' (crossing or blurring boundaries). These 'not-yet-fully-born' individuals only felt they had a properly delineated identity when they literally and mentally put on paramilitary uniform (which Theweleit calls evocatively 'body armour'), for this legitimized their need to externalize their violence and aggression. These men were demonstrably haunted by a constant anxiety that their 'soldier-ego' may disintegrate at any moment, thus precipitating them into dissolution, isolation, and pain. However, in the pathological state of integration and control achieved by being part of a fighting machine they could also feel an ecstatic sense of spiritual community, of redemption, of the divine. In psychoanalytical terms they then lived out a 'fantasy of rebirth'.

The correspondence between Theweleit's model and the new consensus on the nature of fascism is surely too close to be coincidence. It may well only account for the highly atypical constituency of Nazis who were directly attracted by its appeal to an instinctual predisposition to violence, destruction, and sadism. Yet it rings true as part of a multi-causal analysis of fascism once we assume that the many other highly distinctive psychological groups who undergo an active conversion to fascism[16] in its many permutations (even within the 'same' movement) experience their own equivalent sense of ecstatic rebirth or reawakening. They do so by projecting the psychic drama of their individuation and psychological regeneration onto the fate of the nation, precisely what Nazi propaganda, culture, and social engineering urged them to do.[17]

Having considered cultural, socio-political, international, ideological, psycho-historical, and psychoanalytical levels of causation separately, Stanley Payne's multi-causal analysis of the various factors which contributed to fascism gaining a 'significant following' in inter-war Europe is particularly valuable. It reassembles several of the preconditions which have already been considered into a synoptic overview, adding a few more for good measure. In doing so it provides an instant synopsis of some of the ground covered so far in this Reader while anticipating some issues which it will raise later. Moreover, the multi-causal approach presented here naturally ties in closely with Payne's own tripartite typological definition (Reading 13), since it is that definition which establishes the conceptual framework for the historical analysis presented in the rest of the book. By managing to be both complex and accessible, Payne's 'retrodictive theory' demonstrates just how far academic scholarship on fascism has progressed since the crude or abstruse monocausal analyses of the early years. It is no coincidence if the chapter opens with a pointed remark about the failure of so many theorists in the past to provide an adequate account of fascism, and a warning against the dangers of reductionism when dealing with something so complex in its sources and causes. His own causal model highlights the role of cultural, political, social, economic, and international factors, which are summarized in a table so as to be easier to grasp.[18]

Payne goes on to point out that the conjuncture of preconditions which produced fascism disappeared after 1945. This point is central to understanding how radically post-war fascism has had to adapt to a very different cultural climate in order to survive, and will be explored at length in Diethelm Prowe's final contribution (Reading 25). The conclusion also draws attention to the misleading connotations of the phrase 'the era of fascism' when applied to the period 1918–1945 as a whole, and underlines the ultimate unsustainability of fascism even when it seizes power. In short, the history of generic fascism is the history of marginalization and failure, even if the Third Reich demonstrated that its potential for destruction knows no bounds if one of its more radical manifestations ever gets the chance to try to turn its palingenetic fantasies into reality.

Notes

1 This is why Gregor's use of fascism applies to practically as many regimes as any Marxist one.
2 See above Introduction, p. 14.
3 For Sternhell's ideal type of fascism see Reading 2.
4 Linz's most extensive discussion of this important concept is to be found in his chapter 'Political space and fascism as a late-comer', in S. U. Larsen, B. Hagtvet and J. P. Myklebust (eds), *Who Were the Fascists* (Oslo, Universitetsforlaget, 1980), pp. 153–89.
5 See above p. 10.

6 Sauer's analysis in Reading 10 is similarly vague about precisely which movements are being alluded to in his sweeping geo-political references.

7 J. Linz, 'Some Notes Towards a Comparative Study of Fascism in Sociological Historical Perspective', in W. Laqueur (ed.), *Fascism: A Reader's Guide* (Harmondsworth, Penguin, 1979; 1976), pp. 13–78.

8 A theme already emphasized by Mosse: see 1st edition, Reading 12.

9 R. Eatwell, *Fascism: A History* (London, Chatto & Windus, 1995), p. 11. See also Introduction pp. 14–15.

10 This perspective leads to the realization that 'Hitlerite' Nazism, which Linz has misgivings about calling fascist because it lacks the Strasserite 'socialist' element, merely represents another type of syncretism within the same spectrum of ideological permutations.

11 In his later article 'On defining the "Fascist Minimum"': the centrality of ideology', *Journal of Political Ideologies* 1: 3 (1996), pp. 303–19, Roger Eatwell explains how fascism's syncretism accounts for its ability to attract a wide spectrum of support on economic and psychological grounds.

12 The 'authoritarian personality' was a psychological model to explain fascism elaborated by a team of *emigré* researchers of the Frankfurt School of (Marxist) social scientists in the USA shortly after the Second World War: see R. Griffin, *Fascism* (Oxford, Oxford University Press, 1995), p. 289.

13 In such cases aesthetic considerations of finding 'neat' explanations seem again to have prevailed over a 'messy' empirical engagement with the complexity and subtlety of fascist realities.

14 Platt's source on Nazism is Fred Weinstein, *Germany's Discontents, Hitler's Visions: The Claims of Leadership and Ideology in the National Socialist Movement* (New York, Academic Press, 1980).

15 See Griffin, *Fascism*, op. cit. pp. 95–6.

16 Activists are to be distinguished from those who passively 'went along with fascism' once it became the orthodoxy of a regime, such as the *Märzgefallene* or 'those who fell in March', the millions who flocked to join the Nazi party *after* the establishment of the Third Reich in March 1933.

17 Cf. the observation of an expert on film in the Third Reich, a scholar seemingly oblivious of the debate over generic fascism, that 'Nazi cinema originated as a site of transformation, an art and technology implemented to engineer emotion, to create a new man – and to recreate woman in the service of the new order and the new man': Eric Rentschler, *The Ministry of Illusion: Nazi Cinema and its Afterlife* (Cambridge, MA., Harvard University Press, 1996), p. 57.

18 While impressive in the sense of organized complexity which Payne displays here, it is to be noted that even his account is typical of orthodox historiography in its omission of any reference to the psychohistorical/psychological dimension of causation. This leaves a gap all too readily filled by those prepared to produce accounts of fascism's pathological origins which are essentially speculative, and fail to take adequate account of non-psychological factors, or of the empirical complexity of fascism as an ideological and social phenomenon.

14

The crisis of fin-de-siècle *thought**

ZEEV STERNHELL

In February 1936 the French review *Combat*, which was sympathetic to the fascists, published an article entitled *Fascisme 1913*,[1] by Pierre Andreu, one of the most faithful and authentic of Georges Sorel's disciples, in which he remarked on the curious synthesis of syndicalists and nationalists centered around the author of *Reflections on Violence*, and in nationalist circles connected with Action Française, immediately before the outbreak of the First World War. At about the same time, a similar comment came from Pierre Drieu La Rochelle, who a few months later – and in company with Bertrand de Jouvenel, a young economist of the left – became one of the leading intellectuals in the Parti Populaire Français (PPF), the largest of the French fascist parties. He observed that,

> looking back on that period, we can see how by 1913 certain elements
> of the fascist atmosphere had already come together in France, before
> they did in other countries. There were young men from all classes of
> society, fired by a love of heriosm and violence, who dreamed of
> fighting what they termed the evil on two fronts – capitalism and
> parliamentary socialism – while culling from each what to them
> seemed good. Already the marriage between nationalism and social-
> ism was on the cards.[2]

The self-same formula had already been used in 1925 by Georges Valois, the founder of the first non-Italian fascist movement, Le Faisceau, to define the idea in which the substance of the phenomenon was contained: 'Nationalism + socialism = fascism'.[3] Some ten years later Sir Oswald Mosley picked it up in his turn: 'If you love our country you are national, and if you love our people you are socialist'.[4] It was a powerfully clear and simple idea, possessing immense attraction, and by the time the former Labour minister came to found the British Union of Fascists it was already shared by all the European fascist movements.

The shock of the war and its immediate consequences no doubt pre-cipitated the birth of fascism as a political movement, but its ideological roots in fact go back to the years 1880–90, when an alliance sprang up

* Extract from Zeev Sternhell, 'Fascist Ideology', in W. Laqueur (ed.), *Fascism: A Reader's Guide* (Harmondsworth, Penguin, 1979; 1st edition, 1976), pp. 332–8.

between theories deriving from one or another type of socialism – whether non-Marxist, anti-Marxist, or indeed post-Marxist – and from nationalism. Those were the incubation years of fascism, as is attested to by Valois or Drieu, and equally by Gentile or by Mussolini. For on the eve of the First World War the essentials of fascist ideology were already well defined. The word did no exist yet, but the phenomenon it would eventually designate had its own autonomous existence, and thenceforward awaited only a favourable combination of circumstances in which to hatch into a political force. Fascist ideology is seen therefore as the immediate product of a crisis that had overtaken democracy and liberalism, and bourgeois society in all its fundamental values: the break-away was so disruptive as to take on the dimensions of a crisis in civilization itself.

Fascism was not a reflection of Marxism, nor did it come into existence simply as a reaction to organized Marxism; it had the same degree of autonomy that Marxism had, in that both were products of bourgeois society and reacted against that society, compared to which they each presented a radical alternative; both were agreed in that they put forward a new pattern of civilization. The growth of fascism therefore cannot be understood, or fully explained, unless it is seen in the intellectual, moral, and cultural context which prevailed in Europe at the end of the nineteenth century.

The changes that took place at this time, within the space of a single generation, were so profound that it would be no exaggeration to speak of them as constituting an intellectual revolution,[5] which in its themes and style was to pave the way for the mass politics of our own century. For the vast movement of thought of the 1890s was above all a movement of revolt: revolt against the world of matter and reason, against materialism and positivism, against the mediocrity of bourgeois society, and against the muddle of liberal democracy. To the *fin-de-siècle* mind, civilization was in crisis, and if a solution were possible it would have to be a total one.

The generation of 1890 – which included among others, d'Annunzio and Corradini in Italy, Barrès, Drumont, and Sorel, in France, Paul de Lagarde, Julius Langbehn and Arthur Moeller van den Bruck in Germany – took as its point of departure not the individual, who as such had no importance in himself, but the social and political collectivity, which, moreover, was not to be thought of as the numerical sum of the individuals under its aegis. The 'new' intellectuals therefore inveighed violently aginst the rationalistic individualism of liberal society and against the dissolution of social links in bourgeois society. In identical terms sometimes, they one and all deplored the mediocrity and materialism of modern society, its instability and corruption. They decried the life of the great cities, which was dominated by routine with no room for heroism, and to the claims of the individual's powers of reason they preferred the merits of instinct, sometimes even of animality. Such is the soil to which Giovanni Gentile traces the root-origins of fascism, which he defines as a 'revolt against positivism'[6] and against the way of life fostered by industrial society, which revolt broke out at a time when the intellectual atmosphere was saturated with Darwinian biology and Wagnerian aesthetics, Gobineau's racialism, Le Bon's psychology, as well as the black prophecies of Nietzsche and Dostoevsky, and, later, the philosophy of Bergson.

Of course neither Bergson's philosophy nor Nietzsche's are to be confused with the use to which they have been put at the hands of the 'dread simplificators' and other exponents, any more than we attribute to Darwin the social Darwinism touted by the generation that came after him. And yet, though philosophers and scientists cannot be held responsible for the uses made of their teachings, for the way they are interpreted and the meaning read into their thoughts, it was nevertheless their teachings which, when put into the hands of a thousand minor intellectuals who frequently had little aptitude for careful philosophical reasoning, shaped a new intellectual climate. In the aftermath of the dreadful shock of the war, the Soviet revolution, and the economic crisis, that intellectual climate allowed fascism to burgeon and grow into a powerful mass movement. For the masses were by then well conditioned to accept a new interpretation of the world and of human realities, and even a new morality, as the foundations of a new order.

The contributions made by scientists and pseudo-scientists to this new vision of the world were in point of fact legion. As the notion of social Darwinism gained widespread acceptance, it stripped the human personality of its sacramental dignity. It made no distinction between the physical life and the social life, and conceived of the human condition in terms of an unceasing struggle, whose natural outcome was the survival of the fittest. Positivism also felt the impact of social Darwinism, and underwent a profound change. In the latter half of the century its emphasis on deliberate and rational choice as the determining factor in human behaviour gave way to new notions of heredity, race, and environment.[7] Thus, social Darwinism played a large part in the evolution of nationalism and the growth of modern racialism. So too its influence is clearly to be seen in the interest taken by the generation of 1890 in the study of psychology and the discovery of the unconscious. For the new theories of social and political psychology rejected out of hand the traditional mechanistic concept of man, which asserted that human behaviour is governed by rational choice. Opinion now dictated that sentiment and feeling count for more in political questions than reasoning, and fostered contempt for democracy and its institutions and workings.

Throughout Europe the same fears and the same passions began to find expression at the same moment, and men from very different backgrounds, engaged in fields of study that were often quite unrelated to one another, each played their part in the formulation of the new ideology. The onslaught on bourgeois society went hand-in-hand with the wholesale condemnation of liberal democracy and parliamentary government, for one of the ideological tenets common to this whole vast protest movement was the reforming of all institutions in the authoritarian mould. The call for a leader, a saviour embodying all the virtues of the race, was to be heard throughout Europe, at the turn of the century. When the march of events gainsaid these theories, the setback was invariably blamed on a plot, and the instigators, also invariably, identified as Jews and Freemasons hand-in-glove with the international financiers. The men who at the turn of the century revolted against positivism, and also against liberalism and socialism which they regarded as a vague form of positivism to be treated in a similar manner, joined forces not merely to attack certain social structures or the nature of political institutions, but also to impeach Western civilization itself, which in their eyes was fundamentally corrupt.

It must be stressed too that these rebels were not men relegated to the fringes of contemporary opinion. Whatever the verdict of the historian of ideas on the intrinsic worth of their individual writings, it must be said that it is not the historians who fashion the sensibilities of a bygone generation. The men who put together the ingredients of fascist ideology, as it was on the eve of the Great War, were well-known interpreters, rendering into common language the work accomplished by the giants of their own or of the previous generation. They brought within reach of the general reader a system of ideas which was not easily understood, and which they themselves from time to time deformed or oversimplified. Such are the writers who in point of fact inform the everyday reader of newspapers and popular novels, the average university and high school student, and the people who in the counties and country towns make up a social élite, and who in their day enjoyed a tremendous success. Julius Langbehn was renowned from the year 1890, when he published *Rembrandt als Erzieher*, the book in which he denounced the intellectual and scientific bent of German civilization, and sang instead the praises of irrationalism. The two ensuing decades saw Arthur Moeller van den Bruck steadfastly renewing the attack on liberalism and democracy, until he came to fame in 1922 with *Das Dritte Reich*.[8] The same is true of the Italian and French writers: d'Annunzio, Barrès, and Maurras ranked among the most important intellectuals of their generation, while Drumont's works went into more reprints than any other publication of the last century. Their thinking took root throughout the Latin- and French-oriented regions of Europe: they had an immense influence not only in Italy and France but in Spain, Switzerland, Belgium, and Eastern Europe, particularly in Romania. There was a professor at the Sorbonne, by the name of Jules Soury, who in 1902 published a book called *Campagne Nationaliste* – along the same lines as *Mein Kampf* – and was acclaimed as the equal of Bergson, while Gustave Le Bon was quoted at some length by the father of psychoanalysis and was sometimes seen as another Freud. Given the number of men writing on the subject, one may wonder if their prolific output does not account in some measure for the inattentive reception accorded to Hitler; for the author of *Mein Kampf* had nothing to say which had not already been said, and not by men of the lunatic fringe, but rather by the ranking intellectuals of the day.

In the years preceding the First World War Europe experienced an extraordinary revival of nationalism. Well before 1914 *völkisch* ideology, the set of ideas which are crucial to the understanding of Nazism, had found a widespread acceptance in German society, notwithstanding a remarkable flowering of the intellectual disciplines in that country, reminiscent of the classical period around 1800, over which *völkisch* ideology nevertheless gained the upper hand. It must not be forgotten that, as Professor George Mosse had pointed out, the Nazis found their greatest support among respectable and educated people. Their ideas were eminently respectable in Germany after the First World War, and indeed had been current among large segments of the population even before the war. The essential element here is the linking of the human soul with its natural surroundings, with the 'essence' of nature, that the real and important truths are to be found beneath surface appearances. According to many *völkisch* theorists, the nature of the soul of a *Volk* is determined by the nature of the landscape. Thus, the Jews, being a desert people, are regarded as shallow and dry people, devoid of profundity and totally lacking in creativity. Because of the barrenness of the desert landscape, the Jews are a spiritually barren people.[9]

The self-same themes are to be met in the nationalist ideology of France: the Frenchman, nurtured by his soil and his dead, cannot escape the destiny shaped for him by past generations, by the landscapes of his childhood, the blood of his forebears. The nation is a living organism, and nationalism is therefore an ethic, comprising all the criteria of behaviour which the common interest calls for, and on which the will of the individual has no bearing. The duty both of the individual and of society is to find out what this ethic may be, yet only those can succeed who have a share in the 'national consciousness', shaped over the course of the centuries: the Jews, as a foreign race, cannot enter upon this quest.[10]

In Italy, d'Annunzio and Corradini were the best-known spokesmen for a nationalist movement which reached far and deep, feeding on external defeat, as it had done in France in the aftermath of 1870. It was this movement indeed which by 1915 had brought Italy into the war, looking to war for glory. In France the young men of the coming generation were fired by patriotism, by a zeal for order, authority, and discipline, and were morally at the ready for war, many years before August 1914.

This resurgence of nationalism accounts, at least in part, for the failure of international socialism, and explains why the working class set off for war on a wave of patriotism, regardless of their long-standing tradition of anti-militarism and of countless resolutions adopted at each and every Socialist Congress. Throughout the years separating the two wars, the workers' movement did not recover, morally speaking, from this defeat, and it would weigh heavily in the balance when the fascist movements began to come to a head, and particularly, of course, in Italy. [. . .]

Notes

1 *Combat*, no. 2 (February 1936).
2 Quoted in Michel Winock, 'Une parabole fasciste: Gilles de Drieu La Rochelle', *Le Mouvement Social*, 80 (July 1972), p. 29.
3 Georges Valois, *Le Fascisme* (Paris, 1927), p. 21.
4 Oswald Mosley, *Tomorrow we live* (London, Abbey Supplies, 1938), p. 57.
5 Cf. the recent studies by H. Stuart Hughes, *Consciousness and Society: the Reorientation of European Social Thought 1890–1930* (New York, Knopf, 1961); Gerhard Masur, *Prophets of Yesterday: Studies in European Culture 1890–1914* (London, Weidenfeld & Nicolson, 1966); W. Warren Wagar, ed., *European Intellectual History since Darwin and Marx [Selected Essays]* (New York, Progress, 1966); John Weiss, ed., *The Origins of Modern Consciousness* (Detroit, Wayne State University Press, 1965).
6 Giovanni Gentile, 'The Philosophic Basis of Fascism', *Foreign Affairs*, VI (1927–8), pp. 295–6.
7 H. Stuart Hughes, op. cit., pp. 38–9. Cf. in particular Carlton J. H. Hayes, *A Generation of Materialism 1871–1900* (New York, Harper & Row, 1963) and Jacques Barzun, *Race: a Study in Superstition* (New York, Harper & Row, 1965), p. 162.
8 Fritz Stern's *The Politics of Cultural Despair* (Berkeley, CA., University of California Press, 1961) is the best treatment of Langbehn, Lagarde, and Moeller van den Bruck.
9 George L. Mosse, *The Crisis of German Ideology: Intellectual Origins of the Third Reich* (New York, Grosset & Dunlap, 1964), pp. 4–5.
10 Zeev Sternhell, *Maurice Barrès et le nationalisme français* (Paris, A. Colin, 1972), pp. 263–73.

15

The crisis of democracy after the First World War*

JUAN LINZ

Mobilizational authoritarian regimes in postdemocratic societies

The Western European democratic revolution initiated in the eighteenth century spread liberal democratic institutions to societies of very different economic, social, cultural, and institutional development. In many of them there was no possibility of returning to traditional legitimate rule after political revolutions and often major social and economic changes. In a number of them the sequence of development crises – state-building legitimation, participation, incorporation of new social forces, representation in legislative organs, and ultimately share in executive power – cumulated in a short period of time. More often than not economic development did not keep pace with political change. Protest ideologies formulated in more advanced societies diffused and new movements combined demands for redistribution and participation with the hostility to the changes resulting from early industrialization and disruption of traditional economic and social patterns (Borkenau, 1933). Other countries, particularly those that had not experienced the Protestant Reformation and the disestablishment of religion that went with religious pluralism in earlier centuries, faced a crisis of secularization. Some like Italy and Germany as late-comers to statehood, whose boundaries did not coincide with those of the culture nation, experienced a heightened need for a sense of national cohesion. The success of the United Kingdom and France and to a lesser extent the Netherlands and Belgium in the colonial expansion created in other medium-sized powers the consciousness of the 'proletarian nation'. The loss of the last remnants of Spain's empire and the English veto of Portugal's expansion also created crises of national consciousness. The coincidence of these quite different but cumulated crises through the period of rapid political democratization, particularly in the absence or

* Extract from Juan Linz, 'Totalitarian and Authoritarian Regimes', in F. I. Greenstein and N. W. Polsby (eds), *Handbook of Political Science: Macropolitical Theory*, Vol. 3, (Massachusetts, Addison-Wesley, 1975), pp. 313–21.

weakness of traditionally legitimate institutions and elites, prevented the successful and slow institutionalization of democratic political processes capable of incorporating the demands of new social groups awakened to class or cultural consciousness. In contrast to the Eastern European societies, those of Western Europe already before World War I had experienced the introduction of liberal freedoms, constitutional or semiconstitutional government, and an increasing importance of modern political parties, including Marxist, syndicalist, and Christian labor movements. The crisis caused by war interventions, post-war economic dislocations, and the psychological impact on the underprivileged masses of the Russian Revolution and with it the split of the socialist movement led to the delegitimation and ineffectiveness of democratic regimes in process of consolidation. In contrast to the less politically, economically, and socially developed Eastern European nations, purely bureaucratic–military–oligarchical authoritarian solutions could not be the response to the crisis. It could not be because even the oligarchic institutions of the establishment had accepted the notion that politics could not be reduced to administration and realized that a purely coercive repression was condemned to failure because in all social classes, including the privileged middle class, democratic ideas had gained considerable loyalty. In such societies the crisis of democracy would lead to new political formulas including the plebiscitarian pseudodemocratic component: the mass single party. On the other hand, those societies had reached a level of development and complexity that made it difficult for the leadership of such a single party to move in a totalitarian direction, except in the case of Nazi Germany. It is no accident that the first manifestation in Europe of a plebiscitarian, nonliberal authoritarian solution to the crisis of democracy should have been Bonapartism, considering that France was the country of Europe in which revolutionary change had brought the biggest break with traditional authority and had led to the highest political mobilization with the 1848 revolution. It is no accident that some Marxists like Thalheimer (1930) should have turned to Marx's analysis in *The Eighteenth Brumaire* to understand the novel authoritarian regimes created by fascism.[1]

The crisis of European societies at the end of World War I led to the emergence of two political movements that broke with the liberal democratic systems that seemed on the ascendancy: Leninism and fascism. Both were based on the rule by the minority, by an elite, self-appointed to represent the majority, the proletariat or the nation, at the service of an historical task. Parties led by a self-confident elite defined not by ascriptive characteristics or by professional achievements but by its will to gain power and to use it to break through social and historical constraining conditions, appealing for the support of the masses but unwilling to allow them to interfere in the pursuit of its goals. The strength of the democratic heritage of Marxism and the scientism of Marxist social science, while allowing a break with the liberal tradition, assured the persistence of an ideological commitment to democracy. Fascism as a nationalistic response to the ideological internationalism of Marxism, by linking with other ideological traditions of the nineteenth century – romantic irrationalism, social Darwinism, Hegelian exultation of the state, Nietzschean ideas, Sorelian conceptions of the role of the myth, imagery of the great man and the genius – turned explicitly antidemocratic (Gregor, 1969; Nolte, 1969; E. Weber, 1964). In contrast to other conceptions of authoritarianism as a modern response to the crisis of society, it searched for a new and different form of democratic legitimation, based on the emotional identification of the followers with the leader, in a plebiscitarianism that had found its first postrevolutionary manifestation in Napoleonic Caesarism. In a complex way we cannot analyse here, fascism combined and perverted many stains of Western intellectual tradition that directly or indirectly put into question the assumptions of liberal democratic pluralist society and politics.

The special circumstances of Italian society after World War I led to the emergence under the leadership of Mussolini of a new type of non-traditionalist, popular antidemocratic movement, initially carried by a small number of activists recruited among the interventionists; nationalists; the veterans of the war who found reintegration into civil society difficult; a certain type of intelligentsia heady with nationalism, futurism, and hostility for the clientelistic politics of Giolittian *transformismo* and for the selfishness of the bourgeoisie; together with revolutionary syndicalists who had discovered their national identity (De Felice, 1966, 1969, 1970; Delzell, 1970). The poet D'Annunzio discovered a new style, new symbols for this generation of rebels (Hamilton, 1971). It was, however, the mobilization of the Italian working class by a Maximalist social labor movement, unable to implement a revolutionary takeover of power and still unwilling to follow a reformist path toward integration into democracy in the making, that created the conditions for success of this minority of activists. The red domination of the northern Italian countryside, which scared landowners and wealthier peasants, and occupation of factories in the industrial centers, particularly Torino, led a scared bourgeoisie to join and support the incipient movement (Salvemini, 1961). Its leaders, hostile to the socialists on account of their anti-interventionism and to the workers who had stayed in the factories and received with hostility the returning veterans, were ready for the alliance. The ambivalent attitude of the state and its representatives toward the terrorist activities of the *squadrismo*, the failure of the reformists to turn to support the demo-liberal state, and the tensions between the old liberal parties and both the socialists and the new democratic Christian populist party, combined with the ruthlessness and opportunism of Mussolini, led the new movement to power. A new and multifaceted ideology, a new form of political action, and a new style had been born and would find echo in much of Europe (Nolte, 1966, 1968; Laqueur and Mosse, 1966; Rogger and E. Weber, 1966; Woolf, 1969; Carsten, 1967; Kedward, 1969; Hayes, 1973) and even in Latin America (Trindade, 1974) and Asia (Maruyama, 1963; Morris, 1968). Initially it was possible to conceive of fascism as a peculiar outcome of the Italian crisis (De Felice, 1966, 1969, 1970; Nolte, 1967). Later, even as far as the 1930s, it could be interpreted as a response to the problems created by late and unsuccessful economic development and modernization (Borkenau, 1933). But with the success of Hitler it became necessary to explain it in terms of certain basic characteristics of Western society (Nolte, 1967, 1969; Gregor, 1968, 1974a, 1974b; Woolf, 1968; Turner, 1972).

In the context of our analysis of types of political systems we cannot enter into an analysis of the variety of forms the fascist antidemocratic ideology and movement took, nor an explanation of the conditions for its success (Lipset, 1960; Nolte, 1968; Linz, 1976). The nature and definition of fascism itself are a subject of lively debate. We would characterize fascism as an ideology and movement defined by what it rejects, by its exacerbated nationalism, by the discovery of new forms of political action and a new style. The anti-positions of fascism are essential to its understanding and its appeal, but they alone do not account for its success. Fascism is anti-liberal, anti-parliamentarian, anti-Marxist, and particularly anti-communist, anti- or at least aclerical, and in a certain sense anti-bourgeois and anti-capitalist; while linking with the real or imagined historical national tradition, it is not committed to a conservative continuity with the recent past or a purely reactionary return to it but is future-oriented. Those negative stances are a logical outcome of its being a latecomer on the political scene, trying to displace liberal, Marxist, socialist, and clerical parties and win over their supporters. They are also the fruit of the exacerbated nationalism that rejects the appeal to class solidarity across national boundaries and puts in its place the solidarity of all those involved in production in a nation against other nations, seizing on the notion of the proletarian nation: the poor countries against the wealthy plutocracies, which happened to be at that time also powerful democracies. Communist internationalism is defined in this context as the enemy. The latent hostility to a church that transcends the national boundaries and whose divisive effect on the national community with the struggle between clerical and secularizers interferes with the goal of national greatness, hostility that becomes bitter hatred in cases like Nazism, is another logical consequence that differentiates the fascist from other conservative anti-democratic parties. To the extent that modern capitalism is, particularly in its financial institutions, part of an international system, fascists tend to idealize pre-industrial strata like the independent peasant, the artisan, and the entrepreneur, particularly the founder directing his own firm (Mosse, 1964; Winkler, 1972). Masonry, as an organization emphasizing links across nations and closely identified with the liberal bourgeois, secularized strata that created the democratic liberal regimes, is another obvious enemy. Anti-Semitism in the Europe of the turn of the century, particularly Eastern Europe (Pulzer, 1964; Massing, 1949), had a long tradition, and wherever there were Jews fascism seized on those tendencies, stressing the anational, cosmopolitan character of the Jews and particularly of Zionism.

Those negative appeals, however, had a kind of distorted positive counterpart. The anti-Marxism is compensated by an exultation of work, of the producers of *Faust* and *Stirn*, 'hand and brain', in that way appealing to the growing white-collar middle class, which rejected Marxist demands that it should identify with the proletariat (Kele, 1972). The populism of fascism leads it to support welfare-state policies and to engage in loose talk of national socialism, socialization of the banks, etc., which justifies in fascist authoritarian regimes economic intervention- ism and the development of an important public sector in the economy. The anti-capitalism that appeals to pre-capitalist and petit bourgeois strata is redefined as hostility to international financial stock exchange and Jewish capitalism and as exultation of the national entrepreneurial bourgeoisie. The emphasis on a national common good, which rejects the assumptions of individualism, is easily combined with hostility to the free play of interests of economic liberalism and finds expression in protec- tionist and autarchic economic policies that appeal to industrialists threa- tened by international competition. The hostility of a secularized intelligentsia of exacerbated nationalists to clerical politics and their competition with Christian democratic parties for a similar social basis account for the anticlericalism that gets combined with an affirmation of the religious tradition as part of the national, cultural, historical tradition. Already the Action Française in secularist France had taken this path, appealing to the Catholics who rejected the secularizing, liberal democratic state. The Iron Guard, the only successful fascist movement in a Greek Orthodox country, confronted with the denationalized, secularized bour- geoisie and an influential Jewish community, was the fascism that most directly linked with religious symbolism. In the case of Germany the confused programmatic statements about positive Christianity and the identification of many Protestants with a conservative state religion were used by the Nazis, but ultimately the racist ideology became incompatible with any commitment to Christianity (Lewy, 1965; Buchheim, 1953). The anti-religious stands of Marxism and particularly communism in the Soviet Union allowed the fascists to capitalize on the ambivalent identification with the religious heritage. The anti-clericalism facilitated the appeal to secularized middle classes unwilling to support the clerical and Christian democratic middle-class parties, while their anti-liberalism, anti-Masonic, and even anti-Semitic stands, combined with their anti-communism, facilitated the collaboration with the churches when they came to power. The anti-bourgeois affect, the romanticization of the peasant, the artisan, the soldier, contrasted with the impersonal capitalism and selfish bourgeois rentiers, appealed to the emotional discontent of the sons of the bourgeoisie, the cultural critics of modern industrial and urban society. The rejection of the proletarian self-righteousness and the bourgeois egoism and the affirmation of the common national interests above and beyond class cleavages exploited the desire for interclass solidarity developed among veterans of the war (Linz, forthcoming; Merkl, forthcoming) and the guilt feeling of the bourgeoisie, and served well the interests of the business community in destroying a labor movement that threatened its privileges and status. The populist appeal to community against the pragmatism of society, *Gemeinschaft* versus *Gesellschaft*, had considerable appeal in democratic societies divided by class conflict and mobilized by modern mass parties.

The deliberately ambiguous and largely contradictory appeals we have just described would have been, and were, unsuccessful in those societies in which war and defeat had not created a serious national crisis. In the defeated nations or those, like Italy, being victors, felt unjustly deprived of the fruits of their victory, an upsurge of nationalism was channeled by the new parties. The efforts to establish an international political order through the League of Nations under the leadership and to the benefit of the Western, capitalistic, plutocratic democracies became another issue in the armory of the fascists. The lack of coincidence between the national–cultural boundaries and those of the states, the irredenta on the borders, and the existence of nationalities that had not become nation–states, combined with the pan-nationalist movements, were another source of strength for fascism, particularly in the case of Nazis.

Fascist ideology had to reject totally the assumptions of liberal democratic politics based on pluralist participation, the free expresson of interests, and compromise among them rather than the assertion of the collective interests above individuals and classes, cultural and religious communities. The obvious distortion of the idea of democracy in the reality of the early twentieth century and the incapacity of the democratic leadership to institutionalize mechanisms for conflict resolution provided the ground for the appeal of fascism. On a less lofty level, all the interests threatened by a powerful labor movment with revolutionary rhetoric, particularly after some of its revolutionary attempts had been defeated, could support the fascist squads as a defense of the social order. In societies that had reached the level of political, economic, and social development of Western Europe, that defense could not be left to the old institutions – the monarchy, the army, the bureaucracy, and the oligarchical political elites. In that context the fascist ideology offered a new alternative, which promised the integration of the working class into the national community and the assertion of its interests against other nations, if necessary through military preparedness and even aggression (F. Neumann, 1963). This position would appeal to veterans not reintegrated into civil society and army officers and would neutralize the armed forces in the course of the struggle for power.

Neither the ideological appeals nor the interests served by or expected to be served by fascism are sufficient to account for its rapid success. Fascism developed new forms of political organization, different from both the committee electoral-type of parties and the mass-membership, trade-union-based socialist parties, as well as the clerically led religious parties. It was the type of organization that, like the communist counter-part, offered an opportunity for action, involvement, participation, break-ing with the monotony of everyday life. For a generation that had lived heroic, adventurous actions of war and even more for the one that had lived that experience vicariously, due to its youth, the *squadrismo* and the storm troopers offered welcome relief. Many of those who found their normal careers and education disrupted by the war and economic crisis, and probably some of the unemployed, provided the party with many of its activists, whose propaganda and direct action in support of specific grievances – of farmers to be evicted, peasants onto whom the labor unions were imposing the employment of labor, industrialists threatened by strikers – gained them support that no electoral propaganda could have achieved. This new style of politics satisfied certain psychological and emotional needs like no other party could except some forms of cultural protest and to some extent the communists.

Finally, fascism is characterized by a distinctive style reflected in the uniforms – the shirts – which symbolized the break with bourgeois con-vention, the individualism of bourgeois dress; and the mass demonstra-tions and ceremonies, which allowed individials to submerge in the collective and and escape the privatization of modern society. The songs, the greetings, the marches, all gave expression to the new myth, the hopes, and illusions of part of that generation.

This ideal–typical description of fascism as a political movement ignores national variants in ideology, appeal, social basis, and alignments on the political scene. We cannot go into the complex question of whether National Socialism, with its extreme racism, its biologic conception of man, fits into the broader category of fascism (Nolte, 1963; Mosse, 1964, 1966), particularly since many fascists felt quite critical of Nazism and many Nazis felt ambivalent toward Mussolini and his movement (Hoepke, 1968). Our view is that National Socialism, particularly the northern left wing of the movement, rather than 'Hitlerism', fits into the more general category (Kühnl, 1966). Nazism did not reject the identification as fascism, but it also acquired unique characteristics making it a quite different branch of the common tree into which German ideological traditions

(Mosse, 1964; Sontheimer, 1968; Lukácz, 1962) had been grafted and one that had its own distinct fruits.[2] The strength of that branch growing with the resources of German society made it an appealing competitor of the first fascist state.

The ambiguities and contradictions of the fascist utopia, combined with the inevitable pragmatic compromises with many of the forces it initially criticized, account for the failure of the model, except in Italy (to a certain point) and in Germany. To have been successful the initial nucleus would have had to gain support in all strata of the society and particularly among the working class in addition to the peasantry. However, the organizational penetration, except perhaps in Hungary, Rumania, and (if we consider Peronism as a deviant of fascism) in Argentina, of the socialist, communist, and anarcho-syndicalist (in Spain) labor movements was such that such hopes were condemned to failure. In some countries the Catholic peasantry, middle classes, and even many workers had identified with clerical and/or Christian democratic parties in the defense of religion and found in the social doctrine of the Church the answer to many of the problems to which fascism presumed to be a response. Unless deeply scared by unsuccessful revolutionary attempts, disorganized by continuous economic crises – inflation, depression, unemployment, and bankruptcies – or uprooted by war, the middle and upper-middle classes remained loyal to old parties (including, before the March on Rome, most of the Italian south) in countries like France, Belgium, the Netherlands, Scandinavia, and the UK (Linz, 1976; Kaltefleiter, 1968; Lepsius, 1968). Fascism's success in these countries was a minority, largely generatioal phenomenon, strengthened in nationalist border areas and gaining broader support in crisis periods. The heterogeneous basis and the failure to gain strata to which its appeal was directed, ultimately explainable by its latecomer role on the political scene, led the leaders to an unremitting struggle to gain power and to a policy of opportunistic alliances with a variety of established groups and a- or antidemocratic conservative forces, which in turn hoped to manipulate its popular appeal and youthful activist following for their own purposes. In societies that had experienced a serious crisis but no political, social, and economic breakdown comparable to czarist Russia, this meant that the way of power was open only in coalition with other forces, particularly the conservative authoritarian parties like the Partito Nazionalista in Italy and the DNVP in Germany, the powerful anti-labor interest groups, and the army, and by neutralizing the churches. Such groups well entrenched in the establishment and the state could provde men more capable of governing than were the activists of the first hour. The result was the establishment of authoritarian regimes – with a seriously limited and muted pluralism – with a single party whose rule ranged from fairly dominant and active, approaching in some moments the totalitarian model, to regimes in which it was only a minor partner in the coalition of forces, or absorbed like in Portugal, or suppressed, like in Rumania. Only in Germany would the party and its many – and competing – organizations become dominant. In all of them fascism introduced a moblizational, populist component, a channel for some degree and some types of voluntary political participation, a source of ideological discontent with the status quo and justification for social change, which differentiates authoritarian mobilizational regimes from other types. Even where that mobilization was ultimately deliberately demobilized, like in Spain (Linz, 1970), the half organic-statist, half bureaucratic–expert-military authoritarian regime emerging after the 1940s would never be the same as for example the regime of Salazar, where fascism as we have characterized it never had taken root.

The struggle against a powerful, particularly a social democratic, labor movement and the effort to undermine the authority of a democratic state exacerbated the romantic love for violence into an end in itself and generally, consciously or unconsciously, transformed the movement into an instrument of vested interests (often verbally and even sincerely denounced), transforming the 'national integrative revolution' into hateful counter-revolution. The Marxist interpretation (Abendroth, 1967; Mansilla, 1971; *International Journal of Politics*, 1973; Galkin, 1970; Lopukhov, 1965[3]), while inadequate to explain the emergence of the ideology, its complex appeal, and its success in capturing the imagination of many youthful ideologists and misunderstanding the motivation of the founders and many leaders, is largely right in the analysis of the 'objective' historical role played by fascism (F. Neumann, 1963). This obviously does not mean to accept the thesis that the fascists were the hirelings of capitalism based on subsidies that started coming only when the party had gathered strength and in proportion to its success relative to other anti-Marxist parties, or that fascism was the last possible defense of capitalism, or that in power it only and always served its interests. Even less does it absolve the Marxist movement of having undertaken and failed in revolutionary attempts to gain power in relatively democratic societies or of holding onto a maximalist revolutionary rhetoric that mobilizes its enemies and prevents the democratic governments from functioning effectively – a policy that prevents the government from imposing the order desired by those supporting it, while not making a serious effort to impose (at least in part) the policies favored by those movements by participating actively in democratic policy-making by either supporting or even entering government. Fascism, among other things, is a response to the ambivalence of the Marxist ideological heritage toward the importance of political institutions, toward 'formal' liberal democracy, toward reform rather than revolution. Mussolini reflected this dialectical relationship when he said that if the red menace had not been there it would have had to be invented. The anti- or at least ademocratic behavior of the left made

possible the more effective one of the right, even when in turn the manip-
ulative attitude of the liberals toward democratic institutions explains the
reaction of the left.

Fascist–mobilizational authoritarian regimes are less pluralistic, more
ideological, and more participatory than bureaucratic–military or
organic–statist regimes with a weak single party. They are further from
'liberalism' and closer to 'democracy', further from individual freedom
from political constraint but closer to offering citizens a chance to parti-
cipate, less conservative, and more change oriented.[4] Probably the greater
ideological legitimacy and the greater mobilization of support made them
less vulnerable to internal opposition and overthrow than other types of
authoritarian rule, and in fact only external defeat destroyed them.

Notes

1 Significantly, Trotsky (1937, pp. 278–9), in attempting to describe and analyse
   Stalinism also uses the term Bonapartism in this text. We cannot resist quoting
   it since it also reflects his view of the symmetry of Stalinism and Fascism 'in
   spite of deep differences in social foundations'.

   > Bonapartism is one of the political weapons of the capitalist regime in its
   > critical period. Stalinism is a variety of the same system, but upon the
   > basis of a workers' state torn by the antagonism between an organized
   > and armed soviet aristocracy and the unarmed toiling masses. [. . .]

   > In the last analysis, Soviet Bonapartism owes its birth to the belatedness
   > of the world revolution. But in the capitalist countries the same cause
   > gave rise to fascism. We thus arrive at the conclusion, unexpected at first
   > glance, but in reality inevitable, that the crushing of Soviet democracy by
   > an all-powerful bureaucracy and the extermination of bourgeois democ-
   > racy by fascism were produced by one and the same cause: the dilatori-
   > ness of the world proletatriat in solving the problems set for it by history.
   > Stalinism and fascism, in spite of a deep difference in social foundations,
   > are symmetrical phenomena. In many of their features they show a deadly
   > similarity. A victorious revolutionary movement in Europe would imme-
   > diately shake not only fascism, but Soviet Bonapartism.

2 The literature on national socialism as an ideology, a movement and a party in
   power fills libararies. For a bibliography see Herre and Auerbach and supplement edited by Thile Vogelsang *Vierteljahrshefte für Zeitgeschichte* (since
   1953). Basic in English is Bracher (1970), with bibliography, pp. 503–33. For
   annotated critical bibliography, Orlow (1969, 1973). See also Bracher and
   Jacobsen (1970). Useful reviews are Broszat (1966), Nolte (1963), the anthologies of documents with introductions by Hofer (1957), Remak (1969), and
   Noakes and Pridham (1974), and for the period 1933–5, Wheaton (1969). Still
   indispensable is the classic work by Franz Neumann (1963; originally published
   1944), *Behemoth*. An interesting overview of German politics, society, and
   culture under the Nazis is Grunberger (1971). For excellent biographical
   sketches of the Nazi leadership, Fest (1970). To place Nazism in the context

of German society and history see Dahrendorf (1967). An excellent documentary collection is Tyrell (1969). A most stimulating review of conflicting or complementary interpretations of Nazism is Sauer (1967).

3 In addition to the more sophisticated Marxist analyses of fascism we cannot ignore the partisan interpretations of Aquila, Zetkin, Togliatti, Dutt discussed by Nolte (1967), De Felice (1969, 1970), and Gregor (1974b), the Trotskyite Guerin (1939), and more recent writings of Lopukhov (1965), Galkin (1970), and Vajda (1972), reviewed by Gregor (1974c, pp. 370–84), as well as the responses of the Third International (Fetscher, 1962; Pirker, 1965).

4 The relation of fascism to modernization is a complex issue, object of a recent debate (Turner, 1972; Gregor, 1974c; Turner, forthcoming). See also Organski (1965) and the early essay by Borkenau (1933).

References

Abendroth, W. 1967: *Faschismus und Kapitalismus: Theorien über die sozialen Ursprünge und die Funktion des Faschismus*. Frankfurt: Europäische Verlagsanstalt.

Borkenau, F. 1933: Zur Sociologie des Faschismus. In Ernst Nolte (ed.), *Theorien über den Faschismus*. Cologne: Kiepenheuer & Witsch.

Bracher, K. D. 1970: *The German Dictatorship*. New York: Praeger.

Bracher, K. D., and Jacobsen, H.-A., (eds) 1970: *Bibliographie zue Politik in Theorie und Praxis*. Düsseldorf: Droste Verlag.

Broszat, M. 1966: *German National Socialism, 1919–1945*. Santa Barbara: Clio Press.

Buchheim, H. 1953: *Glaubenskrise im Dritten Reich: Drei Kapitel Nationalsozialistischer Religionspolitik*. Stuttgart: Deutsche Verlags-Anstalt.

Carsten, F. L. 1967: *The Rise of Fascism*. Berkeley: University of California Press.

Dahrendorf, R. 1967: *Society and Democracy in Germany*. Garden City, NY: Doubleday.

De Felice, R. 1966: *Mussolini il fascista. I: La conquista del potere. 1921–1925*. Torino: Einaudi.

——— 1969: *Le Interpretazioni del Fascismo*. Bari: Laterza.

——— 1970: *Il Fascismo: Le Interpretazioni dei contemporanei e degli storici*. Bari: Laterza.

Delzell, C. F. (ed.) 1970: *Mediterranean Fascism 1919–1945*. New York: Harper & Row.

Fest, J. C. 1970: *The Face of the Third Reich: Portraits of the Nazi Leadership*. New York: Pantheon Books.

Fetsher, I. 1962: Faschismus und Nationalsozialismus: Zur Kritik des sowjetmarxistischen Faschismusbegriffs. *Politishce Vierteljahresschrift* 3, 42–63.

Galkin, A. 1970: Capitalist society and fascism. *Social Sciences* (Published by the USSR Academy of Sciences) 1, 128–38.

Gregor, A. J. 1968: *Contemporary Radical Ideologies*. New York: Random House.

—— 1969: *The Ideology of Fascism: The Rationale of Totalitarianism*. New York: Free Press.

—— 1974a: *The Fascist Persuasion in Radical Politics*. Princeton: Princeton University Press.

—— 1974b: *Interpretations of Fascism*. Morristown, NJ.: General Learning Press.

—— 1974c: Fascism and modernization: some addenda. *World Politics* 26, 370–84.

Grunberger, R. 1971: *The 12-Year Reich: A Social History of Nazi Germany 1933–1945*. New York: Holt, Rinehart and Winston.

Hamilton, A. 1971: *The Appeal of Fascism*. New York: Avon.

Hayes, P. M. 1973: *Fascism*. New York: Free Press.

Herre, V. F. and Auerbach, H. 1955: *Bibliographie zur Zeitgeschichte und zum Zweiten Weltkrieg für die Jahre 1945–1950*. Munich: Instituts für Zeitgeschichte.

Hoepke, K. P. 1968: *Die deutsche Rechte und der italienische Faschismus*. Düsseldorf: Droste Verlag.

Hofer, W. (ed.) 1957: *Der Nationalsozialismus: Dokumente 1933–1945*. Frankfurt am Main: Fischer Bücherei.

International Journal of Politics 1973: Vol. 2, no. 4. Critiques of fascism theory from the West German New Left. Several essays.

Kaltefleiter, W. 1968: *Wirtschaft und Politik in Deutschland: Konjunktur als Bestimmungsfaktor des Parteiensystems*. Cologne: Westdeutscher Verlag.

Kedward, H. R. 1969: *Fascism in Western Europe 1900–45*. Glasgow: Blackie.

Kele, M. H. 1972: *Nazis and Workers: National Socialist Appeals to German Labor, 1919–1933*. Chapel Hill: University of North Carolina Press.

Kühnl, R. 1966: *Die nationalsozialistische Linke 1925–1930*. Meisenheim am Glan: Anton Hain.

Laqueur, W. and Mosse, G. L. (eds) 1966: *International Fascism, 1920–1945*. New York: Harper & Row.

Lepsius, R. 1968: The collapse of an intermediary power structure: Germany 1933–1934. *International Journal of Comparative Sociology* 9, 289–301.

Lewy, G. 1965: *The Catholic Church and Nazi Germany*. New York: McGraw-Hill.

Linz, J. J. 1970: From Falange to Movimiento-Organización: the Spanish single party and the Franco regime 1936–1968. In S. Huntington and C. Moore (eds.), *Authoritarian Politics in Modern Societies: The Dynamics of Established One Party Systems*. New York: Basic Books.

—— 1976: Some notes towards a comparative study of fascism in socio-logical-historical perspective. In Walter Laqueur (ed.), *A Guide to Fascism*.

Linz, J. J., and Stepan, A. (eds) (forthcoming). *Breakdown and Crises of Democracies*.

Lipset, S. M. 1960: 'Fascism' – left, right, and center. In S. M. Lipset, *Political Man: The Social Bases of Politics*. Garden City, NY: Doubleday.

Lopukhov, B. R. 1965: Il problema del fascismo italiano negli scritti di autori sovietici. *Studi storici* 6, 239–57.

Lukács, G. 1955: *Die Zerstörung der Vernunft*. Berlin: Aufbau-Verlag.

Mansilla, H. C. F. 1971: *Faschismus und eindimensionale Gesellschaft*. Neuwied: Luchterhand.

Maruyama, M. 1963: *Thought and Behaviour in Modern Japanese Politics*. London: Oxford University Press.

Massing, P. W. 1949: *Rehearsal for Destruction: A Study of Political Anti-Semitism in Imperial Germany*. New York: Fertig.

Merkl, P. H. (forthcoming). *Political Violence under the Swastika: 581 Early Nazis*. Princeton: Princeton University Press.

Morris, I. (ed.) 1968: *Japan 1931–1945: Militarism, Fascism, Japanism?* Lexington, MA.: D. C. Heath.

Mosse, G. L. 1964: *The Crisis of German Ideology: Intellectual Origins of the Third Reich*, New York: Grosset & Dunlap.

—— 1966: *Nazi Culture: Intellectual, Cultural and Social Life in the Third Reich*. New York: Grosset & Dunlap.

Neumann, F. 1963: *Behemoth: The Structure and Practice of National Socialism 1933–1944* (first edn 1944). New York: Octagon.

Neumann, S. 1942: *Permanent Revolution: Totalitarianism in the Age of International Civil War*. New York: Harper.

Noakes, J., and Pridham, G. (eds) 1974: *Documents on Nazism 1919–1945*. London: Jonathan Cape.

Nolte, E. 1963: *Der Nationalsozialismus*. München: R. Piper & Co.

—— 1966: *Die faschistischen Bewegungen*. München: Deutscher Taschen-buch Verlag.

—— (ed.) 1967: *Theorien über den Faschismus*. Cologne: Kiepenheuer.

—— 1968: *Die Krise des liberalen Systems und die faschistischen Bewegungen*. Munich: Piper.

—— 1969: *Three Faces of Fascism: Action Française, Italian Fascism, and National Socialism*. New York: Mentor Book.

Organski, A. F. K. 1965: *The Stages of Political Development*. New York: Knopf.

Orlow, D. 1969: *The History of the Nazi Party: 1919–1933*. Pittsburgh: University of Pittsburgh Press.

—— 1973: *The History of the Nazi Party: 1933–1945*. Pittsburgh: University of Pittsburgh Press.

Pirker, T. (ed.) 1965: *Komintern und Faschismus, 1920–1940: Dokumente zur Geschichte und Theorie des Fascismus*. Stuttgart: Deutsche Verlag-Anstalt.

Pulzer, P. G. J. 1964: *The Rise of Political Anti-Semitism in Germany and Austria*. New York: Wiley.

Remak, J. (ed.) 1969: *The Nazi Years: A Documentary History*. Englewood Cliffs, NJ: Prentice Hall.

Rogger, H., and Weber, E. (eds) 1966: *The European Right: A Historical Profile*. Berkeley: University of California Press.

Salvemini, G. 1961: *Scritti sul fascismo*. Milano: Feltrinelli.

Sauer, W. 1967: National Socialism: totalitarianism or fascism? *American Historical Review* 73, 404–24.

Sontheimer, K. 1968: *Antidemokratisches Denken in der Weimarer Republik*. Munich: Nymphenburger Verlagshandlung.

Thalheimer, A. 1930: Über den faschismus. *Gegen den Strom: Organ der KPD (Opposition)*. Reprinted in O. Bauer, H. Marcuse, and A. Rosenberg (1967), *Faschismus und Kapitalismus*. Edited by Wolfgang Abendroth. Frankfurt: Europäische Verlagsantalt.

Trindade, H. 1974: *Integralismo: O Fascismo Brasileiro na Decada de 30*. São Paulo: Difusão Europeia do Livro.

Trotsky, L. 1937: *The Revolution Betrayed*. New York: Doubleday.

Turner, H. A. 1972: Fascism and Modernization. *World Politics* 24, 547–64.

——— (forthcoming): Fascism and Modernization: A Few Corrections. *World Politics*.

Tyrell, A. (ed.) 1969: *Führer Befiehl . . . Selbstzeugnisse aus der 'Kampfzeit' der NSDAP Dokumentation und Analyse*. Düsseldorf: Droste.

Weber, E. 1964: *Varieties of Fascism*. Princeton: Van Nostrand.

Wheaton, E. B. 1969: *Prelude to Calamity. With a Background Survey of the Weimar Era*. Garden City, NY: Doubleday.

Winkler, H. A. 1972: *Mittelstand, Demokratie und Nationalsozialismus, Die Politische Entwicklung von Handwerk und Kleinhandel in der Weimarer Republik*. Cologne: Kiepenheuer und Witsch.

Woolf, S. J. (ed.) 1968: *The Nature of Fascism*. London: Weidenfeld and Nicolson.

——— (ed.) 1969: *European Fascism*. New York: Random House (Vintage).

16

*The drive towards synthesis**

ROGER EATWELL

The spectral–syncretic model

The problem of producing a model of generic fascism can best be understood by considering it within the context of four themes: (a) 'natural
history'; (b) geopolitics; (c) political economy; and (d) leadership,
activism, party and propaganda. The problems of list-approaches have
already been considered, and the above four themes are not proposed as
a new form of list. Rather they are issues through which it is possible to see
both the central syntheses of fascism and the spectrum of positions which
could derive from this. Hence, it is called 'the spectral–syncretic' model.

It is based on a study of primarily European fascism, both as a movement and as a regime. It is particularly important not to ignore the former.
Whilst it is vital never to lose sight of what fascist regimes actually did,
policy should not necessarily be seen as providing the true key to fascist
ideology. The two classic regimes were relatively short-lived and, like
communism in the Soviet Union, they found it necessary at times to
accommodate both internal and external forces. Thus post-1945 intellectual fascists have sometimes claimed that inter-war fascism exhibited
'immaturity and incoherent ideology' (*Rising*, No.4, 1983, p. 5). Moreover,
fascism in Italy during its closing stages sought a return to the early
movement's radicalism, and some of the more thoughtful European neo-
fascists have held that both the Hitler and Mussolini regimes betrayed, or
deformed fascism by accommodating more conservative groups. Some
attention is thus also paid to European neo-fascist views, especially as
they highlight the possibility of a fascist ideology which is dialectical, which
reacts to a changed world. Indeed, far too much discussion of fascist
ideology sees it as locked in a narrow time-periodization. (Must the conservative heirs of Burke be judged solely within the intellectual and social
context of Britain at the turn of the nineteenth century?!). The model itself
is thus a spectral–syncretic distillation of different phases of fascism. As
such it tries to limit the problem which afflicts some ideological models,
namely a tendency to focus exclusively on the more interesting fascist

* Extract from Roger Eatwell, 'Towards a New Model of Generic Fascism', *Journal of
Theoretical Politics*, 4(2) (1992), pp. 174–85, 189–90.

intellectuals, like Drieu La Rochelle, who, according to one leading critic, had minimal influence over actual fascist leaders and parties (Allardyce, 1979: 378).

Natural history

There is something dangerous about talking of 'in the beginning' when discussing fascist ideology. Those present at the creation of the first twentieth-century fascist movements were political activists, individuals who were mainly lightweight theoretical magpies, borrowing from diverse sources, and developing ideas to accommodate both contextual and principled changes. Moreover, in view of the violence and atrocities which characterized fascism from the outset, it is important to underline that many of its activists need understanding in terms of psychopathology rather than political theory. Nevertheless, a relatively constant set of ideas and debates can be discerned among early fascists – from which most other positions subsequently tended to derive. Arguably the most central of these in early twentieth-century Europe were views on what could be termed 'Natural History', which were linked to the idea of the creation of a 'new man'.

The idea of nature as a model of human existence exercised a profound attraction on Nietzsche, whose thought influenced many fascists (though it was corrupted in the process). The word 'nature' occurs throughout Hitler's *Mein Kampf*, but he was only picking up a theme to be found earlier within Italian Fascism, and intellectuals linked in some way to Fascism. The Mussolini–Gentile entry in the 1932 *Enciclopedia Italiana* begins by arguing that 'In order to know men it is necessary to know man; and in order to know man it is necessary to know reality and laws' (Mussolinni, 1936: 68). These laws were partly derived from views about human nature, and a tendency to use biological explanations can be found in many fascist writers. These views derived mainly from the late nineteenth-century attack on positivism, and more specifically from Social Darwinism.

Fascism was influenced by Social Darwinism in at least two senses. The first was the emphasis on a hierarchical, evolutionary chain. Man was not born equal, nor was he essentially rational. He was easily swayed, and tended to be lazy, to lack goals, to be decadent. As Valois's thought shows, fascism in a sense reversed Rousseau. In nature man was an ignoble savage until civilized by strong leaders. Fascism held that man needed to be welded into a new community, with a less materialist set of goals. At the core of this community would be the traditional, male-dominated family, but in terms of wider values there would be dramatic changes. Indeed, even the emphasis on family was countered by youth organizations, which in some ways threatened the autonomy of the family. The new community fascism sought would end the alienation and decadence which came from the individualistic, mercenary and inherently divisive liberal democratic–capitalist form of society. Fascism thus sought to remake man, not least in a more martial form. For the second aspect of Social Darwinism which was picked up by fascism was more the emphasis on survival of the fittest, the need to maintain a society based on the willingness to wage war, or at least healthy enough to avoid falling into the false cosiness of individualistic–materialistic domesticity. Indeed, Lorenz warned the Nazis that domestication was a greater danger than race mixing.

The implications of these views for fascism have, understandably in view of fascism's historical record, tended to be seen by commentators in a one-sided way. Thus the emphasis has been on hierarchy or manipulation rather than on the alleged freedom which would flow from a consciousness of nature, and the creation of new values which broke away from alienating capitalist plutocracy. Similarly, militarism has been analysed largely in terms of aggressive male values, of foreign conquest and the subjugation of 'lesser peoples'. A more careful study of historical reality would show that some forms of fascism, for example the Iron Guard, were not expansionary. Moreover, militarism had another side: a sense of 'blood socialism', of the community of the trenches, of the willingness to die for a cause rather than to 'live' in the pursuit of alienating individual material reward (Jünger, 1920; Röhm, 1928). Here we begin to see the impact of history, in particular the vivid memories of the First World War in the formative years after 1918.

Fascism's more general philosophy of history can be glimpsed through the views of Rocco, an Italian Fascist professor of law. He held a typical cyclical vision. This was no liberal or Marxist linear view of history as the story of progress. Rather, it was a tale of the unending struggle of state authority against centrifugal forces of disintegration. Italian Fascism's interest in Ancient Rome was not simply a question of using its glories for propaganda purposes. The fall of Rome was important as a source of historical lessons. Rome fell because of decadence and a lack of discipline (see, in particular, Evola's works on the decline of 'Traditional' society). It was defeated by less sophisticated, but more virile primitive peoples who had not experienced the debilitating effects of domesticity.

Yet this was no fatalist cyclical philosophy. In the Classical world decadence was regarded almost as a law of nature. Civilizations rose and fell with recurring regularity. Fascism synthesized natural and historical arguments by adapting vitalist and activist ideas. The human will was capable of freeing man, and shaping destiny and history. Or more exactly, the will of a small number of those born to rule could bring about such changes. Following Machiavelli and Pareto, these natural rulers were not necessarily equated with the existing ruling elite. Indeed, a central aspect of the fascist critique was the belief that existing elites had failed in important ways.

History thus reinforced the biological views: it taught a whole series of lessons about what man was like, and how societies developed. For example, it confirmed the importance of property: did not each regiment at Verdun fight to defend its own 'patch'! (Valois, 1921: 265 ff.). For Gentile, history showed how the rise of secularism and individualism had destroyed faith and heroism. He saw fascism as the continuation of the struggle between the idealist spirit of Mazzini and the materialist scepticism of Giolitti, the two souls of Italy (Gentile, 1961: 15–50). More generally, history was seen to show the need for elites. Bourgeois conceptions of history were wrong: it was great men, exercising power and vision who produced significant changes. History was sometimes even taken to show that a particular nation had a unique destiny (Poliakov, 1974).

Interpretations of the lessons of nature and history also helped reconcile apparently different groups. Thus in Italy Fascism had strong continuities with earlier nationalist and syndicalist groups (De Grand, 1978; Roberts, 1979). One of the core points which helped bring some of their members together during and after the First World War was a belief that myths, particularly nationalism, could be used to mobilize the people. Indeed, they were seen as vital to counter socialist myths, notably the dream of equality (Corradini is a good example of someone who sought to free the people from socialist myths – and Giolittian corruption).

The result was not an irrationalist philosophy, or a 'non-intellectual, even anti-intellectual' position, as many critics have argued (O'Sullivan, 1983: 40; Trevor-Roper, 1968: 21). It was more an anti-rationalist philosophy in the sense of its hostility to liberalism and Marxism. There was nothing irrational in believing that man had certain traits, or that history taught certain lessons. Nor was there anything irrational in believing than an individual, or group of dedicated individuals, might change the course of history – though clearly the possibilities of such vitalist views are open to debate.

Presented in this way, the argument helps differentiate fascism from other ideologies. For example, an emphasis on decadence was common within reactionary thought, but this was much more pessimistic overall. To a lesser extent this was true of conservative thought, which often featured natural and historical views close to fascism (Blinkhorn, 1990). What it did not feature, except where it began to shade into fascism, was the existentialist side, and the revolutionary implications of fascism.

However, the argument presented above is also too clear-cut, too heuristic. Differences of stress and interpretation can be found on these issues among fascists. For example, what exactly did revolution mean? Was it the violent overthrow of the existing system, or could it come more peacefully, encompassing a fundamental spiritual change? Gregor Strasser often wrote of revolution as spiritual change (Lane and Rupp, 1978: xix). Would it be necessary to destroy existing socializing agencies, notably the church, or could they be used? Was decadence so deep-rooted that even after the revolution it would be necessary for extended indoctrination in order to create the new man? Or would decadence disappear with the passing of the old order, allowing a less authoritarian-organized form of state subsequently to emerge?

Papini argued that development to higher forms requires some sacrifice of the mass, of little man (Lyttelton, 1973: 24). Ideas such as duty and sacrifice were central to fascism, but the point being highlighted here is that fascism was not the pure celebration of the people to be found in more populist thought. This was not simply a question of the inherent inequalities in people. There was at times even a kind of contempt for the masses.

This raises the vital problem of how the basic unit of the people, the community, was perceived. The standard answer is that the nation, or race was this unit. Indeed, fascism is universally portrayed as the very epitome of hyper- or ultra-nationalism. However, whilst this is a *vital* perspective, there is a misleading aspect to the focus on nationalism [and racism, especially as such views were pervasive in European culture (Mosse, 1978)]. If nationalism is conceived in ethnocentric rather than polycentric terms, how is it possible to explain the thousands who volunteered from many countries to fight with the Nazis against Bolshevism? (Degrelle, 1969a).

The Mussolini–Gentile entry in the 1932 *Enciclopedia Italiana* noted that the nation is '[n]ot a race, nor a geographically determined region' (Mussolini, 1936: 72). This was accompanied by the view that the nation does not constitute the state so much as the state makes the nation. The boundaries of the nation were thus fluid, and a form of Fascist Internationalism appears at least as early as 1930. Later, the Salò Republic's constitution encompassed a form of Europeanism. However, this internationalism did not encompass a view of equal-community with, say, black Africans. Indeed, parts of Africa were seen as ripe for colonization. On the other hand, Italian Fascism had no indigenous theory of racial superiority (the tall, blond, Aryan male eulogized in Nazi propaganda was hardly designed to appeal in southern Mediterranean cultures, though it might be added that Nazi leaders hardly corresponded to this ideal either). Moreover, central to the Italian colonial idea was a quest for land to provide work and opportunities. The theme of colonies as something to be exploited was a minor one (De Felice, 1976: 65–7).

National Socialism placed much greater emphasis on biology and race, though some Nazis did not hold deep-rooted anti-semitic views. Hitler held that 'The Jewish doctrine of Marxism rejects the aristocratic principle of Nature' (1969: 60), whilst simultaneously arguing that Jewish materialism lay behind capitalism. To explain this paradox, Hitler held that there was a Jewish conspiracy to destroy Western civilization. In the words of the propaganda film, *The Eternal Jew* (1940), 'This is no religion . . . this is a conspiracy against all non-Jews, of a cunning, unhealthy, contaminated race' who believed that *they* were the 'Chosen People'. This view owed much to Rosenberg's anti-Semitism, which was more cultural, holding that Jews were a distinct race, from which dangerous cultural characteristics could be deduced (Rosenberg, 1982). On the other hand, Eckhart saw Jewishness as something spiritual, a materialistic bent which exists in everyone. Thus, whereas the former views were inherently genocidal, Eckhart's interpretation pointed more to the need for Germany to retain a sense of 'Jewishness'. In terms of actual policy, Jews were allowed to leave Germany as late as 1940 (though having suffered terrible persecution), and Nazi policy until the start of the war seems to have been to make Europe as a whole 'Jew Free' through forced emigration (Marrus, 1989).

Although Nazi racism was based mainly on biology, it was not uniquely nationalist. Biological argument was in some ways a geopolitical defence of *all* Aryan peoples, and involved an embryonic Europeanism (Herzstein, 1982). In the short run, there was the threat from Bolshevism, not just at home, but in terms of Bolshevik hordes from the East. Bolshevism's ideological commitment to class politics, ultimate equality, internationalism and other principles was anathema to most fascists. (NB. There were some who saw affinities with communism.) In the longer run there was the problem of the USA. Hitler's *Secret Book* (1962) raises the spectre of a future conflict between Europe and the USA. Especially in Nazi ideology, the USA was seen as the epitome of capitalist decadence, a *Gesellschaft* linked only by the pursuit of wealth, and riddled with divisions [see the Nazi propaganda film, *Round the Statue of Liberty* (1941)]. However, this was countered by the expansionary implications of its capitalist culture and the military implications of its ever-growing wealth. Europeanism could even have a socio-economic as well as geopolitical aspect: it was part of a 'third way' (between communism and capitalism) vision of social organization.

Some leading non-German/Italian, fascists, for example Degrelle, Mosley and Szálasi, increasingly saw a European rather than national dimension to their politics (Degrelle, 1969b; Mosley, 1958). Since 1945 the more thoughtful and intellectual European fascists have shown an even greater tendency to some form of Europeanism rather than nationalism (though with the inevitable spectrum of opinions as to what was sought, and disputes over past intra-national border grievances). A leading European neo-fascist thinker, Bardéche, even entitled his seminal journal *Défense de l'Occident*, and wrote in one of the most interesting overt expositions of neo-fascist thought that fascism's 'mission of the Defence of the West has remained in the memory, and this is still the chief meaning of fascist ideas' (Bardèche, 1961: 88). Geopolitics now included the general defence of Western culture, even outside Europe, against the multiple threats of communism, Third World liberationism, and the rise of Japanese economic power (Evola, 1979; Yockey, 1948). One leading commentator has argued that 'fascist internationalism was a contradiction in terms' (Woolf, 1981: 17). In fact, it is one of the most under-researched aspects of fascism.

Nevertheless, it is important not to lose sight of the nationalist theme. Nationalism, like racism, also had a mythical dimension (much less true of Europeanism, which appealed more to the 'intellectuals'). Thus, following Sorel, the crucial point was not the prior truth or logic of an argument, but its ability to motivate and thus take on an objective force. As a radical ideology, a central question for classic fascism was how to rouse the masses from their slumbers. Here again the influence of natural and historical arguments combined. From natural arguments fascists derived a belief that people wished to combine in like groups, that they were only fulfilled in such groups. History taught that one of the great mobilizers of the people was racism or nationalism. Thus Hitler in *Mein Kampf* clearly stresses the role of anti-semitism in attracting working-class support in turn-of-the-century Vienna (1969: 51, 90 ff.). The impact of the First World War, when left-wing dreams of proletarian unity shattered in the face of mass jingoism, offered a far more important pointer.

Before the Second World War, these factors led many in Germany and Italy to the idea of the need for a new empire, or *Lebenstraum* (the idea of 'Eurafrica' lingered on after 1945). Marxist critics have often seen such policies as a reflection of the influence of business on fascism, in particular the quest for new markets and sources of cheap labour at a time of declining profits. However, studies of Nazi policy in particular have shown that its East European vision was largely developed before significant business donations were made to the party. More important were the desires both to counteract Bolshevism and to provide a basis for the economic health of the state. For most fascists, this was not a step on the path to world domination, though Nazi imperialism had rather confused motives (Smith, 1986). Hence both Germany and Italy could sign a pact with Japan, which did not threaten their interests, but which shared a common fear of the Soviet Union. Some were also interested in pacts with Arab countries, though here motives encompassed anti-Semitism and economic interests too. British and French fascists similarly tended to have no concept of world domination, more a sense of 'natural' spheres of interest. Among the smaller European countries a few fascists dreamed of new, or restored empires, but most were realistic of their state's potential. Their fascism tended, therefore, not to be expansionary (with the exception of the specific 'rectification' of boundaries, somewhat capriciously drawn by the post-1918 peace treaties).

Political economy

Hitler in *Mein Kampf* wrote that 'economics is only of second- or third-rate importance' (1969: 206) in comparison to factors such as politics or the blood. Speer has even argued that the Führer's dream was to use technology to colonize Eastern Europe, and then to institute a kind of back to the land policy, though the neglected testimony of Degrelle (Hitler said he would have chosen Degrelle as his son) portrays Hitlerism as essentially technological-modernizing (Degrelle, 1968b; Speer, 1982). Certainly there were other fascists who placed great emphasis on economics. One of the central ideas in Valois's thought was how to make work meaningful. Economics was even more central to Mosley: the 1929 depression was arguably the key factor in his conversion to fascism (Mosley, 1932). Nevertheless, there were some linking strands in fascist thought about economics, though it is important to separate policies developed in a particular context from more fundamental principle. In particular, fascism sought to find a 'Third Way' between capitalism and communism. There was also an element in Nazism which sought to synthesize 'the antimodernist, romantic, and irrationalist ideas present in German nationalism and . . . modern technology' (Herf, 1984: 1).

Fascist thought essentially defended private property, a factor which stemmed from both natural and historical theories about social organization. Early Italian Fascism had a distinct *laissez-faire* element within it, but private property was never seen as sacrosanct. There was a willingness both to accept extensive state interference in the market and state ownership. Thus the Nazi Economic Emergency Programme of 1932 made it clear that private property must work in the state's interests. This synthesis of private and state, which had some similarities with emerging social democratic thought as can be seen especially in the work of De Man and Mosley, was part of a widespread fascist quest for a 'Third Way' between communism and capitalism (De Man, 1932). However, it is important to stress that the 'socialism' of fascism was essentially propagandistic, or more specifically anti-capitalist. Fascists never held what are usually key socialist ideas, most notably conceptions relating to equality (though there was a strong element of 'welfarism' in fascism) and ownership.

The extent to which such policies were propaganda rather than rhetoric has been the subject of much dispute, particularly among Marxism who see fascism as essentially operating in the interests of business. Although in the early years Nazi policies and propaganda seemed designed to win *Mittelstand* support, in general after 1933 Nazi policy increasingly operated against the interests of small business, and proto-ecological and *völkisch* propaganda largely disappeared (Noakes and Pridham, 1974). This might point more to policies operating in the interests of big business.

Certainly after 1923 the Nazis began to court larger business, increasingly playing down some of the anti-capitalist rhetoric. But here too there are problems. These can be seen by considering fascim's autarchy, a policy which did bring some gains to small business, especially in the agricultural sector (the Fascist policy of wheat autarchy is a particularly good example of political determination: it was clearly designed to foster rural support rather than suit industrial needs).

There is little in *Mein Kampf* about autarchy, but Hitler seems to have feared that extensive trade outside Germany would leave it at the mercy of hostile powers and international Jewish finance. He also feared that increasing industrialization elsewhere threatened employment at home. The last point was especially important to Mosley too, though he believed that the application of Western science and technology might help preserve a competitive lead. However, the autarchy envisaged was not within a single country. The Nazi vision was linked to eastern European expansion; Mosley's to maintaining the British empire; and Italian autarchy was linked to creating a new empire. Moreover, these policies were political more than economic, and were certainly not determined by business interests. Italian business was divided, but much of it was worried by the colonial expansion and the resulting imposition of sanctions. Hitler had to reassure German businessmen in the early years of the regime that autarchy would only apply to some vital goods, adding that to a large extent the policy was being forced on Germany by a general rise in protectionism (Hayes, 1987; Sarti, 1971).

It seems best to consider autarchy as part of the context of classic fascism rather than a fundamental principle. This is not simply a question of the economic position of Germany or Italy in the 1930s, or the fact that in some of the smaller European countries fascist autarchy could be realistic in the light of the extremely limited international trade which took place. The autarchy policy was also very much part of an expansionary foreign policy. Indeed, the whole development of economic policy in the two classic examples of fascism cannot be separated from their foreign policy goals. Thus in Germany small industrial businesses, which still formed an important part of the economy, were increasingly being leant on by 1939 to improve efficiency as part of the armaments drive. At the more theoretical level, there might seem a contradiction in Valois's thought between his emphasis on production, and the anti-hedonist side of his fascism. In fact, Valois's technocratic side was designed to provide the funds for both extensive welfare and the arms necessary for defence in the modern age (1906: 169–81).

In order more fully to understand the underlying principles behind economic policy, it is necessary to turn to fascim's views on social and political institutions (Broszat, 1981). A common belief among fascists was that capitalism produced not just alienation, but was enslaving. Mosley saw capitalism as unfreedom, holding that the beginning of liberty is the end of economic chaos. Thus economic revival, not possible under free market capitalism, was essential to increase positive freedom. José Antonio's key speech on 29 October 1933 argued in a similar vein:

> [. . .] the liberal state came to offer us economic slavery, saying to the workers, with tragic sarcasm: 'You are free to work as you with [. . .] Since we are rich, we offer you the conditions that please us; as free citizens, you are not obliged to accept them [. . .]; but as poor citizens you will die of hunger'. (Payne, 1962: 38)

The liberal state included parliamentary institutions as well as capitalism. Such 'democratic' forms were universally despised by fascists, though they could use them where it suited their purposes. Parliamentary politics were seen as leading to weakness and lack of authority. The multi-party systems which characterized much of Europe were seen as part of this cancer, especially as they helped create false social divisions.

So what did fascism propose to replace this despised capitalist–liberal–democratic system? The answer, according to previous commentators, is the strong state. Certainly Mussolini and Mosley wrote extensively about the state, though there were a few fascists, like Brasillach, who seemed suspicious of permanent central authority (Tucker, 1975). Exactly what was meant by this strong state, however, was not always clear. It has been claimed that 'Never did [. . .] any major Nazi writer before 1933, prophesy a dictatorship' (Lane and Rupp, 1978: xii). In *Mein Kampf* Hitler wrote that '[t]he state is a means to an end' (1969: 357), adding little about what a Nazi state would be like. In terms of state theory it is interesting to consider the Action Française, given the usual high level of its theorizing. Many commentators have not seen this group as fascist, mainly on account of its lack of mass-mobilizing policies. However, in 1923 Maurras called Italian Fascism close cousins even twin sisters to his group; if he later stressed differences with fascism this stemmed mainly from a need to fend off other French nationalist groups by avoiding any tainting with foreign doctrine, and later by his anti-Germanism. Interestingly, Maurras called for a decentralization of government and less Jacobin *étatisme*, though this was to be under elite control.

Italian fascist often talked of creating a totalitarian state in a positive sense, meaning in particular the achievement of social unity. However, it is particularly important when discussing political and economic forms to be wary of separating propaganda from ideology for two main reasons. First, like Marxism, fascism was more a critique- and transition-based ideology than a utopian one. It was notably vague about basic economic and political institutions. Indeed, it has been claimed that 'When the Nazis took office, they had no coherent economic programme' (Noakes and Pridham 1974: 375). Second, there was a philosophical explanation for this as well as the obvious historical point that the classic fascist movements went relatively quickly from small opposition groups to running the government. This was the Bergsonian idea, common among some fascists, that all is flux, that ultimate reality is a continuous, unpredictable process of creation which could not be grasped by the intellect but only intuited, lived. This was hardly a philosophy suited to the practicalities of government, and policy-oriented fascist thinkers developed more concrete ideas.

Thus fascism in practice was often a strange mix of ill-thought out and *ad hoc* policies. For example, Point 19 of the 1920 Nazi programme had called for replacement of Roman Law, 'which serves a materialist world order', with German common law. However, after 1933 the regime operated a weird mixture of Weimar continuities in some areas, on to which were grafted often inconsistent new Nazi policies (Koch, 1989). Thus judges were encouraged to consider principles such as 'healthy popular feeling' and 'the Führer's Will'. The rule of law was not simply broken through the bestialities of fascism, conducted after 1933 on a daily basis by non-state agencies such as the SS. It was dismantled in a piecemeal attempt to create a new order in which legalistic individual rights had no meaning. The ending of the rule of law even received academic support. Heidegger, in his Rectorial address to Freiburg University in April 1933, justified the elimination of academic freedoms and accepted Hitler's will as the primary guiding light. Schmitt, in an attempt to resolve the dualism of individual and state which cursed liberal democracy, defended the *Führerprinzip*. Only subsequently, after the full horrors of Nazism had become clear, did some of the more thoughtful European neo-fascists, like Mosley, begin to question the precise role of law and the limits of state power (Mosley, 1961).

The most consistently advocated socio-economic institution by fascists in Europe was corporatism. Indeed, one leading authority on France has argued that 'Every French fascist movement in the interwar period posited corporatism as the answer to Marxism' (Soucy, 1986: 160–1). Corporatism was meant to institutionalize social unity by linking workers, management and the state. Italy created the facade of such a system, as did Franco's Spain and Salazar's Portugal. Hitler wrote in *Mein Kampf* of a 'future economic parliament or chambers of estates' (1969: 546), but the Nazis never created an elaborate facade of corporatism. Rather, as in Italy, corporatist rhetoric was used to hide the brutal suppression of free trade unions by the state. This points to dangers in seeing corporatism as a key defining aspect of fascism, especially as the term is open to significantly different interpretations. For example, was the system essentially authoritarian–statist, or more syndicalist. Moreover, some European neo-fascists have been highly critical of corporatism, arguing that it managed to combine the worst aspects of capitalism and socialism/communism: namely continuing division between workers and employers on the one hand, and increasing state bureaucracy on the other (*Vanguard*, No. 18, 1988: 14–15).

Nazi attempts to end worker alienation focused more on welfarist policies. Within factories this incorporated what one commentator has called 'the aesthetics of production'. This was the Beauty of Labour programme, which sought to return to the worker the feeling for the worth and importance of his labour (Rabinbach, 1976). More generally, there were social welfare programmes and promises to satisfy growing consumer demand. The Volkswagen car is the best-known aspect of this, though none had been marketed by the time war began (its factory was an interesting example of the beauty programme). Italian Fascism too increasingly developed a welfare side, for example through institutions like the *Dopolavoro*. This provided activities such as cheap outings to the seaside, or cultural visits, and was an important organization in terms of penetrating working-class culture (Tannenbaum, 1973).

These arguments indicate that fascist economic and political structures were flexible, and are largely to be understood in terms of context or other principles. Thus the increasing technological rather than *völkisch* theme in Nazi propaganda after 1933 reflected the move towards war footing, with its concomitant demands on production. Italian propaganda films such as *The 9th May, The 17th Year* (1939) clearly point the link between modernization, welfare, colonial expansion and national greatness. And in the post-1945 period some neo-fascists have paid more attention to economic growth as a way of ensuring national/European security. In this sense, it is clearly wrong to see fascism as a form of resistance to modernization. However, it is also misleading to see it as purely developmental. Fascism never worshipped economic growth for its own sake. Indeed, it was highly critical of purely material goals. Particularly in some forms of Nazi thought, and some European neo-fascist thought, it is even possible to discern a form of middle-way proto-ecologism, though it is important not to confuse ideology and propaganda and to be wary of subtle attempts to rehabilitate fascism (Bramwell, 1985; Pois, 1986). [. . .]

Conclusion

Most attempts to produce a generic definition of fascist ideology have been linked to a particular conception of where fascism stands on the left–right spectrum. It is normally seen as 'extreme right', though right-wing terminology is often used erratically, and fascism is sometimes also conceived as 'radical right', 'far right' and 'ultra right'. Moreover, left–right terminology fails to bring out that ideologies are better seen as multidimensional, and that at some levels there can be significant overlaps between ideologies (Eatwell, 1989).

One recent definition from a major commentator holds that: 'fascism was primarily a new variety of authoritarian conservatism and right-wing nationalism which sought to defeat the Marxist threat and the political liberalism which allowed it to exist in the first place' (Soucy, 1991: 163). Such a definition completely fails to see fascism's radical side. In an attempt to solve this problem, others have seen fascism as 'neither left nor right', as a doctrine of the 'revolutionary centre' (notably Sternhell's major works, 1978, 1983). The problem here is the opposite one; such approaches fail to see fascism's right-wing aspect.

The approach delineated above tries to resolve this problem by seeing fascism as a spectral–syncretic ideology. In other words, there was a series of core themes in European fascist ideology, notably synthesis, but these did not produce a unique set of conclusions. Some commentators, notably Sternhell, have already stressed Valois's formulation of: nationalism + socialism = fascism. However, there are misleading aspects to this formula. Moreover, fascism sought a much broader set of syntheses. Among the most important were: between a conservative view of man constrained by nature and the more left-wing view of the possibilities of creating a 'new man'; between a commitment to science, especially in terms of understanding human nature, and a more anti-rationalist, vitalist interest in the possibilities of the will (one of the factors which attracted the philosopher Heidegger to Nazism was his belief that the fall into an inauthentic mode of existence in modern society was reversible); between the faith and service of Christianity and the heroism of Classical thought; between private property relations more typical of the right and a form of welfarism more typical of the left. The Mussolini–Gentile entry in the 1932 *Enciclopedia Italiana* underlines this point when it notes that fascism was '[a]nti-positivistic, but positive', that the fascist state was 'the synthesis and unity of all values' (Mussolini, 1936: 69, 71).

Limitations on space mean that the full implicatons of the arguments set out above cannot be developed. In particular, it has not been possible to specify more precisely through specific case studies where fascism ends and where related typologies begin. This can be seen by highlighting one crucial question – what was meant by the creation of the 'new man'. The term 'new man' can be found in what might be classed 'extreme right' thought before 1914, but this reveals crucial differences with fascism, differences which underline the problems of placing fascism clearly on the left–right spectrum. For the more reactionary aspects of the extreme right, the 'new man' was essentially a misnomer: what was sought to re-instil in man old values, notably religious ones. Others on the extreme right were more artistic individuals, writing of self-actualization and distinguishing themselves from both decadent culture and the masses. Fascism sought to create what social science would call a new 'political culture'. It was in this sense that it was most totalitarian, though it never totally sought to elminate intermediate organizations such as private enterprise and the Church. Rather it sought to control them, and believed that in the long run the 'national revolution' would lead either to their withering away or to conformity.

This brief gloss on the argument does not solve all the problems of this approach, but there is clearly a series of regimes, yet alone movements, which exhibit strong affinities with fascism viewed in a spectral–syncretic way. Among the major fascist movements which have existed outside Europe was the Brazilian Integralistas. This was not simply a mimetic copy; it clearly demonstrates the need for a successful movement to adapt to local conditions and traditions (Trinidade, 1983: 312). This last point underlines the fact that it is vital not to adopt too narrow a cultural or chronological conceptualization of fascism. The same point can be made in relation to regimes. Franco's Spain and Perón's Argentina, to take two of the problem cases, had periods when they seemed able to be fitted into the model. This is not to deny that there were differences compared to the two classic regimes, but there are enough ideological points of similarity to make comparison valid. A model of generic fascism thus seems to have been delineated which can incorporate a relatively larger number of cases, but at the same time can offer grounds for rejecting such alleged examples of fascism as Pinochet's Chile (in particular, its free-market economic policies).

References

Allardyce, G. 1979: What Fascism Is Not: Thoughts on the Deflation of a Concept, *American Historial Review* 84, 367–98.

Bardèche, M. 1961: *Qu'est que le fascisme?* Paris: Les Sept Couleurs.

Blinkhorn, M. (ed.) 1990: *Fascists and Conservatives.* London: Unwin Hyman.

Bramwell, A. 1985: *Blood and Soil: Walther Darré and Hitler's Green Party.* Bourne End: Kensal Press.

Brozat, M. 1981: *The Hitler State.* Longman: London.

De Felice, R. 1976: *Fascism.* New Brunswick, NJ: Transaction Books.

De Grand, A.J. 1978: *The Italian Nationalist Association and the Rise of Fascism.* Lincoln: University of Nebraska Press, Lincoln.

Degrelle, L. 1969a: *Front de l'est.* Paris: La Table Ronde.

—— 1969b: *Hitler pour 1000 ans.* Paris: La Table Ronde.

De Man, H. 1932: *Nationalisme et socialisme.* Brussels: L'Eglantine.

Eatwell, R. 1989: Part One: Approaching the Right. In R. Eatwell and N. O'Sullivan (eds), *The Nature of the Right.* London: Pinter.

Evola, J. 1979: Sur les fondements spirituels et structuraux de l'unité européene, *Defense de l'Occident*, 167, 17–28.

Gentile, G. 1961: *Il fascismo: antologia di scritti critici*. Bologna.

Hayes, P. 1987: *Industry and Ideology.* Cambridge: Cambridge University Press.

Herf, J. 1984: *Reactionary Modernism*. Cambridge: Cambridge University Press.

Herzstein, R. 1982: *When Nazi Dreams Come True*. London: Abacus.

Hitler, A. 1962: *Hitler's Secret Book*. New York: Grove.

—— 1969: *Mein Kampf*. London: Hutchinson.

Jünger, E. 1920: *In Stahlgewittern*. Hanover: published privately.

Koch, H. 1989: *In the Name of the Volk: Political Justice in Hitler's Germany.* London: I. B. Tauris.

Lane, B. M. and Rupp, L. J. (eds) 1978: *Nazi Ideology before 1933*. Manchester: Manchester University Press.

Lyttleton, A. 1973: *Italian Fascisms: From Pareto to Gentile*. London: Jonathan Cape.

Marrus, R. 1989: *The Holocaust in History*. London: Penguin.

Mosley, O. 1958: *Europe: Faith and Plan*. London: Euphorion Books.

Mosse, G. L. 1978: *Toward the Final Solution*. New York: Howard Fertig.

Mussolini, B. 1936: *Scritti e discorsi di Benito Mussolini: (1932–33)*. Milan: Ulneo Hoepli.

Noakes, J. and Pridham, G. (eds) 1974: *Documents on Nazism, 1919–1945*. London: Jonathan Cape.

Organski, A. F. K. 1965: *The Stages of Political Development*. New York: Alfred A. Knopf.

O'Sullivan, N. 1983: *Fascism*. London: Dent.

Payne, S. G. 1962: *Falange: A History of Spanish Fascism*. Stanford: Stanford University Press.

Pois, R. 1986: *National Socialism and the Religion of Nature*. London: Croom Helm.

Poliakov, L. 1974: *The Aryan Myth*. London: Chatto and Windus.

Rabinbach, A. 1976: The Aesthetics of Production in the Third Reich, *Journal of Contemporary History* 11: 43–74.

Roberts, D. D. 1979: *The Syndicalist Tradition and Italian Fascism*. Manchester: Manchester University Press.

Röhm, E. 1928: *Die Geschichte eines Hochverraters*. Munich: Eher.

Rosenberg, A. 1982: *The Myth of the Twentieth Century*. Torrance: Noontide Press.

Sarti, R. 1971: *Fascism and the Industrial Leadership in Italy, 1919–1940*. Berkeley: University of California Press.

Smith W. D. 1986: *The Ideological Origins of Nazi Imperialism*. Oxford: Oxford University Press.

Soucy, R. 1986: *French Fascism: The First Wave, 1924–1933*. New Haven, CT: Yale University Press.

—— 1991: French Fascism and the Croix de Feu: A Dissenting Interpretation, *Journal of Contemporary History* 26, 159–88.

Speer, A. 1982: *The Slave State*. London: Weidenfeld and Nicolson.

Sternhall, Z. 1978: *La droite révolutionnaire, 1885–1914. Les origines française du fascisme*. Paris: Seuil.

——1983: *Ni droite, ni gauche*. Paris: Editions du Seuil.

Tannenbaum, E. R. 1973: *Fascism in Italy*. London: Allen Lane.

Trevor-Roper, H. R. 1968: The Phenomenon of Fascism, in S. J. Woolf (ed.) *European Fascism*. London: Weidenfeld and Nicolson.

Trinidade, H. 1983: La question du fascisme en Amérique Latine, *Revue Française de Science Politique* 33, 281–312.

Tucker, W. R. 1975: *The Fascist Ego: A Political Biography of Robert Brasillach*. Berkeley: University of California Press.

Valois, G. 1921: *D'un siècle à l'autre*. Paris: Nouvelle Librairie Nationale.

Woolf, S. J. 1981: *Fascism in Europe*. London: Methuen.

Yockey, F. P. 1948: *Imperium: The Philosophy of History and Politics*. London: Westropa.

17

*A sense-making crisis**

GERALD M. PLATT

An alternative theory

[. . .] An alternative theoretical framework is needed that can subsume and surmount the inadequacies of categorical analysis and can explain the forces producing heterogeneous populations in revolutions while offering a detailed understanding of the complexity of revolutionary events. Such a theory would focus on individuals' subjectivities, but not in terms of preconceived categories. Rather, individuals' subjectivities would be linked to the particularities of their historical circumstance.[1]

This kind of theory is important because it remains oriented to scholarly standards of adequate description and analysis similar to categorical

---

* Extract from G. Platt, 'Thoughts on a Theory of Collective Action: Language, Affect, and Ideology in Revolution', in M. Albin (ed.), *New Directions in Psychohistory* (Lexington, MA., Lexington Books, 1980), pp. 69–94.

analysis while it generates recognizably 'correct' descriptions, that is, adequate descriptions from the subjective viewpoint of the participants in revolutionary activities. This last criterion of adequate is crucial because of the unavailability of contemporary subjects for personal and close examination. Less adequate descriptions of revolutionary actions, depictions inconsistent with the data and contrary to our empathic understanding of the individuals involved in a historical event, are no more than glosses that satisfy the theorist's, but not the participant's, version of events.

The central conceptual terms of empirically adequate theory are language, affect, cognition, and ideology. It is by linking these concepts that we can develop a subjectively adequate theory of revolution, explaining simultaneously the heterogeneous composition of revolutionary movements and the complexity of revolutionary events. A theory based on these concepts will be acceptable to historical demands for detail while fulfilling the sociological demands for generalization.

The point of departure is the link between individuals' subjectivities and social contexts organized in terms of interpretive responses to the historical circumstances. However, it is first necessary to develop theoretically interpretive specific rules employed by revolutionaries who must integrate cognitive and affective responses to real circumstances. Once we develop such rules we have a basis for understanding the shared experiences of people involved in revolutions. In addition, these rules must provide a unified conception of the ways in which individuals construct their worlds and the meanings these constructs have for them in revolutionary situations. (The means by which we develop interpretive rules are applicable to all revolutionary situations but the rules are specific to particular revolutions.)

We can discover the interpretive bases for action through language used to organize cognitive and affective processes. Language codified in revolutionary ideology, whether written or spoken, is crucial for our analysis. The ideological language allows us to know the subjective experiences of revolutionaries. This is not to substitute a one-sided idealist conception of revolution for a one-sided materialist conception. On the contrary, real individuals and groups struggle over real economic and political grievances and interests, but these can only be reconciled and reorganized in terms of coherently elaborated, believable standards to which people can become cognitively and emotionally attached and by which they can organize and orient actions.

Thus, the analysis of the language of social process is not an example of idealism. Gadamer denies 'that the linguistically articulated consciousness claims to determine all the material being of life-practice'. Rather, as Gadamer has claimed in his debate with Habermas,

It only suggests that there is no societal reality, with all its concrete forces, that does not bring itself to representation in a – consciousness that is linguistically articulated. Reality does not happen 'behind the back' of language; it happens rather behind the backs of those who live in the subjective opinion that they have understood 'the world' (or can no longer understand it); that is, reality happened precisely *within* language.[2]

Additionally, I should note that a subsection of British Marxists are aware, and have been aware, of the need to integrate language and social process to the material base. It is the contemporary American political economists still wed to American positivism that have reified the material base into a mechanistic determinant of process, class consciousness, language, ideology, and so on. In contrast to this attitude, Coward and Ellis wrote:

For Marxism, the question of language posed the problem of subject in two ways. First, Marxism asked whether the role of language in the social totality is determined or determining, whether language is superstructural or not. In admitting – as linguists seemed to insist – that it is neither of these oppositions, Marxism had also to admit the possibility that the theoretical opposition base/superstructure were inadequate and that analysis of language was not possible within a rigid and false distinction between objective (mode of production) and subjective (individual identity).[3]

In short, the different contending ideological positions, the codified images of the past, present, and future worlds are the repositories of the principles by which revolutionaries orient themselves to action. Ideology therefore, is not the cause of action, but rather a mode through which action is made subjectively meaningful. And ideology is the mechanism by which diverse populations are bound together.

Although more can and will be said of the role of language and ideology in revolutionary situations, affective and cognitive processes are more fundamental to action. At one point Weinstein and I suggested that aggressive impulses released by moral transgressions served as the basis for revolutionary activities, particularly as this occurred in traditional societies.[4] At a later point we generalized this position, suggesting that experiences of loss in real social circumstances generated affective responses mobilized in the service of revolutionary action, a notion that stemmed from Freud's conceptions of signal affect.[5] That is, affective experiences in the face of threatened or actual external social losses (for example, the failure of the economy, the incapacity of the political system to integrate divergent political interests, and so on) are reactive responses to failed or failing aspects of society. Affective states of depression, anxiety, anger, and so on caused by societal failures threaten the personal sense of continuity and act motivationally to produce collective action rectifying the social failures. However, although these formulations are generally correct, they must not reify society on the one hand nor anthropomorphize affect on the other.

What after all, can affect signal? And what do we mean when we speak of societal failures and a sense of loss accruing from such failures? Externally or internally provoked arousal is by itself meaningless. An interpretive theory of collective action must give meaning to and integrate affect to the intersubjective experience of constructing reality. Societal failures, loss, affect, personal continuity, and the production of conceptions of society are inseparable in an interpretive theory stressing the subjective construction of meaningful social action.

Every aspect of social action is viewed in an emotional context, and every social setting demands a certain experience of emotion.[6] To be sure, this is not reflected on or in awareness when interactions are routinized, that is, conceived as consistent with familiar past experiences. However, the disruption of routine interactions results in heightened physiological arousal.[7] Meaning placed on such arousal, or emotional labeling, is achieved through socially evaluative cognitive processes.

This relation of cognition to emotion is spelled out by Schacter as follows: 'The cognition, in a sense, exerts a steering function. Cognitions arising from the immediate situation as interpreted by past experience provide the framework within which one understands and labels his feelings. It is the cognition which determines whether the state of physiological arousal will be labeled "anger", "joy", or whatever.'[8] Schacter's notions regarding cognition, and emotion stem from his laboratory studies. It is necessary, however, to generalize these notions to all forms of situated action.

We can begin by suggesting that meaningless action never occurs. Action and meaning are associated by definition. Thus people are continuously engaged in producing meaning in their lives, in making sense of their activities and their situations, interpreting the conditions in which their activities occur, rendering meaningful their feelings and the activities of others and so on. People will not and cannot live in chaotic meaningless worlds, as Susanne Langer observed.[9] People are constantly involved in constructing their worlds, employing several devices for providing meaning to activities. (It is impossible to present an exhaustive list of devices or sources persons employ in conceiving their worlds.)

In the widest sense biographical and social history provide people with cognitive standards for organizing experiences in particular settings. Individuals may also rely on some cognitive features of their categorical identities (that is, class, age, sex, religion, and so on) to bring situated experiences to coherent closure. People derive private or idiosyncratic cognitive standards in various ways; moreover situations require the emergent shaping of standards.[10] However, there is no way to suggest what portion of any population will employ various combinations of sources to construct their experiences. Nevertheless, it can be said with some certainty that it is the routine 'sense making' of daily life, in providing for one's sense of membership and worth, in giving meaning to everyday emotions, and in giving the commonplace world a sense of meaningful social order that the language of culture, class, situations, and so forth offer standards to organize experience. It is in the organization of the routine sense of everyday life that such sources for cognition play a paramount role.

We may then say that revolutionary activities follow from perceived interferences with routine attempts to construct a familiar world. Economic unemployment, productive reorganization, geographic and social mobility, changes in the distribution of wealth, redistribution of resources, changes in spending and purchasing power, inflation and deflation, political disenfranchisement, redistribution of power, arbitrary uses of power, failure of effective political authority, illegitimate decision making, and so on, all constitute shared disruptive situational conditions that interfere with constructive processes. Prolonged and/or severe and rapid forms of change inhibit the capacity to construct images consistent with familiar personal and social experiences. The routine modes of organizing the world cannot be managed under these conditions, the result being a world that is inconsistent with previous experiences.

Loss is experienced when the familiar modes of cognizing and experiencing the world, and familiar forms of action, are no longer available. Loss is experienced when the routine sources, including the familiar ways of integrating the material aspects of social action, become ineffective in constructing meaningful orders and one's place in them. What is lost, then, is the experience of a familiar social order and one's place in it, or the capacity to rely on the routinized sources of belief and action to produce familiar social situations. This type of experience has ramifications in several directions.

The loss of familiar social orders and one's place in them is potentially chaotic. People who cannot sustain a biographically achieved sense of personal identity, continuity, feelings of worthiness, self-esteem, membership in a community, and so on, are easily overwhelmed by affective experiences. When these conditions are widespread the society is undergoing a sense-making crisis.[11]

In the face of a sense-making crisis, of course, different people perceive the situation differently; there will not be a single response to the crisis throughout the population. For private reasons people may be capable of denying the disorder or of perceiving the disorder and not responding to it. Other persons in the society may continue to use the routine sources for sense making despite their ineffectiveness and the personal and social discomfort experienced with producing variant and even deviant forms of familiar world views. These individuals attempt to normalize the experience of chaos by retrospectively reviewing their accomplishments as only temporary variants on traditional and familiar experience. Another class of people may use its categorical identities for making sense of the chaotic situational conditions. These people interpret the world, even disruptive economic and political events, in terms of class, religion, age, psychological disposition, and so on, make the events meaningful and thus cognitively and emotively organized according to subjective interpretive principles embedded in the categorical identities.

This last type reaction is most important and consistent with expectations derived from categorical subjectivities. However, we cannot expect, and the evidence indicates, that not all people in any category will be so affected and will employ their identities to make sense of the world and their place in it. And further, there is no way to predict which of the many categories a person holds or identifies with will act as the basis for action and therefore will be effective in these terms. A Catholic man of working-class background with 'authoritarian' tendencies in pre-Nazi Germany could employ any of these identities singly or in combination to make sense of the world and his place in it. The result being that such a man could account for and experience the world in terms of religion, class, 'authoritarianism', and so on, thus making sense of the world in a variety of ways including pro- or anti-Nazi affiliation.

A substantial portion of the population whose relation to material conditions, to their place in the world and their relations to others is undermined by these circumstances; that portion of the population who experience these circumstances as enduring unendingly, unresolvable in traditional terms, experiences a sense-making crisis. Those individuals cannot continue to employ routine sources of sense making to organize their meaningful actions and they experience bewilderment and loss. They cannot make sense of the emotional arousal they experience. They cannot harness and give direction to the emotional arousal. Once the familiar sources are inapplicable, unavailable, or disrupted individuals experiencing this cannot resolve and make meaningful the sources of arousal in constructive directions.

It is at this point that situationally produced chaos leads to the search for new situated rules for interpreting the world; that is, the search for new methods for cognizing and experiencing the world and making sense of the emotional arousal. These situated rules of interpretation provide meaning to the experienced chaos by providing for alternate world views. They harness emotional arousal and they guide persons to a renewed sense of meaning in the world. The emerging interpretive rules accomplish this by informing their adherents of the meaning of chaotic experiences, pointing to the modes for resolving such experiences.

However, the system of rules which arises is characterized by an intermingling of the traditional with the new interpretive sources. A population thus is being offered simultaneously both an explanation of the failure and a reason for hope. A temporal relationship exists between the routine sources of meaning and the new interpretive rules. The latter slowly emerge from and are dialectically related to the former. The new system incorporates parts of the old system as the new rules are being institutionalized in a significant portion of the population. This evolution permits a transition to the new sources of meaning, a new mode of constructing meaning without a total abdication of the past. As the dialectical interplay between the failing and rising modes of construction of the new system is sharpened, the population becomes attuned to the failures of the traditional sources and the effectiveness of the new interpretive procedures. Finally, a leadership for the new sources arises in society either expressing or simply codifying the new rules of interpretation. And if this leadership gains access to sources of power it makes attempts at superimposing the new interpretive system upon broad ranges of the society's population.

The new interpretive system is codified in the language of ideology, determining the meaning of emotional arousal, suggesting the reestablishment of a coherent world and one's place in it. The language of ideology points to new modes of cognizing and making sense of the material circumstances, past failures, present circumstances, future hopes, and the meaning of the whole society.

Thus, it is in the language of ideology that the meaning of the social senses of a failing society are formulated. It is the language of ideology that the experiences of chaos and emotional arousal are harnessed and the sense of loss resolved. Moreover, personality and social order are formulated as inseparable in this theoretical context. There is no duality of self and society, rather they are unified. Cognition, emotion and the sense of society and one's place in it are all features of the social process.

Of course, ideology does not serve all people equally in a society during a sense-making crisis. Portions of the population are not drawn into the new system but remain attached to other sources of morality, other sources for constructing the world. Additionally, ideology itself is not the same to all people who accept it. Rather, ideological language is itself a complex fabric of social rules of interpretation, which draws together different persons for different reasons. In no sense is the language of ideology a coherent logical statement. Further, the language of ideology is itself situationally interpreted so that its meaning changes with changing private and/or collective interests of its use, with changing time and social space of its application and so forth.[12]

Engels has formulated ideology as, '[. . .] a process accomplished by the so-called thinker consciously, it is true, but with a false consciousness. The real motive forces impelling him remain unknown to him; otherwise it would simply not be an ideological process.'[13] If we are to fit Engel's definition of ideology to collective action it must be elaborated in terms of its purposes for sense making, that is, for organizing personal and social events in a sense-making crisis. First, we accept Engels implicit distinction between the conscious sense-making experience and unconscious interpretive rules embedded in ideology for producing sense making. Although the latter constructive methods are never entirely beyond the ideological adherent's reflexive comprehension such effort at understanding is without purpose, for ideological adherence necessitates that certain interpretive rules are intractably part of the adherent's ideological sense-making process. The sense of the world and methods of production are tied to one another; world views are dependent for their sense on their methods of production.[14] Thus, in a sense-making crisis, it is not only the ideological conception of the world that adherents accept but also the methods for its production. And it is the latter that are transferable from situation to situation. It is the latter rules of interpretation that lend the ideology whatever degree of coherence it may have in different social settings of its application.

These interpretive rules in ideology may be likened to Chomskian deep structures but not simply native language rules. Rather they are social rules interpretively fitted to situational exigencies in the manner similar to that suggested by Cicourel's investigation of rule use.[15] That is, ideological language rule use is accomplished through social interpretive procedures fitted to situated sense making. We may extend these thoughts in another direction especially pertinent to our analysis. For example, it is possible to think of psychoanalytic defense mechanisms, situationally employed, as a lexicon of interpretive rules for sense making. Such a formulation generalizes defenses from personal modes for controlling internal drives and external information to shared interpretive rules for patterning experience and social content. It is from such a perspective that we can come to understand the ways in which movements take on particular dynamic appearances. However, such accomplished appearances are not forms of mental illness but rather the expression of particularly institutionalized defenses as methods in the constructive process.

Thus, an ideological orientation that allows for the construction of the meaning of the world in terms of external factors may give a movement the appearance of being 'paranoid'. Such an interpretive orientation could produce a movement resembling, for example, the paranoid-aggressive style of the Nazis, but it could also produce certain movements along Diaspora Jews characterized by a paranoid-passive appearance. The interpretive lexicon of ideology is not constituted by a simple system of rules but rather by a complex of interconnected interpretive language rules comprising the total rule set embedded in the ideology. Thus, characteristic appearances of movements, perhaps dominated by a particular practice, will appear as more than the product of a single rule always supplemented in its production by the work of other rules. The result is that even movements with dominant social characteristics are always many-sided.

There are advantages to formulating defenses in terms of a lexicon of language rules. On the one hand, this formulation is consistent with Anna Freud's use of defenses; on the other hand, it also incorporates recent interpretive approaches to psychoanalytic theory, approaches that are more readily articulated to sociological analysis.[16] Additionally, this formulation of defenses ties them to all aspects of the constructive process, whether the reference is to dream work, the construction of daily life, pathological life, or revolutionary movements. It is in this sense that defenses are generalized to all social processes.

But the most significant analytic point presented here is that through an empirical investigation of ideology we may develop a set of language rules that act as orienting principles for ideological adherents in constructing a viable world in the face of a sense-making crisis. Neither the scope of such interpretive rules nor the particular rules can be worked out without turning to a specific revolution. For while the particular rules may be transferable from situation to situation in a particular revolution, they are not transferable from revolution to revolution.

The subjective experience of revolutionary situations, thus, is tied to a particular dominant ideology. We become intimately acquainted with the revolutionary experience through an investigation of the interpretive rules embedded in that ideology. Although this is a general approach to revolutionary experience, the specifics of the subjective orientation to and experience of revolution must be reworked in each historical setting.

I should stress that the analytic development of these rules and the ideological content are situationally accomplished rather than deduced from generalized abstractions about revolution. Thus, Engels is correct in suggesting that the real circumstances that persons face are inseparable from their developing ideology. But we must supplement Engel's thinking in three ways. First, we should note that social conditions sufficient to produce such an ideology for collective action do not arise from a failure of sense making in a single societal dimension. Rather, ideologies that can mobilize collective revolutionary activities arise from the real failures in multiple dimensions of society. Ideology directed to revolutionary action builds on the experiences of sense-making failures in several dimensions of society. The result is that revolutionary ideology becomes a total fabric regarding the total society, one that draws together multiple issues and populations. The characterizations of the specific real problems the society faces are integrated in the language of ideology. The ideology offers formulas for making sense of the experiences being felt and offers methods for their solution. The ideology becomes a composite of the heterogeneous issues that plague the society. And a composite ideology is the medium through which the many events confronting society are interpreted.

The second point by which we should amend Engel's definition is that real circumstances cannot interpret themselves. The objective character of social events offer no unequivocal conception of themselves and of their meaning. Evaluated events in the world such as the inequitable distribution of power, the unjust allocation of resources, the exploitation of labor, the oppression of religious factions, the discrimination against classes of persons, and so on, are so experienced because the interpretive rules embedded in ideology inform its adherents that particular activities in the world should be ascribed with such meanings.

In addition, although ideological adherents' ordering of interactions in society is accomplished according to the interpretive rules embedded in the ideology, these interpretive rules are bound not only to sense making in the present but also to the achievement of future circumstances, that is, the manner in which the real events should proceed in the society in light of the ways in which past and future worlds are envisioned.

Finally, while adherents experience a sense of unity and solidarity in their ideologies, in a strict sense ideologies do not enjoy such coherence. Different aspects of an ideology serve different purposes and not all aspects of an ideological fabric are important to all adherents. Particular members are drawn to particular subfeatures of the ideological interpretive system of rules. Frequently this is an outgrowth of people's interests or the result of a segment's need to resolve a sense of crisis confined to less than the total array of issues falling within the perview of the ideological fabric. The result is that different segments of an ideological movement construct shared but incongruent views of the world while appearing to be committed to, and not questioning the commitment of others to, the ideological whole. An ideology therefore, appears as shared and held in common by all adherents, giving the illusion of welding its heterogeneous members together for a single purpose or for all purposes in common.

Thus, it is the ideology that appears to hold together the heterogeneous populations but does so not for a single purpose. Ideological adherents are really oriented to and by multiple moralities.[17] Each adherent constructs from his circumscribed commitment to and conception of the ideology his particular conception of the movement. And yet from the point of view of the ideological whole adherents can envision themselves as members unified into a single movement. Similarly, outsiders may envision a unified movement although it is only at the surface. Finally, it is because ideology is so many things to so many people that it can be situationally and practically interpreted, and thus it can draw together such diverse sociological and psychological populations.

A significant analytic feature of treating ideology in this fashion is that it turns ideology from the theorists' formulation about the ways in which persons proceed in the world to the ways in which ideological adherents conduct their own lives in their worlds and the ways in which ideology affects that performance. This formulation removes ideology from an objective category of analysis, which the analyst superimposes on persons, describing the ways in which actors may or may not be motivated to action, and focuses on the subjective uses of ideological rules that persons in collective movements use to interpret the real interests of their lives, to evaluate the actions of others, to construct meaning, and to give sense to their emotions. It is through ideology that real worlds are experienced and made cognitively and emotively meaningful for revolutionary activities.

This approach calls for special research strategies. How people decide which way they must identify themselves in a revolutionary struggle can in part be explained in terms of the traditional sociological and psychological categories such as class, religion, age, and so forth, as stated. As for the rest, it is necessary to proceed by analysing their subjective experiences, feelings, conceptions of the world, and so on as these are spelled out in a multidimensional ideology. From this perspective, the revolutionary process is not conceived in crass political, economic, or social terms but in terms of standards for organizing life, including the yearnings and moralities as well as expressions of interest. A second methodological refinement then follows from this position, one that requires the analyst to start with the given ideology working backward to the individuals and the groups that develop these statements to understand how, why, and the ways in which heterogeneous populations become committed to them. This involves something quite different from the traditional technique of distinguishing people according to the social locations and particular social and psychological spaces and then assuming shared interests and shared yearnings because of shared location and disposition. It is precisely this assumption that has led to the contradictory positions noted and particularly to the inability to explain the heterogeneity of participants in revolutionary action in any comprehensive or parsimonious way.

Notes

1   We [Fred Weinstein and Gerald Platt] asserted this point in both *The Wish to Be Free* (Berkeley, CA., University of California Press, 1969) and in *Psychoanalytic Sociology* (Baltimore, Johns Hopkins University Press, 1973); that is, revolution arises out of realistic circumstances beyond the control of individual wishes. However, this does not imply that revolutionary events arise outside the formulating processes of individuals. Recently a similar point regarding social structure in revolution was suggested by Skocpol and Trimberger, 'We have a different conception from Marx about what creates objectively revolutionary crises, but our analysis, like his, hinges on discerning how revolutionary situa-

tions arise out of structural relations and historical processes outside of the deliberate control of acting groups'. See Theda Skocpol and Ellen Kay Trimberger, 'Revolutions and the World-Historical Development of Capitalism', *Berkeley Journal of Sociology* 22 (1977–1978), pp. 101–3.

2 Hans-Georg Gadamer, 'On the Scope and Function of Hermeneutical Reflection', in *Philosophical Hermeneutics*, trans. and ed. David E. Linge (Berkeley and Los Angeles, University of California Press, 1976), p. 35.

3 Rosalind Coward and John Ellis, *Language and Materialism, Developments in Semiology and the Theory of the Subject* (London: Routledge and Kegan Paul, 1977), p. 154. E. P. Thompson also has correctly insisted that class and class consciousness are not determined by objectified class positions but rather in terms of historical and social process. Thompson's Marxism integrates base and superstructure in a manner that is absent from the works of his American counterparts. Recently, Thompson reasserted this formulation in his polemic against Althusser. See E. P. Thompson, *The Making of the English Working Class* (York, Vintage Books, 1963), pp. 9–14; also see, E. P. Thompson, *The Poverty of Theory and Other Essays* (New York and London, Monthly Review Press, 1978), pp. 56–7, pp. 103ff. I am indebted to Rick Fantasia for calling these points to my attention.

4 Weinstein and Platt, *The Wish to Be Free*, chap. 1, 'The Sociology of Value Change', pp. 20–44; recently Barrington Moore, Jr. made a similar point in his *Injustice: The Social Bases of Obedience and Revolt* (New York, Pantheon Books, 1978).

5 Fred Weinstein and Gerald M. Platt, *Psychoanalytic Sociology: An Essay on the Interpretation of Historical Data and the Phenomena of Collective Data* (Baltimore, Johns Hopkins University Press, 1973), see especially chaps. 3 and 4. Weinstein, 'Events and Affects'; and F. Weinstein, *Germany's Discontents, Hitler's Visions: The Claims of Leadership and Ideology in the National Socialist Movement* (New York, Academic Press, 1980), chap. 2.

6 Parsons made this point in 1951. See Talcott Parsons, 'The Superego and the Theory of Social Systems', reprinted in his *Social Structure and Personality* (New York, Free Press of Glencoe, 1964), reprinted from *Psychiatry*, February 1952.

7 Garfinkel demonstrated this in his paper, 'Studies of the Routine Grounds of Everyday Activities', reprinted in his *Studies in Ethnomethodology* (Englewood Cliffs, NJ, Prentice Hall, 1967). Reprinted from *Social Problems*, Winter 1964.

8 Stanley Schacter and Jerome E. Singer, 'Cognitive, Social and Physiological Determinants of Emotional State', *Psychological Review* 69 (September 1962), pp. 379–99; Stanley Schacter, 'The Interaction of Cognitive and Physiological Determinants of Emotional State', in *Advances in Experimental Social Psychology*, ed. L. Berkowitz, vol. 1 (New York, Academic Press, 1964), pp. 49–80, quote from p. 51. Schachter's work on cognition and emotion has influenced my thinking on this issue. Most studies indicate that physiological states of arousal are indistinguishable when described by such diverse emotional terms as joy, anxiety, depression, anger. The very terms of emotion have social connotations. To be happy or anxious implies deviation from standard levels of societal emotions in the direction of excessive positive and negative excitation. The language of emotion is socialized in individuals and is socially produced. We are made happy by joyful events, by social successes, by the warmth and concern of friends and kin. We are angered and depressed by contrary circumstances, by the perceived hostilities of others, by death of friends and loved

ones, by social failures. Persons who profess such arousal without apparent social cause are deemed simpletons, deviants, and insane.

9 Susanne K. Langer, *Philosophy in a New Key* (New York, Mentor, 1951), p. 241.
10 Ralph H. Turner formulated this type of emergent norm devised by people in exigent situations; see his '*Collective Behavior* (Englewood Cliffs, NJ, Prentice Hall, 1972), pp. 394ff. We should also note Peter McHugh's work, which demonstrates people's use of similar emergent cognitive devises; see his *Defining the Situation: the Organization of Meaning in Social Interaction* (Indianapolis and New York, Bobbs-Merrill Company, 1968), chap. 4.
11 Tom Juravich suggested this metaphor.
12 Karl Mannheim, *Ideology and Utopia: An Introduction to the Sociology of Knowledge*, trans. L. Wirth and E. Shils (New York, A Harvest Books, Harcourt Brace and World, 1936), pp. 68, 83.
13 Karl Marx and Friedrich Engels, *Selected Correspondence* (Moscow, International Publishers, 1954), p. 541.
14 Garfinkel, 'What is Ethnomethodology?', *Studies in Ethnomethodology*, pp. 1–34.
15 Aaron V. Cicourel, 'Cross-Modal Communication: The Representational Context of Sociolinguistic Information Processing', in his *Cognitive Sociology, Language and Meaning in Social Interaction* (New York, Free Press, 1974), p. 141–71, especially pp. 164–71.
16 Anna Freud, *The Ego and the Mechanisms of Defense*, trans. C. Baines (New York, International Universities Press, 1946); Paul Ricoeur, *Freud and Philosophy: An Essay on Interpretation* (New Haven, CO., Yale University Press, 1976).
17 Mannheim, *Ideology and Utopia*, p. 58; Alfred Schutz, 'On Multiple Realities', in his *Collected Papers*, vol. 1, *The Problem of Social Reality*, ed. M. Natanson (The Hague, Martinus Nijhoff, 1962), pp. 207–59.

18

*The ecstasy of rebirth**

KLAUS THEWELEIT

[. . .] Almost any fascist text with even minimum pretensions requires the same perception of processes as if 'in a dream', the writer's sense of unrealities, the threatening knowledge that the ground on which he moves is unstable.

Escape was impossible from whatever it was that was approaching, feeling its way forward, enveloping me in stifling gloom incomprehensibly, indescribably. Then it was upon me! Overcome by paralys-

* Extract from K. Theweleit, 'Male Bodies and the "White Terror"', in *Male Fantasies* (Cambridge, Polity Press, 1989: 2 vols), Vol. 2, pp. 227–43.

ing fear, a desire to run, felt some weight attach itself to me, a barrier. In swooning submission I tried to confront it directly, but it refused to make itself visible – the intangible!

It approached, inexorable. [. . .] I felt how it would be to antici- pate murder in some dark alleyway, to suffocate slowly in a gully filled with rubble, with the last vestige of my strength, I resisted the ultimate horror: death! 'All of this is a dream – only a dream!': the thought rose up as a last hope within me.[1]

And it *is* only a dream, the dream the body-armor dreams. These are moments of fragility, when the 'inner dungeon' and its inhabitants surface. The same moments return in sleep. Hardly has the armor relaxed its tension than it is seized by the dream. Salomon gives the following account of a dream:

I suddenly found myself having to escape from a confined space, pursued by some tentacled creature that continually dissipated into vague and shadowy forms. The only exit led down a steep and winding stairwell to bottomless depths. But the creature was faster than I was, I could still see its tentacles clutching at me; I extended failing legs into the darkness . . .

In his dream, he remembers 'with blissful excitement' that he can fly, and he flies, always slightly above the creature from which the threat emanates – and once 'over the heads of the enemies into which the figure of the demon had transformed itself', then across water:

As I crossed the dark sea, I saw the demon in the shape of some gruesome polyp moving through the water's depths and *watching* me from a round eye that goggled mockingly from the center of its spongy stomach.[2] Though I was moving at some considerable height, my feet were still sodden from flailing across lashing water, and I felt the flesh on my limbs drawing in the liquid that still dragged me downward.[3]

The extreme concreteness of Salomon's description seems to me to suggest that the body-armor had become extremely well molded and functiona- lized; it seems unlikely to fragment in the face of minor threats such as these. Saturation by the 'dragging liquid' of his interior does not immedi- ately drown him; he does not feel the river's waves crashing above him. For the same reason, perhaps Salomon, like Jünger, seems able to use *writing* to gain stability. In both authors, the threshold of collapse is raised ever higher so that when collapse eventually comes, it is described with more than usual intensity. By contrast, in texts by such comparatively ineffectual authors as Goote, it is left to the reader to imagine collapse in the numerous spaces between hyphens. Goote 'invokes' the horror from extreme distance; he dares not approach too close; this is perhaps why Goote, like the majority of fascist authors, appears particularly tedious to the critical reader.

When Rudolf Höss was imprisoned for his part in a *Vehme* murder, he developed what the prison doctor called 'prison psychosis':[4]

> I paced back and forth in my cell like a wild animal. Sleep now evaded me though I had always slept deeply and almost without dreaming the whole night through.

Höss then reports 'confused anxiety dreams':

> Chaotic dreams in which I was constantly being followed, or set upon, or falling into some abyss. The nights were pure agony. I heard the clock in the clocktower strike every passing hour. The closer it came to morning, the more I dreaded the day and the company it would bring – men I wished never to set eyes on again. I failed in every attempt to pull myself together; I could not fight it. I wanted to pray, but could summon only a feeble and fearful stammering, I had lost the ability to pray, and with it the pathway to God.[5]

And this was a man whose desired profession had been the priesthood. In prison, he becomes bitterly self-recriminatory; his whole past returns, approaching ever closer:

> My inner agitation grew daily, indeed hourly. Something approaching frenzy threatened to take hold of me. I went into increasing physical decline.[6]

He begins to hallucinate, and returns to a state of parental symbiosis.

> Can it be possible to communicate with the departed? Often, in the hours of my greatest agitation, in the moments before my mind was invaded by chaos, my parents would appear to me in flesh-and-blood, I would see them and speak to them as if they were still my guardians. I still find it impossible today to think clearly about these things; and after all these years, I have still spoken of them to no one.[7]
>
> I had plunged to the very depths, to the verge of breakdown, but from that point on, my life here in prison continued with no particular difficulty. I settled down to a more balanced existence.[8]

Höss takes refuge in 'work'; but still any reminder of the 'low point' he once reached has what he describes as a 'whip-like' effect on him.[9]

What happens here to Höss? I believe that what he acquires is a 'substitute' ego; he makes the transition from the machinery of the troop to that of the prison and is rebuilt as a functioning component within a new totality-machine (in his later capacity as commandant of Auschwitz, his greatest concern was that the camp should run smoothly and that each individual should perform the tasks allotted to them). As his old ego, the soldier-ego, crumbles and eventually perishes, he inevitably returns to the symbiotic situation. A new form of the ego then becomes visible in his unreserved affirmation of the daily round of prison life. This capacity to disintegrate and then re-emerge equipped with a new 'ego' seems to me to be a peculiar characteristic of the not-yet-fully-born; it arises from their dependence on external egos which are first assembled around them, then dismantled, reassembled, and so on. And in the interim they experience breakdown, blackout, coma, they know nothing . . . where am I?

It should also be borne in mind that Höss, unlike Salomon for example, was not a product of the drill machinery. He left home at seventeen and immediately became a soldier. Thus his muscular body-ego is likely to have been significantly less stable, more susceptible of rapid fragmentation during imprisonment, than the body-ego of drill veterans such as Killinger. Having passed through the military academy, war, and the Ehrhardt Brigade, Killinger maintained himself as an upstanding man by putting himself through half an hour of physical training before the official start of his day. The whole process (which he called 'milling') involved washing his whole body daily in 'ice-cold water',[10] chin-ups by clinging to the ledge of a wall only by his fingertips.[11] He too describes 'work' as crucial for his survival.

As he once wrote, having himself been through the experience of prison: 'If I were in the shoes of the examining magistrate, I would give these men nothing – no books, no newspapers, no letters, nothing to write or tinker with. These men are hard as glass; they should be given no more than a piece of soap and a towel'.[12] And he who admits having stolen only three apples confesses to murder for no other reason than that he desires to be put to 'work' as before.

Höss hankers after work primarily as a means of discipline; what he considers important is its capacity to occupy a large part of the day to the full and to impose a certain regularity. 'My essential consideration was to impose strict, but voluntary limits on myself. [. . .] Work saved me from grueling and fruitless brooding.[13]

In 1946, from his cell in Cracow, Höss wrote: 'What I miss most in my current imprisonment is work. Mercifully, I have applied myself to a writing exercise that I find absolutely and completely fulfilling'.[14] The 'writing exercise' Höss refers to is his autobiography, whose existence it can thus be assumed we owe to his fear of reverting to the 'low point' at which, in the breakdown of his body-ego, he might potentially have had to re-live Auschwitz 'from the inside'. The scrupulous detail of the biographical report he wrote for the Polish court seems likely to have had little to do with any hope of milder punishment; more probably, it was a form of request for mercy, a plea not at any cost to be left alone with ('I will say anything if you only allow me to write – a form of working'.)

Writing – and diary writing in particular – appears to perform the same function for many soldier males: this is why we are so richly endowed with fascist biographies. In the evening when their duties are completed, they compress themselves into line upon line of methodical handwriting and compacted syntax; all the elements that threaten to rip their bodies to shreds are restrained through writing.[15] Fountain pen and paper together form a unification-machine whose totality-blocks – rows of lettering and bound pages – are devoted to the preservation of the self in body-armor.[16] Writing is a means of avoiding both feelings and degeneration. In descriptions of battle, by contrast, blood-ink is allowed to stream forth ecstatically. The crucial feature of the fascist understanding of work seems, then, not to be its ability, as wage labor, to guarantee his material reproduction; instead it is its capacity to keep the man living.[17]

The activity of work screens his ego against fragmentation and collapse and thus also protects it from the onset of devouring symbioses. 'Arbeit macht frei' (Work makes free) was the motto that crowned the gates of Auschwitz; and it was meant more or less literally. The phrase was not coined by Höss, but he did appropriately defend it:

> The motto 'Arbeit macht frei' should be understood in the sense given to it by Eicke, who resolved to release any internee from no matter what category whose consistent achievement in work raised him *above the mass*,[18] even in the face of opposition from the Gestapo and Reichskriminal-Polizeiamt (the Headquarters of the Criminal Police).[19]

For Höss, the intentions of such as himself had been benevolent; it was war that had thwarted them. Had he himself been a prisoner, he would have been among those for whom the Auschwitz motto was beneficial; as commandant he certainly derived support from it:

> To fulfill my duties adequately, I had to become the motor that tirelessly and restlessly regenerated impulses to work at building the camp. I had incessantly and repeatedly to drive every inmate onward, to haul SS men and prisoners forward together.[20] I was aware of nothing but my work.[21]

It was source of pain to Höss that his SS subordinates did not hold the notion of work in sufficiently high regard.

From 1942, the concentration camp increasingly lost meaning for him, as it became no more than a site of destruction. The Hössian labor, his labor, had been one of building and extending the camp. This was how he had been able to continue to function. It had, of course, involved imposing a certain number of penalties, torture, and executions. But once these had become the principal purpose of his work, it lost its attraction. Höss had been required to move through the camp as a force of inspiration, intervention, observation, command. He had been secure in the knowledge of his own absolute control, his status as a man respected.[22] He perceived Eichmann's extermination order as a more or less flagrant sabotage of his activities (Eichmann spent his days behind a desk and lacked the unmediated satisfaction of camp labor). Extermination nullified all the efforts Höss had expended to contain the camp inmates within boundaries that can ultimately be equated with the boundaries of his own ego.[23]

The means he had used to subdue them were the same he had employed to imprison his own interior; inmates had been annihilated only if the maintenance of his boundary-order so demanded. By working on the object of his drives, Höss had been able to 'stabilize' himself – to escape feeling to a point at which it was no longer necessary to exterminate the securely dammed-in forms of his interior. (What he found most threatening, by contrast, was *escape* from the concentration camp . . . taking flight . . .)[24]

In the opening sections of Goebbels's *Michael*, 'work' similarly appears as a key concept; later, however, it is revealed to be a subordinate form of battle; this, alongside war, is the most essential. 'Work brings redemption',[25] says Michael – redemption being the longed-for state toward which all his work is directed. What he means by it is redemption from humanity in its traditional form, from the 'inner swine', his 'tempter' who appears in the diary at certain points in the guise of Michael's debating adversary, Iwan Wienurowsky.[26]

At the end of the book, Michael joins the ranks of the 'workers'; he begins work in a mine. This offers him above all an opportunity to invoke the intensities of work as a form of *intoxication*, which, like the black-outs and intoxications of the drill, guarantees 'redemption': 'I have no wish to be a mere inheritor'. The purpose of 'work' is instead to allow Michael to become a new and self-born man within an apparatus that strips him of ego boundaries.[27] 'I am no longer human. I am a Titan. A god!' Goebbels notes in his diary at the end of a first day of labor.[28] He is already strong enough to strangle his inner Ivan. In his invocations, the object worked on in mining figures as little as does the object worked on in his glorifications of writing: 'Now the same grasp, the tone returns to me. My pen flies across the pages. Creation! Creation!'[29]

Goebbels accords to the writing process the very same function as hewing coal underground or muscle-training in the barrack square.

My freedom was now absolute. A miracle had been enacted within me: the miracle of a new world emerging. The pathway was now open – a pathway whose foundations had been laid by my own labor. All of us are faced at some time or another with the task of performing the labor of redemption, first on ourselves, then on others.

. If we are to be strong enough to form the life of our era, it is our own lives that must first be mastered.[30]

A new law is approaching – the law of a labor realized in battle and of the spirit that is labor. The synthesis of these three will be internally and externally liberating; labor will become battle, and spirit labor. Herein lies redemption![31]

Goebbels's use of the term synthesis is merely a rhetorical device to allow him to invoke 'labor' as part of a philosophical terminology. In fact, he sees the two simply as synonymous, distinguished from each other only by the difference in their methods of functioning. Both are dams: but while 'labor as battle' works through the control of the body, in 'spirit as labor' the control is mental. Both forms, however, involve suppression both of the self and others. I do not believe it is at all exaggerated to claim that Höss and his contemporaries treated concentration camp internees in precisely the same way as they treated their own desires, the productive force of their unconscious: for both they had nothing to offer but incarceration, the labor of dam-building, and death.

The Nazi term 'Community of Workers' (*Arbeiterum*) was used by Goebbels to describe a laboring community battling to maintain the *front* of politics. No sense was ever made of the fact that it was to this conception of *Arbeitertum* that the 'A' in NSDAP referred:

The working community (*Arbeitertum*) is not a class. While class derives from the economy, the working community is rooted in the political domain. It is a historical estate. [. . .] Its task is the internal and external liberation of the German people.[32]

Nazi references to 'work' are, then, never simply nonsensical; they refer to men's actual exertions to give birth to themselves as men of stable ego; men *released* from their own history, their feelings, their origin and parents. Their escape route from their own history leads through a German history that is the product of their own labor – 'we shall rise again through the efforts of the political community of workers'.

The process traced here has been described psychoanalytically as a 'fantasy of rebirth'. In a clear attempt to defuse their significance, and with some elegant side-stepping, psychoanalysis has traced fascist endeavors to escape the family by becoming 'new men' to origins in the mama–papa relationship. Jung presents mama, and incest, as the actual object of these men's desires. (The symbol-seeker will have no difficulty identifying supporting evidence in Goebbel's text, where the writer in search of renewal enters the interior of the mother through the mine as vaginal passage and hammers himself out anew in the ectasy of labor.)

In a more sophisticated account, Freud criticizes Jung's position; for him, what these men were seeking was papa, the papa inside mama. For Freud, something akin to a penis was everpresent in the (maternal) body; the man thus penetrated her in search of redemption. Freud saw the fantasy of rebirth as obscuring a latent homosexual fantasy, whose object was the father.[33] And for anyone looking for such things, they can indeed be identified in Goebbels's text: Michael is guided and directed by the pit forman, Mathias Grötzer, who is alone among the miners in accepting and protecting him. In the interior of the earth, Michael meets an affectionate paternal friend.[34]

However, no reference is made in any of the literature to what seems to me to be the essence of the renewal desired by such as Goebbels. Since he is 'no longer . . . God', he is also no longer the son of any mother; how then can he wish for incest? Or wish to love a father? Instead, he is the son of the earth and of himself, and made to dominate the earth and whatever remains in it of 'humanity'.

If I understand correctly, what we are dealing with here is what structural anthropology calls 'direct filiation';[35] an attempted specification of origins in which any human line of descent is eradicated. In direct filiation, a single man sets himself up independently as son of God and his mother as nature.[36] The filiative power that thereby accrues to him supersedes all other forms of social power; the ego it engenders is massive, its limits measured only by the limits of the world. Fascism produces a construction of rebirth that is similar in structure to direct filiation, but involuted; the new-born ego is not the son of God, but the son of himself and of history. Thus, as Goebbels's novel progresses, Michael relinquishes his attempt to become Christ. In a world where fathers are nonexistent, there can be no God the Father. Under fascism, there exists only the new ego as part of a greater totality (whose boundaries are, however, synonymous with its own) and the 'world': the two stand in mutual opposition. Their relationship is necessarily one of domination, since it is only from a position of dominance that this ego can endure life and avoid breakdown.

The fascist form of direct filiation appears then to create an immediate link between desire and the full body of the earth − a link theoretically capable of causing all streams to flow. Yet here, desire itself is compelled to wish to be dam, boundary, *ego*. What fascism, therefore, produces is not the microcosmic multiplicity of a desire that longs to expand and multiply across the body of the world, but a 'desire' absorbed into the totality machine, and into ego-armor, a desire which wishes to *incorporate* the earth into itself. This is the basis on which the typically fascist relation between desire and politics arises: politics is made subject to *direct* libidinal investment, with no detours, no imprints of mama-papa, no encodings through conventions, institutions, or the historical situation. Under fascism, the most common form of the 'I' is as a component within a larger totality-ego – the 'I' as 'we', pitted in opposition to the rest of the world, the whole starry galaxy . . .

> Yes, we are the masters of the world and kings upon the sea . . . Masters of the air, the truest sons of Germany, men more battle-worthy than any the earth has ever borne . . . Our motto is that of the sunbird: the watchword of the Erhardt brigade.'[37]

Jünger prepares for battle: 'Waiting to be swept forward and formed in the grip of the world spirit itself. Here, history is lived at its very center.'[38]

This, then, is 'megalomania' – the desire of men to shake off what they consider to be meaningless parental origins – 'history will absolve me'. These men desire to execute the hidden design of history from a position of dominance within the largest of all imaginable symbiotic unities: 'I/We and History. "Freedom". Never shall we rest until the day. . .'[39]

In their attempts to manufacture themselves as the I/We that safeguards them against threatening disintegration, the not-yet-fully-born are forced to engage in unremitting labor (the labor of subjugation). Only thus can they stave off dissolution and achieve redemption. Their ultimate need is for the whole body of the earth, as the symbiotic body that guarantees their survival. Only within the absolute totality does life arise.

To achieve that totality is the goal of all fascist 'labor'. 'Labor, War!': [40] these are the last whispered words of Goebbels's *Michael*, as he is crushed to death by falling coal. [. . .]

Notes

1 Thor Goote, *Wir tragen das Leben. Der Nachkriegsroman* (Berlin, 1932), p. 128.
2 My emphasis.
3 Ernst Salomon, *Die Geächteten* (Berlin, 1930). Translated as *The Outlaws* (New York, P. Smith, 1935), pp. 328–9.
4 Rudolf Höss, *Kommandant in Auschwitz* (Munich, 1963), p. 48. Höss's own title for his memoirs was *Meine Psyche, Werden, Leben und Erleben*.
5 Ibid., p. 47.
6 Ibid., p. 47.
7 Ibid., p. 48. Von Selchow's dreams are of a similar nature, when he collapses following his training as a naval cadet (*Hundert Tage aus meinem Leben*, Leipzig, 1936), pp. 66–7.
8 Höss, *Kommandant*, p. 49.
9 Ibid., p. 49.
10 Jünger's writing days begin with the same immersion in a cold bath. He once referred to this in an interview as 'my formula' (Südwestfunk 3, January 1979).
11 Manfred von Killinger, *Ernstes und Heiteres aus dem Putschleben* (Berlin, 1928), p. 111.
12 Ibid., p. 110. See also T. Weller, *Peter Mönkemann* (Berlin, 1936) and the

volume edited by Hartmut Plaas, *Wir klagen an. Nationalisten in den Kerkern der Bourgeoisie* (Berlin, 1928).

13 Höss, *Kommandant*, p. 65.

14 Ibid., p. 65.

15 'Save us from internal chaos and deliver us to the literal cosmos', demands Blüher in *Der Rolle der Erotik in der männlichen Gesellschaft* (Stuttgart, 1962), p. 263, also describing it as the step from 'the feminine to the masculine'. Berthold calls his diary 'dear diary' and 'my best council, my friend in times good and bad' (L. Gengler, *Rudolf Berthold*, Berlin, 1934), p. 97. His entry for 21 January 1919: 'I wish to continue my diary. I wish to have someone in these times to whom I can entrust my whole inner being, someone who will patiently bear me out . . .' (pp. 101–2). Fritz Kloppe: 'You too, my dear and trusted diary . . .' in Ernst Jünger (ed.) *Der Kampf um das Reich* (Eisen, 1929), p. 242. Josef Goebbels, *Michael. Ein deutsches Schicksal in Tagebuchblättern* (Munich, 1929), p. 146: 'This diary is my best friend, I can confide in it totally. There is nobody else I can tell all these things to. And I have to be honest, I'd never get anything off my chest otherwise. It would all burn my heart out'. (And so on.) It is here that the function of writing as ego maintenance is most clear. 'The old must be expelled to make room for the new. The human soul is too small for things to live side-by-side'. (p. 46).

16 The counterpart to blood-ink gushing forth in ecstatic battle descriptions.

17 Perhaps prison labour in the Federal Republic of Germany is deemed as such because there is barely a need for remuneration. Prisoners work for themselves, not for money. The fact that they are allowed to do so is a sufficient blessing. On the function of prison labour when it was introduced in the eighteenth and nineteenth centuries, see Michel Foucault, *Discipline and Punish* (New York, Pantheon Books, 1977), p. 231ff. It was introduced by the prison *administration* and its aim was to discipline individuals for the world of work (not to perform the arduous task of preventing ego disintegration).

18 My emphasis.

19 Höss, *Kommandant*, pp. 65–6.

20 Ibid., p 98.

21 Ibid., p. 96, standard for the tenor of the whole book.

22 Ibid., p. 90ff. But his underlinings, particularly the women prison team leaders, failed to pick that up: 'They far outdid their male counterparts in their toughness, despicableness, cruelty and depravity. Most of them were whores with a considerable number of previous convictions. Usually vile pieces . . . I don't believe men can ever turn into such creatures.' (p. 116).

23 Ibid., p. 131ff. 136ff.

24 Ibid., p. 87ff.

25 Goebbels, *Michael*, pp. 95, 124, 149.

26 It is against the bearer of this name, who gruesomely embodies Vienna and the Slav, psychoanalysis and communism together, that Goebbels marshals his forces in the battle against Bohemia. Like all 'political writers' of his time (from Becher to himself), Goebbels emerges victorious from his struggle with the devouring morass of Bohemia. When Bohemia perished, the writers who had inveighed against it themselves took on the gruesome qualities they had so despised within it.

27 Ibid., p. 124.

28 Ibid., p. 127.

29 Ibid., pp. 69, 137.

30 Ibid., p. 147.
31 Ibid., p. 147.
32 Ibid., p. 118.
33 Sigmund Freud, *From the History of an Infantile Neurosis, Standard Edition of the Complete Psychological Works of Sigmund Freud*, 24 vols, (London, Hogarth Press, 1959), vol. XVII, p. 100. Criticism of Jung is also to be found there.
34 Goebbels, *Michael*, p. 127.
35 See Gilles Deleuze and Felix Guattari, *Anti-Oedipus: Capitalism and Schizophrenia*. Translated from the French by R. Hurley *et al.* (Minneapolis, University of Minnesota Press, 1983), p. 205ff.
36 At the beginning of Leni Riefenstahl's film *Olympia, Festival of Peoples* (completed in 1938), she has the bodies of athletes emerge equally directly from the ancient birth places of Olympia and from the body of the earth.
37 Plaas, 'Das Kapp-Unternehmen', in Ernst Jünger (ed.), *Der Kampf um das Reich* (Eisen, 1929), p. 170. Also Friedrich Freska, *Kapitän Ehrhardt* (Berlin, 1924), p. 158.
38 Ernst Jünger, *Feuer und Blut* (Berlin, 1929), p. 125.
39 See also the order for the day given by Röhm on the 'Führer's' 45th birthday, in Charles Bloch, *Die SA und die Krise des NS-Regimes 1934* (Frankfurt, n.d.), pp. 84–5; the exclusion by the leader of the Hitler Youth rituals in Hans Steinhoff's film *Hitlerjunge Quex 1933*; Dieter Thomas Heck announcing the ZDF record charts; or Salomon, *Nahe Geschichte* (Berline, 1935), p. 33, where the *Freikorps* member feels 'needed by the forces of history itself'; or Goebbels, *Michael*, p. 148: 'The globe belongs to whomsoever takes it'. See also Ferdinand Crasemann, *Freikorps Maercker, Erlebnisse und Erfahrungen eines Freikorpsoffiziers seit der Revolution* (Hamburg, 1920), p. 23; Kurt Eggers, *Der Berg der Rebellen* (Leipzig, 1937), p. 145: 'He knows a well-aimed shot can unleash a world war. That's why he wants to bear the responsibility all by himself'; Eduard Stadtler, *Als Antibolschewist 1918/19* (Dusseldorf, 1935), p. 106; Herbert Volck, *Rebellen um Ehre* (Gütersloh, 1932), p. 10; Kurt Eggers, *Von der Freiheit des Kriegers* (Berlin, 1940), p. 48; Ferdinand Solf, *Deutschlands Auferstehung: 1934* (Naumberg a. d. Saale, 1921), p. 45. In addition, see the portrayal of historic battles as a direct attack on the body of the earth in Friedrich Hielscher, 'Die grosse Verwandlung', in *Krieg und Krieger*, ed. by Ernst Jünger, (Berlin, 1930), pp. 129–34.
40 Goebbels, *Michael*, p. 157.

19

A retrodictive theory of fascism*

STANLEY PAYNE

The search for an adequate theory or interpretation of fascism has generally ended in failure, so that over the years the residue left by such discussions has come to resemble, in MacGregor Knox's phrase, the remains of a desert battlefield littered with abandoned or burned-out wrecks. Most theories of fascism can be easily shown to lack general or even specific validity. They mostly tend toward the monocausal or reductionist and can either be disproved or shown to be inadequate with greater or lesser ease. Moreover, most of those who deal with fascism are not primarily concerned with a common or comparative category of diverse movements and/or regimes but refer exclusively or primarily to German National Socialism, which reduced the scope and application of such arguments.

It is doubtful that there is any unique hidden meaning in, cryptic explanation of, or special 'key' to fascism. It was an epochal European revolutionary movement of the early twentieth century of great complexity, fomented by the new ideas and values of the cultural crisis of the *fin de siècle* and the ideology of hypernationalism. Fascism possessed distinctive political and social doctrines, as well as economic approaches, but these did not stem from any one source and did not constitute an absolutely discrete new economic doctrine. Fascist movements differed more widely among themselves than was the case with various national movements among other political genera. Fascism was not the agent of any other force, class, or interest or the mere reflection of any social class, but was produced by a complex of historical, political, national, and cultural conditions, which can be elucidated and to some extent defined. Above all, fascism was the most revolutionary form of nationalism in Europe to that point in history, and it was characterized by its culture of philosophical idealism, willpower, vitalism, and mysticism and its moralistic concept of therapeutic violence, strongly identified with military values, outward aggressiveness, and empire.

On the basis of broad inductive study of the principal fascist movements, it should be possible to arrive at the constituents of a kind of

* Reprinted in full from S. Payne, 'Elements of a Retrodictive Theory of Fascism', in *A History of Fascism, 1914–1945* (Madison, Wisconsin, University of Wisconsin Press, 1996; London, UCL Press, 1996), pp. 487–95.

retrodictive theory of fascism – that is, an elucidation of the particular circumstances that would have to have existed in an early twentieth-century European country in order for a significant fascist movement to have developed. Such movements – gaining the support of as much as about 20 per cent or more of the electorate – emerged in only five countries: Italy, Germany, Austria, Hungary, and Romania. The only other two lands where significant fascist movements developed were Spain and Croatia, but the growth of Spanish fascism developed only after incipient civic breakdown and then civil war – circumstances of such crisis as to cloud the issue there – whereas in Croatia the Ustashi had remained a comparatively small movement before Hitler overran Yugoslavia and awarded power to Pavelić as a second choice.

The elements of such a retrodictive theory would include many factors, including the cultural, political, social, economic, and international (Table 19.1). Obviously not all these factors existed in every case where a significant fascist movement developed, but the great majority of them did, and the absence of certain factors may explain the ultimate failure of one or two of the stronger movements.

The cultural roots of fascism lay in certain ideas of the late nineteenth century and in the cultural crisis of the *fin de siècle*. The chief doctrines involved were intense nationalism, militarism, and international Social Darwinism in the forms that became widespread among the World War I generation in greater central Europe, coupled with the contemporary philosophical and cultural currents of neo-idealism, vitalism, and activism, as well as the cult of the hero. Fascism developed especially in the central European areas of Germany, Italy, and the successor states of Austria-Hungary most affected by these cultural trends. It was also to be found in varying degrees outside greater central Europe, but elsewhere fascism was more effectively counterbalanced by opposing cultural influences. The impact in France may have been nearly as great as in central Europe, since some of these concepts originated there. Yet the overall effect in France was less, because the ideas were counterbalanced by other elements and because the overall sense of crisis was less acute. Moreover, most of the other variables were scarcely present in France. The case of Romania is somewhat peculiar, for the *fin de siècle* crisis seems initially to have been less intense there. Among the smaller Romanian intelligentsia, nonetheless, the general sense of crisis grew after World War I. A Marxist response was ineffective for domestic political and for geopolitical reasons, while more moderate nationalist populism proved ineffective. Spain was another peripheral country in which the effect of the *fin de siècle* crisis was weaker, and in fact fascism had little presence there before the final breakdown of 1936.

Fascism could not become a major force in countries where a reasonably significant nationalist ideology or movement had not preceded it, at least by half a generation if not more. So radical and intense a doctrine could

Table 19.1 Elements of a retrodictive theory of fascism

Cultural Factors

1. Comparatively strong influence of the cultural crisis of the *fin de siècle*
2. Pre-existing comparatively strong currents of nationalism
3. Perceived crisis in cultural values
4. Strong influence (or challenge) of secularization

Political Factors

1. A comparatively new state, not more than three generations old
2. A political system that temporarily approximates liberal democracy but has existed for no more than a single generation
3. A fragmented or seriously polarized party system
4. A significant prior political expression of nationalism
5. An apparent danger, either internally or externally, from the left
6. Effective leadership
7. Significant allies
8. In order to triumph, a government that is at least semidemocratic at the time of direct transition to power

Social Factors

1. A situation of pronounced social tension or conflict
2. A large sector of workers and/or peasants-farmers that are either unrepresented, underrepresented, or outside the main party system
3. Major middle-class discontent with the existing party system because of either underrepresentation or major party/electoral shifts
4. Existence of a Jewish minority

Economic Factors

1. Economic crisis either of dislocation or of underdevelopment, caused by or nominally imputable to war, defeat, or 'foreign' domination
2. A sufficient level of development in politics and economics to have neutralized the military

International Factors

1. A serious problem of status humiliation, major status striving, and/or underdevelopment
2. Existence of a fascist role model

gain momentum only as the second stage in ongoing nationalist agitation and mobilization. This was the case in each example of a vigorous fascist movement, while the virtual absence of any previously mobilized nationalism in Spain was a major handicap for the Falange that could not be overcome under seminormal political conditions.

Fascism seems also to have required the kind of cultural space opened by a process of secularization or, in one or two cases, the challenge of a kind of secularization not otherwise being met. In most of the more heavily secularized countries, conversely, fascism was not a challenge either because the secularization process had been effectively completed or because most of the other preconditions did not exist. In a number of

central European countries, fascism was able to take advantage of the
space left by secularization, and it was less successful in nonsecularized
areas. In Spain, political Catholicism sought to meet the challenge of leftist
secularization directly, and under seminormal political conditions it had
no need of fascism. In Romania, however, fascism itself provided perhaps
the main political challenge to secularization, creating a hybrid religious
fascism, though necessarily of a semiheretical character. The core fascist
movements were anticlerical and fundamentally even antireligious, but this
was not so much the case in the geographically and developmentally more
peripheral areas. As the main example of a nominally religious or
Christian fascism, the Legion of the Archangel Michael was the most
anomalous of fascist movements, for the somewhat heretical or potentially
schismatic character of its mysticism nonetheless did not obviate its peculiar religiosity.

In every case, the significant fascist movements emerged in comparatively new states, none more than three generations old. In general, fascism
was a phenomenon of the new countries of the 1860s and 1870s – Italy,
Germany, Austria, Hungary, and Romania – their unsatisfied status striv-
ings, defeats, or frustrations, and late-developing political systems.
Fascism has sometimes been called the product of a decaying liberal
democracy, but that notion can be misleading. In no case where a liberal
democratic system had been established either before World War I or had
existed for a full generation did the country succumb to fascism. This,
rather, was a significant phenomenon only in certain relatively new countries during the period in which they were just making, or had very recently
made, the initial transition to a liberal democracy that was as yet uncon-
solidated. Simultaneously, and again seemingly paradoxically, conditions
approximating liberal democracy were in fact necessary for fascist movements to develop and flourish. They did not function as Communist-style
insurrections but as broad European nationalist movements which required
the liberty to mobilize mass support – liberty offered only by conditions
equivalent to, or closely approaching, liberal democracy.

Another, and fairly obvious, requirement was fragmentation, division,
or sharp polarization within the political system. Countries with stable
party systems, such as Britain, France, and the Low Countries, were largely
immune to fascism. The larger fascist parties required not merely some
preparation of the soil by a pre-existing movement of intense nationalism
but also significant fragmentation or cleavage among the other forces. A
partial exception to this stipulation might appear to be the rise of the
Arrow Cross in Hungary during the late 1930s, in a situation in which
Horthy's government party still enjoyed a nominal majority. In this case,
however, the system was one of only semiliberal democracy at best. The
elitist ruling party was increasingly unpopular and maintained its status to
that point only by sharp electoral restrictions, accompanied by some

corruption. Fascism (or more precisely the multiple national socialisms, in the Hungarian nomenclature) thus became the main vehicle for a deeply felt popular protest that had few other means of expression. The structure of the Hungarian electoral system stood apart from that of most other European parliamentary regimes.

The existence of a menace from the left – either real or perceived – has often been held necessary for the rise of fascist movements, and this is generally correct. Italian Fascism could probably never have triumphed without the specter, and the reality, of revolutionary social maximalism. Germany was the home of the strongest Communist party in Europe outside the Soviet Union, always perceived as a serious threat by many. In the minds of others, the broad base of support enjoyed by German Social Democrats only added to the problem. The even greater strength of socialism in Austria was at first a basic catalytic factor there, while the Spanish Civil War represented the ultimate in left–right polarization.

Conversely, the left would not seem at first glance to have played an equivalent role in Hungary and Romania, but certain other features of politics in these countries must also be kept in mind. At the beginning of the inter-war period, Hungary was briefly the only country outside the Soviet Union ruled by a revolutionary Communist regime. This colored Hungarian politics for the next generation, exacerbating anti-communism and anti-leftism in general and also helping to create the conditions in which only a radical non-leftist movement such as Hungarian national socialism would have both the freedom and the appeal to mobilize broadly social discontent. In Romania, the Communist Party was effectively suppressed and the Socialists weak, but Romania now shared a new border with the Soviet Union, which never in principle recognized the Romanian occupation of Bessarabia. Anti-communism thus remained a significant factor in Romanian affairs, and Soviet seizure of Bessarabia and Bukovina in 1940 (together with Hitler's award of much of Transylvania to Hungary) created the condition of extreme trauma in which Antonescu and then the Legion could come to power.

Fascist movements were no different from other political groups in needing effective leadership. In fact, because of their authoritarian principles they required a strong leader – with at least some degree of ability – more than did more liberal forces. Not all the leaders of the larger fascist movements were charismatic or efficient organizers, Szalasi being perhaps the best negative example. But in many cases leadership was a factor in helping to determine the relative success of the movement, even though other conditions were more determinative. The difference between the relative success of a Mosley and a Szalasi did not lie in their respective talent and ability but in the totally distinct conditions of their two countries.

Leadership was more important the higher any particular fascist movement rose. It became vital for any serious attempt to take power, except in the cases where Hitler simply awarded authority to puppets of limited ability such as Pavelić and Szalasi. When Horia Sima, a relatively incompetent leader, was awarded a share of power in Romania, he was unable either to consolidate or to expand it. Given the inability of fascist parties to employ insurrectionary tactics because of the institutionalized character of European polities, allies were in every case essential for taking power. No fascist leader ever seized power exclusively on his own, as leader of a fascist movement and no more. Since semilegal tactics were required, and even the most popular fascist movement never gained an absolute majority, allies – who almost always came from the authoritarian right – were indispensible in bringing a fascist leader to power and even to some extent in helping to expand that power.

Though fascism battened on the weakening of democracy and consensus, it was important for such movements that relative pluralism and some degree of a representative process be preserved up to the time of initially taking power. Without conditions of at least relative freedom – even if not the purest constitutional democracy – a fascist leader could not expect to be able to take power (again, with the standard exception of Hitler's puppets). Authoritarian government closed the door to fascism in Austria and Portugal, in Vichy France, and in a number of eastern European countries. Authoritarian government also controlled and limited the participation of fascists in power in Romania and Spain, subordinating them in the latter and eventually eliminating them altogether in the former.

As far as international circumstances are concerned, significant fascist movements took root in countries suffering from severe national frustration and/or ambition, or in some cases a combination of both. The classic examples of fascist movements battening on a national sense of status deprivation and defeat were the national socialisms, German and Hungarian. To a lesser degree, the whole complex arising from the sense of a *vittoria mutilata* (mutilated victory) in Italy stimulated the growth of Mussolini's movement, though it was not necessarily the prime cause thereof. In Spain, the Falange finally benefited not merely from the challenge of the revolutionary left in 1936 but also from the strong, if paranoid, perceptions of the roles of foreign ideologies and powers therein. Once more the Romanian case seems anomalous, for, despite an ignominious military effort, Romania was one of the biggest winners in World War I, doubling in size and being awarded more territory than it could digest. The deprivation perceived by Romanians did not stem from military defeat or loss of territory (as in Germany and Hungary) but from the failure to achieve dignity, development, and national unity or integration, from the perception of a breakdown in culture and institutions as much as in politics.

Another international factor of importance was the existence abroad of a fascist role model, at least in the case of nearly all the movements except for those in Germany and Italy. To prosper, any fascist movement had to develop autochthonous roots, but foreign examples were factors in encouraging the majority of them, for only in Italy and Germany did they develop absolutely on their own. Conversely, it was of course also true that a fascist movement primarily (rather than only secondarily) dependent on foreign example, ideology, inspiration, or funding was not likely to develop much strength of its own, and thus all the purely mimetic movements – with the exception of Austrian Nazism and perhaps the partial exception of Spanish Falangism – failed.

No aspect of the analysis of fascist movements has generated more controversy than the issue of social bases and origins. It is true that fascism had little opportunity in stable societies not undergoing severe internal tensions. A significant degree of internal stress or social conflict was a sine qua non, but that is about as far as agreement has gone. There is relative consensus that the lower middle class was the most decisive social stratum for fascism, but even this has been somewhat exaggerated. Italian Fascism, for example, had approximately as much support from workers, farmers, and farm laborers during its rise as it did from the lower middle class, the mesocratic stratum coming to dominate membership only after formation of the dictatorship. The decisiveness of different social classes varied from case to case and country to country. The lower middle class was ultimately the most important social sector for the movements in Germany, Austria, Italy, and probably Spain. In these cases, the failure to represent or incorporate the lower middle sectors adequately in the liberal system was important, together with the fragmenting of middle-class parties in Germany and Spain.

In Hungary and Romania, the role of the middle and upper classes was significant primarily for the leadership. The ordinary members were more likely to be peasants and workers. In these countries, it was the failure to incorporate or represent the lower classes that provided available space for mass social recruitment.

In the majority of cases, the existence of a Jewish minority was important for the development of the movement as well. In Italy, on the other hand, this proved to be irrelevant, the Fascist Party itself being disproportionately Jewish. In Poland and Lithuania, conversely, the presence of Jewish minorities as large or even larger than those in Hungary and Romania did not 'elicit' significant fascist movements, though a great deal of less lethal anti-Semitism existed. Once again, no single factor is of crucial importance by itself, but only insofar as it converged, or was unable to converge, with other influences.

In economic structure, influence, or development, no single key common to all significant fascist movements can be found. Such a movement was powerful in one of the best educated and most advanced of European countries, and also in one of the most backward and illiterate. Those seeking to explain the social and economic basis of Hitlerism have often referred to the very high German unemployment statistics of 1930–33, but equally high unemployment existed in various other countries that did not develop significant fascist movements, and the percentage of unemployed was almost as high in the democratic America of Hoover and Roosevelt.

The only economic common denominator was that in every country in which a strong fascist movement was found, there existed a broad perception that the present economic crisis stemmed not merely from normal internal sources but also from military defeat and/or foreign exploitation. The further down the development ladder, the greater the economic hatred of the 'capitalist plutocracies'.

One factor concerning the level of development that was more clear-cut was the need for the country to have achieved a plateau in economic and political development in which the military was no longer a prime factor in political decisions. Otherwise the Mussolini and Hitler governments would probably have been vetoed as both irrelevant and even as harmful by a politically dominant military. Such military powers largely throttled fascism in eastern Europe.

Not one of the factors providing elements for a retrodictive theory was of any great significance by itself, or even in combination with one or two others. Only if the majority of them converged in a given country between the wars was it possible for a truly fascistogenic situation to develop.

To recast the retrodictive design in simpler and shorter terms, then, we can say that the necessary conditions for the growth of a significant fascist movement involved strong influence from the cultural crisis of the *fin de siècle* in a situation of perceived mounting cultural disorientation; the background of some form of organized nationalism before World War I; an international situation of perceived defeat, status humiliation, or lack of dignity; a state system comparatively new that was entering or had just entered a framework of liberal democracy; a situation of increasing political fragmentation; large sectors of workers, farmers, or petit bourgeois that were either not represented or had lost confidence in the existing parties; and an economic crisis perceived to stem in large measure from foreign defeat or exploitation.

Fascism was, as Nolte, Mosse, Weber, and Griffin have explained, a revolutionary new epochal phenomenon with an ideology and a distinctive set of ambitions in its own right. It was also the product of distinctive national histories, being primarily confined to the new nations of the 1860s – new state systems that had failed to achieve empire and status, and in some cases even reasonable economic development. Sufficient conditions existed for strong fascisms in those countries alone, the only exception being the sudden rise of fascism in Spain amid the unique civil war crisis of 1936 – itself sufficient explanation of this apparent anomaly in the Europe of the 1930s.

Conversely, sufficient conditions for the growth of fascist movements have ceased to exist since 1945, even though the number of neofascist or putatively neofascist movements during the past half century has been possibly even greater than the number of genuine fascist movements during the quarter century 1920–45.

To call the entire period 1919–45 an era of fascism may be true in the sense that fascism was the original and vigorous new type of radical movement in those years, and also in the sense that Germany for a time became the dominant state in Europe. The phrase is inaccurate, however, if it is taken to imply that fascism became the dominant political force of the period, for there were always more anti-fascists than fascists. Anti-fascism preceded fascism in many European countries, and among Italian Socialists – in their opposition to Mussolini's early 'social chauvinism' – it almost preceded the original Fascism itself. Down to 1939, anti-fascists, both voters and activists, always outnumbered fascists in Europe as a whole.

Crises and semi-revolutionary situations do not long persist, and fascist movements lacked any clear-cut social class or interest basis to sustain them. Their emphasis on a militarized style of politics, together with their need for allies, however temporary the association, greatly restricted their opportunities as well as their working time, requiring them to win power in less than a generation and in some cases within only a few years. The drive of a fascist movement toward power threatened the host polity with a state of political war (though normally not insurrectionary civil war) quite different from normal parliamentary politics. No system can long withstand a state of latent war, even if a direct insurrection is not launched. It either succumbs or overcomes the challenge. In the great majority of cases the fascist challenge was repelled, though sometimes at the cost of establishing a more moderate authoritarian system. At any rate, the 0.7 per cent of the popular vote won by the Spanish Falange in the 1936 elections was much nearer the norm than the 38 per cent won by the Nazis in 1932.

FASCIST THEORIES OF FASCISM

Presentation

We have seen how liberal theorists agonized over the definition of fascism before a fairly cohesive, partially consensual theory eventually emerged in the hands of such academics as Mosse, Payne, Eatwell, and myself, one which treats it cogently as a revolutionary form of modern nationalism. The premise to this approach, one generally repellent to earlier generations of scholars, is to take fascist ideology at its face value, and to recognize the central role played in it by the myth of a national rebirth to be brought about by finding a 'Third Way' between liberalism/capitalism and socialism/communism. One of the advantages of the new consensus is that it brings fascism in line with the way other major political 'isms' are approached in the human sciences by defining it primarily as an ideology inferrable from the claims made by its own protagonists, rather than assuming it refers essentially to a type of state system or treating it as intelligible only as the by-product of another historical or socio-psychological process. At this point the opinions of fascists on the nature of their ideology, so rarely consulted in the past, offer valuable corroboration of the heuristic value of the models which liberal academics operating from within the new paradigm are currently seeking to refine.

It is appropriate to start with Mussolini's definition of his own movement (Reading 20) first published in the *Enciclopedia Italiana* in 1932, and reprinted in *Fascism: Doctrine and Institutions*, a compilation of declarations about the nature of Fascism translated into English for the benefit of the Anglo-Saxon world. Not only is this the most famous encyclopedia definition ever printed of the historical singularity which gave rise to the generic term, but in it the *Duce* claims that his regime is setting an example to be followed by other countries in the spirit of 'Universal Fascism'.[1] The first part of the original encyclopedia article (omitted here) was in fact written by the idealist philosopher Giovanni Gentile who gave a ponderous Hegelian gloss to the principles underlying the Fascist state. Writing as the regime's creator and charismatic leader, Mussolini's tone is less analytical, more defiantly anti-intellectual. He makes no bones of the lack of a specific doctrine hitherto, proud of the fact that as a Fascist activist he had been too busy to worry about providing a rigorous theoretical basis to what he was doing. Consistent with this assertion of the primacy of action over intellectual theory, he presents Fascism as the heir of the French 'national socialist' Péguy, of his close associate Sorel, who extolled the vital role played in historical transformation by mobilizing myths, and of French and Italian brands of revolutionary socialism (particularly national syndicalism) inspired by Sorelianism.

The period leading up to the March on Rome saw the rise of *squadrismo* which turned the minute movement into a national political force. It is consistent with the extreme anti-materialism and anti-individualism of the Fascist mindset that Mussolini portrays this period as one in which the readiness to be martyrs, the ultimate test of faith to the Fascist cause, was 'more important and sacred' than discussions. As with the allusion to Sorel, such passages bear out the profound role played in the genesis of fascism of the *fin-de-siècle* 'revolt against positivism' which was highlighted by Sternhell.[2] Mussolini qualifies this anti-intellectualism by pointing to the books, articles, and campaign speeches published in the revolutionary years as proof that a Fascist doctrine did exist embryonically from the beginning, if only as denunciations of what Fascists were against. The legislation and institutions of the new regime also supply evidence that a doctrine was emerging to accompany deeds, even if it has had to wait till now to be fully elaborated.

The cornerstones of Fascist doctrine which Mussolini then identifies are initially a series of negations, anticipating the emphasis which Linz and Payne gave to them in their definitions, as well as fascism's need as a late-comer to elbow its way into a space already occupied by existing ideologies. They include: (a) the rejection of pacifism and the celebration of war, associated with a vitalistic 'love of life' and the virtues of duty, heroism, and self-sacrifice;[3] (b) the rejection of universal solidarity in favour of national pride; (c) the rejection of Marxism and the materialistic conception of life and class struggle which underpins it; (d) the rejection of democratic ideologies based on universal suffrage and egalitarianism; (e) the rejection of liberalism's claim to be the ultimate stage of history; (f) the rejection of any conservatism which attempts to recreate the feudalism and oppression of the *ancien régime*.[4]

As for what Fascism stands for positively, Mussolini adumbrates Eatwell's emphasis on the syncretic dimension of fascist ideology when he claims its right to draw on any vital element which still survives in all the ideologies it rejects. It is at this point that he prophesies that Fascism is destined to become for the twentieth century what liberalism was to the nineteenth, underlining his vision of his movement as a future-oriented, progressive, international force. This force he evokes once again in vitalistic terms, this time Nietzschean rather than Sorelian, as will to power and will to live. Distinctly un-Nietzschean, though, is the emphasis on (implicitly militaristic) violence,[5] and on the State as a transcendent, ethical entity which gives meaning to individual lives,[6] a conception which reflects the influence of Gentile's Hegelianism. By resolving the fragmentation produced by parliamentary democracy, the economic tensions generated by class-division, and the ethical crisis created by individualism, the State, as the institutional embodiment of the nation, is presented as a revolutionary force which liberates and channels human energies rather than oppressing them, and fosters Christianity rather than replacing it. At the end Mussolini alludes once more to the universality of Fascism, implying that all countries in the vanguard of history will create their own form of it (or, to put it less rhetorically, become individual permutations of generic fascism).

Fascism is thus characterized by its leader in terms which correspond in every respect to the definition of generic fascism proposed by the new consensus. It is a revolutionary force, breaking with conservatism and sweeping away rival modern ideologies such as liberalism and socialism whose historical moment has passed. Its populism is clear from the pledge to 'go towards the people' and to create a new form of democracy capable of coordinating and intensifying all the productive energies of the nation. Its palingenetic thrust emerges from the identification of the

State's essential goal as that of creating a new type of political, economic, and ethical order, one which will usher in 'a new style of Italian life', and preside over a revival of the Roman spirit of imperialism in which the vitality of the people will triumph over apathy ('indifferentism') and decadence. In short, it is a manifesto of what I have termed 'palingenetic populist ultra-nationalism', though it is equally consistent with Payne's tripartite typology,[7] or with Eatwell's definition.[8]

The 'interpretation of fascism' offered by Claud Sutton in 1937 in the *British Union Quarterly* (Reading 21) echoes many of Mussolini's sentiments, though his opening remarks express a scepticism about the appropriateness of the term 'fascism' employed outside its Italian context which a number of academics would endorse decades later when exasperated by the seemingly endless wrangles over its precise meaning.[9] However, he recognizes that it has gained a wider currency (i.e. has become a generic concept)[10] because of the wide-spread intuition that Fascism embodies 'something new and of world-wide import', just as Mussolini claimed in the previous text, and as his own leader, Oswald Mosley, also firmly believed.[11] He is quick to point out that, far from being internationalist in the Marxist sense, fascism's universality lies in the way quite different nationalist movements can still share the same basic world-view first manifested in the new Italy. This is because they are arising as a response to the same two global processes, the decay of liberal democracy and the rise of Marxism.

Sutton then launches into a critique of the philosophical foundations of liberal democracy, notably its egalitarianism, the belief that the function of government is solely to protect individual rights (cf. Mussolini's attack on the 'night-watchman' state), and the supreme value it places on individual freedom and personal happiness. This is followed by a damning verdict on Marxism's attempt to enforce egalitarianism by attempting to create an authoritarian state charged with establishing the dictatorship of the proletariat, and hence actively fomenting a class-war within the nation. He is particularly scathing about Stalinism, portraying it as the product of the decay of communism. This inner collapse, he suggests sarcastically, may eventually result in Russia's transformation into a truly nationalistic, and hence fascist state, but only at terrible human cost.

At this point fascism is presented as the alternative to both. While it originated in an instinctive response to the diseases of liberalism, 'disorder, materialism, plutocracy and cosmopolitanism' (i.e. a 'negative' force), as a mature ideology it is rooted in the ('positive') conception of the nation as an organism which confers meaning on the life of each individual through the vital links it provides with the past and the future. The vitality of a true nation is sapped by internal divisions and the domination of any particular group or faction, and demands the rule of an inspired leader who will prevent the process of moral, physical and ecological decay. The fascist state plays a central role in maintaining the health of the nation. It raises the living standards of the poorest, though not in a spirit of egalitarianism, but for the sake of the national community as a whole. It runs the economy in the national interest to prevent it being abandoned to the vagaries of international trade and consumer demand. It acts as the protector of the cultural and material resources of the nation, and so becomes the steward of national life in which each individual existence finds meaning.

A Fascist contemporary of Sutton would have had little problem sensing the kinship between his ideals and the ones proclaimed here, a kinship underlined by the direct quotation from Mussolini concerning the natural inequality of human beings. However, he might well have been disconcerted by a number of statements which specifically point to the influence of the Third Reich. Thus the assertion that a 'Jewish gang' controlled Russia before Stalin came to power smacks of rabid anti-Semitism (Italy had not yet introduced its racial legislation). Also the will of the (unnamed) fascist countries to make the best of the national resources in the spirit of a noble landowner is referred to as 'the religion of Blood and Soil', a somewhat misleading allusion to the Nazi cult of the nation's roots in the peasantry and the countryside – in fact Sutton's concern with 'the decay of land and forests' is much closer to the spirit of *Blut und Boden*. In the same paragraph there is also a reference to 'the decay of mental fitness', a phrase which has sinister eugenic connotations irrelevant to Mussolini's Italy, where the Nazi euthanasia campaign was unthinkable even after the introduction of racial legislation in 1938. Race is also listed along with nationality and management at the end as one of the forces of 'modernity' which made fascism possible. The admiration for Nazism becomes explicit when Sutton cites Hitler's declaration that the state's purpose was not to be worshipped (as in Mussolini's Italy), but purely to act as a container for a people 'conceived as an enduring biological and cultural entity'. Indeed, a major difference between Fascism and Nazism was that the reverence encouraged in Italy for the state was in Germany directed towards the *Volk*, a concept which fused ideas of biological and cultural purity which had no genuine counterpart in Italian. Thus it is no coincidence if the article traces the fascist idea of the organic community back to the Teutonic idea of loyalty rather than to the Roman precepts which a Fascist would have invoked.

Sutton's concept of generic fascism thus represents a curious amalgam of Fascism and Nazism, faithfully reflecting the eclectic ideological make-up of the BUF itself, which by the time he wrote had renamed itself the British Union of Fascists and National Socialists. There is also one element in his analysis which corresponds to neither: the idea of 'minding one's own business as the basis for foreign policy' and cooperation with 'coordinate' (i.e. fellow fascist) nations alludes to the official BUF policy of appeasement which was designed to let Fascist Italy and the Third Reich satisfy their voracious imperial ambitions unhindered, on condition that the British Empire was left intact. But whatever the idiosyncrasies of the piece, the basic features of fascism which it identifies again confirm the heuristic value of the new paradigm as an ideal type of what fascists themselves generally recognize as the core of fascism. It is an international, revolutionary, modern movement which seeks to save individual nations from decadence and regenerate the whole of Western civilization by finding a 'third alternative' to both liberalism and Marxism.[12]

With the next Reading we enter a quite different intellectual universe. During the 1970s its author, Marco Tarchi, was one of the most prolific, scholarly, and original thinkers of the Italian post-war radical right. By the time he wrote the article reproduced here (1978), his numerous books, articles, and translations or editions of other people's works had made him a major influence on those keen to reorient the ideology of radical right-wing culture away from its inter-war Fascist role models, particularly by blending into it ideas drawn from the Italian fascist philosopher Julius Evola, the French philiosopher of the New Right, Alain de Benoist, and the leading representatives of the so-called 'Conservative Revolution'.[13] As cultural director of the periodical *Diorama letterario* Tarchi helped establish it as an important forum for debate between intellectuals of Italy's highly diffuse radical right and ideologues associated with the Italian neo-Fascist party, the Movimento Sociale Italiano. However, even before his formal break with the Italian MSI in 1980, he had become disillusioned with politics and was dedicating his time increasingly to scholarship of an academic nature – he is now professor in the Department of Political Science and Sociology at the University of Florence. In this capacity he has written a historical work of impeccable scholarship on the role played in the origins of Fascism and Nazism by the crisis of collective identities[14] (cf. Platt's concept of a 'sense-making crisis' in Reading 17).

In the mid-1980s Tarchi devoted an issue of *Diorama letterario* (he was still its cultural director) entirely to the theory of generic fascism. The various articles written by right-wing intellectuals, which are published alongside a piece by Juan Linz, demonstrate a thorough grounding in the intricacies of the 'orthodox' academic debate over fascism which puts some contemporary 'liberal' experts to shame. They readily cite approvingly the theories of distinctly non-fascist academics, such as Renzo De Felice, Zeev Sternhell, and George Mosse, and it would take a trained eye to spot that some of the analyses are written not in order simply to understand generic fascism, but to elaborate a coherent conceptual framework in which to pursue the revision of the Italian and European fascist tradition (of which, in the eyes of many neo-fascists, Mussolini's regime was but one deeply flawed manifestation). It should be stressed, however, that in his correspondence with me concerning the inclusion of this piece Tarchi emphasized that the reprinting of his article in the issue had no revisionist intent, for by this time he had comprehensively distanced himself from fascism. His main purpose even when he wrote it seven years earlier was 'to elaborate an *authentic* interpretation of Fascism which could be used to counter those manipulated by scholars prone to write about it in a denigratory spirit'. He also points out that he has always been equally critical of 'the apologists of Fascism,' and that his writings have made him extremely unpopular in nostalgic neo-Fascist circles, the traditional backbone of MSI support.

He starts with an account of the extraordinary blindspot which prevented academics in various disciplines from taking generic fascism seriously as a legitimate object of study. The failure of sociology to give a cogent account of its dynamics let in aberrant psychohistorical theories (such as Reich's *The Mass Psychology of Fascism*), while political science had recourse to crude theories such as totalitarianism. The result was a failure to recognize the existence of a species or genus of fascism, and concentration focused instead on the economic groups which supported it (producing the fallacious 'categorical analysis' identified by Platt), and the fascist concern with 'order' (i.e. its manifestation as an authoritarian regime). Later Tarchi takes side-swipes at Marxist and modernization theories as well. He sees the breakthrough to a less simplistic understanding of generic fascism as occurring in the 1970s, when academics such as Renzo De Felice and George Mosse started arguing that fascism had to be investigated in terms of its ability to recruit a mass (not a class) following.

The rest of the article is a thoroughly documented exposition of the idea that the key to fascism is the concerted attempt it made to regenerate society with a new type of party. Born of the war experience, it would not be a conventional electoral organization, but a militarized, charismatic movement which through a blend of activism with a ritualistic style of politics would mobilize a mass following drawn from all social strata and integrate all those it touched into the regenerated nation, uniting them within a 'community of destiny'. Fascism was thus simultaneously a revolution and a civic religion or 'festival'. It promised its supporters not new programmes, but the radical renewal of society, not representation, but participation in a communal experience of 'festive' or 'sacred' time which would put an end to alienation and anomie.[15] Far from being anti-modern, or the symptom of a pathological modernization, fascism formed as a response to the crisis of modernity, an alternative modernity. In its diverse inter-war forms (there are references in the article to Fascism, Nazism, the Romanian Iron Guard, the Hungarian Arrow Cross, and the Spanish Falange), 'all fascism' (i.e 'generic fascism') sought to resolve the prevailing political, social, and spiritual crises with creation of a totally new type of community whose product would be the birth of a new type of human being.

Writing now as a scholar, but perhaps with a feeling for his subject still informed by his time as a spokesman of the radical right's campaign for Italy's cultural regeneration, Tarchi's analysis uses the testimonies of conventional academics to make a powerful argument to see fascism in positive terms as a profoundly innovative response to the crisis of democracy, one which is to be understood as much in social, cultural, and psychological terms as in strictly political ones. He also implies that without a grasp of generic fascism the individual movements and events it subsumes cannot be fully comprehended. The main thrust of the argument is once more profoundly compatible with the 'new consensus', and since it was composed in 1978 can be seen as one of the earliest formulations of its basic principles: fascism is a charismatic movement of social renewal based on an organic conception of the national community. So orthodox does his approach seem from the vantage point of the late 1990s that the legacy of the intense period which Tarchi spent with radical right intellectual circles is only detectable in what he (perhaps unconsciously) neglects to point out: it was precisely the Fascist and Nazi regimes' attempts to create a fully integrated 'community of destiny' and maintain its dynamism at all costs which led to the 'catastrophe of war' referred to at the end. (Note that he also reminds the reader that the 'open, painful wound' inflicted on the generation which survived the war was experienced both by 'victors and *vanquished*'.)[16]

The fourth sample of fascist theory of fascism to be considered has been chosen to throw into relief just how far from universal the new consensus is, and the paradoxical results it can lead to when applied to putative fascist movements. It is taken from the biennial periodical *The Crusader* published by the contemporary English Nationalist Movement whose declared goal it is to lay the foundations of a 'national revolution'. The ENM's programme conforms in every respect to the ideal type of generic fascism which has been the organizing principle of this Reader. As its literature makes clear, it vehemently attacks materialism, individualism, liberalism, capitalism, Marxism, cosmopolitanism, the Europe of Maastricht, the internationalism of NATO, and Zionism (claiming the Holocaust to be a hoax and selling the infamous anti-Semitic forgery *Protocols of the Elders of Zion*). It wants to restore the sovereignty of England, Alba (Scotland), Cymru (Wales), Ulster, Mannin (Isle of Man), and Kernow (Cornwall) in a new political order based on direct democracy and a new economic order based on a principle called 'distributism'. The national revolution will create a new community conscious of its roots in blood and soil. This will stem both ecological breakdown and moral degeneration, as well as instituting a programme of 'humane' repatriation of 'immigrants' so as to put an end to the racial and cultural intermixing which the ENM believes lies at the root of the identity crisis now threatening the English. There is more than a suggestion that the ENM conceives national identity in eugenic terms as well, since its book catalogue for 1997/8 includes *The Racial Elements of European History*, by Hans Günther, the Third Reich's foremost academic expert on 'racial science'.

In its literature the ENM claims to be seeking a Third Position between capitalism and communism, and counts among its heroes Otto Strasser, the German 'national socialist' who founded his own fascist party in opposition to Nazism, and Gadhafi, leader of Libya's popular revolution. It hopes for the appearance of a New Man who instinctively devotes his life to his nation and helps usher in the New Dawn.[17] The national revolution will be led by a cadre of political soldiers who combine military qualities with the readiness to sacrifice themselves to a higher goal in the spirit of José Antonio de Rivera, leader of the Spanish Falange, and Corneliu Codreanu, leader of the Romanian Iron Guard. One could hardly find a more perfect specimen of an ideology of 'palingenetic ultra-nationalism' or of a movement preaching 'the need for social rebirth in order to forge a *holistic-national radical Third Way*'.[18]

Yet, as the article reproduced here shows, ENM spokespersons adamantly refuse to accept that their movement is 'fascist'. Writing under a pseudonym, the author's definition of fascism (which at least demonstrates an awareness of the need for a consciously constructed ideal type) specifies five criteria: strong leadership, anti-liberalism, imperialism, anti-Marxism, and a maintenance or tolerance of capitalism. She then applies these criteria to three putative fascist movements: the

Falange, Belgian Rexism, and the Iron Guard. Citing evidence from established historians she argues that all three contained a leadership cult, but one which never degenerated into fanatical obedience. Moreover, they did not pursue expansionist policies, and, most importantly of all for the ENM, rejected capitalism as much as they hated Marxism. The conclusion she draws is that Falangism, Rexism, and the Iron Guard were not fascist, but formations of 'national revolutionaries' or 'political soldiers' like the ENM itself. By contrast, the fascism embodied in Mussolini's Italy and Hitlerite (but not Strasserite) Germany was at bottom not revolutionary, but reactionary, as its retention of capitalism demonstrates only too clearly. The article stresses the way José Antonio came to repudiate the term 'fascism', Degrelle betrayed Belgian nationalism for Nazism, and the Iron Guard was crushed by the Third Reich. Hence fascism not only perpetuates capitalism, but its imperialism crushes genuine nationalism. By implication, the reader is meant to infer that the ENM is a truly revolutionary movement which intends to renew the economy along with every other aspect of English society, and create an England which will live in harmony with other nations which have found their Third Way.

What are students and researchers to make of ideologues of movements which clearly fit their working definition of generic fascism, yet who deny being fascist on the basis of their own, conflicting definition? In such a situation it is good to remind ourselves of the ideal–typical nature of all definitions of generic terms in the social sciences. Their purpose is not to produce definitive classifications or legally watertight criteria, but to serve as heuristic devices to research further into human realities. There is no 'objective' use of a generic term, but if it throws into relief empirically observable patterns and interconnections between phenomena then it increases understanding rather than hindering it. In the case of the ENM, for example, to classify their ideology as fascist not only fits in with the way it celebrates a number of inter-war figures (Gregor and Otto Strasser, José Antonio, Codreanu) to whom few historians would deny fascist credentials, but makes it unremarkable that some of its activists are known to have previously been involved in Britain's National Front. In the 1970s the tactics and programme of this party were not 'Third Positionist', but deeply indebted to Nazism (which the ENM article accepts was indeed fascist). Before this the NF had been chaired by A. K. Chesterton, former BUF member and biographer of Mosley in the 1930s, but fiercely independent of Mosley after the war. To see the ENM as a unique, 'unclassifiable' nationalist revolutionary movement is thus to rip it out of the historical context of British and European fascism in which it is so clearly embedded. Furthermore, once the new consensus is applied to the issue, a distinct pattern of political affiliation emerges which would otherwise be invisible. It can be demonstrated empirically from the evidence provided by primary sources that what links the BUF, the political world-view of Chesterton after 1945, British neo-Nazism, and contemporary Third Positionism is the vision of a post-liberal new order brought about by a populist movement of revolutionary nationalism which will put an end to decadence and inaugurate Britain's (or in the ENM's case England's) rebirth.

Clearly the ENM do not see things this way. They want to distance themselves from forms of ultra-nationalism whose revolutionary zeal did not extend to the destruction of the capitalist system itself. They want to assert their own identity and not be absorbed into an all-embracing category. Hence their ideal type differs from mine. There may also be another factor at work. The perennial problem with 'fascism' is that it is not just any political 'ism'. It is widely used colloquially as a term of abuse, and even in dispassionate contexts is readily associated with totalitarianism, racism, militarism, the use of terror, and genocide. Few academics nowadays would treat any of these pheomena as definitional components of fascism. Nevertheless, if a contemporary movement is described as fascist its supporters may well take this classification as a misrepresentation of their ideals, and even as libellous. I would exhort them, however, to recognize that in a serious work of social science or history such as this Reader, the use of the term is neither an insult nor a condemnation, but a matter of 'value-free'[19] classification ('taxonomy').[20]

Notes

1   See Introduction, pp. 1–2.
2   See Reading 14.
3   Cf. Theweleit's diagnosis of the pathology of the 'soldier male' in Reading 18.
4   The portrayal of liberalism as a historically played out force in this section indirectly testifies to the importance of the post-war crisis of democracy in providing a precondition to the rise of fascism. See Reading 15.
5   Sorel's *Reflections on Violence* (London, Collier-Macmillan, 1961; first French edition 1908) had a major influence on early twentieth-century revolutionary theory. See David Ohana, 'Georges Sorel and the Rise of Political Myth', *History of European Ideas*, 13(6) (1991), pp. 733–46.
6   Cf. Platt's theory that fascism resolves a generalized 'sense-making crisis' in Reading 17.
7   See Reading 13.
8   See Introduction p. 14–15.
9   Notably G. Allardyce: see Introduction p. 9.
10 Note that Sutton retains the capital letter for all political ideologies, including what we would call (generic) fascism.
11 See for example Oswald Mosley, 'The World Alternative: European Synthesis within the Universalism of Fascism and National Socialism', *Fascist Quarterly*, 2(3) (July 1936), pp. 377–95.
12 This corroborates the emphasis placed by Mosse and Eatwell on fascism as 'a Third Way' (see Reading 12 and Introduction p. 15).
13 See Roger Griffin, *Fascism* (Oxford, Oxford University Press, 1995), pp. 346–57.
14 Marco Tarchi, *La 'rivoluzione legale'. Identità collettive e crollo della demo-crazia in Italia e Germania* (Bologna, Il Mulino, 1993).
15 As with Tarchi's book on Fascism's and Nazism's 'legal revolution' cited in note 13, his analysis of the socio-psychological dynamics of fascism correspond

closely to Platt's analysis of revolution as the solution to a generalized sense-making crisis (see Reading 17). 'Alienation' in the way Tarchi uses it here corresponds closely to what the sociologist Durkheim called 'anomie', a sense of having no communal values to give meaning to existence, a concept which in turn corresponds closely to what Platt refers to as a situation in which available ideologies no longer make sense of the world.

16 My emphasis. In the mid-1990s the Alleanza Nazionale, the 'modernized' version of the MSI, was campaigning for the members of the Italian militias who fought for the Nazi puppet state, the Republic of Salò, to be honoured as heroic patriots on a par with the partisans who fought them.

17 See especially *The Crusader*, Issue 4, 1995, dedicated to exploring the theme 'A new individual, a new society'.

18 Roger Eatwell, *A History of Fascism* (London, Chatto & Windus, 1995), p. 11.

19 'Value-free' only in the sense which it acquires within the context of the social scientific quest for 'truth' once conceived in Weberian terms. See H. S. Hughes, *Consciousness and Society* (Brighton, The Harvester Press, 1979) pp. 296–315.

20 It is presumably because it associated fascism with a term of abuse, that the South African Afrikaner-Weerstandsbeweging resolutely refused to allow its programme to be reprinted in my Reader *Fascism* (Oxford, Oxford University Press, 1995), claiming adamantly that it is 'not a fascist movement'.

20

The ideology of the twentieth century*

BENITO MUSSOLINI

Political and social doctrine

When in the now distant March of 1919, speaking through the columns of the *Popolo d'Italia* I summoned to Milan the surviving interventionists who had intervened, and who had followed me ever since the foundation of the *Fasci* of revolutionary action in January 1915, I had in mind no specific doctrinal program. The only doctrine of which I had practical experience was that of socialism, from 1903–04 until the winter of 1914 – nearly a decade. My experience was that both of a follower and a leader – but it was not doctrinal experience. My doctrine during that period had been the doctrine of action. A uniform, universally accepted doctrine of Socialism had not existed since 1905, when the revisionist movement, headed by Bernstein, arose in Germany, countered by the formation, in the see-saw of tendencies, of a left-revolutionary movement which in Italy never quitted the field of phrases, whereas, in the case of Russian socialism, it became the prelude to Bolschevism.

Reformism, revolutionism, centrism, the very echo of that terminology is dead, while in the great river of Fascism one can trace currents which had their source in Sorel, Péguy, Lagardelle of the *Mouvement Socialiste*, and in the cohort of Italian syndicalists who from 1904 to 1914 brought a new note into the Italian socialist environment – previously emasculated and chloroformed by fornicating with Giolitti's party – a note sounded in Olivetti's *Pagine Libere*, Orano's *Lupa*, Enrico Leone's *Divenire Sociale*.

When the war ended in 1919 Socialism, as a doctrine, was already dead; it continued to exist only as a grudge, especially in Italy where its only chance lay in inciting to reprisals against the men who had willed the war and who were to be made to pay for it.

The *Popolo d'Italia* described itself in its sub-title as 'the daily organ of fighters and producers'. The word 'producers', was already the expression of a mental trend. Fascism was not the nursling of a doctrine previously drafted at a desk; it was born of the need of action, and was action; it was

* Reprinted in full from B. Mussolini, *Fascism: Doctrine and Institutions* (Rome, Ardita, 1935; first published in Italian in 1932), pp. 7–22.

not a party but, in the first two years, an anti-party and a movement. The name I gave the organisation fixed its character.

Yet if anyone cares to reread the now crumpled sheets of those days giving an account of the meeting at which the Italian *Fasci di combattimento* were founded, he will find not a doctrine but a series of pointers, forecasts, hints which, when freed from the inevitable matrix of contingencies, were to develop in a few years time into a series of doctrinal positions entitling Fascism to rank as a political doctrine differing from all others, past or present.

'If the bourgeoisie – I then said – believe that they have found in us their lightening-conductors, they are mistaken. We must go towards the people . . . We wish the working classes to accustom themselves to the responsibilities of management so that they may realise that it is no easy matter to run a business . . . We will fight both technical and spiritual rear-guardism . . . Now that the succession of the régime is open we must not be faint-hearted. We must rush forward; if the present régime is to be superseded we must take its place. The right of succession is ours, for we urged the country to enter the war and we led it to victory . . . The existing forms of political representation cannot satisfy us; we want direct representation of the several interests . . . It may be objected that this programme implies a return to the guilds (*corporazioni*). No matter! . . . I therefore hope this assembly will accept the economic claims advanced by national syndicalism . . .'.

Is it not strange that from the very first day, at Piazza San Sepolcro, the word 'guild' (*corporazione*) was pronounced, a word which, as the Revolution developed, was to express one of the basic legislative and social creations of the régime?

The years preceding the March on Rome cover a period during which the need of action forbade delay and careful doctrinal elaborations. Fighting was going on in the towns and villages. There were discussions but . . . there was something more sacred and more important . . . death . . . Fascists knew how to die. A doctrine – fully elaborated, divided up into chapters and paragraphs with annotations, may have been lacking, but it was replaced by something far more decisive, – by a faith. All the same, if with the help of books, articles, resolutions passed at congresses, major and minor speeches, anyone should care to revive the memory of those days, he will find, provided he knows how to seek and select, that the doctrinal foundations were laid while the battle was still raging. Indeed, it was during those years that Fascist thought armed, refined itself, and proceeded ahead with its organization. The problems of the individual and the State; the problems of authority and liberty; political, social, and more especially national problems were discussed; the conflict with liberal, democratic, socialistic, masonic doctrine and with those of the *Partito Popolare*, was carried on at the same time as the punitive expeditions.

Nevertheless, the lack of a formal system was used by disingenuous adversaries as an argument for proclaiming Fascism incapable of elaborating a doctrine at the very time when that doctrine was being formulated – no matter how tumultuously, – first, as is the case with all new ideas, in the guise of violent dogmatic negations; then in the more positive guise of constructive theories, subsequently incorporated, in 1926, 1927, and 1928, in the laws and institutions of the régime.

Fascism is now clearly defined not only as a régime but as a doctrine. This means that Fascism, exercising its critical faculties on itself and on others, has studied from its own special standpoint and judged by its own standards all the problems affecting the material and intellectual interests now causing such grave anxiety to the nations of the world, and is ready to deal with them by its own policies.

First of all, as regards the future development of mankind, – and quite apart from all present political considerations – Fascism does not, generally speaking, believe in the possibility or utility of perpetual peace. It therefore discards pacifism as a cloak for cowardly supine reunciation in contra-distinction to self-sacrifice. War alone keys up all human energies to their maximum tension and sets the seal of nobility on those peoples who have the courage to face it. All other tests are substitutes which never place a man face to face with himself before the alternative of life or death. Therefore all doctrines which postulate peace at all costs are incompatible with Fascism. Equally foreign to the spirit of Fascism, even if accepted as useful in meeting special political situations – are all internationalistic or League superstructures which, as history shows, crumble to the ground whenever the heart of nations is deeply stirred by sentimental, idealistic or practical considerations. Fascism carries this anti-pacifistic attitude into the life of the individual. 'I don't care a damn', (*me ne frego*) – the proud motto of the fighting squads scrawled by a wounded man on his bandages, is not only an act of philosophic stoicism, it sums up a doctrine which is not merely political: it is evidence of a fighting spirit which accepts all risks. It signifies a new style of Italian life. The Fascist accepts and loves life; he rejects and despises suicide as cowardly. Life as he understands it means duty, elevation, conquest; life must be lofty and full, it must be lived for oneself but above all for others, both nearby and far off, present and future.

The population policy of the régime is the consequence of these premises. The Fascist loves his neighbor, but the word 'neighbor' does not stand for some vague and unseizable conception. Love of one's neighbor does not exclude necessary educational severity; still less does it exclude differentiation and rank. Fascism will have nothing to do with universal embraces; as a member of the community of nations it looks other peoples straight in the eyes; it is vigilant and on its guard; it follows others in all their manifestations and notes any changes in their interests; and it does not allow itself to be deceived by mutable and fallacious appearances.

Such a conception of life makes Fascism the resolute negation of the doctrine underlying so-called scientific and Marxian socialism, the doctrine of historic materialism which would explain the history of mankind in terms of the class struggle and by changes in the processes and instruments of production, to the exclusion of all else.

That the vicissitudes of economic life – discoveries of raw materials, new technical processes, scientific inventions – have their importance, no one denies; but that they suffice to explain human history to the exclusion of other factors is absurd. Fascism believes now and always in sanctity and heroism, that is to say in acts in which no economic motive – remote or immediate – is at work. Having denied historic materialism, which sees in men mere puppets on the surface of history, appearing and disappearing on the crest of the waves while in the depths the real directing forces move and work, Fascism also denies the immutable and irreparable character of the class struggle which is the natural outcome of this economic conception of history; above all it denies that the class struggle is the preponderating agent in social transformations. Having thus struck a blow at socialism in the two main points of its doctrine, all that remains of it is the sentimental aspiration – old as humanity itself – toward social relations in which the sufferings and sorrows of the humbler folk will be alleviated. But here again Fascism rejects the economic interpretation of felicity as something to be secured socialistically, almost automatically, at a given stage of economic evolution when all will be assured a maximum of material comfort. Fascism denies the materialistic conception of happiness as a possibility, and abandons it to the economists of the mid-eighteenth century. This means that Fascism denies the equation: well-being = happiness, which sees in men mere animals, content when they can feed and fatten, thus reducing them to a vegetative existence pure and simple.

After socialism, Fascism trains its guns on the whole block of democratic ideologies, and rejects both their premises and their practical applications and implements. Fascism denies that numbers, as such, can be the determining factor in human society; it denies the right of numbers to govern by means of periodical consultations; it asserts the irremediable and fertile and beneficient inequality of men who cannot be levelled by any such mechanical and extrinsic device as universal suffrage. Democratic régimes may be described as those under which the people are, from time to time, deluded into the belief that they exercise sovereignty, while all the time real sovereignty resides in and is exercised by other and sometimes irresponsible and secret forces. Democracy is a kingless régime infested by many kings who are sometimes more exclusive, tyrannical, and destructive than one, even if he be a tyrant. This explains why Fascism – although, for contingent reasons, it was republican in tendency prior to 1922 – abandoned that stand before the March on Rome, convinced that the form of government is no longer a matter of pre-eminent importance, and because the study of past and present monarchies and past and present republics shows that neither monarchy nor republic can be judged _sub specie aeternitatis_, but that each stands for a form of government expressing the political evolution, the history, the traditions, and the psychology of a given country.

Fascism has outgrown the dilemma: monarchy v. republic, over which democratic régimes too long dallied, attributing all insufficiences to the former and proning the latter as a régime of perfection, whereas experience teaches that some republics are inherently reactionary and absolutist while some monarchies accept the most daring political and social experiments.

In one of his philosophic Meditations Renan – who had pre-fascist intuitions – remarks:

> Reason and science are the products of mankind, but it is chimerical to seek reason directly for the people and through the people. It is not essential to the existence of reason that all should be familiar with it; and even if all had to be initiated, this could not be achieved through democracy which seems fated to lead to the extinction of all arduous forms of culture and all highest forms of learning. The maxim that society exists only for the well-being and freedom of the individuals composing it does not seem to be in conformity with nature's plans, which care only for the species and seem ready to sacrifice the individual. It is much to be feared that the last word of democracy thus understood (and let me hasten to add that it is susceptible of a different interpretation) would be a form of society in which a degenerate mass would have no thought beyond that of enjoying the ignoble pleasures of the vulgar.

So far Renan. In rejecting democracy Fascism rejects the absurd conventional lie of political equalitarianism, the habit of collective irresponsibility, the myth of felicity and indefinite progress. But if democracy be understood as meaning a régime in which the masses are not driven back to the margin of the State, then the writer of these pages has already defined Fascism as an organized, centralized, authoritarian democracy.

Fascism is definitely and absolutely opposed to the doctrines of liberalism, both in the political and the economic sphere. The importance of liberalism in the nineteenth century should not be exaggerated for present-day polemical purposes, nor should we make of one of the many doctrines which flourished in that century a religion for mankind for the present and for all time to come. Liberalism really flourished for fifteen years only. It arose in 1830 as a reaction to the Holy Alliance which tried to force Europe to recede further back than 1789; it touched its zenith in 1848 when even Pius IXth was a liberal. Its decline began immediately after that year. If 1848 was a year of light and poetry, 1849 was a year of darkness and tragedy. The Roman Republic was killed by a sister republic, that of France. In that same year Marx, in his famous *Communist Manifesto*, launched the gospel of socialism. In 1851 Napoleon III made his illiberal *coup d'état* and ruled France until 1870 when he was turned out by a popular rising following one of the severest military defeats known to history. The victor was Bismarck who never even knew the whereabouts of liberalism and its prophets. It is symptomatic that throughout the nineteenth century the religion of liberalism was completely unknown to so highly civilized a people as the Germans but for one parenthesis which has been described as the 'ridiculous parliament of Frankfort' which lasted just one season. Germany attained her national unity outside liberalism and in opposition to liberalism, a doctrine which seems foreign to the German temperament, essentially monarchical, whereas liberalism is the historic and logical anteroom to anarchy. The three stages in the making of German unity were the three wars of 1864, 1866, and 1870, led by such 'liberals' as Moltke and Bismarck. And in the upbuilding of Italian unity liberalism played a very minor part when compared to the contribution made by Mazzini and Garibaldi who were not liberals. But for the intervention of the illiberal Napoleon III we should not have had Lombardy, and without that of the illiberal Bismarck at Sadowa and at Sedan very probably we should not have had Venetia in 1866 and in 1870 we should not have entered Rome. The years going from 1870 to 1915 cover a period which marked, even in the opinion of the high priests of the new creed, the twilight of their religion, attacked by decadentism in literature and by activism in practice. Activism: that is to say nationalism, futurism, fascism.

The liberal century, after piling up innumerable Gordian knots, tried to cut them with the sword of the world war. Never has any religion claimed so cruel a sacrifice. Were the Gods of liberalism thirsting for blood?

Now liberalism is preparing to close the doors of its temples, deserted by the peoples who feel that the agnosticism it professed in the sphere of economics and the indifferentism of which it has given proof in the sphere of politics and morals, would lead the world to ruin in the future as they have done in the past.

This explains why all the political experiments of our day are antiliberal, and it is supremely ridiculous to endeavor on this account to put them outside the pale of history, as though history were a preserve set aside for liberalism and its adepts; as though liberalism were the last word in civilization beyond which no one can go.

The Fascist negation of socialism, democracy, liberalism, should not, however, be interpreted as implying a desire to drive the world backwards to positions occupied prior to 1789, a year commonly referred to as that which opened the demo-liberal century. History does not travel backwards. The Fascist doctrine has not taken De Maistre as its prophet. Monarchical absolutism is of the past, and so is ecclesiolatry. Dead and done for are feudal privileges and the division of society into closed, uncommunicating casts. Neither has the Fascist conception of authority anything in common with that of a police-ridden State.

A party governing a nation 'totalitarianly' is a new departure in history. There are no points of reference nor of comparison. From beneath the ruins of liberal, socialist, and democratic doctrines, Fascism extracts those elements which are still vital. It preserves what may be described as 'the acquired facts' of history; it rejects all else. That is to say, it rejects the idea of a doctrine suited to all times and to all people. Granted that the ninteenth century was the century of socialism, liberalism, democracy, this does not mean that the twentieth century must also be the century of socialism, liberalism, democracy. Political doctrines pass; nations remain. We are free to believe that this is the century of authority, a century tending to the 'right', a Fascist century. If the nineteenth century was the century of the individual (liberalism implies individualism) we are free to believe that this is the 'collective' century, and therefore the century of the State. It is quite logical for a new doctrine to make use of the still vital elements of other doctrines. No doctrine was ever born quite new and bright and unheard of. No doctrine can boast absolute originality. It is always connected, if only historically, with those which preceded it and those which will follow it. Thus the scientific socialism of Marx links up to the utopian socialism of the Fouriers, the Owens, the Saint-Simons; thus the liberalism of the nineteenth century traces its origin back to the illuministic movement of the eighteenth, and the doctrines of democracy to those of the Encyclopaedists. All doctrines aim at directing the activities of men towards a given objective; but these activities in their turn react on the doctrine, modifying and adjusting it to new needs, or outstripping it. A doctrine must therefore be a vital act and not a verbal display. Hence the pragmatic strain in Fascism, its will to power, its will to live, its attitude toward violence, and its value.

The key-stone of the Fascist doctrine is its conception of the State, of its essence, its functions, and its aims. For Fascism the State is absolute, individuals and groups relative. Individuals and groups are admissable in so far as they come within the State. Instead of directing the game and guiding the material and moral progress of the community, the liberal State restricts its activities to recording results. The Fascist State is wide awake and has a will of its own. For this reason it can be described as 'ethical'. At the first quinquennial assembly of the regime, in 1929, I said:

The Fascist State is not a night-watchman, solicitous only of the personal safety of the citizens; nor is it organised exclusively for the purpose of guaranteeing a certain degree of material prosperity and relatively peaceful conditions of life, a board of directors would do as much. Neither is it exclusively political, divorced from practical realities and holding itself aloof from the multifarious activities of the citizens and the nation. The State, as conceived and realised by Fascism, is a spiritual and ethical entity for securing the political, juridical, and economic organisation of the nation, an organisation which in its origin and growth is a manifestation of the spirit. The State guarantees the internal and external safety of the country, but it also safeguards and transmits the spirit of the people, elaborated down the ages in its language, its customs, its faith. The State is not only the present, it is also the past and above all the future. Transcending the individual's brief spell of life, the State stands for the immanent conscience of the nation. The form in which it finds expression change, but the need for it remains. The State educates the citizens to civism, makes them aware of their mission, urges them to unity; its justice harmonises their divergent interests; it transmits to future generations the conquests of the mind in the fields of science, art, law, human solidarity; it leads men up from primitive tribal life to that highest manifestation of human power, imperial rule. The State hands down to future generations the memory of those who laid down their lives to ensure its safety or to obey its laws; it sets up as examples and records for future ages the names of the captains who enlarged its territory and of the men of genius who have made it famous. Whenever respect for the State declines and the disintegrating and centrifugal tendencies of individuals and groups prevail, nations are headed for decay.

Since 1929 economic and political development have everywhere emphasized these truths. The importance of the State is rapidly growing. The so-called crisis can only be settled by State action and within the orbit of the State. Where are the shades of the Jules Simons who, in the early days of liberalism proclaimed that the 'State should endeavor to render itself useless and prepare to hand in its resignation'? Or of the MacCullochs who, in the second half of last century, urged that the State should desist from governing too much? And what of the English Bentham who considered that all industry asked of government was to be left alone, and of the German Humbolt who expressed the opinion that the best government was a 'lazy' one? What would they say now to the unceasing, inevitable, and urgently requested interventions of government in business? It is true that the second generation of economists was less uncompromising in this respect than the first, and that even Adam Smith left the door ajar – however cautiously – for government intervention in business.

If liberalism spells individualism, Fascism spells government. The Fascist State is, however, a unique and original creation. It is not reactionary but revolutionary, for it anticipates the solution of certain universal problems which have been raised elsewhere, in the political field by the splitting-up of parties, the usurpation of power by parliaments, the irresponsibility of assemblies; in the economic field by the increasingly numerous and important functions discharged by trade-unions and trade associations with their disputes and ententes, affecting both capital and labor; in the ethical field by the need felt for order, discipline, obedience to the moral dictates of patriotism.

Fascism desires the State to be strong and organic, based on broad foundations of popular support. The Fascist State lays claim to rule in the economic field no less than in others; it makes its action felt throughout the length and breadth of the country by means of its corporative, social, and educational institutions, and all the political, economic, and spiritual forces of the nation, organized in their respective associations, circulate within the State.

A State based on millions of individuals who recognize its authority, feel its action, and are ready to serve its ends is not the tyrannical state of a mediaeval lordling. It has nothing in common with the despotic States existing prior to or subsequent to 1789. Far from crushing the individual, the Fascist State multiplies his energies, just as in a regiment a soldier is not diminished but multiplied by the number of his fellow soldiers.

The Fascist State organizes the nation, but it leaves the individual adequate elbow room. It has curtailed useless or harmful liberties while preserving those which are essential. In such matters the individual cannot be the judge, but the State only.

The Fascist State is not indifferent to religious phenomena in general nor does it maintain an attitude of indifference to Roman Catholicism, the special, positive religion of Italians. The State has not got a theology but it has a moral code. The Fascist State sees in religion one of the deepest of spiritual manifestations and for this reason it not only respects religion but defends and protects it. The Fascist State does not attempt, as did Robespierre at the height of the revolutionary delirium of the Convention, to set up a 'god' of its own; nor does it vainly seek, as does Bolschevism, to efface God from the soul of man. Fascism respects the God of ascetics, saints, and heroes, and it also respects God as conceived by the ingenuous and primitive heart of the people, the God to whom their prayers are raised.

The Fascist State expresses the will to exercise power and to command. Here the Roman tradition is embodied in a conception of strength. Imperial power, as understood by the Fascist doctrine, is not only territorial, or military, or commercial; it is also spiritual and ethical. An imperial nation, that is to say a nation which directly or indirectly is a leader of others, can exist without the need of conquering a single square mile of territory. Fascism sees in the imperialistic spirit – i.e. in the tendency of nations to expand – a manifestation of their vitality. In the opposite tendency, which would limit their interests to the home country, it sees a symptom of decadence. Peoples who rise or rearise are imperialistic; renunciation is characteristic of dying people. The Fascist doctrine is that best suited to the tendencies and feelings of a people which, like the Italian, after lying fallow during centuries of foreign servitude, is now reasserting itself in the world.

But imperialism implies discipline, the coordination of efforts, a deep sense of duty and a spirit of self-sacrifice. This explains many aspects of the practical activity of the régime, and the direction taken by many of the forces of the State, as also the severity which has to be exercised towards those who would oppose this spontaneous and inevitable movement of twentieth century Italy by agitating outgrown ideologies of the nineteenth century, ideologies rejected wherever great experiments in political and social transformations are being dared.

Never before have the peoples thirsted for authority, direction, order, as they do now. If each age has its doctrine, then innumerable symptoms indicate that the doctrine of our age is the Fascist. That it is vital is shown by the fact that it has aroused a faith; that this faith has conquered souls is shown by the fact that Fascism can point to its fallen heroes and its martyrs.

Fascism has now acquired throughout the world that universality which belongs to all doctrines which by achieving self-expression represent a moment in the history of human thought.

21

*The third alternative**

CLAUD SUTTON

Fascism, in the sense in which it will be used in this article, is an awkward and inconvenient term to describe the world movement which has emerged in our time to compete with Marxism and Liberal-Democracy for men's allegiance. It should undoubtedly be confined to naming the special form which this movement has taken in Italy. Nevertheless, the popular mind, feeling that in Italian Fascism something new and of world-wide import had emerged, persists in using the term in a wider sense.

Fascism is not international as Communism is, in the sense of being a dogma to be thrust down the throat of every nation, regardless of its

* Reprinted in full from Claud Sutton, 'An Interpretation of "Fascism"', *British Union Quarterly*, (2) (April–July 1937), pp. 67–77.

history and circumstances. It is rather an underlying similarity of outlook which can be detected in various modern national movements, and which may be seen to emerge with a kind of necessity from the situation in which our European culture finds itself at present. We in England share in the common cultural inheritance of Europe; just as we were most profoundly affected by the ideas of the French Revolution, so we are bound to be deeply affected by the ideas of the Fascist movement, and to react to these ideas in our own particular national way.

The two factors which are everywhere giving birth to this movement are the decay of Liberal-Democracy and the rise of Marxism.

It needs but a slight acquaintance with history to realize that there is nothing inevitable or eternal about Liberal-Democracy. Compared with other forms of government, democratic governments have neither been common nor stable, nor have they contributed as much of enduring value to human culture as have aristocratic and monarchical governments. Of course it is possible – and often done – to define Democracy in such a way as to include in it all tolerable forms of government whatever, – for instance, to describe England under Queeen Elizabeth or under Pitt as a democracy. But this is a gross misuse of language and a debasing of the intellectual currency. 'Democracy' should not be used to denote every government which rules by the consent of nearly all the governed; nor one which consciously pursues the welfare of the whole people; nor one which is tolerant of a variety of opinions and encourages free discussion; nor one which rules according to settled and known law, impartially applied. Many democratic governments have failed conspicuously in these respects; many non-democratic governments have exhibited these virtues in a high degree. It is absurd to call 'democracy' any government which is not tyrannical; democracy is one particular historical form of government, which has sometimes worked to the general satisfaction, sometimes not. Its chief feature would seem to be the decision of all important questions by majority vote, either of the whole people or of large representative assemblies.

Democracy as we know it in Western Europe and America – which I shall hereafter term 'liberal-democracy' – is a special product of the French Revolution, and based upon the peculiar theories of certain influential thinkers of that era. The underlying philosophy of human nature on which it is based has not always been accepted by thinking men, and there is no reason to suppose that its sway over men's minds will be eternal. On the contrary, there is considerable evidence that this philosophy of the 'Rights of Man and of the Citizen' no longer carries conviction, and that the system of government based upon it is therefore doomed to pass away.

Like other political philosophies, it did not win general acceptance without a struggle. But today, who can detect any difference between Conservatives, Liberals and right-wing (non-Marxian) Labour in respect of their ideals or the general character of the methods by which they propose to realize them?

What are the philosophical assumptions, or axioms, of this system of Liberal-Democracy?

They may be reduced to three.

The first is, that all men are equal, at least to the extent that they must have an equal share in government. The second is, that government only exists in order to prevent any man interfering with the equal liberty of others (J. S. Mill); or as more forcibly expressed to me by a student: 'government only exists to enable every man to go to hell in his own way'. The third, that such individual liberty results in the greatest possible satisfaction of all.[1]

Fascism is based on the denial of all these principles. To the first it replies that all men are not equal in their capacity for cooperative enterprise, – and government is a cooperative enterprise. Men differ markedly in respect of their courage, fairness, loyalty, veracity and other qualities of character which are required for any corporate undertaking. Such qualities are not the monopoly of any class, nor dependent on education in the ordinary sense of the word. Some men are markedly deficient in them – all the Old Bolshevik leaders for example, if we are to believe their confessions; anyone of us would try to exclude them from power in any organization for which he was responsible. Political representation must be based on a selective system of real groups whose members are personally acquainted with one another. A good political system should not even try to ensure that all opinions have equal weight.

To the second principle it observes that equal liberty is impossible, for men do not all want to do the same things; that every system of law presupposes some positive ideas as to what is objectively good or bad for everyone; that the principle is either meaningless or disastrous.

To the third, that owing to the nature of man and society, the greatest possible sum of satisfaction cannot be achieved by the system of maximum individual liberty; nor is this 'greatest happiness of the greatest number, every-one to count for one and no one for more than one'[2] the end of life. Men are and should be more interested in the welfare of their own family, their own profession, their own neighbourhood, their own nation; and good government should take account of this fact. We shall return to these points later.

Liberal-democracy is a lazy philosophy. Instead of making up one's mind what ought to be done and fighting tenaciously to get it realized, the good democrat waits and sees which way the majority will jump, secure in his belief that the voice of the masses is the voice of God. We must not even seek to persuade people.[3] Today the driving power of Liberal-Democracy has everywhere run down. Few people wholeheartedly believe in its slogans. Half its present-day advocates are really timid Marxists.

Their avowed end is equal wealth for all, and democracy merely a means to this. They fondly imagine that this end can be achieved by mere voting, without force, at least in the distant future. They frequently betray their contempt for individual liberty as such. They are envious, but they care for their skins. Such are the Lib-lab Social-democrats.

What is the philosophical basis of the unholy alliance between Communists and Democrats, wherever Fascism appears on the scene? To this problem we must now turn our attention.

Communism – or better Marxism, for there are many Marxists outside of the Communist Party – is altogether a product of the individualistic, equalitarian philosophy of Liberal-democracy. Frequent in history have been revolutionary movements of the less fortunate classes; this one has taken over the peculiar ideology of the early Victorian era in which it was born. It too conceives the community as a collection, and social happiness as a sum. It accepts the first two principles of Liberal-democracy; all men are equal – though there is no God – and therefore they ought to have not merely equal political rights, but equal wealth.[4] Again, happiness is to be achieved by giving everyone equal wealth and then letting them do what they like with it; when once economic equality is achieved, the state is to 'wither away'. But it most emphatically rejects the third principle of Liberal-democracy, that this happy condition of things comes about by letting people alone. *Laisser-faire* is the ultimate aim, when once economic equality has been achieved; but this has to be achieved by the forcible dicatorship of the proletariat, that is, of the unskilled factory-worker.

Its central doctrine is the Class-war between proletarians and capitalists. It persists in herding all mankind into these two pens, although no economist any longer takes seriously the 'surplus-value' theory upon which the distinction was based. How unreal the two pens are! There is indeed conflict between groups, and such conflict is of the essence of a live community. But a large proportion of the inhabitants of the modern state, who live on the joint proceeds of their work and of the property needed to make that work fruitful, cannot be squeezed into either pen except by a *tour-de-force*. And are not the conflicts of interests between townsmen and countrymen, between manufacturers and financiers, between craftsmen and unskilled labourers, between racial groups and religious groups, just as real and vital as this alleged one between capitalists and proletariat?

The keynote of Marxism is the class-war, in which all methods are allowable. That is why, wherever it raises its head, politics become so embittered and so 'dirty'. It destroys all sense of the moral unity of the nation which previously mitigated conflicts between groups. That is why it must be fought to the death.

But, it will be said, has nothing of any value been achieved through the Communist experiment in Russia? And is there no resemblance between the 'dictatorships' of Communism and Fascism?

It is impossible to understand the development of Communism in Russia, unless we distinguish the present stage of 'Bolshevism in Retreat', as it has been termed, from the earlier stage in which doctrinaire Communism had full sway. This earlier stage was marked by an unparalleled destruction, for the sake of the class-war theory, of the human and material resources of the nation – of farmers, technicians and teachers, of cattle, machines, buildings and art-treasures. The same phenomenon has manifested itself in Spain and elsewhere, wherever Bolshevism has seized power. When after some ten years production had reached such a low level that it seemed the limit of human endurance had been reached, the doctrines were largely abandoned; and with the help of capitalist credits, foreign technicians and machinery and Stakhanovist driving of the workers, a beginning was made to build up again. Certainly the change of heart is far from complete. One symptom of it seems to be the present conflict betwen Stalin, the robust and undoctrinaire brigand from the Caucasus, and the Jewish gang who hitherto controlled Russia and are now largely eliminated. Russia has not abandoned the Comintern and the Marxian ideal of world-revolution. But for herself she seems to have tacitly abandoned the equalization of wealth and the dictatorship of the proletariat, and to be building up a powerful nationalistic state. Under Stalin, there are signs of a sort of shame-faced Fascism with a guilty conscience emerging. If this was to be the end, at what a cost has it been achieved![5]

'Fascism' has arisen out of the decay of Liberal-democracy and in response to the menace of Bolshevism. Unlike Bolshevism, it was not the putting into practice of an academic theory; it arose in response to an actual situation, and can therefore only be understood in the light of the two world-movements which it is destined to supersede. Originally it was a kind of instinctive reaction of European man to the forces of disorder, materialism, plutocracy and cosmopolitanism. It is at one with Communism in denying absolutely that there is a pre-established harmony which makes the greatest happiness of all result from the greatest liberty of each. But this is all that it has in common with Communism. It takes a radically different view from both Communism and Liberal-democracy with regard to the 'happiness' which the state is to secure. For it conceives the nation as an organic unity of many different functional groups; each of these represents a certain unique contribution to the nation, with its own type of life which must be fostered. If the right relationships between these groups are disturbed, there can be no enduring happiness or soundness in the state. 'We could,' said Plato, 'make our potters much happier by allowing them to lie on couches before the fire, eating and drinking, and turning their wheel when they felt like it . . . But do not advise us to do this, for our potters would no longer be potters, nor our farmers farmers.'[6]

Moreover, it conceives the nation, in the words of Burke, as ' a partnership not only of the living, but of the living with the dead and with those that are yet unborn'.[7] It is something that endures, with human and natural resources, which may be wasted or which may be made more fertile.

A movement has come into power in each of the 'Fascist' countries with a will to make the best out of the national estate, as the old noble land-owner did out of his own family and estate. This is what has been called the religion of Blood and Soil.

It is evident that these movements cannot admit the unlimited rights of majorities. They cannot for instance permit a present majority of towns-men to wipe the countrymen out of existence, nor to enjoy the utmost possible present wealth at the expense of future power. The evils which the rule of short-sighted majorities brings – the decay of public honesty and the spirit of self-help, the decay of the family, of mental and physical fitness, the decay of lands, forests and ships – can only be cured by giving great scope and independence to leaders.

Fascism evidently must, and does, devote its chief efforts to strengthen-ing the weakest links in the national chain, that is, in improving the conditions of those groups which are hardest pressed. It cannot, however, admit equality between the lazy and the active, between imaginative and routine work, even as a far-off ideal. 'Fascism affirms the immutable, beneficial, fruitful inequality of men' (Mussolini).

Liberal-democracy is paralysed by the rivalry of functional groups, whose existence it pretends to ignore. Fascism recognizes these and bases its representative system upon them, believing that it can master their potential conflicts through the strengthened national sense of unity, and the 'leadership-principle', the principle of individual responsibility. 'Democracy' – the principle of control by anonymous majorities – is on its trial in the industrial no less than in the political field.[8]

In the economic sphere the aim of Fascism, conforming to its general outlook, is to achieve the utmost possible security and stability for all producers – not the maximum freedom of choice for consumers. To this end international trade must be reduced to a subordinate and auxiliary position, in the interests of national planning. And ethical considerations – considerations as to the kind of life which should be encouraged or discouraged – must often override economic.

There is nothing in Fascist nationalism which is incompatible with the well-understood interests of other nations. Its foreign policy is based on the principle of minding one's own business and being really ready to fight for certain well-known vital interests and only these. It is naturally opposed to the democratic, equalitarian and universalistic principles of the League of Nations. It wants friendly cooperation with those coordinate nations with whom it actually has interests in common, based on the planned elimination of possible causes of friction. It wants leadership in international affairs as at home. In Europe its task is to rebuild the Concert of Europe which the founders of the League of Nations destroyed.

Finally we may attempt to answer the objection so often heard that Fascism subordinates the individual utterly to the state, a living being to an unreal abstraction. The answer to this is implicit in the foregoing. Government, the Fascist conceives, does not exist merely to increase the happiness of the individual citizens. It is a trustee for the enduring national culture and for the material resources which form its necessary basis. Without this the individual would be nothing; nor can he divest himself of it even if he leaves the territory of the state; it is the whole sum of ancestral traditions which differentiate him from a Stone Age man. A government which secures the harmonious development of the different culture-bearing groups and prevents them annihilating one another has a claim on our allegiance. But the state is a mere piece of machinery, a mere 'container', as Hitler said, for the people, conceived as an enduring biological and cultural entity. Fascism is not *étatiste*; unlike the Hegelians, it does not worship the state as such.

Historically considered, it presents analogies with the ancient European state-form as it was 'before the Orontes began to flow into the Tiber' – before the rise of abstract individualism and the desire for salvation in another life. Again, it presents analogies with Feudalism, with its conception that government must be based on the personal loyalty of man to man – the primeval Teutonic idea of the *comitatus*. Further, it reminds one of the aim of the medieval guilds to regulate production in the interests of all categories of producers. Like every big movement, it has its roots in the past. But it is no mere harking back to outworn systems. It is unintelligible apart from the essentially modern conceptions of Nationality, Race, Voluntary Trade Associations, the Divorce of Ownership from Management, the idea of Liability without Fault, interacting Cultures as opposed to a 'one-track' Civilization – and many others[9] It is through and through modern, and a creature of our time. Five years ago, it seemed to many of us that there was no choice except between the not very palatable alternatives of individualist liberal-democracy and Marxian Socialism. Now there is a third alternative.

Notes

1 This third axiom, as E. Halévy has pointed out, takes two forms. On one version, maximum social satisfaction results automatically from maximum individual liberty, whatever the laws and institutions of the society. On the other, certain legal restrictions are necessary to achieve this greatest sum of satisfactions. Most writers do not stick quite consistently to the one version or the other; but they have no doubt about the end, nor about the means – individual

liberty restricted as little as possible. (E. Halévy, *The Growth of Philosophic Radicalism*, London, Faber & Faber, 1934).

2 J. Bentham, *An Introduction to the Principles of Morals and Legislation* (Oxford, Clarendon Press, 1907).

3 Follett, *The New State*, p. 27.

4 Contrast Aristotle, *Politics* (London, Heinemann, 1932), III, 9 and 12: 'Justice is giving equal treatment to equals, and unequal treatment to unequals. Men omit one factor or the other, as it suits them; for they are not good judges in their own cause'. But this should not free us from the duty of judging as well as we can.

5 Stalin himself seems a very different type from the 'Old Bolshevik' Jewish bosses of Russia. It is striking that the two really big men the Russian Revolution has produced have not been Jews. But we do not know the extent of the influence of Stalin's father-in-law, Lazarus Moiseivitch Kaganovitch, who seems to be the second man in the state.

6 Plato, *Republic* (London, J. M. Dent, 1920), 420.

7 Burke, Edmond, *Reflections on the French Revolution* (London, J. M. Dent, 1935).

8 M. S. Miller and C. P. Campbell, *Financial Democracy* (London, L. and V. at the Hogarth Press, 1933), a recent research by two economists of Liverpool University into the operation of British industrial companies.

9 A. Toynbee, *A Study of History* (London, Oxford University Press, 1934). Vol. I, p. 149 ff.

22

*Between festival and revolution**

MARCO TARCHI

When fascism – by which is meant a global phenomenon: a doctrine, a political system, a historical event, and a myth of collective identification – left the stage so abruptly once it had been defeated at the hands of the Axis forces, it did so in a climate of tragedy which at the time it was impossible to imagine ever being parallelled. One of the consequences of this defeat has been generally ignored, namely, what could be called 'a loss of historical bearings'.

Let me explain. In contrast to what happened to those political forces which were its contemporaries and, whether they were in conflict with it or under its influence, were caught up in its fate – democracy, socialism, liberalism, communism – fascism did not attract a plurality of analytical

* Reprinted in full from M. Tarchi 'Tra festa e rivoluzione', *Diorama letterario*, 31, May–June 1985, pp. 29–34. Originally published in *Intervento*, 31 (May–June 1978), pp. 113–132. Translation by Roger Griffin.

approaches for over a quarter of a century. Placed under a curse which condemned it to appear in scholarly texts and academic writings as an impetuous and ephemeral tide of irrationality, as a 'parenthesis' in which civic virtues were eclipsed, as a 'cultural transgression' which flew in the face of the predetermined and self-evident Purpose of History, fascism tended to be classified by the social sciences, in whatever branch, as devoid of intrinsic value and legitimacy.

Naturally political philosophy could not tackle it, since its task was to concentrate on scanning the horizons for the common good, and churn out value judgements. Sociology could not tackle it, since it was so disconcerted by the hold which authoritarian nationalistic regimes had enjoyed over the masses that it left the field free for psychological ramblings and typologies of pathology. Political science was unwilling to tackle it, despite what Max Weber had taught about 'value-free' methodology, because to do so ran the risk of compromising its conceptual heritage (indeed, when it was prepared to do so, fertile but controversial new concepts resulted such as totalitarianism, revolution from above, and the opposition 'participation/mobilization'). Even legal theory, though it could not ignore the normative implications of the institutional structure of the 'total state', seemed reluctant to go beyond investigations into the 'material' ways in which the constitutions evolved.

What fascism could not be eradicated from was memory, that is to say from history. Like a painful, open wound, whether the mind which had experienced it was that of the victor or the vanquished, the trace of over two decades of domestic and international upheavals could not be wiped out. Having lost its power as a political force, fascism thus became consigned to historiographical one-dimensionality, with all the risks that entailed. For decades scholars persisted in dissecting it and analysing it in the style of that all too familiar method: the one which involves rigorous particularizing and a wariness of generalizations; an awareness of the immediate context, but obliviousness of the internal dynamics of movements and regimes; a keenness to find analogies with the past, but insensitivity to forces of innovation. What emerged were some highly durable stereotypes: the inimitable 'singularity' of each national case (and the subsequent refusal to recognize a political 'species' of fascism), the interminable debate about fascism's dependency on economic groups, its association or identification with an ideology of 'order'.

The first signs of a breakthrough only came in the 1970s, when the taboos surrounding the subject started to fade, and when it became clear that a strictly historiographical account was incapable of doing justice to the 'novelty' of fascism and to its capacity to involve the popular masses in its support. Taking their cue from the debate about 'consensus' stimulated by de Felice (and then so badly conducted once opponents took up conflicting positions), numerous studies started to adopt an interdisciplinary method and to probe into the phenomenon under discussion in some depth, making connections between elements and criteria derived from different specialisms and thus going beyond the stage of critical reconstruction to experiment with typologies and analytical models. Among the authors who have contributed to this process of clarification which has thrown into relief new themes central to the study of the fascist phenomenon, George L. Mosse deserves a special mention. After producing a number of weighty and erudite tomes which were well received by experts in the field, he risked unpopularity with a slim synoptic work, *Nazism: A Historical and Comparative Analysis of National Socialism*[1] that blended intellectual non-conformism with some intuitions, which, even if they are not elaborated, are of considerable significance. We would like to take these as the starting point to developing some thoughts on the hitherto largely neglected relationship between fascism and collective identity in secularized societies.

In the work referred to, the political scientist from the University of Wisconsin sets out to 'formulate a new interpretation of Nazism as a cultural phenomenon' and to 'analyse the elements which link it to Mussolini's Fascism as well as those which set them apart'. Building on the results of previous studies in this area,[2] Mosse carries out a series of concise analyses which challenge the conceptual frameworks that had always handicapped the type of research into the fascist movement in which the author might have recognized a general, supranational pattern, even if it was one only detectable through the filter of familiarity with its particular manifestation in each country. He first demystifies reductionist analyses of fascism which see it as the expression of the mentality (or even the vested interests) of particular social classes or segments of them, or as a fundamentally reactionary or conservative movement which was led to base its own consensus on the disintegration of traditional social hierarchies and on the advent of the so-called 'mass man'.[3] He goes on to suggest an autonomous perspective within which to locate the various national attempts at political self-expression between the two wars:

> Everywhere after 1918 there was a tendency in Europe for what we might call a radicalism of the Right – a radicalism that went beyond conservatism, and which posited a certain revolution. What sort of revolution? I think that we find that it is a revolution of the spirit which was supposed to have concrete consequences. That is to say, this radicalism of the Right wanted to do away with the traditional hierarchical structures of the society and of the state. It did not want to abolish the state, but to substitute instead hierarchies based on function rather than on status. [. . .] I should also, of course, mention that all fascisms were mass movements. [. . .] So there are enough things in common to *all* fascism that I think you must say

there is such a phenomenon as fascism and that within that phenomenon there are variations.[4]

Hence, not only do fascisms (or rather the individual expressions of the fascist phenomenon) lead an autonomous existence within the political context of their own time, but they tend to modify profoundly the historical setting in which they operate by proposing a revolution in the categories of political action. Rejecting a social ideal founded on superimposed horizontal stratifications (the 'classes' of Marxist analysis), they work towards a collective based on a new structural model, one which is vertically stratified (according to 'functions') following a principle of practical differentiation without ethical implications of the sort which Marx imputed to the bourgeois-capitalist system based on the 'division of labour'.[5] In this framework Mosse attempts to identify the salient contents of the fascist alternative. These contents find their organic synthesis in one overriding value, that of the community in the sense of the unified and qualitative expression of the wills, forces, and individual energies which make up the substratum of a national collective:

> [. . .] all fascism – more than any other revolutionary impetus between the wars – stressed the idea of community. The idea of leadership [. . .] came out of the idea of community – a community of affinity, not an enforced community; the kind of longing for *camaraderie* which came from the war. It's very important – not only the idea of struggle which comes from the war, but the idea of *camaraderie*.[6]

Thus fascism, starting out from a living and real experience – that of overcoming differences of background in the bloody crucible of war, that of negating the egoisms of social position in the life and death community of the trenches which was capable of creating new mentalities, new styles, new forms of behaviour (in a word, a new culture in the anthropological sense) at the end of the conflict – gives rise to a new myth: that of national integration and the end of alienation; a process no longer to be realized, as Marxism envisaged it, by overthrowing relationships *within* the structures, but through a revolution *of* the structure.

> I think it is quite clear that another element [which fascism has] in common (and yet different according to national context) is this matter of alienation. All fascism promised an end to alienation and indeed Hitler had a very startling passage in *Mein Kampf* where he says that when a man comes out of his factory and into a mass movement he becomes a part of a community and ends his alienation. But what is of course different are aspects of the idea of the community [. . .] Hitler, D'Annunzio, and Mussolini believed that the

community climaxes in the nation, but to D'Annunzio and Mussolini this community is the state and not the *Volk* or the race.[7]

The profound sense of spiritual, human community fostered by the experiences of camaraderie pervades the anti-Marxist and anti-democratic movements of the immediate post-war period to the point of forming a distinctive feature of the ideology, one expressed in a whole series of external signs which bring the militants together, unify their style, and try to win the attention, and then the active support, of sympathizers. The whole symbology which typifies fascism conforms to this logic. The shirts of various colours which movements, akin but originating in differing national and cultural contexts, adopt as an external uniform epitomize the discourse. They are the external signs of a mindset which is anti-bourgeois and contemptuous of the habitual 'normality' of the man in the street, and which the unifying logic of the war, though fought out on opposing fronts, has brought to the fore in a generation bound together less by a common year of birth than by shared attitudes. The problem of alienation caused by the uprooting of individuals and families from their natural, traditional environment, the consequence of a progressive process of urbanization, commercialization, and industrialization, is resolved in the *new* community, no longer taken for granted as something hereditary, but achieved through an act of will. Hannah Arendt stresses that:

> Nor did national distinctions limit the masses into which the postwar elite wished to be immersed. The First World War, somewhat paradoxically, had almost extinguished genuine national feelings in Europe, where, between the wars, it was far more important to have belonged to the generation of the trenches, no matter on which side, than to be a Frenchman or a German. The Nazis based their whole propaganda on this indistinct comradeship, this 'community of fate'. [. . .]

And again, in a glimmer of lucidity about the opposition which had been growing up between society and community, and which had increasingly come to resemble the *pays legal* and *pays réal* in Maurrassian thought, she writes:

> Activism, moreover, seemed to provide new answers to the old and troublesome question, 'Who am I?' which always appears with redoubled persistence in times of crisis. If society insisted, 'You are what you appear to be,' postwar activism replied: 'You are what you have done.'[8]

If society conditioned by ideological fashions and currents banishes veterans, these 'outlaws', which von Salomon will portray so effectively, forge their own unifying, communal bonds, more immediate, alive, and real than the ones which a document of citizenship or an identity card can create.

> The war had provoked a disintegration of society and had created a mass of persons who in the sociological sense were 'displaced', i.e. a mass of people or groups deprived of status but who, in the course of the war, had developed a political awareness, albeit a muddled one, and derived from it motives and ambitions to succeed in civilian life and become upwardly mobile. The social order which had been shattered now had to reconstruct its normality, not by returning to the old situation, but by legitimizing the upheavals which had occurred. Rather than feeling they belonged to a class, the veterans felt a sense of solidarity by virtue of having survived the war. [. . .] The ideology of these 'displaced persons' was a legitimation of the identity between the nation and soldiers which confirmed the gulf between materialist Italy and idealist Italy.

These lines written by Emilio Gentile[9] sum up the vision of the world of these socially marginalized groups who had already gathered enough influence to constitute 'a state within the state', and hence a community within society. The fascination of the ideal community envisaged by the nascent fascist movements is twofold: on the one hand, it presents itself as the agent of dissolution for social bonds judged to be anachronistic, such as ones of profession or 'class'; on the other, it is to act as a binding force in the name of a reality which is no longer and not only material. The result of this mixture is shattering:

> For the young, war and revolution were aspects of the same revolt against the established order and for social renewal, and between the war which had been and the revolution which was under way there was, as far as they were concerned, no break in continuity: both represented the flight from order, from a regulated life, from the defined status of social conventions: both were a festivity in the sociological sense, that is to say a collective euphoria which subverts the boundaries between the sacred and the profane, between the licit and the illicit. [. . .] The habits formed by warfare became the methods of the 'revolution' and the festivities continued.[10]

The fascist parties, typical movement-parties, thus came into being as what Duverger terms 'community parties', in other words parties whose membership was not motivated by material interests, but by spiritual motives, by instinctive impulses, by demands of idealism. Historical and political analyses converge on this point. Emilio Gentile writes:

> having returned from the war with anti-political sentiments [. . .] they scorned politics and celebrated life: they substituted words with

action which was violent but intended to resolve things; parliamentary discussions with the concrete and rapid methods of military life; the divisions and struggles between parties with the almost religious unity and solidarity of all those who had for years been through the same experience of *camaraderie*, sharing the glories and risks of front-line combat to the point of death, and thus becoming the living embodiment of the unity of the nation. [. . .] Parliament and parties no longer represented the nation.[11]

Maurice Duverger explains in these terms the dynamics behind the membership of community parties:

The community seems a way of joining together which is natural and spontaneous, based on closeness, whether geographical, parental, or spiritual. [. . .] At the same time it is a grouping which is not based on vested interests, a grouping which is by nature disinterested. [. . .] What binds the community together is something disinterested, is precisely the phenomenon of shared blood or closeness, an affinity which comes from a feeling of identity or happiness, of the identity which comes from living together. [. . .] Tönnies' classification could be complemented with the sociological category described by another German author in 1922, Schmallenbach, who talks of the *Bund* or Order. [. . .] 'The Order implies a much more total, deeper and binding commitment than that found in other groupings, [. . .] the *Bund* is distinguished from other groups by the degree of social integration. Social integration is much deeper in the *Bund*, much more complete.' It might be fruitful to see how far this concept explains some aspects of certain modern parties which try to create a profound and total sense of community between certain groups of individuals like the religious or military Orders did in the Middle Ages. The terminology of the Order can be found in the language of some fascist parties.[12]

The fundamental thesis of Tönnies which had such influence in the German cultural world especially after the First World War (even though the volume which expounded it, *Community and Society* had appeared in 1887), is that in their human context the ideas of community and society take on distinctive, mostly conflicting values: the one, community (*Gemeinschaft*) generated by the irrational, non-utilitarian, organic will, the motor of every act and source of every creation; the other, society (*Gesellschaft*) stemming from the reflexive will, the pure product of instrumental, rational thought. Opposition and at the same time complementarity rule the two models. The modern world, by stressing its own technical and utilitarian character, tends to reduce the sphere of the organic, qualitative, spontaneous, pluralist, 'natural' will to make way for new 'instrumental' relationships with no bonds of heredity or common faith. It is only logical that one response to this 'societal' dehumanization of our time consists in a rediscovery of the community, which is seen as a natural product of authenticity, but also as a choice in favour of spiritual, anti-material values. Without being 'scientifically' conscious of it, but rather living it out as a cultural reality in the anthropological sense of the term, it was this philosophy which was imbibed by veterans, demobbed soldiers, youths, idealists, political militants who came together in fascism, turning it into a force to be reckoned with. This characteristic of disinterested attachment to the 'cause of revolution' came to exert profound influence on the political style of Italian Fascism and the European movements akin to it, to the point of constituting a genuine typological feature which has been detected by numerous authors.

It was another political scientist, Juan Linz, the Spanish academic who teaches in the USA, who described the message of movements such as the Romanian Iron Guard, the Hungarian Arrow Cross, or the Spanish Falange in the following terms:

> The populist appeal to the community as opposed to the pragmatism of society, *Gemeinschaft* versus *Gesellschaft*, had considerable appeal in democratic societies divided by class conflict and mobilized by modern mass parties.[13]

The theme is echoed in Franz Neumann's classic though debatable work on the German National Socialist Party *Behemoth*: 'Not man, but the community is placed at the centre of the system', and, even more clearly, 'On this structure of society, National Socialism imposes two ideologies that are completely antagonistic to it: the ideology of community and the leadership principle.'[14] As we fleetingly saw above, the substantial consensus of academics on the thesis of the 'community' as the vehicle of the fascist message makes nonsense of those interpretations which reduce generic fascism to a heterogeneous assembler of amorphous masses flung onto the stage of history by the maelstrom of modernization. On the contrary, there are some acute critics who stress how there is an adequate fascist response to every aspect of modernization,[15] and how, throughout the various forms and characteristics adopted by movements and regimes in various contexts, whether as a systemic or an anti-systemic force, the theme of community persists as a fundamental element: even 'integral fascism', which the author in question, Garruccio, defines as 'conspiratorial' – anti-oligarchic, anti-urban, mystic – 'presents itself as a modernizing force in that it aims to integrate into a homogeneous community forces which have become marginalized from it',[16] and its structure, based fundamentally on solidarity and community, leads it to present itself as antithetical to capitalism, not as a socially alienating factor, but as a *nationally* alienating one.

All fascisms, in their many permutations of expression, remain true to this model. It is a coherence which De Felice himself recognizes, underlining the effort which the Fascist regime made to integrate the masses whose social activities had been hitherto so indeterminate and uncoordinated:

> Fascist mass policy became the fulcrum of the Fascist system – trade unions had an important role that Togliatti saw well – along with a series of social, recreational, and sporting initiatives – because for Fascism the consensus and participation of the masses in the regime had to be active. For Fascism it was necessary that the masses feel mobilized and integrated into the regime. [. . .] This revolutionary process was supposed to create a new moral community in Italy, with its own ideals, models of behaviour (for example, the use of *'voi'* instead of *'lei'*) and hierarchy. The creation of this community awaited the new generations. [. . .] Had Fascism succeeded in creating this desired community, this political power would have become increasingly autonomous and prevalent compared to that (in large part economic) still firmly in the hands of the flankers.[17]

In some areas of the movement (and of regimes where they formed), the project reached the point of complete self-consciousness to the point of being formulated theoretically and debated. In Italy, for example, this was the case of the School of Fascist Mysticism in Milan whose official publication, *Dottrina Fascista*, contained passages such as this:

> The individual, as a historical reality, has never existed. [. . .] The social personality of every group is always greater than the private personality. What follows is that [. . .] the subject sees his individual power and personality enhanced as a direct function of the power, coherence, and stability of the group into which he is hierarchically inserted. [. . .] Historically the need for this cohesion and stability, linked to ethnic and geographical factors, leads to the formation of ever larger groupings till they form nations.[18]

Here we see at work what Garruccio calls in his essay 'The Three Ages of Fascism', the 'ideology of total commitment, psychological rather than technical'.

Thus in the context of the immediate post-war period characterized in many European countries by sacrifice and disillusionment, movements of a fascist stamp come to form part of a generalized trend to reject the fractures, conflicts, and divisions which derived from the existing social and economic structures. The only divide recognized was between those who honoured the service paid to the nation in the war, the courage, the faith in the values for which the supreme effort had been made, and those who did not. The society which even during the years of trench warfare had carried on living out its life practically unscathed in the factories and drawing rooms, in the lecture halls and parliaments, or in bourgeois circles, was increasingly experienced as alien, as imposed, as out of touch. For the generation which had gone through the war there were two ways to come to terms with it, once so-called 'normality' had returned: either one of total, destructive nihilism, or the path of drastic, surgical reform inspired by the radically new communal values which had grown out of the recent and bloody experience of war. The visible fruit of this second alternative is the parallel 'militarization' of the political extremes of various nations, the partial convergence of styles and symbols (one only has to think of the 'Arditi del Popolo' or the paramilitary units of the Social Democrats during the Weimar Republic).

The 'communal style' of politics takes over from the rules previously imposed on society, which had for decades been dominated by the spirit of the club or faction. The distinction between the private and the public, which the cultural world will again interrogate so intensely in the 1960s and after, had already been resolved and rejected in the experience of the post-1918 avant-gardes: the Action Squads, the SA, the Green Shirts of Codreanu in Romania. Politics was no longer a spare-time activity or a well-paid occupation: the idea of the 'disinterested' revolution, or the 'community party' in the sense given it by Duverger created the political soldier, the militant, the 'believer' in the Party, in a welter of contradictory experiences which tended towards the birth of the same type of human being: *arditism*, revolutionary syndicalism, the nihilistic sense of revolt which spread among university students tired of an ascetic and over-specialized culture.

The Dannunzian adventure in Fiume was already marked by this new style of politics, which was festive in the sense outlined above, communal, disinterested. Ritual arose as a mediator between the realm of values and the indistinct mass of citizens, and what it forged was a community which was simultaneously sacred and profane. In Germany too the new politics made headway:

> In any Christian liturgy, so a tract on political festivals tells us, one person speaks on behalf of us all, and the congregation participates in the form of short appeals to God, through the Credo and, above all, through the hymn sung by the congregation. This order of service must be kept intact for secular festivals, the tract continues, because it expresses a fundamental psychological truth – it recognizes symbols as expressing, in a binding form, the spirit of the community. The theme of a Christian liturgical rite is therefore always the same: the confession of its sins by the congregation, the Credo, the explanation of the Scripture, and, as a climax, common prayer and blessing. For the National Socialist this basic form could not be abandoned, but should simply be filled with a different content.[19]

The choice of the qualitative and organic community, first of all as a rejection of a quantitative and indifferent 'society', and then within that society once 'the revolution' has established itself, is a constant of fascist movements transcending the level of historical contingencies to find articulation in the realm of cultural expression in the full sense of the term, namely in political philosophy and doctrine: the myth of the 'community of destiny', the moment of supreme collective identification, and the pivotal concept of the 'new politics' intuited by Mosse and buried by the catastrophe of the Second World War, are both its emblem and its culmination.

Notes

1 George L. Mosse, *Nazism: A History and Comparative Analysis of National Socialism; an Interview with Michael A. Ledeen* (Oxford, Basil Blackwell, 1978).

2 See George L. Mosse, *The Crisis of German Ideology* (New York, Grosset and Dunlap, 1964); *The Nationalization of the Masses* (Ithaca, Cornell University Press, 1975).

3 The first of these interpretive approaches, typical of Marxist thought, has undergone continual evolution and modification, but is still present in contemporary authors, such as Nicos Poulantzas.

4 Mosse, *Nazism*, op. cit., pp. 86–7.

5 Theoretical starting points for moving beyond analyses of social stratification based on class conflict were widely available in contemporaries of Marx or appeared shortly after him. We might cite, for example, Max Weber. A 'functionalist' school is still alive and productive in the field of sociology: among its best known exponents of the recent past are Pitrim A. Sorokin and Talcott Parsons.

6 Mosse, *Nazism*, op. cit., pp. 87–8.

7 Ibid., pp. 91–2.

8 Hannah Arendt, *The Burden of Our Time* (London, Secker and Warburg, English edition of *The Origins of Totalitarianism*, 1951), pp. 322, 324.

9 Emilio Gentile, *Le origini dell'ideologia fascista* (Laterza, Bari, 1975), p. 69.

10 Ibid.

11 Ibid., p. 71.

12 M. Duverger, 'Classe sociale, ideologia e organizzazione partica', in Giorgio Sivini ed. *Sociologia dei partiti politici* (Bologna, Il Mulino, 1971).

13 Juan Linz, 'Totalitarian and Authoritarian Regimes', in *Macropolitical Theory*, volume 3 of *Handbook of Political Science* (Reading, MA., Addison-Wesley, 1975), pp. 317–18.

14 Franz Neumann, *Behemoth: The Structure and Practice of National Socialism* (London, Victor Gollancz, 1942), pp. 128, 130.

15 Cf. Ludovico Garruccio, *Le tre età del fascismo* (Bologna, Il Mulino, 1971).

16 Ibid., p. 56.

17 Renzo de Felice, *Fascism: An Informal Introduction to Its Theory and Practice* (New Brunswick, New Jersey, Transaction Books, 1976), pp. 75–6.

18 A. Gracis, cited in Daniele Marchesini, *La scuola dei gerarchi* (Milan, Feltrinelli, 1976), p. 107.
19 Mosse, *The Nationalization of the Masses*, op. cit., pp. 79–80.

23

Revolutionary charlatanism*

BERNADETTE ARCHER

[In the last issue] I examined whether Hitler or Mussolini actually developed a distinctive brand of Fascist economics in its own right, concluding that Fascism itself was and remains a bastardized form of Capitalism which has frequently hijacked genuine Nationalist sentiment for its own ends. But what of the other organizations in Europe around this period, many of which were considered to be very similar?

Intellectual establishment

During the latter part of the twentieth century, political, social and historical analysts have frequently employed the Fascist epithet in order to describe the nature of those individuals and groups considered to resemble the German and Italian regimes. Indeed, many politically motivated individuals in the intellectual Establishment have used this sweeping term to conveniently disregard the philosophical trappings of Nationalism elsewhere. The fact that the objectives of an organization happen to accord with the aspirations of Fascism on one or two ideological points, does not make it Fascist *per se*. Despite portraying themselves as opponents of Fascism, Right-wing conservatives have often been known to steal Nationalistic imagery and fool the more radical elements within a nation subject to political instability.

Characteristics

In this chapter, I intend to examine three expressions of European Nationalism: the Spanish Falange, the Belgian Rexists and the Romanian Iron Guard. I have chosen to reject the various other examples across Europe, simply because the aforementioned groups reflect the different approaches

* Reprinted in full from Bernadette Archer, 'Were "Fascisms" outside Germany and Italy Anything More than Imitators?', *The Crusader*, 6 (1996), pp. 20–3.

to liberal-democracy during the time when Fascism was rather fasionable in Italy and Germany. Furthermore, each group will be studied in accordance with what I consider to be five fundamental characteristics of Fascism: strong leadership, anti-Liberalism, imperialism, anti-Marxism and a maintenance (or tolerance) of Capitalism. In addition, it is worth noting how such groups viewed their German and Italian counterparts. However, before going any further, here is a brief sypnosis of how each organization arose in the first place.

Romanticism

The Spanish Falange was formed in Madrid on 29 October 1933, although the organization and its charismatic leader, José Antonio Primo de Rivera [1903–36], did not become a force to be reckoned with until it had merged with the J.O.N.S. (National-Syndicalist Councils of Action) on 13 February 1934. José Antonio's father had led the military dictatorship which ruled Spain from 1923 to 1930 and, despite his many faults, the General's loyal and devoted son expressed a bitter contempt towards those he felt to have let his father down: namely the aristocracy and the property-owning classes. In the early days of the Falange, José Antonio won the support of many Right-wing conservative elements, although his poetic romanticism also inspired many students to join his political crusade. Like so many other Nationalistic entities, the Falange was a reaction towards what it perceived to be weak government; in this case, the moderate conservatives which had triumphed at the 1933 elections.

Tense

But whilst Spain has always had a tense political atmosphere, in Belgium people seemed less prone to Nationalism. According to Eugen Weber, Belgium was 'a country whose problems were in no way dramatic and whose people, solid and often stolid, inclined neither to excesses nor to histrionics'.[1] Indeed, in the 1930s Belgium had merely been torn between two distinct forms of popular expression. On the one hand, Flemish activists were campaigning vigorously to preserve their own independence from the French-speaking Walloons, and on the other, reactionaries and imperialists were perpetuating the rule of the privileged aristocracy. In the wake of this sterility came Rex, a Movement which had its roots in the Association of Belgian Youth (A.C.J.B). Its founder. Léon Degrelle [1906–94], began his political adventure by contributing to Léon Daudet's *Action Française* newspaper, before emerging as the leader of the Rexist Movement in 1935.

Conspiracy

Elsewhere, Corneliu Codreanu's Iron Guard was established after many people became alarmed at the disproportionate number of Jews in positions of power and influence. Indeed, many of them saw the need for an alternative to the twin evils of Capitalism and Marxism: materialist philosophies controlled by a Judaeo-Masonic conspiracy. Codreanu [1899–1938] had formed his group after a split with the more conservative League of Christian National Defence in 1927. The Iron Guard, also known as the Legion of St Michael Archangel, became a bastion of spiritual warriors, their ranks an antithesis to the decadence of Romanian Liberalism. But how do these three manifestations of Nationalism compare with the fundamental traits of Fascism?

Strong leadership

Strong leadership is certainly one of the main characteristics of Fascism, and the Falange undoubtedly embraced such a concept. But whilst more orthodox Fascism is dependent upon a form of uncompromising dictatorship, José Antonio believed that the 'leader should obey the public; he should serve it, which is a different thing'.[2] On the other hand, he was of the opinion that leadership should be administered in the interests of the people 'even though the people itself be unaware what good is'.[3] Elsewhere. José Antonio noted that German totalitarianism was peculiar to the German people, and that for Spain, a different form of leadership was required; one which, in accordance with the Spanish tradition of confederations, blocks and alliances, would allow a leader to emerge from 'the union of several dwarfs'.[4] In Belgium, leadership was essential to the whole Rexist philosophy. According to George L. Mosse, 'The language and style of Rex was Degrelle. This was its most Fascistic characteristic.'[5] But Degrelle was careful to point out that 'The Leader, in Rex, is the one who sees in the nation, at all levels, not slaves or robots, but collaborators in a common task.'[6] In Romania, Codreanu believed that strong leadership must be founded upon personal morality. In truth, whilst Codreanu was undoubtedly its leader, the Iron Guard was far more decentralized than its Spanish or Belgian counterparts and encouraged initiative from below, rather than authority from above. In fact the Iron Guard was based upon the concept of the Nest, a series of highly disciplined and locally organized branches. In his *Nest Leader's Manual* Codreanu clearly states that a 'Leader must be wise; he must consider carefully before taking a decision so that it may be the right one. He must decide quickly and carry out the decison.'[7] In addition, unlike the blind obedience shown to the Führer and the Duce, he was of the opinion that such a role was there to be earned and that, despite his authority, the Nest Leader 'must be benign and care for the men under his command'[8]. He must also be good-humoured 'in the eyes of his subordinates; not bitter; gloomy; nervy.'[9] Codreanu also believed that leadership should not entitle an individual to any specific privileges, and that a such a figure 'must put himself in the hardest place. A Legionary must not push to fill the best seat at the table or the softest bed to sleep in.'[10]

Anti-liberalism

Our second characteristic, anti-Liberalism, was present in all three examples. José Antonio described Liberalism as 'the mockery of the unfortunate'[11], believing that 'Under the Liberal system the cruel irony could be seen of men and women working themselves to skeletons, twelve hours a day, for a miserable wage, and yet being assured by the law that they were "free" men and women.'[12] In Belgium, Degrelle's right-hand man, Jean Denis, proposed that

> The concept of the individual which forms the erroneous philosophical foundation of the present regime, and which was born of the catastrophic ideologies of the 17th and 18th centuries, must be replaced by the concept of the human being, which corresponds exactly to the reality of man – a social being endowed with a fundamental dignity, which society can help develop, and with which it has no right to interfere.[13]

Meanwhile, Codreanu opposed Liberalism due to the fact that it did not accord with his Christianity and came into conflict with Objective Truth and the Natural Law. In other words, Codreanu rejected the majoritarianism of liberal-democracy because in his view a State 'can not be based only on theoretical conceptions of constitutional law'.[14] But there is no doubt that the Falange, Rex and the Iron Guard each relied upon paramilitary, or extra-parliamentary activity which greatly distinguished them from their liberal-democratic adversaries. By openly rejecting Liberalism, Nationalists were advocating not only the destruction of the existing system from within, but the creation of a viable alternative from without.

Imperialism

Turning now to imperialism, the Falange was not particularly concerned with the extension of Spanish power abroad, at least not in a physical sense. In terms of setting an example to others, however, José Antonio did intend 'to bring it about that the head of the world shall once again be our

Spain'.[15] But depending upon how one views imperialism within Spain itself, the Falange may be considered imperialist in the sense that it opposed an independent Catalonian nation. Catalonian separatism, however, at least during the early 1930s, was also rejected due to the fact that many of its adherents were Moscow-backed Communists. But the seemingly unbridgable gulf between imperialism and parochialism has always presented something of a dilemma for some Nationalists, and for Degrelle it was no different. In the war he raised a battalion of SS volunteers and joined Hitler's forces on the Eastern Front, but as Weber rightly points out, 'though he may have been a "European", Degrelle remained a Belgian Nationalist'.[16] Codreanu, on the other hand, was certainly not an imperialist. Romania had only won its independence from the Ottoman Empire in 1879, and Codreanu himself had fought for his country against the encroaching imperialism of Austria-Hungary in 1916. In terms of propaganda, the Iron Guard only ever referred to the need for a rebirth within the confines of its own borders. This may have been due to the fact that, by emerging victorious from the First World War, Romania had been one of the few nations to have retained her territorial independence. In terms of ethnicity, however, Eastern Europe has always been a hotbed of racial conflict due to its highly potent and proximate concentration of Latinos, Germans, Magyars, Slavs, Jews (Khazars) and Gipsies.

Anti-marxism

But one important factor shared by all three groups, was their fierce opposition to Marxism. José Antonio described Communism as 'an appalling negation of man: this is indeed the absorption of man into a vast amorphous mass, in which all individuality is lost and the corporeal vesture of each individual soul is weakened and dissolved.'[17] But the Falange was still perceived by many to be a Socialist organization, although the Movement was wrongly accused of 'Bolshevism' by its conservative enemies on the Right. The implications of such a smear have an important parallel in that, elsewhere, German Hitlerites attacked the likes of Gregor and Otto Strasser for taking a rather similar stance. By leaving for the Eastern Front, Léon Degrelle obviously intended to engage *his* Communist enemies head on, but even before Rex had encouraged its supporters to join Hitler's SS, the Movement was inevitably perceived as anti-Marxist due to its adherence to Catholicism. But the Rexists were also keen to stress that

> We are not the sort to exploit the funk of frightened bourgeoisie by telling them that Communism and revolution are one and the same. We are those who, having nothing to lose and everything to win, have

decided to replace the decaying liberal regime with a new regime and to create a world in which man can truly live.[18]

So Rexist oppositon to Communism 'was based on the belief that Marxism was a left-over of decaying liberalism'.[19] Codreanu, of course, battled against Romania's Communists during his time as a university student, and even before he had anticipated the formation of the Iron Guard, had little hesitation in climbing to the top of the Nicolina Railway Works in 1920, and hoisting aloft the Romanian tricolour in defiance of the '5,000 armed Communists'[20] gathered below. As far as the Iron Guard was concerned, the realization of a Marxist system would not in any way have liberated the ordinary Romanian worker from the clutches of Capitalism:

> 'If these had been victorious, would we have had at least a Romania led by a Romanian workers' regime? Would the Romanian workers have become masters of the country? No! The next day we would have become the slaves of the dirtiest tyranny: the Talmudic, Jewish tyranny.'[21]

Marxism was also greatly feared due to the fact that, as far as Romanians were concerned, Russia was itself an unpredictable and intimidating entity which, potentially at least, could have launched an attack upon its smaller neighbour at any time.

Capitalism

Fascists in Germany and Italy were renowned for their tolerance of Capitalism, with Mussolini and Hitler being financed both overtly and covertly by wealthy bankers and industrialists. In Spain, however, the Falange was rather different from other Right-wing organizations in that it refused to form an alliance with General Franco and his rich conservative sympathisers. Indeed, José Antonio described capital as 'an economic instrument which must serve the entire economy, and hence may not be an instrument for the advantage and privilege of the few who have had the good luck to get in first'.[22] If set in a rather more conspiratorial context, despite the fact that such an act was carried out at the behest of the ruling Marxist regime. José Antonio's anti-Capitalist attitude may have had a great deal to do with his eventual murder in the Alicante Prison immediately prior to the outbreak of the Spanish Civil War in 1936. Indeed, what better way for Franco to fuse together his Falangist and Carlist (Monarchist) opponents and unite the remaning patriotic elements beneath one banner? In fact the Spanish leader remained opposed to the forces of conservatism right up until his execution, declaring, that

Our triumph will not be that of a reactionary group, nor will it mean the people's loss of any advantage. On the contrary: our work will be a national work, which will be capable of raising the people's standard of living – truly appalling in some regions – and of making them share the pride of a great destiny recovered.[23]

Here lies the very crux which separates genuine Nationalism from conservative imposture. Rexists meanwhile opposed Capitalism just as strongly as they opposed Marxism and, according to George L. Mosse,

Degrelle exploited a mounting distaste for both State Socialism and super-Capitalism, arguing that the lesser bourgeoisie was being sacrificed to the whims and wishes of Capital and Labour: large-scale industrial plant owners and large financier-speculator groups, in collusion with liberal and Marxist politicians, had become the power elite.[24]

But, more importantly, Rexists sought to replace the prevailing atmosphere of selfishness and individualism with something involving the whole nation, believing that

In a century where people only live for themselves, hundreds, thousands of men must no longer live for themselves but for a collective ideal, and be prepared in advance, to endure for its sake every sacrifice, every humiliation, every heroic act.[25]

In Romania, the Iron Guard represented the very antithesis of the existing Capitalist System, with its whole ideology espousing the virtues of self-sacrifice, trust and humility. As far as Codreanu was concerned, 'we were striking a blow at a mentality which placed the golden calf in the centre and as the main purpose in life'.[26] Furthermore,

Through our daring gesture we turned our backs on a mentality that dominated everything. We killed in ourselves a world in order to raise another, high as the sky. The absolute rule of matter was overthrown so it could be replaced by the rule of the spirit, or moral values.[27]

Fascism

To sum up, in order to establish whether or not these three organizations actually *were* imitations of German and Italian Fascism, it is necessary to examine how each group viewed the whole concept of Fascism itself. In 1933, Jose Antonio is said to have embarked upon his political voyage after becoming 'profoundly impressed'[28] by Mussolini. He even wrote an article for a prospective periodical known as *El Fascio*, although it never appeared. In addition, he announced that 'If there is anything which deserves to be called a State of Workers, it is the Fascist State'.[29] However, by 1934 it had become clear that 'No true Spaniard will knowingly follow a foreign model'[30] and when he was asked to attend an international Fascist Congress at Montreux, José Antonio announced that 'the truly national character of the movement he leads is inconsistent with even the semblance of international governance'.[31] He added that the Falange was not a Fascist Movement, declaring that 'It has certain coincidences with Fascism in essential points which are of universal validity: but it is daily acquiring a clearer outline of its own'.[32] Indeed, acording to Hugh Thomas, after visiting Germany in the Spring of 1934 José Antonio 'returned to Spain depressed by the Nazis'.[33] And whilst the Falange was originally inspired by Italian Fascism, he soon became 'almost as ill-impressed by Mussolini'[34] and developed a distinct form of Nationalism in its own right. From that moment on, the Falange leader 'had no other meetings with foreign Fascist groups, and made a conscious effort in succeeding months to distinguish his movement from Fascism'.[35] In Belgium, however, the exact opposite happened and Degrelle's Catholic heritage became gradually incorporated within Hitler's vision of a Germanic Empire. Whilst Degrelle was prepared to trade his Belgian Nationalism for an active role in the Nazi crusade against Bolshevism, he also admired the political aspects of Fascism. Indeed, according to Roger Griffin, 'After the Nazi invasion of Belgium in May 1940. Degrelle threw his efforts into transforming Rex into an openly pro-Nazi party'.[36] But whilst José Antonio had rejected Fascism, and Degrelle had come to embrace it, Codreanu was never part of the Fascist tradition in Europe. The Iron Guard certainly shared many of its ideas with Hitler and Mussolini, but it was essentially a product of an age in which the full effects of Liberalism were beginning to be rejected throughout the Continent as a whole. Although Codreanu sent Hitler his personal greetings on 12 March 1938,[37] he had developed his brand of National Christian Socialism as early as 1919.[38] In fact Condreanu's emphasis upon the supremacy of spirit over matter clearly distinguished the Legionaries of the Iron Guard from their Fascist contemporaries. According to C. Papanace,

> By way of a metaphor, let us say that Fascism will assail the branches of the tree of evil that must be cut down, National-Socialism the trunk, Legionarism the very root feeding the evil, by depriving them of the source of nourishment.[39]

It is also worth noting that when the legitimate Legionary Government was toppled in 1941 by the incoming military dictatorship of General Antonescu, the *coup d'état* was directly backed by the Hitler regime.[40] According to F. L. Carsten, 'Hitler was preoccupied with his plans of domination and conquest in Eastern Europe and for this reason needed an orderly regime in Romania capable of aiding him'.[41] The Iron Guard's vision of an independent Romanian nation obviously did not accord with the concept of a European Fascist Empire.

Reactionary charlatans

On a final note, the Falange, Rex and the Iron Guard were all different in their attitudes to the liberal-democratic sterility which had plunged Europe into chaos in the wake of the First World War. But whilst Degrelle sacrificed his own originality in order to imitate Adolf Hitler, José Antonio soon realized that he did not wish to be connected with a foreign phenomenon and rejected Benito Mussolini almost as quickly as he had adopted him. On the other hand, Codreanu was able to rely upon his own characteristic resourcefulness in order to address a series of very similar problems. It is, then, perhaps significant that the Iron Guard was 'the only "fascist" movement outside Germany and Italy to come to power without foreign aid'.[42] Given the mysterious forces behind the funding of the Hitlerian and Mussolinian regimes, it seems hardly surprising that Codreanu and his followers were dealt with in such a repressive manner. *Capitalism, it seems, will only tolerate Nationalism if it is used to clothe the reactionary charlatans of Fascism.*

Notes

1 Eugen Weber, *Varieties of Fascism* (Princeton, Von Nostrand Co., 1964), p. 122.
2 José Antonio Primo de Rivera, *The Spanish Contribution to Contemporary Political Thought* (Madrid, Ediciones Almena, 1947), p. 92.
3 Ibid., p. 93.
4 Ibid., p. 149.
5 George L. Mosse, *International Fascism* (London, Sage Publications, 1979), p. 309.
6 Eugen Weber, op. cit., p. 181.
7 Corneliu Codreanu, *Legion: The Nest Leader's Manual* (London, The Rising Press, 1984), p. 41.
8 Ibid.
9 Ibid.
10 Ibid.
11 José Antonio Primo de Rivera, op. cit., p. 99.
12 Ibid.
13 Eugen Weber, op. cit., p. 179.
14 Corneliu Codreanu, op. cit., p. 62.
15 José Antonio Primo de Rivera, op. cit., p. 270.
16 Eugen Weber, op. cit., p. 129.
17 José Antonio Primo de Rivera, op. cit., p. 136.
18 Eugen Weber, op. cit., p. 125.
19 *Ibid.*

20 Corneliu Codreanu, *For My Legionaries* (Reedy West Virginia, Liberty Bell Publications, 1990), p. 13.
21 Ibid., p. 9.
22 José Antonio Primo de Rivera, op. cit., p. 112.
23 Ibid., p. 275.
24 George L. Mosse, op. cit., p. 298.
25 Léon Degrelle, *Révolution des âmes* (Paris, Editions de la France, 1938), p. 162.
26 Corneliu Codreanu, *For My Legionaries*, op. cit., p. 214.
27 Ibid., pp. 213–14.
28 José Antonio Primo de Rivera, op. cit., p. 19.
29 Ibid., p. 151.
30 Ibid., p. 19.
31 Ibid., p. 150.
32 Ibid.
33 Hugh Thomas, *The Spanish Civil War* (Harmondsworth, Pelican, 1974), p. 101.
34 Ibid.
35 Ibid.
36 Roger Griffin, *Fascism* (Oxford, Oxford University Press, 1995), p. 204.
37 Corneliu Codreanu, *Circulars and Manifestoes* (Madrid, Editorial 'Libertatea', 1987), p. 229.
38 Corneliu Codreanu, *For My Legionaries*, op. cit., pp. 329–30.
39 Corneliu Codreanu, *Legion: The Nest Leader's Manual*, op. cit., p. 7.
40 Eugen Weber, op. cit., p. 105.
41 F. L. Carsten, *The Rise of Fascism*, (Methuen, 1970), p. 192.
42 George L. Mosse, op. cit, p. 319.

THE REBIRTH OF FASCISM?

Presentation

If fascist prophecies that liberal humanist civilization was giving way to a global era of the authoritarian state seemed horrifically close to coming true by the summer of 1941, the military defeat of the Axis Powers four years later at the cost of millions of lives relegated palingenetic myths of reborn organic nations back to the realm of utopian fantasy once more. Instead the drama of the future seemed to be playing itself out in a struggle to the death between the 'Free World' and state communism, that is until the disintegration of the Soviet Union in the late 1980s created the mood of triumphalism in capitalist democracies in which American president George Bush could talk confidently of a New World Order. It was in this peculiar climate that a highly schematic academic article declaring the imminent victory of liberalism over all rival ideologies and signalling 'the end of history' could make its author world-famous.[1] The common-sense perception after 1945 has thus been that fascism was buried in the rubble of Berlin.

For a long time Western academia (though not its Marxist enclaves) generally shared this perception, and it is significant that for several decades histories of fascism focused exclusively on its inter-war (and usually its European) manifestations, leaving it to political scientists to write the occasional article on specific post-war phenomena. Yet, while the objective conditions for fascism seizing power in Europe may have been destroyed once and for all in 1945, as an ideology and movement it has survived, proliferating organizations, producing vast numbers of publications, and adapting its revolutionary vision both crudely and subtly to a rapidly changing world. By the mid-1980s a meticulous stocktaking of the world's radical right[2] revealed thousands of its groupings still dedicated to overthrowing the 'system' both locally and internationally so as to found a new order. No matter how numerically small in membership and acutely marginalized in terms of main-stream politics, many of them were still important sources of racial tension and violence at a local level, and the larger ones could make major contributions to contaminating the climate of liberal tolerance nationally. Their continued presence and distribution in the 1980s also showed that a habitat for the incubation of the fascist mindset, far from being eradicated, now existed in every capitalist democracy. Indeed, in a handful of countries, notably France, Italy, Austria, and Belgium (and before long in Russia), radical right electoral parties had established themselves, representing sizeable constituencies of public opinion. Nevertheless, fascist studies were still habitually treated as a specialism whose time had passed, and academics trying to make original contributions to them could easily find themselves on the defensive about why they bothered.

In the early 1990s the situation changed rapidly. A succession of high-profile events occurred which cumulatively pointed to an international resurgence of fascism: the flare-up of neo-Nazi violence in the new Germany, the growing strength of the Front National in France, the electoral success of Zhirinovsky in the Russian parliamentary elections of December 1993, the inclusion in

Berlusconi's government coalition in March 1994 of the Alleanza Nazionale, direct heir of the neo-Fascist Movimento Sociale Italiano, the Oklahoma Bombing in April 1995 partially inspired by the paranoid fantasies of *The Turner Diaries* written by the American neo-Nazi William Pearce. Newspaper editorials drew the obvious conclusions. Fascism was back in business. Fascism was threatening the fabric of liberal democracy. Or was it? As the reader now realizes only too well, in fascist studies no simple questions have simple answers. Whenever the issue is raised of the threat posed by fascism to democracy, and how best to combat it, the diagnosis and prognosis will vary enormously according to the premises adopted concerning the nature of fascism. The concluding section thus presents two Readings which highlight how far from resolution the conundrum of fascism still is over fifty years after Hitler's death. They also highlight the gulf between the academic urge to understand it and an activist concern to 'do something about it'.

For Marxists the stubborn persistence of fascism holds few surprises. After all, if fascism is the product of capitalism in crisis, and indeed reveals the latent capacity of capitalism to transform itself into a repressive system whenever it is under attack, then, like a seed in the desert, it is ready at any time to burst into life whenever conditions are right. As for combating fascism, this cannot be entrusted to the liberal forces of law and order, since it is an intrinsic part of 'their' system. Thus it must be fought by mobilizing the forces of the left and taking to the streets whenever fascist activity threatens the lives of ordinary people. As is only to be expected, tracts on the fascist menace designed to rouse supporters into taking action will be written with an immediacy unadulterated by niceties of hair-splitting definitions and footnotes. Meanwhile in the 'liberal camp' of academics we can expect experts to agonize over which ideal type to use and the problems of applying models based on inter-war fascism to the post-war period. Fascism is thus transformed from being an enemy which is easy to recognize and arouses distinct gut feelings into a topic so complex and debatable that any activistic impulses are likely to drain away in a welter of Byzantine analysis. This difference is illustrated by the two Readings which follow.

The first extract (Reading 24) is taken from a pamphlet published by Britain's Socialist Workers Party in 1992, soon after neo-Nazi outrages in Germany and the growing strength of Le Pen's Front National in France had put fascism firmly back on the agenda of current affairs. It is an analysis of contemporary fascism directed, not at academics dispassionately studying the subject, but at the activists of the SWP-dominated Anti Nazi League which is resolutely committed to stopping fascism by playing it at its own game (the ANL's twin tactics are publicity campaigns and anti-fascist rallies). The linguistic register is thus deliberately unscholarly and propagandistic, with no publishing details given for quotes, and a highly florid, journalistic style.

Nevertheless, the fundamental approach to the question 'what is fascism?' posed in the first section of the pamphlet is unmistakably informed by Marxist premises about the nature of fascism, and more particularly by the Trotskyism on which the SWP is based (see Reading 5). This explains the readiness with which it equates any form of fascism with its most radical manifestation, Nazism. In the case of John Tyndall, the leader of the British National Party alluded to in the third paragraph, this assumption is not without foundation, since the ideas expressed in his most important ideological testament, *The Eleventh Hour: A Call to British Rebirth*, can be shown to be little more than an Anglicized variant of neo-Nazism.[3] The Front National, however, has never been a Nazi party, and even fails the test of palingenetic ultra-nationalism by advocating that the values and advantages of French liberal democracy be upheld exclusively 'for the French' in a spirit reminiscent of the apartheid system of 'white' South Africa. Thus to link Le Pen directly with the Holocaust and with the prospect of a new one, is, from the point of view of the new consensus, a highly misleading, not to say wild, allegation.

In fact, the theory of fascism which underlies the analysis is questionable from any 'liberal' standpoint. Its author, Chris Bambery, cites Trotsky to support the idea that fascism 'is thrown up and carried forward by the failings of capitalism'. He goes on to argue that fascism is the product of social crisis, a point which all experts would agree, though most would have problems with the assertion that what lets fascism in is the despair of 'the bosses' who use fascism to 'terrorise a weakened or divided working class'. It is to be noted that Bambery at least concedes that fascism itself is not identical with capitalism, and that it has its own ideology. However, no glimpse is offered into what constitutes this ideology, though the phrase 'ideologically crazed thugs' either implies that some of its followers become fanatically committed to realizing their ideals at any cost (which is certainly a defensible assertion), or that it is an essentially pathological phenomenon (which is a highly dubious one). What he is primarily concerned to stress is that reactionary forces let fascism in, whether it was the industrialists of Weimar Germany or the Catholic Church of Spain (note the typically Marxist assumption that Franco's regime was fascist: for the new consensus only the Falangist element within Franquism was actually fascist, whatever its opponents believed or Hitler and Mussolini hoped).

The next passage attributes the main cause for the rise of fascism in the 1920s to fears of Bolshevik revolution in the aftermath of the Russian Revolution and the First World War. This made the Establishment (presumably Europe-wide) throw its lot in with fascists to protect its vested interests. The context for Nazism's seizure of power, however, was a second wave of middle-class panic triggered by the Wall Street Crash. Bambery suggests that the middle classes, finding themselves squeezed between 'the bosses' and the proletariat, might actually have sided with the workers had they shown 'the possibility of building something different altogether'. But the reformist Social Democrats failed to deliver effective government, while Communists had become Stalinists – by implication only Trotskyites could offer the genuine socialist alternative of 'building something different altogether'. In this situation Nazism exploited the crisis by playing on national grievances and whipping up anti-Semitism to recruit the despairing bourgeoisie. At this point the analysis becomes confused: it is implied that Mussolini's Fascism filled the political vacuum of the early 1930s, although he came to power in 1922, and scape-goated Jews as an explanation of the crisis, despite the fact that anti-Semitism was not adopted as government policy in Italy till 1938.

Another area of potential confusion for the reader concerns who provided the social basis for Nazism, the petty bourgeoisie or big business. Having earlier claimed that fascism was sponsored by the 'bosses', it is suddenly treated as rallying the mass support of the petty bourgeoisie whose interests we have just been told conflicted with those of the bosses. The paradox is then traced to Trotsky's own interpretation: fascism gains power though the petty bourgeoisie, but once in power serves the interests of big business. Bambery goes on to explain that, in order to smash the working class, fascism needs another constituency of support: the street power provided by a paramilitary instrument of terror (the allusion is presumably to the Fascist *squadristi* and the Nazi SA). The section ends with a number of inferences for the present struggle against fascism, which by now has become completely identified with Nazism: (a) a fascist take-over has horrific consequences for the majority of the population; (b) as a force based on terror 'Nazis' cannot be defeated through debate, and in fact free speech must be denied them: instead they must be confronted on the streets; (c) a United Front of street activists must be formed with as wide a membership as possible. For this to happen it is important not to appease conservatives and liberal businessmen by being excessively moderate since when it comes to the crunch they will support Nazism rather than socialism. It is also necessary to be prepared to form an alliance with reformist socialists: implicit here is memory of the fact that the failure of the German Communists and Social Democrats to unite against Nazism in the 1930s helped secure Hitler's victory (though it was far from being the only factor).

A later section of the pamphlet deals with 'the rebirth of European fascism'. It opens with an account of the emergence of Le Pen's 'Nazi' Front National from a position of total marginalization in 1981 to become a major force in French political and social life. Bambery links the rise to the deteriorating conditions of the French economy, the failure of Mitterrand to deliver genuine socialism, the espousal of racism by all the mainstream parties including the Communists, and the reluctance of the liberal and socialist anti-fascist movements to adopt the tactics of the British Anti-Nazi League by openly denouncing Le Pen's Nazism or confronting NF marches in the streets.

Turning to Germany, he admits that the closest equivalent to the FN, the Republicans, are a minute force, yet suggests that the economic crisis caused by unification, the racism of centre parties, and the lack of an effective (revolutionary socialist) alternative to the present system could create conditions for a significant rise in its fortunes. He points to the arson attacks on asylum seekers and 'foreigners' by skinhead Nazis as a sign of the times, and while conceding that there is a powerful anti-fascist movement in the new Germany, calls for the battle to be taken to the streets of former East Germany where racist violence is concentrated. He ends the section with a reiteration of the verdict pronounced earlier that the rise of fascism can be checked only as long as the anti-fascists are prepared to mobilize to stop it, that is, form a United Front under revolutionary socialist (i.e.

SWP) leadership prepared to fight Nazis in the streets where necessary. They would then be applying the lessons of the 1930s when the failure to adopt this strategy let in Hitler, and the 1970s, when, so the SWP claim, the readiness to adopt it enabled anti-fascists to stop the British National Front in its tracks.

Clearly Bambery assumes that Europe in the early 1990s shows marked parallels to Germany in the early 1930s. The subtext of his argument is surely an exhortation to the SWP to take advantage of the unique opportunity which the flare up of fascist activity offers to gain hegemony over a wide constituency of the anti-fascist left, and thereby give it a role in the political life of the nation denied it hitherto (one which might possibly even form the core of the revolutionary transformation of Britain itself). What it fails to offer the non-Marxist is convincing evidence of a general 'rebirth of European fascism', or a realistic assessment of the threat it poses to society as a whole.

Diethelm Prowe's article (Reading 25) exudes the atmosphere, not of the revolutionary council, but of the study. It has been deliberately chosen as the last text in this Reader because the dense texture of scholarly analysis and references which it weaves and the complexity of the approach to several issues raised by the subject of post-war fascism which it offers are challenging even to those versed in the subject, let alone to those still tentatively feeling their way around it. While it could never inspire activists to take to the streets, it certainly might help a student or researcher who was able to engage with it properly to write a nuanced, subtly argued essay on a number of topics relating to neo-fascism: for example, how fascism might be defined to make a case for the use of the term neo-fascism, the difference between inter-war fascism and the post-war radical right (increasingly called the 'extreme right' in academic parlance), and the problems involved in generalizing about an alleged revival of fascism in the 1990s or evaluating its prospects of breaking through once again as a mass movement.

Prowe's starting point is the general perception in the media of the early 1990s (shared by Chris Bambery) that the rise to prominence of radical right movements and parties is to be seen as a rerun of the 1930s, and the assumption that their precise relation to inter-war fascism is worth careful assessment. He briefly reviews the early phase in the evolution of the debate over fascism in terms which should now be familiar, from the dominance of the totalitarian theory, to the breakthrough in the mid-1960s when non-Marxists such as Nolte sought to define fascism as a discrete phenomenon. He shows sympathy for the intuition that fascism has validity as a generic term despite the arch scepticism expressed in some quarters, but stresses the extreme difficulty scholars have experienced in identifying the fascist minimum, which he agrees is an exercise to be conceived in Weberian terms as a process of abstracting an 'ideal type' of its characteristics. He singles out the contrasting attempts of Eugen Weber, George Mosse, Ernst Nolte, and myself, and distinguishes between approaches which focus on the fascist world-view, political behaviour and goals, which would allow some basic continuity between the contemporary radical right and inter-war fascism to be identified, and those which concentrate on the historical setting, which would put any such linkage in a different perspective.

Prowe then offers his own 12-point check-list of fascism's intrinsic characteristics. Most of them revolve round characteristics already emphasized by Mosse and Payne, except that the admiration for Nolte he expressed earlier comes through in his inclusion of 'resentment against the spirit of modernity', and his omission of any allusion to the quest for national rebirth in an anti-conservative spirit – despite his earlier comment that I had offered a 'splendidly clear', 'remarkably handy' one-sentence definition of fascism based on the concept palingenetic ultra-nationalism, he obviously remains unconvinced by it. As he himself points out, his own typology locates fascism in the tradition of 'militant conservative thought' rather than in that of revolutionary nationalism, a point confirmed by his misgivings about the emphasis placed by Sternhell and myself on the revolutionary, anti-conservative thrust of fascism. Instead, he insists on its fundamental cultural pessimism and resistance to 'transcendence' in the sense of reaching out to 'the Other'. (I accept his charge that my quite different use of the term 'transcendence' in my own theory invalidates it as an argument against Nolte's thesis, but I find his attempt to refute my emphasis on the 'optimism' of the fascist mindset unconvincing: surely the precondition of *all* revolutionary optimism is pessimism about the status quo?). On the basis of his composite ideal type, Prowe concedes that, 'one might thus be tempted to speak of the present-day radical right movements as "fascist"', a term which in the way he has defined it even extends to Le Pen's Front National, which my ideal type places in another category because it lacks a revolutionary vision of a new order.

At this point he abruptly changes tack, and considers the issue of how far the contemporary radical right should be seen as fascist from the point of view of the historical conditions which gave rise to those inter-war movements generally considered fascist. In the section I have omitted, major contrasts with contemporary movements are thrown into relief. Prowe argues that the conditions of growing economic prosperity and political stability which prevailed after 1945 precluded the type of movement which had originated in the 'broken world' of inter-war society, especially once the international tensions generated by the Cold War abated, and a new generation arose to replace the one whose formative experience had been the era of fascism and the Second World War. As a result the radical right changed in two significant respects: first, movements wooing a mass base started adopting the outward trappings of democracy and allying themselves with elements from the non-fascist radical right; second, a new radical right youth emerged which despaired of the electoral route to power, craved direct action, and adopted the tactics of leftist urban guerillas and nationalist revolutionaries by launching campaigns of Black terror.

The excerpt resumes at the point in Prowe's article where he comes to the nub of his argument: 'the current Western European movements of the radical right are essentially different phenomena' from fascism. He identifies the structural reasons for the difference in six main areas of contrast with the inter-war period:

(a) multi-culturalism and the threat of immigration is the major concern of the radical right, and not class struggle and the threat of Bolshevism which obsessed fascists; (b) the context of fascism was a climate of imperialism whereas that of the radical right is an era of decolonization; (c) the traumatic experience of the First World War which informed the ethos of fascism has been replaced by the extended period of peace in which the radical right operates; (d) the profound socio-economic crises of the inter-war period have given way to political stability and prosperity; (e) the radical right has to contend with a general consensus about the validity of liberal democratic norms and institutions, whereas it was the collapse of this consensus which was crucial to the rise of fascism and its break-through in two nation–states; (f) the electoral base of the radical right is generally urban, whereas fascism thrived against a background of wide-spread anti-urbanism and nostalgia for rural life.

As a result of these major shifts in social, international, economic, political, and cultural climate, the radical right is characterized by three salient traits which set it apart from fascism: first, 'concrete racism' has emerged directed at all those perceived to be ethnically or culturally different: this has replaced fascist anti-communism, which has largely disappeared, and anti-Semitism (which was, in any case, not common to all fascisms); second, there has been a general retreat from aggressive, expansionist imperialism, though the radical right may espouse instead an anti-Brussels Europeanism as the framework for domestic renewal; third, the place taken by an animus against the Enlightenment (the 'revolt against positivism') has given way to Holocaust denial. For Prowe, such differences are sufficiently profound for inter-war fascism and the contemporary radical right to be best seen as two discrete manifestations of a more general category, the 'modern secular (far) right', a distinction which would explain why the radical right has prospered, not where historical fascism had its heyday, but in areas of Western Europe where immigration has provoked the gravest social tensions. Thus, despite surviving pockets of nostalgia for the age of Mussolini, Hitler, and Codreanu, the notion that the 1990s is experiencing a rebirth of fascism is a misconception. We are witnessing the rise of something essentially distinct: the populist radical right. It is manifested in 'new movements' which 'represent a new era and are fighting new and different battles'.

Prowe's analysis is a penetrating and powerful argument for abandoning attempts to trace fascism's uninterrupted evolution into the post-war period. It thus implicitly rejects the interpretation which sees the modern radical right as divided between a genuinely revolutionary 'neo-fascist' and a 'pseudo-liberal' wing lacking a palingenetic dimension, the distinction which underlies my analysis in *The Nature of Fascism*, and *Fascism*. And yet it must be remembered that there are no rights and wrongs when such contrasting models are put forward, no question of definitive vindication or refutation. What is at stake is the relative heuristic value of different ideal types. As a 'methodological pluralist' I would argue that anyone seriously engaged in refining a conceptual framework for investigating the extreme right in post-war Europe should experiment with a number of approaches and taxonomic schemes on offer,[4] including Marxist ones,[5] paying careful attention to how each one suggests a differing causal analysis, set of definitions, and taxonomy (classification). On the basis of such a process he or she can adopt a ready-made model, or even, given time, develop a new one, which is the most appropriate for the precise subject under investigation.

My model, for example, suggests that all the genuinely (if camouflaged) revolutionary forms of what Prowe calls the new, non-fascist radical right can be usefully understood as products of fascism's chameleon-like ability to adapt its palingenetic ultra-nationalism ideologically and tactically to a radically changed historical climate. Prowe initially treats this type of approach sympathetically, but then reveals that he finds it more illuminating to regard what normally passes for 'neo-fascism' as a new genus of extreme right politics, even if, as he himself admits, it is strongly influenced by, and has elements of continuity with, the 'fascist era'. Both of us part company radically with Bambery's Trotskyite conceptual framework, and hence his analysis of the current threat which fascism poses to democracy and the tactics for dealing with it. We both agree that the post-war era is not conducive to the revolutionary right and that as a result it does not pose anything like the danger to democracy that it did between the wars. Indeed, its prospects of seizing power in any European state, however poorly established its democratic institutions, are minimal. Moreover, the SWP's idea of orchestrating street confrontations *en masse* by a broad anti-fascist front is reminiscent of the French military's scheme for the Maginot Line, the vast network of military fortifications which France built after the First World War to defend its Eastern borders. It was conceived to fight an enemy which had changed so radically as to render them useless. What all three of us do have in common is the conviction that violent forms of nationalism, whether we call them fascist, Nazi, or radical right, did not die in 1945, and that the 'New Europe' would be well advised to take active steps to monitor their activities and to combat whatever threat they pose to democracy.

Notes

1 Francis Fukuyama, 'The End of History', *The National Interest*, 16 (1989). The article's thesis was expanded considerably and underwent some modifications in his *The End of History and the Last Man* (London, Hamish Hamilton, 1992).
2 C. Ó Maoláin, *The Radical Right: A World Directory* (London, Longmans, 1987).
3 John Tyndall, *The Eleventh Hour: A Call to British Rebirth* (London, Albion Press, 1988).
4 For example, Paul Hainsworth, 'Introduction. The Cutting Edge: The Extreme Right in Post-war Western Europe and the United States', in Paul Hainsworth (ed.), *The Extreme Right in Europe and the United States* (London, Pinter, 1982); Christopher Husbands, 'The Other Face of 1992: The Extreme-Right Explosion in Western Europe', *Parliamentary Affairs*, 45(3), 1992 pp. 267–84;

Hans-George Betz, *Radical Right-Wing Populism in Western Europe* (London, Macmillan, 1994); Herbert Kitschelt, *The Radical Right in Western Europe* (Michigan, The University of Michigan Press, 1995).

5 For example, Chris Bambery's extended and fully referenced essay 'Euro-Fascism: The Lessons of the Past and Current Tasks', *International Socialism*, 60 (Autumn 1993), pp. 3–75.

24

_The revival of the fascist menace_*

CHRIS BAMBERY

What is fascism?: the ultimate barbarism

The last time fascism took hold of an advanced industrialized state, it led to Hitler's Holocaust.

Six million Jews were slain by the Nazis. Two and a half million Poles were exterminated; 520,000 Gypsies and 473,000 Russian prisoners were murdered; 100,000 'inferior' people were done to death because they were mentally ill or physically disabled; tens of thousands of socialists, communists, gays and other 'unhealthy elements' were killed.

The Nazis started out on the road to this slaughter by talking about repatriating Jews. Today Le Pen and Tyndall aim to set off on the same bloody trail by calling for the expulsion of non-white people from France and Britain. We know the end result from history. The head of Hitler's terror police, the SS, boasted:

> I have emptied the largest Jewish ghettoes in the area [. . .] By the end of the year the Jewish question will have been settled in all the occupied countries. Only a few individual Jews who have managed to slip through the net will be left. Then we shall set about tackling the problem of the non-Jewish partner in mixed marriages and the problem of the half-Jew systematically and sensibly, and we shall find a solution and put it into effect [. . .]
>
> All of us have asked ourselves what about the women and children? I have decided that this too requires a clear answer. I do not consider that I should be justified in getting rid of the men – in having them put to death, in other words – only to allow their children to grow up to avenge themselves on our sons and grandsons.
>
> _We have to make up our minds, hard though it may be, that this race must be wiped off the face of the earth._

Just translate these terrible words to Britain today. It would mean the extermination of all black people, all Jews. It would mean the wiping out of anyone married to a black person or a Jew, anyone who had a

* Extract from _Killing the Nazi Menace_ (London, Socialist Workers Party Pamphlet, 1992), pp. 7–14, 35–41.

relationship with a black person or a Jew and any child which resulted from that.

The whole of society was reduced to the level of the barracks. 'There are no private lives', declared the Nazi in charge of the labour force. 'The peoples', he stated 'and the individual human beings within each people are like children. The politician must supervise everything'. The Nazis decided who could be born or not, who could marry and who could not, who could have children and who could not. Tens of thousands of 'unhealthy' people were sterilized or castrated. The Nazi slogan for women was simple – 'Children, Kitchen, Church'.

Any independent or voluntary organization which did not fit such rigid centralization was outlawed – from the YMCA to the Boy Scouts. Any ideas which were slightly different were suppressed – not just socialist ideas but also those of religious groups or scientists.

But fascism is not just an assault on minorities, it is a wholesale attack on the vast bulk of society – the working class. In Italy, Mussolini's fascists seized power in 1922 to put an end to years of working-class insurgency. In Germany too, fascism's objective was to snuff out working-class resistance.

Within two years of Hitler's victory, wages were slashed by up to 40 per cent. Workers' leaders and officials were arrested, tortured and murdered, their property confiscated.

This is terror on the highest scale. But fascism is more than this, it is distinguished from other forms of dictatorship by its aims and methods.

Fascism can take off when the bosses feel compelled to completely destroy, to atomize, working-class organization. They can't do this by the usual methods of other police states. In Britain, for example, 200,000 soldiers and 120,000 police would not be enough to overcome and disperse every last bit of resistance from 23 million workers. Fascism, therefore, relies on a *mass* movement within society to smash the working class. Such movements, as we shall see, have largely been recruited from the middle class. As the Russian revolutionary Leon Trotsky put it,

> the historic function of fascism is to smash the working class, destroy its organizations, and stifle political liberties when the capitalists find themselves unable to govern and dominate with the help of demo-cratic machinery.

Today the grotesque images of the dead and dying of Auschwitz are etched onto most people's minds. Little wonder, then, that fascism is often seen as a form of madness which sweeps whole nations before it. But it is more than that, it has a perverse logic of its own. It is thrown up and carried forward by the failings of capitalism itself.

A battering ram against the working class

Fascism has never 'crept up' on society. It has only ever been successful by storming in at periods of profound social crisis.

Fascist movements can come to power under two conditions. The first is that the bosses – the owners of large industry, the judges, the army chiefs – are in despair. They are so desperate that they will abandon the relative stability of the normal form of rule to risk throwing in their lot with ideologically crazed thugs. The second condition is that the fascists themselves have already proved capable of being of use to the bosses. For this they need to have welded together an organization with the srength to terrorize a weakened or divided working class.

There's no doubt most bosses will make such a choice, if necessary. After all, that is precisely what happened in the 1930s. Hitler took power after the major industrialists and bankers cynically decided to throw their weight behind him. In Spain, when Franco rose against a democratically elected government, the Catholic Church pronounced his cause a crusade.

The Establishment chose fascism because capitalism had staggered out of the First World War to find itself besieged by revolution and recession. Three empires were torn up. In Russia the workers took power. In Germany they nearly followed in 1919 and 1923. In Hungary a workers' republic had to be overthrown by French arms. In Italy the factories were occupied by armed workers. The world returned to deep crisis in the early 1930s. Once more, the spectre of revolution haunted industrialists and bankers. They knew they could not rely on their armies. Even if they were immune to the class conflict around them, there just weren't enough soldiers to suppress every factory and street.

Hitler's thugs, however, had amassed enough strength by 1933 to claim to be up to the job of wiping out the threat of the working class. He could boast 400,000 Storm Troopers, ready to move against any opposition. How had he done it?

The 1929 Wall Street Crash heralded the deepest slump in history. Europe's middle classes suddenly found their world collapsing around them.

They were not the only ones to suffer. The working class too was hammered by the depression. But workers had trade unions, and a tradition of battling against their bosses. They were hit by depression, but they had at least the possibility of an answer to it in the form of collective struggle and organization.

The middle classes were in a different position. They had no tradition of collective solidarity. They didn't have the possibility of waging any real fight against the big bosses. If the working class was on the offensive, and showing the possibility of building something different altogether, then the bulk of the middle class might have fallen in behind them. This was not the situation in Germany, however. The working class was fighting defensively. Its parties failed to inspire: the social Democrats were exposed in government; the Communists held up Stalin's Russia as a model.

There was a vacuum in such a desperate *milieu*. Demagogues like Hitler and Mussolini moved to fill it and gather round large numbers of despairing middle-class people. They could offer simple answers in a world gone crazy. Jewish international financiers and Jewish Communists, they said, were conspiring to destroy society; workers were greedy; trade unions were led by 'Marxists'. The fascist leaders latched on to national grievances in order to give their followers a sense of purpose.

The fascist leaders claimed to champion 'the little man' – the small businessman, the doctor, the lawyer, the soldier fallen on hard times, 'decent people' sucked into the mire. From the depths of despair they seemed to lift the middle class – the petty bourgeoisie – to its feet, to give it a banner around which to rally.

As the Nazis formed their combat groups from such 'human dust' – to use the term employed by Trotsky – the capitalist class began to see the new, mass fascist movements as their saviour. They could deploy this new force to destroy working-class organization and restore their profits.

As Trotsky described it, the fascists',

> political art consisted in fusing the petty bourgeoisie into oneness through its solid hostility to the proletariat. What must be done in order to improve things? First of all, throttle those who are underneath. Impotent before large capital, the petty bourgeoisie hopes in the future to regain its social dignity by overwhelming the workers.

But once in power, fascism serves only the interests of big business:

> German fascism, like the Italian, raised itself to power on the backs of the petty bourgeoisie, which it turned into a battering ram against the working class and the institutions of democracy. But fascism in power is least of all the rule of the petty bourgeoisie. On the contrary, it is the most ruthless dictatorship of monopolist capital. Mussolini is right: the intermediate classes are incapable of independent policies. During periods of great crisis they are called upon to reduce to absurdity the policies of one of the two basic classes. Fascism succeeded in placing them at the service of capital.

But to get to this position, where a fascist movement is of use to the bosses, it must have already proved itself as a terror organization. This is why the street and street power is crucial for the fascists. They can't call on the sort of collective power workers have within the factory. The strike is absent from their armory. Rather, they must create a seemingly invincible army of terror to control whole areas of cities.

Hitler grasped this from the start. 'Mass demonstrations', he wrote, 'must burn into the little man's soul the conviction that though a little worm he is part of a great dragon.' The Nazi propaganda chief Goebbels said: 'Whoever controls the streets also conquers the masses, and whoever conquers the masses thereby conquers the state.'

Big business did not like placing its fortunes with a former house painter like Hitler, but he promised to destroy the Communists, the trade unions and the Social Democratic Party (Germany's Labour Party). Big business was driven towards this solution by the depth of its despair.

Therefore, fascism is a mass movement, based primarily around the middle class, which seeks to smash all forms of opposition, and works ultimately in the interests of big business. It is a cancer which weakens and demoralizes the working class as it grows, proving fatal in the final instance.

A number of points follow. The first is that, if successful, fascism represents an unsurpassed disaster for the vast majority of the population. Even under Tory rule, indeed under much more dictatorial regimes than we have known in modern Britain, people can still fight, they can still organize at least the barest forms of defence. Under fascism, all organization, all resistance, is wiped out for years if not decades.

Second, free speech, and other aspects of democracy which we have been able to win, cannot possibly be defended by allowing Nazis the right to free speech. The charge that is often thrown at those who seek effectively to oppose the Nazis – that it would be better to defeat them through reasonable debate – is completely wrong. For a start, Nazis gain power through *terror*, not through force of argument. And, if they do gain power, then *all* free speech, *all* forms of democracy will be at an end. That is why socialists, who are whole-heartedly for free speech and open debate, say Nazis must be silenced to safeguard it.

The third crucial thing that flows from the nature of fascist movements is that direct confrontation with them on the streets is absolutely necessary. As we have seen, Hitler's Nazis regarded control of the streets as essential. Militaristic marches, drums beating, serve two functions for fascists. One is that, unopposed, they terrorize into silence those people who don't agree with them. The other is that being part of a powerful-looking street movement is the only way in which the unemployed, the middle classes and other marginal elements of society can be convinced that they are part of something important.

They can't feel part of a 'great dragon' if they are repeatedly driven from the streets.

Another key element of any fight follows from this. The only way to oppose the Nazis effectively is by building *united action* against them by as many people as possible.

This means steering clear of two dangers. One is to say that we must avoid any action which would put off those people, such as wet Tory MPs or 'liberal' bosses, who may say they deplore fascism, but who will always shy away from confronting the Nazis. In any case, past experience shows that such people would ultimately prefer the Nazis to a working-class victory. The left often fell into this trap in the 1930s, particularly in Spain; of building Broad Democratic Alliances, or Popular Fronts. The opposite danger, however, is to say that the mass of the working class, who at present follow the likes of Neil Kinnock and Norman Willis, are useless because their leaders are themselves reluctant to wage any real battle. This, as we shall see, was the disastrous policy followed by the Communist Party in Germany.

Instead, a mass anti-Nazi movement is needed which leads wide layers of people in real struggle against the fascists. Just as the Nazis feed off division and passivity, we need to oppose them through unity and activity. This is what is meant by the United Front.

Such unity is made possible by the very nature of the fascist threat. When the shock troops of fascism were unleashed in the 1930s, their victims were not simply the far left. All working-class organizations had to be destroyed, even those which had loyally backed the status quo. The German equivalents of Neil Kinnock and Norman Willis were thrown into the concentration camps. The working class was driven apart, disorganized and terrorized.

Of course many leaders of the Labour Party and the unions habitually duck most struggles, even if it is in their interests at times to fight. But the scale of the threat to all minorities, to all workers, to the mass of society by a movement which ended last time in the gas chambers, means that it is possible to rally these people in opposition – if the right things are done. We have a wealth of historical experience, good and bad, to draw on. [. . .]

The rebirth of European fascism

There was dancing on the streets of Paris in June 1981. Champagne flowed at work. The joy followed the election of the Socialist Party's François Mitterrand as president. He seemed to offer a beacon of hope after 23 years of right-wing rule.

A decade later Mitterand was still in office, but the hope had long faded. Official unemployment had risen from 1.5 million to 2.7 million. Many more were on dead end government training courses or not entitled to benefit.

In 1981 the leader of the French National Front, Jean-Marie Le Pen, could not even find the 500 signatures of elected mayors and councillors he needed to contest the presidency. Ten years on, he had 20 per cent support in opinion polls and had long overtaken the once powerful Communist Party.

Le Pen's Nazi record speaks for itself. It goes back to his student collaboration with the Nazis and the pro-Nazi wartime French government. In the 1965 presidential elections he was an agent for the fascist candidate. In 1968 he was convicted for touting recordings of Hitler's speeches and Nazi marching songs. He was condemned in a French civil court for anti-Semitism as late as June 1986. Today the National Front's 50-point programme on immigration includeds calls for immigrants to be officially discriminated against in jobs and for the creation of a separate, inferior social system with inferior funding.

The NF has capitalized on Mitterrand's failure. Heavy industries such as coal and steel have been slashed. Wages for many workers, particularly civil servants, have been held down and even reduced. Public services – notably transport, education and health – have steadily deteriorated. Meanwhile, profits have flourished.

Against this background, Le Pen began to gain an audience for his arguments that there was nothing to choose between Mitterrand and the mainstream parties of the right and that France was under siege from 'anti-national forces' in the shape of international bankers and multinational capital. Then, in the 1986 general election, in an effort to save his own skin, Mitterrand altered France's proportional voting system to favour smaller parties. Mitterrand knew this new system would give the Nazis seats, but cynically calculated it would split the mainsteam right. As a result, the National Front got 2.7 million votes and 35 MPs and the mainstream right won enough seats to form the government anyway. For the next two years the National Front kept its head down only to re-emerge more brazen about its fascist policies. Le Pen now described the Holocaust as 'a detail of history'.

The Nazis also rose atop a wave of racism fuelled by all the mainstream parties, including the Socialists. When, in the summer of 1991 a number of North African-populated areas in the major cities erupted in riots, the Socialist Party prime minister, Edith Cresson, talked of chartering planes to deport 'illegal immigrants' and asylum seekers. The Gaullist leader, Chirac, claimed French people were fed up with the 'noise' and 'smell' of immigrants.

Le Pen jumped on these remarks, exploiting the racism of his opponents to claim he was right all along. There was some truth to his remark that 'people always prefer the original to the copy'. Mitterrand and the Socialists more or less conceded Le Pen's arguments, but promised to implement them in a more 'humane' way.

The Communist Party very often took a similar position. Until ten years ago it was the main working-class party, larger than the Socialists in membership. It controls the major union federation, the CGT, and publishes a daily paper. But it joined Mitterrand's first government in 1981 and shared responsibility for its austerity measures. And, when racism surfaced in the Communists' 'Red Belt' stronghold around Paris, the Communist Party pandered to it.

At the beginning of 1981 the Communist mayor of Vitry led a 'commando group' to wreck a hostel to prevent 300 immigrants moving in. The party daily, *Humanité*, threw its weight behind the mayor's action. It proudly recorded his words to immigrants before the attack: 'You have no right to take young French workers' accommodation.'

Humanité produced a special free edition with the headline 'No To Immigrant Ghettoes'. Under the heading 'A Frank Look At The Problems Posed By Immigration' was displayed a large photo of a dole queue. Inside, the paper stated: 'Immigration must be stopped so as not to worsen unemployment.'

The Communist Party has done little since to confront the Nazi threat. Le Pen has been able to make serious gains within the 'Red Belt' and amongst Marseilles dockers – a group who traditionally backed the Communists.

Worse still, the Communist Party issued a leaflet in the summer of 1991 which began: 'we say immigration is becoming a real problem today'. It linked the rise in crime, unemployment and the worsening social security system and health service to the number of immigrants.

Fascism cannot be weakened through acceptance of its arguments.

However, the rise of Le Pen has provoked a response. There can be no doubt the basis for a movement against the National Front exists. On May Day 1989 Le Pen called a march through Paris. He turned out 40,000. A rival left wing demonstration drew 100,000 – though mistakenly it did not confront the Nazi march.

Hundreds of thousands marched after a horrific attack on a Jewish cemetery in 1990. Forty three per cent of those polled at the close of 1991 'utterly opposed' everything the National Front stood for.

When, at the end of 1986, students occupied their colleges and took to the streets, black, white and Arab stood together. An Arab student killed by the police became a nationwide symbol among the young. The urban riots of 1991 showed that Arab and black youth are not prepared to be pushed around or to accept second-class status. There is even a significant anti-racist movement formed to oppose the Front, SOS Racisme.

The problem is that none of the anti-racist organizations have given an effective lead in crushing Le Pen.

SOS Racisme refuses to confront the Nazis directly. It organizes anti-racist carnivals and talks of the need to improve people's living conditions in order to root out racism. This is all fine, but does nothing to mobilize people against the fascists. SOS Racisme is also bound by its links to

Mitterrand who is responsible for creating the bitterness Le Pen has exploited.

Tragically, the main far left groups have also failed to build in response to the rise of the Nazis. Lutte Ouvrière won 600,000 votes in the 1988 presidential elections. Yet it refuses to openly label Le Pen and the National Front as Nazis. It barely talks about the threat of Le Pen. Rather it argues racism will be beaten when workers struggle in the factories. This is abstention. It does nothing to defend blacks and Arabs under attack, to stop National Front marches or even to remove their filthy graffiti

Trotsky argued against a similar position in Germany in the 1930s:

> Is it correct that in order to destroy unemployment and misery it is first necessary to destroy capitalism? It is correct. But only the biggest blockhead can conclude from all this that we do not have to fight this very day, with all our forces, against the measures with whose aid capitalism is increasing the misery of the workers.

The far left is large enough to mobilize and to put pressure on the Socialist and Communist Parties to follow their lead. They could follow the model of the Anti Nazi League in Britain.

Le Pen, like fascists everywhere, thrives on building a hard core of Nazi thugs through his racist outbursts and his encouragement of racist violence. However, he wants to surround and disguise his Storm Troopers with a growing body of softer electoral support.

The National Front thrives on the lack of confrontation. Counter-demonstrations and protests would strip away its electoral image, label Le Pen as a Nazi and isolate his fascist thugs.

A journalist discovered this when she infiltrated the National Front in Marseilles. She described the fear provoked among Front supporters attending a rally when it was rumoured that SOS Racisme was organizing a counter-demonstration. But she also described their elation and sense of victory when this proved false.

Millions of people across Europe have been chilled by the rise of the continent's top Nazi in France. They have also been horrified by the re-emergence of fascism in Germany.

The German Nazi organizations have not yet reached anything like Le Pen's support. They have achieved little of his respectability. The main far right outfit is the Republikaner Party which has a solid Nazi core. In the 1989 European elections it gained 2 million votes. Today it claims 25,000 members – an undoubted exaggeration.

However, the Nazis hope that here, as in France, economic misery and the lack of an effective alternative can draw more support.

Their main success came after the fall of the Berlin Wall. The German Nazis targeted eastern Germany and its youth in particular. Decades of Stalinist rule left an ideological vacuum and massive discontent. In the first flushes of joy as the wall fell beautiful ideas flourished – equality, democracy and solidarity. But soon the East German economy collapsed. Unemployment mounted. Prices rose. The dreams were wiped out by the reality of the market.

The Nazis capitalized on the fact that racism had been deliberately stirred up by Helmut Kohl's Christian Democrat government. There was a wave of strikes in both eastern and western Germany in the summer of 1991. The economic minister was bombarded with eggs by strikers.

The Christian Democrats sought a scapegoat to divert this anger and began to blame Germany's problems on refugees. Scare stories spread of 'hordes of immigrants' descending on Germany from eastern Europe and the old USSR. The Social Democratic Party rushed to tighten its policy on immigration.

The Christian Democrats claimed the western city of Bremen was a haven for refugees. Elections were looming. The loccoal SPD president responded by banning Poles and Romanians from the city! The Nazis reaped the harvest of this racism, taking 8 per cent of the vote in the city.

The strong German Green Party was caught too. Sections of it have initiated anti-fascist demonstrations. But Green MPs did a deal with the government which allowed it to make asylum applications more difficult and set up special camps for refugees.

In the east, the hysteria about refugees was a godsend for the Nazis. Eastern German youth wanted change. They hated the old system but felt betrayed after the promises made about the new, united Germany. The Nazis began to make ground. Arson and physical attacks mounted. Matters came to a climax with a firebomb attack in broad daylight by a Nazi gang on an immigrant hostel in Hoyerswerda.

It would be wrong, however, to believe that everything is going the Nazis' way. There is strong anti-Nazi sentiment in both halves of the country and the outrages have sparked a response. There were massive demonstrations against Republikaner leaflets during the 1989 European elections.

In Hoyerswerda itself 4,000 anti-fascists demonstrated on the weekend after the pogrom, including several hundred locals. Across Germany over 100,000 demonstrated against the attack and to mark the anniversary of Hitler's *Kristallnacht* – the nationwide anti-Jewish pogrom.

Yet there has been no concerted attempt by the left and anti-fascists to take to the streets of the eastern towns where the violence is taking place.

Much of the left imagined the old East Germany was socialist. When the Berlin Wall fell they were confused. Workers, it seemed, were celebrating the collapse of 'socialism'. This has led many to simply write off eastern German workers as right wing.

But where the anti-fascists have taken to the streets of eastern Germany they have met with a good response.

In both France and Germany the fascists have benefited from the sur-
render to racism by the established parties and by the effects of recession.
In France they have been allowed a clear run by the lack of any sustained
opposition.

Yet when powerful movements of black and white have fought back – as
in France at the end of 1986 and the beginning of 1987 or in the strikes
which swept Germany in 1991 – the fascists have been pushed aside.

When the fascists have been confronted, the anti-fascists have shown
that they can mobilize far wider forces.

Fascism is far from carrying the day. The conditions for defeating it are
very favourable – provided those who want to fight take note of the lessons
of the struggles against fascism from the 1930s and the 1970s.

25

Fascism, neo-fascism, new radical right?[*]

DIETHELM PROWE[1]

Ever since the end of the Second World War, the connection between the
horrors of the 'classic' fascism of the inter-war years and contemporary
movements of the European radical right has seemed obvious. In the later
1940s and 1950s any extreme nationalist groups were naturally identified as
neo-fascist or proto-Nazi, not least because they harboured so many old
henchmen of the fascist regimes. But even today, news of violent acts or
electoral successes of radical right organizations in Europe raise the spectre of fascism in the minds of observers everywhere. There is hardly a
popular or scholarly article that does not refer to this link at least indirectly, above all in analyses of German politics. Thus one German weekly, in
a report on nationalist activities in the new eastern *Länder*, asked fore-
bodingly: 'Is the ex-GDR sinking into a brown [Nazi] morass? Is the SA
marching again, is the Fourth Reich imminent?'[2] A recent scholarly article
on the German *Republikaner* made the same obligatory references in a
more veiled manner: 'Against the background of the course of twentieth-
century European history, right-wing radical tendencies anywhere in Europe warrant special attention.'[3] No doubt, this will hold true for decades
to come. The link of all present-day right-wing movements with the inter-
war years remains inescapable. The catastrophes associated with fascism

[*] Excerpt from '"Classic Fascism" and the New Radical Right in Western Europe:
Comparisons and Contrasts', *Contemporary European History*, 3 (3) (1994), pp. 289–
96, 303–13.

are the kind of historical experience that shapes the political consciousness of several generations. Both for the adherents of extreme nationalism and for their enemies, inter-war fascism thus provides a basic paradigm through which contemporary rightist groups are defined or define themselves.

Any scholarly discussion of the contemporary European radical right must therefore confront at some point the relationship, continuities and differences between the 'classic' inter-war fascisms and the extreme nationalist movements of today. This is necessary not only because the question is constantly posed by the groups' adherents, opponents and observers. As implied by the typical concerns expressed in the above quotes, it is also an issue of practical significance. Are the present movements sufficiently similar to the inter-war fascist stirrings that they threaten Europe and the world to the same degree and in a similar manner as, say, Hitler's Nazi party or Mussolini's Fascists did, so that an all-out 'anti-fascist' plan of action must always be ready, as communists never tired of asserting over the last fifty years? Or are the new movements sufficiently different to suggest a different range of responses? Of the major scholars who have written on the whole span of inter-war fascism and its contemporary successor movements, only the premier theorist of the younger generation, Roger Griffin, has contested the assumption that the danger of another Nazi/Fascist catastrophe is inherent in the rise of fascist movements by pointing out that fascist movements are typically destined to fail in modern 'liberal-secular' societies, as virtually every one of these groups has done, making Nazism and Italian Fascism highly improbable aberrations rather than the prototypes as which they are usually portrayed.[4]

The topic presented here makes an important assumption, which is implicitly shared by most present-day analyses of radical right activity in Europe. It presupposes that there was, in fact, such a thing as 'classic inter-war fascism' or a 'fascist era', as Ernst Nolte put it in the mid-1960s when the discussion of fascism as a separate definable phenomenon reached a new climax among non-Marxists, replacing the totalitarian thesis which had lumped together communism and fascism or Stalinism and Nazism.[5] Powerful arguments have been advanced in particular by historians that there never was a unified phenomenon of European fascism at all. This assertion was put in its starkest classic form by Gilbert Allardyce in the *Amrican Historical Review* a dozen years ago.[6] Yet he was unable to do without the term in dealing with the variety of inter-war movements usually identified as fascist; he simply put it in quotation marks as he argued what 'fascism is not'.[7] Worse, in dismissing the whole 'anti-fascist' scholarship on the inter-war movements, he lumped the premier totalitarianism theorist, Hannah Arendt, with the fascism theorists, even though she linked only the totalitarians Hitler and Stalin and always denied any important similarity between Hitler and the 'normal tyrant' Mussolini.[8]

Hugh Trevor-Roper modified this view to account for the historical reality of a fascist bloc by asserting that 'fascism' mushroomed into an all-European phenomenon only because of the overwhelming power of Hitler's armies.[9]

There is no question that the differences between the movements commonly lumped together under the category of fascism in the inter-war period are numerous and profound. The differentiation on which most historians insist is that of Italian Fascism and its closest imitators, on the one hand, and German Nazism, on the other.[10] What Michael Geyer calls the 'racist social contract',[11] namely the central role of pseudo-biological racism and Social Darwinism with its horrible realization in the Holocaust, the early reactionary alliance with industrial cartels and the élitist Prussian Military, and the racist *Lebensraum* ideology of genocidal conquest, set Hitler's Nazism apart from the integral nationalist and corporatist movements patterned on Italian Fascism. Similarly, the traditionalist, religious–mystical movements of Eastern–Central Europe and the Iberian Peninsula seem essentially different phenomena from Western and northern European fascisms. The former are more reminiscent of early modern millenarian peasant movements. Even within many individual countries, two essentially different groups were variously associated with the fascist label: élite clerical conservative parties and militant radical–revolutionary armed cells. The two groups frequently formed political alliances of convenience, in which one tried to exploit and gain the advantage over the other – generally to the advantage of the conservatives in traditional societies, while the 'dynamic' basically anti-conservative groups gained the upperhand in modernized Germany and, to a lesser extent, in semi-modern Italy.[12]

Still, such fundamental divergences in movements of different countries should not be surprising. In fact, they point to two important unifying features. The rigidly narrow and exclusivist nationalism that characterizes all forms of fascism naturally precludes the kind of transnationally shared ideology demanded of communists. Moreover, the typical fascist resistance to any change in one's own parochial notions – what Ernst Nolte calls 'resistance to transcendence' and what motivates the 'escape from freedom' of Erich Fromm's petty bourgeoisie – made fascists unlikely to overcome locally rooted prejudices in order to adapt to a unified international ideology. Roger Griffin interprets this as 'the protean quality' of fascism and 'its almost Darwinian capacity for adaptation to its environment'.[13] It might be more accurate to argue that the typically narrow and antagonistic mentalities of those to whom the fascist message of an ultra-nationalist rebirth appeals force fascism into their own present parochial conception of their national 'community'.

The most obvious justification for applying the common term of fascism to all the Nazi, 'fascist' and related movements is their self-identification and the perception of most contemporaries that there was such a thing as a fascist phenomenon throughout Europe. Even though a number of the groups commonly included rejected at various times the label 'fascism', including such notable collaborators as Jacques Doriot and Léon Degrelle, they readily identified with the belief systems and organizational structures of Mussolini and Hitler. This was powerfully reinforced by the successes of the Hitler and Mussolini movments and eventually enforced by the direct influence of Hitler's armies. This unifying and clarifying role of the actually existing fascist states continued to influence the radical right after the Second World War, following the demise of these regimes. In the face of this historical reality, most historians have accepted the term on the basis of those central models, even if they still differ widely on which of the many movements are included under the fascist label. Ultimately most scholars have accepted Stanley Payne's Weberian argument for the use of the term fascism: 'Historical understanding requires us to identify certain common features or qualities of new forces within a given period, if only to recognize and clarify their differences and uniqueness.'[14]

Not surprisingly, this effort to 'identify certain common features' has led to an extraordinary variety of definitions. They range from bare-bones listings such as Eugen Weber's in *Varieties of Fascism* to George Mosse's complex description stressing cultural roots and Ernst Nolte's brilliantly comprehensive three-level definition, which appears to have stood the test of time best of all: anti-Marxism as a 'radically opposed yet related ideology' with nearly identical methods; an 'inwardly antagonistic' life-and-death struggle; and 'resistance to transcendence'.[15] Roger Griffin has most recently added a splendidly clear, even more comprehensive and remarkably handy one-sentence definition: 'Fascism is a genus of political ideology whose mythic core in its various permutations is a *palingenetic form of popular ultra-nationalism*.'[16]

Among this array of definitions it is important for our purposes to distinguish between two types, one of which speaks strongly for equating the present radical right movements with inter-war fascism, while the other argues just as vehemently against such an equation. The first type of definition asks primarily about mentality, general political behaviour, and goals of the fascists, while the second kind stresses the specific historical setting from which the extreme rightist movements of the inter-war years emerged.

In accentuating more timeless features like mentality, political behavior and goals, the classic definitions of the former category place inter-war fascism in a context of militant conservative thought and its violent manifestations that has changed very little since the Enlightenment and the French Revolution. It is perhaps most concisely and elegantly expressed in André Malraux's quip in *Man's Hope*: 'A man who is both active and pessimistic is a fascist or will be one.'[17] Fuller definitions of fascism from this perspective, which could comfortably encompass such diverse interwar movements as Nazism and Italian Fascism, Codreanu's Legionaries, the Finnish Lapua Movement and the Austrian *Heimwher*, the Spanish *Falange* and others, might be summed up in the following list of characteristics:

1. A narrowly exclusivist, angrily antagonistic, often mystical nationalism likely to turn to racism.
2. A faith in direct, violent action not simply to achieve specific goals, but to create a deeper bond of community.
3. A strong leadership principle, to provide a 'saviour' who has absolute power because he intuitively knows both the people and their destiny.
4. Glorification of phyical prowess associated with masculinity, youth and the mobilized masses.
5. Accordingly, replacement of established élites with a dynamic activist 'warrior' élite – a counter-élitism sometimes parading as egalitarianism, but always anti-pluralist.
6. Military-like organizations, formations and rituals, which are, however, contemptuous of established military forces constrained by tradition, institutions etc.
7. The central importance of ritual, myths, symbols, emotionally rousing rallies and ceremonies with a stridently activist, anti-rational 'aesthetic'.
8. A profound pessimism and fear of impending doom, of being physically and especially spiritually threatened, sapped by strange foreign elements.
9. Accordingly, a deep resentment against the *spirit of modernity* (not modern technology as such) which requires attitudinal changes or new ways of understanding, including readjustment of gender roles, and which therefore threatens old identities – what Nolte calls 'resistance to transcendence', practically manifested in anti-liberalism, anti-rationalism, intolerance and a rejection of the values of the Enlightenment, French Revolution and Social Democracy.
10. Correspondingly, a belief in conspiracy by powerful evil (secular) forces (usually identified with communism or Zionism) against the nation – and the tendency, therefore, to establish secret conspiratorial anti-organizations (anti-communist, anti-Jewish) which seek limitless power in the name of security or salvation.
11. An appeal to tradition combined with a hatred of established élites and conservatives, because fascism seeks a permanent state of mobilization and violent militancy, even though fascism shares many of their goals and regards them as its most natural allies.[18]
12. An institutional structure of 'representation' reflecting functions and duties in politics and the economy, such as corporatism, designed to

eliminate traditional material interest group conflicts, building on some mythical past of co-operation and obligation.

In the last decade or so revisionists have introduced important modifications to this composite. Their fundamental disagreement is with the association of fascism with conservatism and pessimism. Both Zeev Sternhell and Roger Griffin stress the socialist (Sternhell) or populist (Griffin) Sorelian-syndicalist revolutionary and thus anti-conservative side of fascism,[19] which does not reject modernity but seeks, in Griffin's words, 'an alternative modernism' ',[20] reminiscent of Jeffrey Herf's argument of a 'reactionary modernism' of the Weimar Republic and the Third Reich.[21] 'Fascism thus embodies a manic charge of cultural *optimism*' rooted in an 'intensely idealistic . . . profound urge to transcend the existing state of society'.[22]

Griffin falsely believes that this observation disproves Nolte's third defining characteristic of fascism, the resistance to transcendence.[23] In reality, it is Griffin who uses the word 'transcendence', in a very different sense from its usual political–philosophical definition. His description of the fascists' fanatical devotion as 'a neurotically based mischannelling of the human drive for self-transcendence'[24] is precisely an *escape* from the self, not its transcendence. It is an escape from behind the lonely boundaries of the self, much like the passion described by psychiatrist M. Scott Peck as experienced in the process of falling in love. It does not move beyond the self to reach out to others in appreciation of their different worlds, in order to develop a freer, more mature perspective, rather it is an 'act of regression'. It allows the fanatical followers to 'reexperience the sense of omnipotence', lost with the discovery of self in early infancy. In that state 'all things seem possible', writes Peck. 'We believe that the strength of our love (fanatical devotion in the case of the radicals) will cause the forces of the opposition to bow down in submission . . .'. This is Erich Fromm's 'escape from freedom' and Nolte's resistance to transcendence. This self-denial in blind devotion is, as Peck argues for falling in love, 'not an extension of one's limits or boundaries' – that is, transcendence – 'it is a partial and temporary collapse of them.'[25] Thus Griffin's 'manic charge of cultural optimism' is in fact a deep cultural, if activist–militant, pessimism because the blindly 'optimistic' faith in an imminent magical rebirth of the nation is born of a boundless pessimism about the reality of the existing nation and the possibility of rational progress. Yet Sternhell's and Griffin's insistence on a complete disassociation of fascism and its vision of a fundamentally different (and therefore 'modern'?) future from conservatism and traditional values has served to sharpen our understanding of fascism and related twentieth-century political phenomena.

Even though all leading radical right movements of Europe deny direct links with inter-war fascism, these defining elements fit the main extreme right parties of present-day Europe quite well.[26] Antagonistic nationalism and racism have perhaps been even more universally characteristic of such parties as Jean-Marie Le Pen's *Front National*, the German *Republikaner*, Deutsche Volksunion (DVU) and National Democratic Party, the British National Front or the Italian MSI (*Movimento Sociale Italiano*), as well as the radical right youth gangs, than they were of inter-war fascism generally before Hitler's armies spread their racist terror. The leadership principle and military-like organizations survive in their old forms mainly in the violent cells of radical young men, but they are also reflected in the rightist parties' demands for strong authoritarian leadership and law and order. Their love affair with rituals, myths, symbols and traditions continues; and the profound pessimism and rejection of the modern, materialist and 'stultifying' West is still primarily directed against the most progressive, liberal reformers such as Willy Brandt in Germany or Simone Veil, 'principal architect of the great social reforms' in France.[27] Visceral anti-communism/anti-Semitism are still among the credos of the radical right; and their propensity for secret, conspiratorial organizations remains strong. 'Apocalypse, persecution syndrome, and a dashing savior,' Gerhard Paul has elegantly summarized the programme of today's radical right and its close kinship in mentality and vision with inter-war fascism.[28] Only corporatist solutions have lost their luster.

On the basis of this definition, one might thus be tempted to speak of the present-day radical right movements as 'fascist'. But such an equation based on the striking similarities in mentalities and general vision omits an essential aspect of inter-war fascism. No political movement develops in a vacuum. Rightists, too, have responded to particular historical contexts which have shaped both their specific programmes and the tools they have used in their political struggle. Here the fascist parties of the inter-war years and the radical right of the last decades show some very significant differences. [. . .]

Thus, even though ideology and even a few of the leaders remain eerily reminiscent of fascism, the current Western European movements of the radical right are essentially different phenomena. The most obvious and the most critical differences are as follows.

1. The social antagonism which fuels the hateful language and violence of the present radical right is that of an emerging European *multicultural society*, clashing along new unblended cultural front lines, in contrast to the 'broken society' of inter-war Europe marked by a deep fissure along the classic lines of the class struggle that Nazis and fascists posed most effectively as the great saviours: 'If it weren't for us National Socialists,' the later Propaganda Minister Joseph Goebbels wrote in *Der Angriff* in the early 1930s, 'the Bolshevist tide would have long swept all across Germany and annihilated the rotten and depraved bourgeoisie.'[29] This genuine fear

of communism by the 'depraved bourgeoisie', which actually included not only much of the political-economic élite, but also the broad middle classes of small holders of property and status, also meant that these groups became ready to accept fascist violence, because they regarded it as a basically justifiable move by the most radical anti-Marxists to control communists and their allies.[30] The fascists' claim to be the most determined and thus allegedly most reliable anti-communists also opened the way to power through alliances with the élites, which the present radical right, in the absence of a communist threat, but with the memory of the fascist catastrophe, cannot achieve.

This is not to say that hatred of foreign immigrants, most particularly Eastern European Jews, played no role in the 1920s and 1930s, but even inter-war anti-Semitism was always clothed in the powerful language and images of the class struggle: the rich Jewish exploitative capitalist bourgeois or the Jewish Marxist collectivists, who were ready to take the hard-earned home, land or small business livelihood from responsible citizens and turn people into soulless proletarians. Those most violent sections of the present radical right, who hope to empower themselves by identifying especially with Hitler, mistakenly believe that the Nazis' virulent hatred of Jews and others was the source of their power, rather than an anti-communism, which was so potent because the threat of a communist revolution appeared real in a society charged with a class struggle mentality.

In contrast, the reality of a multi-cultural society with local concentrations of 'foreigners' of 50 per cent and above, has been a new experience for Western Europeans in recent times, except as rulers over colonies. Contemporary rightist slogans are anti-foreigner and racist pure and simple. The multi-cultural society is the number one issue for voters on the extreme right. Thus in polls conducted after the 1986 French legislative elections 38 per cent of Le Pen voters named immigrants as their greatest concern (as against only 8 per cent for the electorate as a whole), while only 19 per cent of the same voters considered unemployment as the biggest problem (as against 28 per cent for the total electorate), even though the Lepenists attracted a disproportionally high number of unemployed.[31] Interviews with German REP voters suggest a similar conclusion.[32]

2. While the cultural roots of fascism reach back into the soil of a fermenting late nineteenth-century European civilization deeply furrowed by the Imperialist expansion, the new radical right was born in the period of *decolonization and its violent aftershocks*. There can be no question that in the longer-term evolution of modern European society, the racist creeds of inter-war fascism and the radical right movements of today share common origins in the European imperialist experience of the nineteenth and twentieth centuries when large numbers of Europeans participated in the conquest, exploitation and transformation of the colonies, and mass-

circulation newspapers brought the stories of 'heroism' and brutality to the home countries. These imperialist roots of fascism are often over-looked. The argument for the imperialist roots of Nazism was made first and most powerfully by Hannah Arendt in her classic *The Origins of Totalitarianism*, where she identified anti-Dreyfusard mass anti-Semitism and the late nineteenth-century imperialism of Cecil Rhodes, Carl Peters and Lord Cromer as the twin taproots of Nazi totalitarianism.[33] Woodruff Smith and other historians have pointed to this link more recently.[34] For Germans the imperialist bestiality of the near-extermination of the Hereros in south-west Africa certainly remains a far more convincing precedent for Nazi extermination camps than a basically defensive reaction to the 'Asian brutality' of the Bolsheviks, as hypothesized by Ernst Nolte. Those French historians who have accepted radical military–authoritarian mass movements such as Colonel de la Rocque's *Croix de Feu* as fascist have been able to draw a line to fascism from French imperialism, which had always been strongly shaped by the colonial armies, especially the Algerian Army.[35] Mussolini's alliance with a frustrated imperialist army in the assault on Ethiopia makes this connection even more concrete and obvious for that nation, as does the fascist politics of the British League of the Empire Loyalists for Britain. Only in France does this link remain visible in the origins of the present leading party of the radical right, the Lepenists; for it was the battle cry against de Gaulle's Algerian 'Betrayal' by the colonial military officers of the OAS (*Organisation de l'Armée Secrète*) and Joseph Ortiz's French-Algerian fascists in the sultry air of 'dying colonialism' (Frantz Fanon) in Algeria that provided the launching pad for Le Pen's political career.

While the radical right has since the 1970s built on this racism of colonial domination, the end of direct imperial rule reshaped the nature of racism significantly. Aside from old anti-Semite traditions, inter-war fascism had taken its racialist cues from colonial conquest and the oppressive practice of imperial rule. The racism of the imperialist age was therefore conditioned by the experiences of vast, 'glorious' and relatively easy conquests of 'inferior' peoples, of seemingly assured domination, and of labour exploitation that was confidently rationalized by arguments of racial superiority and economic development. The assumptions drawn from these experiences naturally became characteristic foundations of fascist racism, most strikingly of Nazi *Lebensraum* racism. In contrast, the new radical right has absorbed its racism from the racial interactions of decolonization, which were marked by deep fear, by the terrorist racial violence of the decolonization wars and by the continued Third World labour dependency, all of which have in one form or another been brought to Europe itself. Unwittingly the prosperous European nations thus created during the decolonization era multi-cultural societies deeply imprinted with the decolonization experience of both sides, even if particular

European nations like Germany and Italy no longer held colonies themselves after the Second World War.

3. In contrast to classic fascism (and its early post-Second World War
heirs), the new radical right movements of Western Europe evolved in an
extended period of peace. Inter-war fascism had been essentially shaped by
the First World War experience. 'It was the war,' Ernst Nolte writes, 'that
made room for a political phenomenon, which was, so to speak, its very
own child, a child which by innate law strove in turn to engender yet
another war.'[36] Ernst Jünger, the neo-conservative whom the Nazis revered
as their great precursor, called the war the father of all things: 'it hammered us, it chiseled us, it made us what we are . . .'.[37] The cult of the
front soldier, the fallen soldier and the war veteran was at the heart of
fascism.[38] Mythologized and ritualized as they were, these images were
still very close and real experiences that shaped fascism in the 1920s and
1930s.[39] The war had even militarized old, aristocratic conservatism to
open it to an activist, bellicose dynamism to move its younger, radical
fringes towards fascism. The war also promoted a new levelling through
the front experience or its myth that opened the political spectrum for a
violent, antagonistic, vulgar–nationalist movement that was, in Zeev
Sternhell's phrase, 'neither right nor left',[40] and cut across all class lines
as the war had done.

The new radical right, in contrast, emerged from a long period of peace.
Its roots are not in the traumatic, all-absorbing war experience and the
disorienting emptiness that followed, but in a deep feeling of boredom,
alienation and sense of powerlessness. Even in France, the Algerian War,
whose bloody conclusion spawned Le Pen's career, had long faded in
political memory when the Lepenists rode to their first electoral near-
triumphs in the mid-1980s. Inter-war radical nationalists and fascists
had been deeply unfair and vague in their hatreds, but they could still
identify their enemies on the basis of the wartime confrontation: enemy
nationals of the First World War, citizens within their own nation who did
not conform to the narrowest standards of nationality, religion, customs,
etc., political leaders who had advocated peace and thus allegedly robbed
the front soliders of total national support – dubbed 'November Crim-
inals' in Germany – and internationalists of all kinds: socialists, pacifists,
Free Masons and, above all, Jews. Present-day rightists lack such clearly
identifiable enemies in an open democratic society, which appears to be
ruled by nobody, as Hannah Arendt put it.[41] Their anger stems from a
more general malaise and an individual sense of powerlessness in a society
which still glorifies violent heroism and power and, in the media, appears
to put it within the grasp of everyone but denies it in reality.[42] 'The minds
and souls of people here in the West are in the process of stultification',
two German militant rightists put it.[43] The violent rage of young rightist

radicals, like that of nonpolitical but violent skinheads (although, obviously, not all skinheads are violent) and other toughs, was therefore initially undirected, arbitrary terror without clear goals as in the bombings in the early 1980s.

Since the mid-1980s, the violence has increasingly become focused against the only visible symbol of otherness: foreign immigrants who 'irritate' by their very presence because they challenge the most basic sense of power, control over secure, comfortable surroundings. Yet the presence of foreigners obviously does not *per se* cause these irritations, but only the combination of rapid immigration and the particular kind of social crises experienced by Western Europeans, gave rise to violent actions, which 'naturally' focused increasingly along ethnic categories.[44] In the context of societies in an extended period of peace, images of the heroic warrior, like that of the fascists' First World War mythology, have receded in the actual violence, and even street battles along ideological class lines have become rarer. The anti-foreigner violence has typically consisted of indiscriminate attacks by drunken youths or fire bombings against a vague unfamiliar 'foreignness', like the vicious arsonist attacks of Mölln and Solingen in 1992 and 1993, the erstwhile peak years when almost 5,000 such assaults were registered in Germany.[45]

4. Whereas fascism grew out of the naked material despair and violent class struggles of the post-First World War economic shocks, inflation and depression, the new young rightists first emerged unexpectedly from the cracks of a *politically stable and prosperous consumer society,* at a time when that otherwise remarkably successful society's cohesive forces began to fade or ceased to be convincing for mostly young men. Even though regional and branch-specific unemployment and other barriers have unquestionably played a role in drawing some people towards the extreme right, especially in Eastern and Eastern Central Europe, there does not appear to be a very strong correlation between unemployment or other specific economic problems on one hand and voting for radical right parties or even nationalist violence in Western Europe on the other.[46] Empirical research on rightist extremism and youth by Wilhelm Heitmeyer and others even suggests that many of the young men who have shown an affinity with extreme right ideas feel themselves to be socially and economically well integrated. On the other hand, in the socialization of young men their developing sense of social orientation and autonomous identity appeared significantly hampered by perceived societal contradictions and political ambivalences.[47] As the most important long-term study to date on right extremism among young men in Germany argues, the extent or lack of *'formal* [social] integration and even work "security" in the "external" biography of employment' cannot by itself tell us enough about the causes of rightist radicalism. We must look beyond the question

of (un)employment to the degree to which jobs may have failed to meet the young men's expectations for economic and/or social positions or the extent to which the youths have lost any identification with the tasks and their personal goals at the work place. Psychological, rather than necessarily economic, voids, thus created, 'are filled from an available reservoir of ideologies of inequality and/or various forms of violence acceptance'.[48] Any 'egalitarian inclinations of the young man are evidently . . . destroyed when he sees the *cultural* and material basis of his own life threatened or when he anticipates such a threat for the future, which the *presence of foreigners* evidently raises for him'.[49]

This suggests a primary causal link between the resurgence of the extreme right in the early 1980s with the striking decline in the cohesive, integrative power of the successive common goals, fears and myths of Europe in the post-Second World War years: the German 'zero hour' and the French *Résistance* myths, the bootstraps reconstruction efforts all over Western Europe, the Cold War struggle with its anti-communist consensus and finally the great social–liberal programme of social integrational and reform inspired by Kennedy's New Frontier. Perhaps the deepest frustration and loss of faith followed the apparent failure of the last – the great reform governments inspired by the Kennedy/Johnson experiment in the US: Brandt's social–liberal coalition, Harold Wilson's new Labour planners, even de Gaulle's 'Participation Revolution' and Aldo Moro's 'Opening to the Left' – all of which had promised power and prosperity for everyone, but had failed to deliver it. The attempt of the 1980s' conservatives to generate a new sense of common goal and consensus on the model of the Kennedy Era reformers by proclaiming a conservative (Reagan, Thatcher) 'revolution' or, in its German version, *Wende* (the first, internal West German turnabout) was not able to reverse this trend of disorientation and rising extremism on the right because this 'revolution' aimed only at a consensus of the more privileged 'two-thirds' of society – the *Zweidrittelgesellschaft*, as Germans have dubbed it – and because the conservative governments have naturally shown greater tolerance towards ideas, if not actions, of the radical right.

5. The new Western European radical right has grown to its own maturity in a society in which *democratic norms* are no longer questioned by the vast majority of the population. This contrasts with the post-First World War breeding ground of fascism, when European states were still strongly shaped by traditional authoritarian–monarchial–military forces, which were especially influential in the fascist movements. Robert Soucy argues that fascism was, even though different in its methods, in fact 'primarily a new variety of authoritarian conservatism and right-wing nationalism which sought to defeat the Marxist threat and the political liberalism which allowed it to exist in the first place'.[50] While one might argue

with this definition, it is undeniable that inter-war fascism developed in the context of that authoritarian, nationalist and frequently aristocratic conservatism, shared many of its values and basic assumptions and was linked to it in innumerable coalitions and personal connections. The present-day radical right movements lack this aristocratic–authoritarian component and can no longer rely on widely shared traditional authoritarian assumptions, but must either adapt to formal democratic rules or appeal directly to romantic visions of (especially guerrilla) war, terrorist 'direct action' and an unabashed espousal of a military or revolutionary 'leadership principle' – or some combination of all of the above. Its access to established élites and appeal to dominant value systems is far more limited.

6. In contrast with inter-war fascism and even radical right movements of the 1950s and 1960s such as French *Poujadisme* and the SRP and early NPD in West Germany, the electoral base of the new radical right groups has been *much more heavily urban*. This has been true of the French *Front National* (Paris, Marseilles, Alsace-Lorraine), the German *Republikaner* (Berlin, Frankfurt, Bremen as well as rural areas in Bavaria and Schleswig-Holstein), the British National Front (London, northeast England), and in Spain (Madrid, northern Castile), southern Italy (Rome, Naples, Tarento, Brindisi), Belgium and Switzerland.[51] Particularly striking is the concentration of radical right voters and violent nationalist youth in major urban housing developments where social integration is often minimal.[52] Ironically, this milieu of urban anomie is eerily reminiscent of Hitler's experience of radicalization in Vienna. The more heavily urban nature of the new radical right is thus undoubtedly primarily due to the fact that Western Europe had become far more urbanized by the 1980s than it was in the inter-war years when most European countries were still undergoing a painful transition to modern industrial societies.

Regardless of the cause, this shift has had important effects. The rural romanticism of 'blood and soil' and the anti-modernism which accompanied it have all but disappeared. Even though there are references to ecological concerns in the programmes and slogans of the radical right parties, this issue has been pre-empted by the Greens on the left.[53] Even in Germany, the home of the 'blood and soil' myth, the 'ecological right' has been quite small – a 1980 poll found only some 2 per cent of its sample to fit this category.[54] Established parties of the radical right have generally hedged about such concerns carefully so as not to interfere with established economic élites. Thus the *Republikaner*, on their programme cover, label themselves 'a community of German patriots . . . with high social and ecological commitment'. Yet in the programme text they only promise to protect the environment through 'steady and expert work and in harmony with research, technology, industry, commerce, agriculture and the entire national economy'.[55]

These fundamental distinctions between classic inter-war fascism and the new Western European radical right are reflected in a number of key practical differences. Most importantly, the central defining characteristic of the new rightist groups has become a concrete physical racism. Even though racism was surely the ugliest and most irritating feature of inter-war fascisms, most notably of Nazism, not all of those movements were in fact racist or only became so late in their evolution under the pressure of Nazism, as in the cases of Italian Fascism and Oswald Mosley's British Union of Fascists. In contrast, the political breakthrough of the present extremist right in Western Europe has been so critically dependent on the rapid flow and incomplete integration of large numbers of generally non-European immigrants that rightist extremism without racism is just as unimaginable today as fascism was without anti-Marxism in the 1920s and 1930s. This racist hatred is not directed against all foreigners or even all immigrants but is a concrete racism against people of different skin colour or visibly different dress, customs or religion.[56]

This concrete racism overshadows both traditional hallmarks of classic fascism – anti-communism and (in most cases) anti-Semitism – even though both will remain essential credos of the radical right as long as they can arouse emotions of hatred and a sordid sense of righteousness. Anti-communism has been fading on the extreme right for some time, not just since the collapse of the communist system. In the 1980s an affinity with the extreme left as well as links with established communists, most notably the East German leadership, went well beyond the negative alliances of convenience such as that of Hitler and Stalin or the common opposition of Nazis and communists against the Weimar Republic. Anti-Americanism, 'anti-Zionism' and 'anti-imperialist wars of liberation' provided the mythical meeting grounds.[57]

Anti-Semitism still maintains its grip on closed-minded rightists who have always found it difficult to abandon old prejudices. Anti-Semitic acts are still by far the most effective tool for right extremists to achieve the kind of notoriety they seek.[58] But the core of the hatred, the overwhelming majority of cases of violence against persons and most of the threatening graffiti are directed against non-Europeans 'of color'[59] If there is a common denominator which might unite an all-European radical right movement in the future, it will most likely be a re-emergence of anti-Muslimism – a prejudice that can build on very old European traditions. Already a 1988 German poll found that 20 per cent of those surveyed rejected Turks as neighbours, whereas 'only' 12 per cent had similar feelings about Jews.[60] Anti-Semitism undoubtedly remains a central plank of rightists, but in the practical actions of the European radical right it is increasingly overshadowed by anti-Muslim and anti-African hatred.[61]

Perhaps most remarkable has been the change in spatial orientation of the present-day aggressive nationalism from that of inter-war fascism and, indeed, radical nationalists of the nineteenth century. Even though dreams of 'Greater Germany' and so on persist, there has been strikingly little practical interest in foreign conquest. In contrast to inter-war fascism, and also to Eastern European chauvinists of the stamp of Russian demagogue Vladimir Zhirinovsky, the present Western European radical right vents its nationalist aggression almost entirely in domestic racism. When the young rightists feel frustrated as powerless victims of change or some imagined conspiracy, they seek their *Lebensraum* in street battles for urban space against ethnically different 'invaders'. 'There are no more apartments left for us,' is a common battle cry.[62] They do not see *Lebensraum* as conquest of vast territories, but much more literally as 'defence of the place and manner of existence, to which they are attached'[63] against outside competitors.

This spatial orientation also accords with the radical right's rather ambivalent posture towards European integration. While the anti-Europe movement gave strong impetus to the extreme right in Britain and the Scandinavian countries, the attitude has not been stridently or universally negative in France, Germany, Italy and the Low Countries. Thus, the leftist German paper *taz* cited young rightists in 1989: 'Every European, who has not yet fallen victim to the intellectual stultification spreading more or less all around us, strives for the liberation of the European peoples from US and Soviet domination.'[64] In 1988, the *Mouvement de la jeunesse d' Europe*, associated with the Lepenists, took a practical step towards creating such a European front by assembling a European Convention of some 500 representatives from like-minded nationalist groups in Strasbourg.[65] Clearly, Europeanism and the radical right, which has been bred in the rapidly integrating Western Europe, are not incompatible because the radicals' focus is not really the nation, but, even more than in the fascist movements, the physical or cultural ethnic identity of individuals in small groups, in neighbourhoods, and in the workplace.

Finally, transformation of the political culture of Western Europe has also changed the philosophical–ideological discourse of the radical right. The old fascist and nineteenth-century conservative argument against the Englightenment as the source of all evil has virtually faded away. Even though both the established parties of the right – which have adapted their external positions to democracy – and the militant young extremists hold on to an arbitrary authoritarianism and intolerance that are fundamentally in conflict with Enlightenment ideals, their public discourse no longer questions the basic assumptions of republican, democratic institutions. Instead, the Holocaust, as the cataclysmic defining event of our time, which, like the Enlightenment, has raised new moral imperatives for society, has taken the place of the Enlightenment as the central object of hateful rejection and denial for the right today.[66] Together with the physical racism against extra-European immigrants and guest workers, which fundamentally rejects the lessons of the Holocaust, Holocaust denial has swept aside the fascist preoccupation with the anti-Enlightenment struggle.

In conclusion, despite the generic similarities among movements of the modern secular right, which include both classic fascism and the present radical right in Western Europe, critical changes in the historical context set these two phenomena apart in essential ways. Most important has been the conjunction of the transformation of Western European political culture in the decades since the Second World War and the rapidly accelerating (re)emergence of a multi-cultural society in the last couple of decades. Even though the dramatic economic, political and social developments since 1945 have gradually altered the face of rightist extremism from its inter-war fascist predecessors, nothing has been so critical for the nature and reality of the new Western European radical right than the emergence of the new multi-cultural society and the racism that has sprung up against it. Ultimately nothing demonstrates the centrality of this anti-multi-cultural racism more plainly than the fact that the new extremism of the right has grown most disturbingly not in those areas with the strongest inter-war fascist movements, or where economic conditions have been of greatest concern, but where the new immigration has been largest. To be sure, the most radical fringes of the rightists still glorify and sometimes adopt old fascist slogans and myths because this link gives them a dramatic presence and a sense of power far beyond what they could otherwise achieve. But related as they may be spiritually to inter-war fascism, the new movements represent a new era and are fighting new and different battles in Western Europe. In the words of Richard Stöss, 'Grandpa's fascism is dead.'[67]

What radical right movements will bring in Eastern Europe, where many post-Second World War patterns have been preserved and where economic pressures reminiscent of the inter-war years are severely straining the social fabric, remains to be seen. They will undoubtedly differ greatly from the recent radical right activities in Western Europe.

Notes

1 Special thanks to William Brustein, Roger Eatwell, Jürgen Falter, Peter H. Merkle, Stanley G. Payne and Carl D. Weiner for valuable comments and criticisms. Thanks also to J. Kim Munholland for organizing the marvellous Conference on the Radical Right in Western Europe at the University of Minnesota's Center for European Studies in November 1991, which first inspired this chapter.

2 Bartholomäus Grill, 'Auferstanden aus Ruinen: Der Rechstradikalismus in Ostdeutschland ist der extreme Ausdruck einer zerstörten Gesellschaft', *Die Zeit*, 21 June 1991, 3.

3 Hans-Georg Betz, 'Politics of Resentment: Right-Wing Radicalism in West Germany' (thereafter Betz, 'Resentment'), *Comparative Politics*, 23 (1990), p. 46.

4 Roger Griffin, *The Nature of Fascism* (thereafter Griffin, *Fascism*) (New York, St Martin's Press, (1991), esp. p. 116.

5 Ernst Nolte, *Three Faces of Fascism* (thereafter Nolte, *Three Faces*) (New York, Holt, Rinehart and Winston, 1966), 3–16; note also the title of the original German edition: *Der Faschismus in seiner Epoche* (Munich, Piper, 1963). Notably Griffin, who does not accept an inherent link between fascism and the inter-war years, also speaks of a 'fascist epoch' between the World Wars, *Fascism*, pp. 212–19.

6 Gilbert Allardyce, 'What Fascism Is Not: Thoughts on the Deflation of a Concept' (thereafter Allardyce, 'Fascism'), AHA Forum, *American Historical Review* 84: 2 (1979), (thereafter AHA Forum), pp. 367–88.

7 For example ibid., 377, and Allardyce, 'Reply', AHA Forum, p. 397; also Nolte's response, AHA Forum, p. 392.

8 Allardyce, 'Fascism', pp. 383–8. Cf. also the title 'Fascism as Totalitarianism' assigned to the Arendt excerpt in Gilbert Allardyce, ed., *The Place of Fascism in European History* (thereafter Allardyce, *Place of Fascism*) (Englewood Cliffs, NJ, Prentice Hall, 1971), p. 86.

9 Hugh Trevor-Roper, 'The Phenomenon of Fascism' (thereafter Trevor-Roper, 'Phenomenon'), in Stuart J. Woolf, ed., *Fascism in Europe* (thereafter Woolf, *Fascism in Europe*) (London/New York, Methuen, 1981), pp. 19–38; also Stanley Payne's response, AHA Forum, p. 390.

10 Cf. esp. the classic Eugen Weber, ed., *Varieties of Fascism* (thereafter Weber, *Varieties*) (New York, Van Nostrand, 1964), pp. 141–3.

11 Michael Geyer, 'The Nazi State Reconsidered', in Richard Bessel, ed., *Life in the Third Reich* (thereafter Bessel, *Third Reich*) (Oxford, Oxford University Press, 1987), pp. 65–7.

12 Trevor-Roper, 'Phenomenon', pp. 26–36.

13 Griffin, *Fascism*, pp. 116 and 146 respectively.

14 Payne, response, AHA Forum, p. 389.

15 For example, Weber, *Varieties*, pp. 139–43; George L. Mosse, 'Introduction: Towards a General Theory of Fascism' (thereafter Mosse, 'Introduction'), in George L. Mosse, ed., *International Fascism: New Thoughts and New Approaches* (thereafter Mosse *International Fascism*) (London, Sage, 1979), pp. 1–41; Allardyce, *Place of Fascism*, pp. 1–27; Alan Cassels, *Fascism* (New York, Crowell, 1975), pp. 342–9; Roger Eatwell, 'Towards a New Model of Generic Fascism', *Journal of Theoretical Politics*, 4: 2 (1992), pp. 161–94; Nathanael Green, ed., *Fascism: An Anthology* (New York, Crowell, 1968); Pierre Milza, *Fascisme français: passé et présent* (thereafter Milza, *Fascisme français*) (Paris, Flammarion, 1987), pp. 55–9; Stanley G. Payne, *Fascism: Comparison and Definition* (thereafter Payne, *Fascism*) (Madison, Univeristy of Wisconsin Press, 1980) pp. 3–21, 177–90; Hugh Seton-Watson, 'The Age of Fascism and Its Legacy', in Mosse, *International Fascism*, pp. 364–75; Robert Soucy, *French Fascism: The First Wave, 1924–1933* (thereafter Soucy, *French Fascism*) (New Haven, Yale University Press), pp. xi–26; John Weiss, *The Fascist Tradition* (New York, Harper & Row, 1967), pp. 1–9 and 128–33; Woolf, *Fascism in Europe*, pp. 1–38; Stuart J. Woolf, ed., *The Nature of Fascism* (New York, Vintage, 1969); Nolte, *Three Faces*, esp. p. 429. For the most useful brief working definitions cf. Richard Thurlow, *Fascism in Britain: A History, 1918–1985* (thereafter Thurlow, *Fascism in Britain*) (Oxford, Basil

Blackwell, 1987). p. xvii; and Payne, *Fascism*, p. 7. Cf. Also Stanley G. Payne's recent review article, 'Historic Fascism and Neofascism', *European History Quarterly*, 32: 1 (1993), pp. 69–75.

16 Griffin, *Fascism*, p. 26 (my italics).

17 As cited in Hans Rogger and Eugen Weber, *The European Right: A Historical Profile* (Berkeley, University of California Press, 1965), p. 8.

18 Cf. William D. Irvine, 'Fascism in France and the Strange Case of the Croix de Feu', *Journal of Modern History*, 63: 2 (1991), pp. 294–5. In drawing the distinction between conservatism and fascism, Irvine does not distinguish between the *kind* of radical change sought by communists and fascists, however.

19 Zeev Sternhell, *Neither Right nor Left: Fascist Ideology in France* (thereafter Sternhell, *Right nor Left*) (Berkeley, CA, University of California Press, 1986), esp. pp. 5–31, 142–212; Griffin, *Fascism*, esp. pp. 36–7.

20 Ibid., 47.

21 Jeffrey Herf, *Reactionary Modernism: Technology, Culture and Politics in Weimar and the Third Reich* (New York, Cambridge University Press, 1984).

22 Griffin, *Fascism* (author's italics).

23 Ibid., pp. 186–8; Nolte, *Three Faces*, p. 429ff.

24 Griffin, *Fascism*, p. 188.

25 M. Scott Peck, *The Road Less Travelled: A New Psychology of Love, Tradition, Values, and Spiritual Growth* (New York, Simon & Schuster, 1978), pp. 87–9.

26 Cf. Klaus von Beyme, 'Right-wing Extremism in Post-war Europe', (thereafter von Beyme, 'Extremism'), *West European Politics*, 11 (1988), pp. 3–6; Woolfgang Benz, 'Organisierter Rechtsradikalismus in der Bundesrepublik Deutschland: ein Überblick 1945–1984', (thereafter Benz, 'Rechtsradikalismus'), *Geschichte in Wissenschaft und Unterricht*, 38: 2 (1987), pp. 90–1; Gerhard Paul, 'Republik und Republikaner: Vergangenheit, die nicht vergehen will?' (thereafter Paul, 'Republik') in Gerhard Paul, ed., *Hitlers Schatten verblaßt: Die Normalisierung des Rechtsextremismus* (thereafter Paul, *Hitlers Schatten verblaßt*), 2nd rev. edn (Bonn, J. H. W. Dietz Nachf., 1990), pp. 138–45; Klaus-Henning Rosen, 'Rechsterrorismus: Gruppen – Täter – Hintergründe', (thereafter Rosen, 'Rechsterrorismus'), Paul, *Hitlers Schatten verblaßt*, pp. 50–69; Thurlow, *Fascism in Britain*, pp. 275–97; Pierre-André Taguieff, 'Un programme "révolutionnaire"?' in Nonna Mayer and Pascal Perrineau, eds, *Le Front National à découvert* (thereafter Mayer and Perrineau, *Front National*) (Paris, Presses de la Fondation Nationale des Sciences Politiques, 1989), pp. 195–227; Franco Ferraresi, 'The Radical Right in Postwar Italy' (thereafter Ferraresi, 'Radical Right'), 16 (1988), pp. 71–119.

27 Eric Roussel, *Le cas le Pen: les nouvelles droites en France* (Paris, Editions J.-C. Lattés, 1985), pp. 71–2.

28 Paul, 'Republik', p. 142.

29 Cited in Wolfgang Zank, 'Mord auf dem Bülowplatz', *Die Zeit*, 23 Aug. 1991, 13.

30 Cf. Richard Bessel, 'Political Violence and the Nazi Seizure of Power', in Bessel, *Third Reich*, pp. 8–14.

31 IFOP statistics as cited in Jean Chatain, *Les affaires de M. Le Pen* (thereafter Chatain, *Les affaires*) (Paris, Editions Messidor, 1987), p. 168, and Martin Schain, 'The National Front in France and the Construction of Political Legitimacy', (thereafter Schain, 'National Front'), *West European Politics*, 10 (1987), pp. 237–8; Cf. surveys and individual interviews on reactions to the

immigration issue in Jacqueline Blondel and Bernard Lacroix, 'Pourquoi votent-ils Front National', (thereafter Blondel and Lacroix, 'Front National'), in Mayer and Perrineau, *Front National*, pp. 150–68, esp. pp 152–5. Noona Mayer, 'Le vote FN de Passy à Barbès (1984–1988)' (thereafter Mayer, 'Le vote FN'), in Mayer and Perrineau, *Front National*, pp. 250–6; Milza, *Fascisme français*, pp. 402–7.

32 Leggewie, *Die Republikaner*, pp. 17–18, 79–86.

33 Hannah Arendt, *The Origins of Totalitarianism* (New York, Harcourt, Brace & Co, 1951).

34 Woodruff Smith, *The Ideological Origins of Nazi Imperialism* (New York, Oxford University Press, 1986); Jon Bridgman, *The Revolt of the Hereros* (Berkeley, University of California Press, 1981).

35 Cf. Soucy, *French Fascism*, pp. 84–6, 130–1. Cf. also A. S. Kanya-Forstner, *The Conquest of the Western Sudan: A Study in French Military Imperialism* (London, Cambridge University Press, 1969).

36 Nolte, *Three Faces*, p. 5; Cf. also Milza, *Fascisme français*, p. 45.

37 Ernst Jünger, *Der Kampf als inneres Erlebnis* (Berlin, E. S. Mittler & Sohn, 1925), p. 2.

38 Mosse, 'Introduction', pp. 12–15; recently again Robert J. Soucy, 'French Fascism and the Croix de Feu: A Dissenting Interpretation', *Journal of Contemporary History*, 26 (1991), p. 165.

39 George L. Mosse, *Nazi Culture* (New York, Grosset & Dunlap, 1966); Jay S. Baird, *To Die for Germany: Heroes in the Nazi Pantheon* (Bloomington, Indiana University Press, 1990).

40 Sternhell, *Right Nor Left*.

41 Hannah Arendt, *On Violence* (New York, Harcourt Brace & World, 1969), p. 81.

42 Cf. Roland Höhne, 'Die Renaissance des Rechtsextremismus in Frankreich', *Politische Vierteljahresschrift* 31 (1) (1990), pp. 89–91; Betz, 'Resentment', pp. 46–8.

43 *Deutsches Allgemeines Sonntagsblatt*, 12 June 1983, as cited in Hoffman, 'Terrorism', p. 24. Cf. a similar statement in *taz*, 18 Jan. 1989, as cited in Claus Leggewie, *Die Republikaner* (Berlin, Rotbuch Verlag, 1989) p. 133.

44 Cf. German sociologist Wilhelm Heitmeyer 'Zuwanderung und Desintegration zusammen fuhren dazu, daß die ethnischen Kategorien ausgepackt werden.' Quoted in 'Das Unbehagen im Alltag: die Ursachen für Fremdenfeindlichkeit und Gewalt liegen in der Gesellschaft', *DAAD Letter*, April 1992, p. 18.

45 Reports by the head of the Federal Criminal Police of 17 Sept. 1992 and by Interior Minister Rudolf Seiters of 6 Feb. 1993, listing some 2,450 and 2,285 violent actions 'with proven or assumed right-wing extremist motivation' for 1991 and 1992 respectively. Reported in *This Week in Germany*, 18 Sept. 1992, I, 12 Feb. 1993, I; Helsinki Watch, *'Foreigners Out': Xenophobia and Right-wing Violence in Germany* (New York, Human Rights Watch, Oct. 1992), pp. 7–15.

46 Cf. Chatain, *Les affaires*, pp. 105–71; Blondel and Lacroix, 'Front National', pp. 155–63; Christopher T. Husbands, 'Militant Neo-Nazism in the Federal Republic of Germany in the 1980s' (thereafter Husbands, 'Neo-Nazism'), in Luciano Cheles et al., *Neo-Fascism in Europe* (London, Longman, 1991), p. 108; Leggewie, *Die Republikaner*, pp. 18–19.

47 Wilhelm Heitmeyer, *Rechtsextremistische Orientierungen bei Jugendlichen: empirische Ergebnisse und Erklärungsmuster einer Untersuchung zur politischen Sozialisation* (Weinheim, Juventa, 1987), esp. p. 210; cf. also Leggewie,

Die Republikaner, pp. 19–24, 79–86 (interview), and Hans-Georg Betz, *Postmodern Politics in Germany: The Politics of Resentment* (New York, St. Martin's Press, 1991), esp. pp. 114–17.

48 Wilhelm Heitmeyer *et al.*, eds, *Die Bielefelder Rechtsextremismus-Studie: erste Langzeituntersuchung zur politischen Sozialisation männlicher Jugendlicher* (thereafter Heitmeyer, *Rechtsextremismus-Studie*) (Weinheim, Juventa, 1992), p. 574.

49 Ibid., p. 274 (my italics).

50 Soucy, 'French Fascism', p. 163.

51 Jean Vanlaer, 'Opposition centre-périphérie et vote d'extrême droite en Europe', *Espace Population Sociétés* 3 (1987), pp. 476–80. Unfortunately Vanlaer uses only the NPD and not the *Republikaner* for Germany, which makes the German radical right vote appear less urban; Höhne, 'Rechtsextremismus', p. 86; Mayer, 'Le vote FN', pp. 249–69; Milza, *Fascisme français*, pp. 404–9; Leggewie, *Die Republikaner*, esp. pp. 17–18, 71–5.

52 Wilhelm Heitmeyer, *Rechtsextremismus-Studie*, pp. 576–8, also 258–65. The authors remain cautious on this link, however, since it is not confirmed in all cases. Cf. also John D. Ely, 'The "Black-Brown Hazelnut" in a Bigger Germany: The Rise of a Radical Right as a Structural Feature', in M. G. Huelshoff, Andrei S. Markovits and Simon Reich, eds, *From Bundersrepublik to Deutschland* (Ann Arbor, MI, University of Michigan Press), p. 249.

53 Cf. Anna Bramwell, *Blood and Soil: Walter Darré and Hitler's Green Party* (Buckinghamshire, Kensal Press, 1985); Raymond Dominick, 'The Nazis and the Nature Conservationists', *The Historian*, 49 (1987), pp. 508–38.

54 Paul, 'Der Schatten', p. 35.

55 Die Republikaner, *Programm*, cover and p. 5.

56 Cf. Höhne, 'Rechtsextremismus', p. 87.

57 Cf. Bruce Hoffman, 'Right-wing Terrorism in Europe', *Orbis: A Journal of World Affairs*, 28 (1984), pp. 23–5; Ferraresi, 'Radical Right', pp. 98–103.

58 Cf. table of anti-Semitic incidents in Beyme, 'Extremism', p. 5.

59 Cf. listings for all major European countries in 'The Far Right in Europe', pp. 127–46.

60 Paul, 'Der Schatten', 36–8; cf. also the excellent article *Multikulti*: The German Debate on Multiculturalism', *German Studies Review* (forthcoming), esp. fo. 13.

61 For example Michael Billig, 'The Extreme Right: Continuities in anti-Semitic Conspiracy Theory in Post-war Europe', in Roger Eatwell and Noël O'Sullivan. *The Nature of the Right: American and European Politics and Political Thought since 1789* (Boston, Twayne, 1990), pp. 146–66, esp. 154–6.

62 Heitmeyer, *Rechtsextremismus-Studie*, p. 297.

63 Blondel and Lacroix, 'Front National', p. 154.

64 *taz*, 18 Jan. 1989, cited in Leggewie, *Die Republikaner*, p. 133.

65 Jean-Yves Camus and René Monzat, *Les droites nationales et radicales en France* (Lyon, Presses Universitaires de Lyon, 1992), pp. 127–8.

66 Cf. Roger Eatwell, 'The Holocaust Denial: A Study in Propaganda Technique', in Cheles *et al.*, *Neo-Fascism*, pp. 120–43. I owe the view of the historical role of the Holocaust as a fundamental turning point in Western or even global civilization to Michael Geyer, initially from his lecture 'Man-Made Ascendance: The Holocaust in an Age of Mass Violence', Carleton College, 18 Feb. 1991.

67 Richard Stöss, *Politics against Democracy: Right Wing Extremism in West Gemany* (New York, Berg, 1991), p. 224.

Afterword

Readers who have reached this point in the book with a minimum of skipping are now in a position to assess for themselves how far it has fulfilled its objectives. They have been deliberately exposed to a variety of conflicting positions on what constitutes fascism chosen to illustrate the broad outlines of the evolution of the concept. At the same time it has been repeatedly suggested to them that a new consensus or paradigm is emerging which allows fascism to be treated fairly coherently as a generic term, both for a particular genus of revolutionary political ideology and for a type of historical movement which exhibited a wide range of variants and had a number of different if interconnecting causes. It will also have been impressed on them that even today this consensus is still only partial. Not only do deep divisions still exist over the 'fascist minimum', but some experts prefer to classify contemporary phenomena commonly regarded as fascist under a different heading altogether.

The basic methodological point raised by the persistence of such varying definitions is that valuable insights can be drawn by the intelligent application of any conflicting approaches to the 'same' phenomenon. For example, Nazism can be profitably treated as a product of a unique German history, as a form of totalitarianism, *and* as a permutation of generic fascism. Those who doubt this are urged to read Ian Kershaw's chapter 'The essence of Nazism: form of fascism, brand of totalitarianism, or unique phenomenon?' in his seminal work *The Nazi Dictatorship* (third edition: London, Edward Arnold, 1993). After all, particles of light behave both as a wave *and* a beam according to the experiment that is applied to them, and human realities are even more multi-dimensional. The important thing is for each student or researcher to develop an approach informed by 'experts' which makes sense and feels right to them. As William Blake says, 'I must make my own system or be enslaved by another man's' (and it is still usually men who make the systems!). My purpose in compiling this anthology has been to organize a sample of sources relating to international or generic fascism on the basis of my conviction that a new consensus is emerging in the scholarly debate surrounding it, not to brainwash the reader into adopting it as the sole key to all the problems it poses. It is for the individual lecturer and student to assess the merits of the 'new paradigm' as a heuristic tool for historical research.

There is plenty of room for everyone who enters the debate to challenge approaches and to propose new ones. The ultimate aim is for fascism to be progressively demystified and de-demonized. As such it can be treated as a man-made, explicable phenomenon which falls just as much within the remit of the human sciences as any other historical phenomenon. Even the most basic school essay on the subject can be a step in this direction. At the same time, working at any level of expertise on such a highly complex and controversial subject associated with horrendous crimes against humanity can foster humanistic instincts of informed curiosity and understanding. In this way those who work on fascism can be inoculated against the lure of palingenetic utopias of a man-made heaven which, by denying the infinite richness and complexity of the world, inevitably lead to a man-made hell. Education in the humanities is not about certainty and absolutes, but informed doubt, and living more fully with knowledge which is relative and incomplete.

We have come a long way from the three brief articles which opened this anthology with their unsubstantiated assertions and highly condensed summaries of complex data. Indeed, readers might be surprised at just how much more they see to approve of and to criticize in those initial encyclopedia definitions (including mine!) if they read them now. By contrast Prowe's analysis is sustained, cautious, scrupulously argued, methodologically intricate, and steeped in an acquaintance with a wide range of contributions to the debate over fascism and positions taken up within it. It is therefore very demanding. Yet much of the ground he covers should have become familiar to readers who have patiently worked their way through the book to reach this point.

Those who find that this last text is generally intelligible, and that it clarifies rather than obscures the issue of the nature and strength of contemporary 'fascism', should feel encouraged and empowered. They are no longer beginners. They have reached an advanced stage in the understanding of international fascism, and are already in a better position to write methodologically and conceptually sound essays than many 'experts' who have published on the subject in the past. I wish them well in their further studies on this important and disturbing subject, and hope that this Reader has made it both more accessible and more fascinating rather than less. I would be pleased to know if this book has helped them, and how it might be improved were a second edition to be contemplated. My e-mail address is rdgriffin@brookes.ac.uk.

Index

References to the authors of secondary sources cited in footnotes have been omitted.

action, fascist cult of 143, 238, 249, 253, 268, 309
Action Française 49, 114, 153, 179, 198, 276
Adreu, Pierre 169
aesthetic politics 154
  see also civic religion
Allardyce, Gilbert 9, 306
Alleanza Nazionale 2, 287
Allen, William S. 113
anomie 38, 243
Ansaldo, Giovanni 132
anti-Americanism 318
  bourgeois 170, 178, 180, 249
  capitalism 8, 34, 101, 141, 178, 179, 197, 198, 244, 261, 275–84
  clericalism 8, 178
  conservatism 6, 36, 163, 178, 239, 253, 309
  decadence 24, 54, 35, 149, 160, 163, 191, 192–3, 201, 240, 255, 257, 261
  democracy 9, 31, 178, 198, 239, 251, 258–9, 262, 268
  dimension of fascism 6, 8, 9, 11, 13, 14, 48, 53, 178, 239
  egalitarianism 149, 239, 240, 252, 262
  fascist activism 5, 287–9, 296–305
  individualism 31, 37, 170, 191, 240, 244, 259
  Muslim 318
  internationalism 37, 244, 261, 262
  liberalism 9, 31, 36, 37, 108–9, 170, 178, 191, 192, 198, 239, 240, 244, 252–3, 258–9, 276, 278
  Marxism 6, 8, 9, 23, 27, 30–1, 37, 47, 106, 170, 178, 179, 192, 231, 239, 240, 244, 251, 259–61, 268, 276, 279–80, 309, 311, 318
  materialism 6, 31, 32, 37, 141, 149, 170, 190, 191, 239, 244, 251, 261

modernization 12, 45–50, 49, 114–15, 99–124, 127, 158, 196, 309, 310
pacifism 250
parliamentarism 8, 178
pluralism 180, 309
rationalism 149, 170
Semitism 28, 37, 116, 119, 152, 172, 173, 179, 193–4, 195, 233, 241, 244, 280, 289, 291, 295, 298, 302, 309, 311, 312, 313, 314, 319–20
socialism 6, 8, 36, 45, 101, 178
  see also Marxist theories of fascism
urbanism 170
utilitarianism 259
Zionism 318
Anti Nazi League 287, 300–5
Antonescu, General Ion 231
Archer, Bernadette 275–84
Arendt, Hannah 89, 268, 306, 313, 314
Arrow Cross 7, 23, 230, 243
Aryanism 194
Austro-Marxists 44
autarky 197

Baeck, Leo 114
Bambery, Chris 288–90
Bardèche, Maurice 194
Barrès, Maurice 31, 170, 172
Barnes, J. S. 1, 9, 16fn
Bergson, Henri 31, 171, 172, 199
Berlusconi, Silvio 287
Bernstein, Edouard 248
Bismarck, Otto von 253
blacks 295–6
Blake, William 325
'blood and soil' 262, 317
Bonapartism 4, 42, 43, 44, 67, 73–4, 75–85, 86, 93, 176
bourgeois basis of fascism 42, 44, 45, 59–60, 101–6, 108, 110–11, 132, 289

see also Marxist theories of fascism
Brandt, Willy 311
British National Party 287
Burke, Edmund 190, 261
Bush, George 287
Bracher, Karl 8
Brasillach, Robert 32, 198
British Union of Fascists 7, 9, 36, 169,
  240–1, 245, 257–64, 318
Brüning, Heinrich 67, 77

Caesarism 177
  see also Bonapartism
capitalism and fascism 28, 42–5, 49,
  59–66, 113, 275–84, 288–90, 296
  see also Marxist theories of fascism
Carsten, Francis 8, 282
Castro, Fidel 134
'categorical analysis' 164, 165, 243
causes of fascism 158–235
charismatic politics, *see* ritual politics,
  leader cult
Chesterton, A. K. 245
China 51
Chirac, Jacques 301
Christianity, *see* Church and fascism
Church and fascism 27, 91, 92, 102,
  121, 133, 150, 175, 178, 182, 202, 239,
  256, 273
civic religion 52, 54, 138, 150, 161, 243
Codreanu, Corneliu 32, 142, 244, 245,
  273, 277–83, 292, 309
colonialism 27
Comintern 42–3, 54, 59–66, 74, 158,
  261
common denominator of fascism, *see*
  fascist minimum
community 164–5, 166, 180, 190, 191,
  193, 222, 243, 267–75, 309
  see also national community
conservatism 52, 113, 182, 190, 288
corporatism 34, 163, 199, 249, 309
Corradini, Enrico 31, 32, 130–1, 173,
  192
cosmopolitanism
  see anti-internationalism
counter-revolution 45, 52, 116, 117, 141
  see also Marxist theories of fascism

Cresson, Edith 301
Cromer, Lord 313
crisis, role of in fascism 44, 60, 86–93,
  116–18, 170, 171, 175–7, 204–16, 227,
  242, 243, 288, 297
Croce, Benedetto 5
Croix de Feu 313
Cuba 51
cyclic scheme of history 191

D'Annunzio, Gabriele 172, 173, 177,
  267–8, 273
Daudet, Léon 276
De Benoist, Alain 38, 242
De Bono, Emilio 142
De Gaulle, Charles 122, 313
de Maistre, J. 253
de Man, H. 196
Déat, Marcel 32, 33, 46
debate about fascism viii–ix, 2–20, 178,
  228, 264–8, 275, 287
decadence 24, 54, 160, 191, 192–3, 194,
  201, 240, 255, 257
decolonization 312
Degrelle, Léon 32, 33, 196, 276, 277–83,
  308
Delzell, Charles 134
Deutsche Volksunion 311
developmental dictatorship 50, 110, 200
Dilthey, Wilhelm 115
doctrine of fascism 34, 248–50
Dollfuss, Engelbert 36, 46, 92
Doriot, Jacques 32, 46, 308
Dostoevsky, Fyodor 171
Drieu la Rochelle, Pierre 32, 143, 169,
  190
Drumont, Edouard 170, 172
Durkheim, Emile 38, 89
Duverger, Maurice 269

Eastmann, Max 73
Eatwell, Roger 14, 15, 149, 162–4,
  189–204, 238, 239, 240
Eckhart, Dietrich 194
ecology 37, 163, 200, 244, 317
economics 33, 116–17, 119–20, 131,
  133–4, 141, 151, 159, 196–200, 240–1,
  251, 255, 262, 309, 315, 320

elites 192
  see also Pareto

Empire Loyalists 313
Engels, Friedrich 210–11, 212
English National Movement 19fn,
  244–5
era of fascism 48, 111, 120, 121, 167,
  227, 235, 293, 306
Ethiopia 2
eugenics 241, 244
Europeanist fascism/radical right 38,
  193, 194–5, 279, 319
Evola, Julius 38, 191, 242
extreme right
  see radical right

Faisceau, Le 7, 9
Falange 7, 23, 28, 161, 228, 229, 232–3,
  235, 243, 245, 275, 276, 277–84, 288,
  309
Fanon, Frantz 313
Fascism 1–2, 7, 12, 23, 27, 36, 37, 42,
  45, 50, 60, 114, 128–34, 138–46, 198,
  228, 233, 243, 248–57, 306, 309, 318
  and Bolshevism 134–5, 138–40, 151,
    165, 261–2
  and imperialism 59, 152, 195, 240–1,
    244, 255, 256, 276, 278–9, 291,
    312–13, 319
  and modernization 6, 12, 13, 15,
    45–50, 51, 99–124, 127–37, 151,
    158, 175–6, 178, 200, 243, 309
  and the Enlightenment 6, 24, 140,
    149, 308, 309
  and the left 200–1
  and the right 200–1
  as revolution 9, 10, 13, 25, 29, 31, 36,
    49, 53, 54, 114, 118, 137–47, 145,
    149–50, 159, 160, 176–7, 178, 192,
    201, 243, 255, 293, 310
  as metapolitics, *see* Nolte
  as neobarbarism 118, 122
  cult of violence 7, 54, 152, 155, 169,
    227, 250
  fascism/Fascism distinction 12fn
  fascists and fascism 19fn
  in Asia 4, 178

  in Austria 36, 46, 228, 232, 309
  in Belgium, *see* Rexism
  in Brazil 7, 25, 36, 104, 163, 202
  in Britain 7, 9, 19fn, 33, 36, 169, 194,
    196, 197, 231, 240–1, 244–5,
    257–64, 287
  in Chile 25
  in Croatia 228
  in Finland 36, 309
  in France 24, 36
  in Germany, *see* Nazism; neo-Nazism
  in Greece 50
  in Hungary 7, 23, 36, 42, 50, 165,
    182, 228, 230–1, 243
  in Italy, *see* Fascism
  in Japan 42, 62–3
  in Latin America 4, 7, 9, 23, 25, 27,
    51, 103, 178
  in Poland 45, 60, 233
  in Portugal 2, 36, 183, 189, 232
  in Romania 7, 23, 24, 32, 36, 50, 165,
    179, 182, 183, 191, 228, 229, 244,
    245, 275, 277, 309
  in Russia 38
  in South America 4, 7, 9, 23, 25, 27,
    51, 103, 178
  in Southern Africa 4, 9, 36, 38,
  in Spain 7, 23, 24, 28, 32, 36, 54, 183,
    228, 229–30, 232, 243, 244, 288,
    297, 309
  in Yugoslavia 42, 50
  minimum 1, 2, 6, 37, 40–155
  theories of fascism 236–84
  see also Mussolini
Felice, Renzo de 9, 242, 243, 265, 272
feminists 25
  see also gender dimension of fascism
Fetscher, Iring 76, 112
fin-de-siècle, see revolt against
  positivism
Fini, Gianfranco 2
First World War viii, 32–3, 36, 43, 50,
  54, 117, 121, 131, 146, 153, 160, 161,
  165, 169, 172, 173, 176, 177, 191, 192,
  195, 268–9, 288, 291, 297, 314, 315
Fourier, Jean 254
foreigners, *see* fascism and immigration

Franco, General Francisco 2, 104, 199, 202, 276, 288, 297
Freemasons 172, 179
Freikorps 165–6, 219, 224
French Revolution 12, 31, 140, 141, 159, 256, 258, 308, 309
Freud, Anna 212
Freud, Sigmund 173, 206, 222
Fromm, Eric 307, 310
Front National 2, 23, 30, 37, 286, 289, 300–3, 311
Futurism 129–30, 131, 132, 177, 253

Gadamer, Hans-Georg 205
Garibaldi, Giuseppe 253
Garruccio, Ludovico 271–2
gender dimension of fascism 26, 52, 144, 154, 166–7, 190, 309
Geyer, Michael 307
Giolitti, Giovanni 43, 177, 192
Gentile, Emilio 54, 269–70
Gentile, Giovanni 33, 34, 170, 190, 192, 193, 201, 238, 239
Gerschenkron, A. 117
Gobineau, Conte de 171
Goebbels, Josef 221–4, 299
Goote, Thor 217
Gramsci, Antonio 3, 91
Great Depression 1, 47, 116–17, 146, 288, 297
Gregor, A. J. 11, 14, 50–1, 127–37
Griepenburg, R. 84
Griffin, Roger 35–9, 149, 150, 234, 282, 290, 292, 306, 307, 308, 309
Grossdeutsche Volkspartei 46
Günther, Hans 244

Habermas, Jürgen 205
Heavy Metal 164
Heberle, Rudolf 114
Hegel, G. W. F. 31, 115, 177, 238, 239
Heidegger, Martin 199, 201
Heitmeyer, Wilhelm 315
Hennessy, Alistair 7
Herf, Jeffrey 310
Hindenburg, P. von Beneckendorf 60, 67, 145
Hitler, Adolf 2, 3, 36, 77, 85, 119, 161,

173, 182, 190, 194, 198, 263, 267, 282, 292, 297, 298–9, 306, 308
Holocaust denial 292, 319–20
Höss, Rudolf 166, 218–21
Horkheimer, Max 75

ideal type 10, 11, 15, 22, 24, 26, 36, 148, 161, 181, 244, 245, 290, 291, 308
ideology, socio-psychology of 204–16
ideology of fascism 6, 8, 28, 33–4, 49, 53, 87–95, 102, 148–9, 162–4, 164–5, 171–2, 177, 189–204
immigration 30, 244, 301–2, 304–5, 312, 315–16
Internet 164
international fascism 1–3
    see also Universal fascism
Iron Guard 7, 23, 179, 191, 244, 245, 275, 277
    see also Codreanu
Italian National Association (ANI) 153

Jahn, Friedrich 116
Jews, *see* anti-Semitism
Joll, James 130
Jouvenel, Bertrand de 169
Jünger, Ernst 217, 224, 314
Jung, Carl Gustav 223

Kerensky, Alexander 71
Kershaw, Ian 11, 16fn, 325
Kinnock, Neil 300
Kohl, Helmut 304

Labriola, Arturo 32
lack of consensus on fascism 1–20, 22, 26, 286–94
lack of doctrine of fascism 7
Lagarde, Paul de 170
Lagardelle, H. 248
Langbehn, Julius 170, 172
Laqueur, Walter 7, 19fn, 161
Lasswell, Harold 101
late-comer, fascism as 178, 182, 239
law under fascism 199
leader cult 28, 34, 52, 54, 119, 138, 144–5, 155, 172, 177, 245, 276, 277–8, 309, 311, 317

League of Nations 262–3
Le Bon, Gustave 31, 33, 142, 171, 172
Leone, Enrico 248
Le Pen, Jean-Marie 2, 37, 287, 289, 291, 295, 300–3, 312, 314, 319
Liberal Democratic Party of Russia 2
Lenin, (V. I. Ulyanov) 68, 109, 119, 134, 176
Linz, Juan 8, 11, 14, 160–2, 164, 175–88, 239, 242, 271
Lipset, Seymour 4, 46–7, 48, 49, 50, 101–6, 112–13, 121
list approaches to fascism 189, 291, 309–10
Lorenz, Konrad 191
Louis-Napoleon (Napoleon III) 44, 77, 81, 253
see also Bonapartism

Macdonald, Dwight 67, 71
Machiavelli, Niccolò 191
Malraux, André 308
Mao Zedong 134
Maritain Jacques 5
Marinetti, F. T. 129
Marx, Karl 77–83, 109, 253
Marxist theories of fascism viii, ix, 3–5, 15, 25, 42–5, 49, 59–97, 102, 112–13, 119, 176, 183, 243, 267, 287–90, 293, 295–305
Mason, Tim 13
masses, role of the 176
see also mass mobilization
Maurras, Charles 31, 172, 198, 268
Mazzini, Giuseppe 192, 253
Meinecke, Friedrich 5
Mezzetti, Nazareno 133
metapolitics 47, 106–12, 114–16
Michels, Robert 32, 33, 154
middle classes 45, 46–7, 49, 101–6, 113, 132, 288–9, 297–8
see also Marxist theories of fascism
militarism 121, 314
Mill, J. S. 259
Milward, Alan 8, 113
Mitterrand, François 289, 300
mobilization of the masses 93, 140, 155, 176, 177, 192, 266, 309

modernization theories of fascism 45–50, 98–137
Moeller van den Bruck, Arthur 170, 172
Moltke, Hellmuth von 253
Mommsen, Hans 8
Montreux 1, 282
Mosca, Gaetano 154
Mosley, Oswald 9, 33, 169, 194, 196, 197, 231, 240, 245, 318
Mosse, G. L. 9, 10, 14, 51–3, 137–47, 173, 234, 238, 242, 243, 266–8, 274, 277, 290, 291, 308
Movimento Sociale Italiano 23, 37, 242, 287, 311
multi-culturalism 292, 312–13, 320
Mussolini, Benito 1, 9, 11, 27, 32, 33, 34, 36, 46, 54, 85, 129, 170, 177, 183, 190, 193, 201, 238, 239, 241, 242, 248–57, 262, 267–8, 281, 288, 292, 298, 306, 308
myth 7, 33, 192, 195, 267
see also Sorel

national community 9, 31, 36, 37, 142, 145, 153, 161, 181, 240, 243, 244, 250, 267
National Front 30, 290, 311
'national revolutionaries' 245
nationhood and fascism 6
Nationaldemokratische Partei Deutschlands (NDP) 23, 311
National Socialism, *see* Nazism
Nazism 2, 3, 7, 8, 12, 13, 23, 28–9, 36, 37, 46, 47, 60, 63, 112, 114, 119, 128, 138, 139–46, 158, 161, 164, 165, 173, 178, 196, 228, 234, 235, 241, 243, 263, 271, 273, 295–6, 306, 309, 313, 318
Nazism and fascism 8, 16fn, 24, 52, 181, 266–8, 309
neo-Nazism 286, 287, 289, 295–305
Neumann, Franz 271
New Age 25, 37
new civilization 10, 23, 32, 34, 161, 170, 201, 267
new culture, *see* new civilization
new consensus on fascism ix–x, 13–15, 24, 49, 50–5, 158–9, 161, 165, 238, 243, 245

new man 9, 10, 52, 53, 54, 144–5, 161, 163, 201, 222, 243, 244
new order 52, 171, 240, 245
New Right 25, 38, 242
New World Order 286
Nietzsche, Friedrich 109, 143, 171, 177, 190, 239
nihilism of fascism 149
Nolte, Ernst viii, 6, 7, 11, 14, 47–8, 49, 50, 106–12, 112–16, 150, 151, 234, 290, 291, 306–8, 309, 310, 313, 314

Oklahoma bombing 287
Olivetti, Angelo 248
Orano, Paolo 32, 248
organic nation
  see ultra-nationalism
Organski, A. F. K. 134
Ortiz, Joseph 313
Owen, Robert 254

palingenetic myth 9, 10, 23, 32, 34, 52, 53, 54, 144–5, 161, 163, 170, 201, 222, 239–40, 243–4, 245, 250, 267, 293
palingenetic ultra-nationalism 13, 24–5, 35–9, 160, 244
  see also new man; new order
Pamyat 38
Panunzio, Sergio 32, 133, 134
Papanace, C. 282
Papen, Franz von 77
Papini, Giovanni 193
paradigm 14, 19fn, 53
para-fascism 24
paramilitarism 28, 52, 177, 180, 181, 273
Pareto, Vilfredo 31, 33, 154, 191
Parsons, Talcott 102
Parti Populaire Français 46
Paul, Gerhard 311
Paveli_, Dr. Ante 228, 232
Paxton, Robert 14
Payne, Stanley 10, 14, 51, 53–5, 147–55, 161, 163, 164, 167, 227–35, 238, 239, 240, 291, 308
Pearce, William 287
Perón, Juan 8, 104, 202
Peronism 2, 103, 182

Pétain, Marshal Henri 43, 67, 73–4
Peters, Carl 313
Péguy, Charles 238, 248
Pinochet, Augusto 202
Pitt, William 258
Pius XII, Pope 120
Platt, Gerald 164, 204–16, 242, 243
political space 152, 161, 162
Popular Front 66, 300
populism 13–14, 36, 101, 103, 138, 155, 179, 239, 245, 249, 256, 292
positivism, see revolt against positivism
post-war fascism 25, 235, 286–324
Poujadisme 46
Poulantzas, Nicos 42, 44–5, 86–97, 161
Primo de Rivera, José Antonio 32, 33, 34, 198, 244, 245, 276, 277–82
productivism 132
progress 191
proletariat and fascism, see Marxist theories of fascism
propaganda 52
Prowe, Diethelm xi, 167, 290–3, 305–24
psychology of fascism 15, 26, 28, 33, 159, 171, 190, 204–16, 216–26, 242, 272, 310

racism 28, 37, 152, 163, 171, 179–80, 191, 193–4, 241, 263, 279, 289, 291, 307, 309, 312–13, 318–19
radical right 292–3, 305–24
Ranke, Leopold von 115
Rassemblement National Populaire 7, 46
reaction, fascism as 102, 118, 283, 288
  see also Marxist theories of fascism
rebirth 155, 166, 222–3, 279
  see also palingenetic ultra-nationalism 155
Reich, Wilhelm 242
Renan, E. 252
Republikaner (REP) 37, 289, 303, 305, 311, 312, 317
resistance to transcendence 6, 48, 106–12, 114–16, 158, 291, 308, 309, 310
  see also Nolte

revolt against civilization 118, 172
revolt against positivism 6, 34, 37,
  159–60, 161, 170, 171, 227, 228, 239
revolution, psychodynamics of 204–16

Rexism 7, 24, 32, 36, 245, 275, 276,
  277–83
Rhodes, Cecil 313
ritual politics 28, 34, 53, 119, 138, 140,
  142, 153, 181, 243, 273, 309, 311
Rizzi, Bruno 135
Robinson, Robert 14
Rocco, Alfredo 33, 191
Rocque, Colonel de la 313
Romanità 50, 129, 191, 240
Rosenberg, Alfred 194
Rostow, W. 117
Rousseau, Jean-Jacques 140, 190
Russian Revolution viii, 60, 64–6, 68–9,
  109–10, 171, 176, 260–1

Saint-Juste, Louis 140
Saint-Simon, Claude 254
Salazar, Dr. Antonio 2, 36, 183, 199
Salvatorelli, Luigi 132
Saposs, David 101
Sarti, Roland 134
Sauer, Wolfgang 49–50, 51, 112–24
Schleicher, Kurt von 67
Schmitt, Carl 199
Schutzstaffel (SS) 29, 295
Schweitzer, Arthur 49, 112, 113
Scruton, Roger 12
Second World War 70, 117, 195, 274,
  305
secularization and fascism 229–30
  see also church and fascism
sense-making crisis 164–5, 204–16
Sima, Horia 232
skinhead Nazism 289
social basis of fascism 37, 45–6, 101–6,
  113–14, 118–19, 145–6, 164–5, 182,
  213–14
  see also Marxist theories of fascism
social fascism 43, 60–1
social democracy 59–66, 74, 288, 289,
  298, 309

social Darwinism 31, 152, 171, 177,
  190, 191, 307
socialism of fascism 31
Salomon, Ernst von 165, 217, 268
Scott Peck, M. 310
Socialist Workers' Party 287, 293
Sonderweg 6
Sorel, Georges 7, 24, 31, 32, 33, 169,
  170, 177, 195, 238, 239, 248
SOS Racisme 302–3
Soury, Jules 172
Spanish Civil War 2, 28, 261
squadrismo 181, 249, 273, 289
Stalinism 24, 34, 42, 51, 70, 119, 134,
  135, 138, 240, 241, 303, 306
state under fascism 33, 34, 198, 241,
  249, 254–7, 263
  see also Marxist theories of fascism
Sternhell, Zeev viii, 8, 9, 11, 12, 14,
  23–4, 30–5, 159–60, 161, 163, 169–74,
  201, 239, 242, 310, 314
Stöss, Richard 320
Strasser, Gregor 161, 181, 193, 245, 279
Strasser, Otto 245, 279
Sturmabteilung (SA) 29, 273, 289, 297,
  303, 305
Sutton, Claud 240–1, 257–64
syndicalism 31–2, 129, 132, 169, 192,
  238, 248, 276
synthesis 53, 145, 160, 163–4, 189–204,
  239, 254
Szálasi, Ferencz 142, 194, 231–2

Talmon, Jacob 140
Tarchi, Marco 17fn, 242–4, 264–75
Tasca, Angelo 12, 77
terror 36, 52, 59, 61, 239, 289, 298–9
Thalheimer, August 43, 66, 77, 83, 84,
  176
Thälmann, Ernst 66
Theweleit, Klaus 165–7, 216–26
Third Force 52, 141, 244
Third Reich 1, 3, 45, 161
  see also Nazism
Third Way 52, 145, 163, 194, 196, 238,
  240–1, 244, 245, 247–64
Third World 51
Thomas, Hugh 282

Tjaden, K. H. 84
Tönnies, Ferdinand 270–1
totalitarianism 6, 24, 34, 36, 49, 51,
    89–92, 114, 128, 135, 138–40, 141,
    151, 182, 198, 201, 242, 254, 306, 313
Trevor-Roper, Hugh 307
Trotsky, Leon 42, 43, 60, 67–75, 77, 83,
    135, 287–90, 296, 298
Trow, Martin 103
Turner, Henry A. 50, 127–9
Tyndall, John 288, 295

ultra-nationalism of fascism 8, 10, 13,
    24, 27, 28, 30, 36, 37, 54, 152, 160,
    173, 178, 193, 195, 227, 240, 261–2,
    270, 283, 309
Universal fascism 1–2, 9, 238, 239, 240,
    254, 257–8
USA 43, 61, 69, 74, 194, 258
Ustashi 228
utopia x, 5, 7, 52, 54, 119, 129, 134,
    144, 149, 167, 182, 198, 254, 286, 326

Valois, Georges 32, 169, 190, 196, 197,
    201
Vargas, Getulio 7, 104
Vajda, Mihaly 42, 43–4, 75–86
Vaterlandspartei 46
Veblen, Thorstein 89
Veil, Simone 311

veterans 217, 248–9, 269, 314
Vichy 2, 14
Victor Emmanuel III 145
vitalism 37, 149, 155, 227, 239, 250, 269
völkisch 28, 173, 196, 200
Volpe, Gioacchino 133

Wagner, Richard 171
Wall Street Crash, *see* Great
    Depression
war and fascism 142, 250, 314
    see also First World War
Weber, Eugen 7, 24, 49, 112, 121, 234,
    279, 290, 308
Weber, Max 10, 38, 102, 112, 120, 265,
    290, 308
Weinstein, Fred 206
Wiles, Peter 135
Wilkinson, Paul 22–3, 27–30
Willis, Norman 300
Wippermann, W. 12
women under fascism 25
work, fascist cult of 218–23

xenophobia, *see* fascism and
    immigration; racism; anti-Semitism

youth 27, 28, 142, 154, 191

Zhirinovsky, Vladimir 2, 286, 319